# BRITISH–OTTOMAN RELATIONS, 1661–1807

# BRITISH–OTTOMAN RELATIONS, 1661–1807

## COMMERCE AND DIPLOMATIC PRACTICE IN EIGHTEENTH-CENTURY ISTANBUL

*Michael Talbot*

THE BOYDELL PRESS

First published 2017
The Boydell Press, Woodbridge

ISBN 978 1 78327 202 0

The Boydell Press is an imprint of Boydell & Brewer Ltd
PO Box 9, Woodbridge, Suffolk IP12 3DF, UK
and of Boydell & Brewer Inc.
668 Mt Hope Avenue, Rochester, NY 14620–2731, USA
website: www.boydellandbrewer.com

A catalogue record for this book is available from the British Library

Typeset by Fakenham Prepress Solutions, Fakenham, Norfolk NR21 8NN

*In memory of my grandmother, Esther*

# Contents

# Tables and figures

# Acknowledgements

I owe many debts of gratitude to teachers, colleagues, and friends. In particular, I am very grateful for the guidance and instruction of my doctoral supervisor, Professor Benjamin Fortna, whose MA class at the School of Oriental and African Studies rekindled my fascination with the Ottoman Empire. His advice, and guidance during and following the research and writing of the PhD thesis from which this book stems has made all the difference. Numerous friends, colleagues, and teachers have commented on earlier drafts of that thesis and of this book, greatly shaping my thoughts and their presentation, in particular Lauren Banko, Sotiris Dimitriades, Aparajita Mukhopadhyay, Fabian Stremmel, Stefano Taglia, and Philipp Wirtz during my time at SOAS, and since then William O'Reilly, Şevket Pamuk, Colin Heywood, Harriet Rudolph, and Antonis Hadjikyriacou. I would also like to thank Mari Shullaw at Boydell & Brewer, whose careful readings and extremely helpful comments and critiques on a number of drafts of this manuscript have greatly improved it.

My thanks go to the patient and unfailingly friendly staff at the archives, libraries, and museums I visited during the course of my research, in particular those at The National Archives, Kew, the British Library, London, and the Başbakanlık Osmanlı Arşivleri in Istanbul. My research in Istanbul was made easier and more enjoyable by a number of people. I should particularly like to thank: Hülya Tezcan; Abdülmecid Arıgüzel, Esra Müysseroğlu, and Selin İpek at Topkapı Palace; and Fatih Tetik at Dolmabahçe Palace. I am grateful for the friendship and company provided by Alaaddin Tok, Kazım Baycar, Celali Yılmaz, and Ercan Uzunoğlu.

My eternal gratitude goes to my wife, Dikla Braier. She has embraced (or at least tolerated) my love of history, and of Turkey and the Ottomans in particular, keeping me company, and indeed sane, in person and in spirit, during the long hours of data input, translation, note taking, and writing. None of this would have been possible without her love and friendship.

# Note on languages, place names, dates, and currencies

## 1. Languages

The research into this book has included material in a number of languages, most prominently English, French, Italian, Latin, and Ottoman Turkish. All translations, unless otherwise stated, are my own. The following transcription and transliteration conventions have been employed:

**English, French, Italian, Latin, and Spanish**
I have updated archaic spellings in those languages to reflect modern conventions. This is also true for eighteenth-century orthography, so that I have written 's' rather than 'ſ', 'ss' for 'ß', 'que' for 'q̃', and 'ii' instead of 'ij' or 'ÿ', and so on. Contemporary renderings of Ottoman Turkish names and words are given with the original spelling followed by the transliterated term: 'I was called to my audience by a chaus [çavuş] and a letter from the chimacham [*kaymakam*].' Grammatical forms are otherwise retained as in the original texts.

**Ottoman Turkish and Arabic**
The majority of Ottoman Turkish sources used are handwritten manuscripts with a high proportion of Arabic and Persian vocabulary and grammatical forms, and it has seemed more appropriate, therefore, to provide a full transliteration rather than attempting to render them in modern Turkish. This is given for terms and phrases taken from primary source documents, and not for names, place names, and official titles. The transliteration system used is based on Eleazar Birnbaum's conventions and the *International Journal of Middle Eastern Studies* guide, combined with the main lexicographical source employed in Sir James Redhouse's *English and Turkish Dictionary* of 1856.[1] A table giving the transliterated equivalent of each letter is written below (transliterations from Arabic and Persian which differ have the alternative character in brackets):

[1] Eleazar Birnbaum, 'The transliteration of Ottoman Turkish for library and general purposes', *Journal of the American Oriental Society* 87:2 (1967) 122–56 at 134–52; 'IJMES Transliteration System for Arabic, Persian, and Turkish', online document [http://web.gc.cuny.edu/ijmes/docs/TransChart.pdf]; Sir James Redhouse, *An English and Turkish Dictionary, In Two Parts, English and Turkish, and Turkish and English* (London, 1856).

| ا | - | خ | ḫ (kh) | ص | ṣ | ك | k/g/ğ*/ñ |
|---|---|---|---|---|---|---|---|
| ب | b | د | d | ض | ż (ḍ) | ل | l |
| پ | p | ذ | ẕ (ḏ) | ط | ṭ/ḍ | م | m |
| ت | t | ر | r | ظ | ẓ | ن | n |
| ث | s̱ (th) | ز | z | ع | ʿ | و | v (w) |
| ج | c* (j) | ژ | j* | غ | ġ (gh) | ه/ة | h/t |
| چ | ç* | س | s | ف | f | ى | y |
| ح | ḥ | ش | ş* (sh) | ق | ḳ (q) | ء | ʾ |

Starred letters (*) indicate the use of the Turkish pronunciation of that letter that may be unfamiliar to the English-language readers:

‘c’ is ‘j’ as in ‘*j*am’;
‘ç’ is ‘ch’ as in ‘*ch*eese’;
‘j’ is ‘zh’ as in the pronunciation of the ‘s’ in ‘plea*s*ure’;
‘ş’ is ‘sh’ as in ‘*sh*eep’;
‘ğ’ is always silent (as ‘ġ’ is on occasion too), but lengthens the preceding vowel.

There are eight vowels, which are equivalent to English long vowels. Sometimes they are signified by the letters ا, ي, or و, sometimes by letter combinations such as اي or او, and sometimes by largely unmarked diacritics (-ِ, -َ, -ُ). The four ‘back vowels’ are ‘a’, ‘ı’ (a schwa sound), ‘o’ and ‘u’; and the four ‘front vowels’ are ‘e’, ‘i’, ‘ö’, and ‘ü’ (that last two sounding like their German equivalents). Long vowels in words of Arabic or Persian origin are marked with macrons (ا ā, ى ī, و ū).

## 2. Places

Ottoman place names are given in their modern form, so that it is Izmir rather than Smyrna, Iskenderun rather than Alexandretta, and Ankara rather than Angora; this simply reflects the language of the Ottoman documents, and not the European language texts that reflected older Byzantine or Roman names. In that regard, the capital city of the Ottoman Empire is always referred to as Istanbul rather than Constantinople, unless specifically referring to the city prior to the Ottoman conquest of 1453. Certainly, the Ottoman state employed the term Kostantiniye, and in several documents also the name İslambul, but on the whole it was İstanbul when not using terms more common terms such as Dersaadet (the abode of felicity).

Britain is understood as the kingdoms of England and Scotland, as there really was almost no differentiation between the two by the ambassadors and even less by the Ottoman government. Ireland is a different case in terms of Levant Company regulations, but the Capitulations and official Ottoman letters also made reference to the kingdom of Ireland as part of a singular British polity. Britain is therefore employed as the generic term for the *de jure* and *de facto* realms of the kingdoms of England and Scotland before 1707, the kingdom of Great Britain after 1707, and the United Kingdom after 1801.

## 3. Dates

As a general rule, the British ambassadors in Istanbul generally used the Julian calendar until September 1752, after which the Gregorian calendar was uniformly employed. Prior to 1752, New Year began on 25 March, and often ambassadors provided both the Julian and Gregorian years in the period between 1 January and 24 March when the two calendars differed, for instance 20 February 1694/5, indicating the Julian year of 1694, but the Gregorian year of 1695.

Ottoman dates from the Islamic *hijrī* calendar – in Ottoman Turkish *hicrī* – are provided occasionally on documents in the British archives and more often on documents in the Ottoman archives (but not always). I have provided dual years in the text and in the footnotes, with dates in the text given as '*hicrī*/Gregorian', e.g. '1086/1675', and in the footnotes in square brackets, e.g. '1 Receb 1086 [5 October 1675]'. To give a rough idea on dates based on 1 January in the Gregorian calendar:

| | | | | | | | |
|---|---|---|---|---|---|---|---|
| 1660 | 1070 | 1700 | 1111 | 1740 | 1152 | 1780 | 1193 |
| 1670 | 1080 | 1710 | 1121 | 1750 | 1163 | 1790 | 1204 |
| 1680 | 1090 | 1720 | 1132 | 1760 | 1173 | 1800 | 1214 |
| 1690 | 1101 | 1730 | 1142 | 1770 | 1183 | 1810 | 1224 |

As far as possible, dates are made as clear and as accurate as the sources themselves allow, and on occasion only month and year, year alone, or approximate year can be provided.

## 4. Currencies

This study uses a number of financial and commercial records, which necessarily involves a number of different currencies. The most common currencies cited are the British pound (£) and the Ottoman *guruş*, both silver-based coins. The British pound was divided into 20 shillings (s) or 240 pence (d), and remains largely unchanged over the period under examination. The Ottoman *guruş* was known by the British as the 'piaster', and its constituent units, the *para*, and the *akçe,* known as the 'asper', although the currency changed at the end of the seventeenth century (as will be explained in detail in Chapter 3). The *guruş* for most of the eighteenth century was made up of 40 *para*s or 120 *akçe*s.

# Abbreviations

| | |
|---|---|
| BL | British Library, London |
| BM | British Museum, London |
| BOA | Başbakanlık Osmanlı Arşivleri (Prime Ministry's Ottoman Archives), Istanbul |
| GAC | Government Art Collection, United Kingdom, online collection (http://www.gac.culture.gov.uk) |
| LMA | London Metropolitan Archives |
| MOL | Museum of London |
| NMM | National Maritime Museum, London |
| NPG | National Portrait Gallery, London |
| POG | Proceedings of the Old Bailey, online archives (http://www.oldbaileyonline.org/) |
| SOAS | School of Oriental and African Studies, London |
| *TLG* | *The London Gazette*, online (http://www.thegazette.co.uk) |
| TNA | The National Archives, London |
| VAM | Victoria and Albert Museum, London |

# Introduction: De/re-constructing the history of British–Ottoman relations

## Approaching eighteenth-century diplomatic history

The history of British–Ottoman relations in the long eighteenth century begins and ends with a voyage at sea. In March 1661, the Earl of Winchilsea arrived at his residence in Istanbul's Galata district after a rough winter's journey of four months aboard HMS *Plymouth*. Winchilsea was one of the first ambassadors appointed by the new King Charles II (r. 1660–85), and was perhaps the highest ranking of the ambassadors that the British dispatched to the court of the sultan. Full of confidence in himself and the reputation of his monarch, Winchilsea wrote that '[t]here is no public minister at this Porte that hath the like esteem as I find here'.[1] This formal re-establishment of relations after the uncertainty of the Commonwealth – when king and parliament had rival ambassadors in Istanbul – was full of promise, with British merchants plying a successful trade in Ottoman marketplaces, and with Britain seen to be in greater diplomatic favour than France following French intervention in the long-standing siege of Crete on the side of the Ottoman's enemy, Venice.[2]

Fast-forward almost 150 years later to January 1807, and we find another British warship anchored in the harbour of Galata. In the midst of a new phase in the wars that had been engulfing Europe, the Ottoman Empire had embarked on a war with Britain's ally and coalition partner, Russia, as part of an alliance with France. The British ambassador in Istanbul, Charles Arbuthnot, had strict instructions from his superiors in London to do his best to lessen French influence over Sultan Selim III (r. 1789–1807), and to bring a swift end to the Russian conflict that was detracting from that state's efforts against France. However, the Ottomans refused to bow to British pressure, and so the British warship HMS *Endymion* was stationed at the imperial capital to send a serious message to the government of the Sublime State. As tensions continued to build, it became clear that Arbuthnot's position was untenable. On 29 January, the ambassador invited the British merchant community to dine with him upon

1 TNA/SP97/17 Earl of Winchilsea to Charles II, 3/13 March 1660/1.

2 Mark Fissell & Daniel Goffman, 'Viewing the scaffold from Istanbul: The Bendysh-Hyde affair, 1647–1651', *Albion* 22:3 (1990), 421–48; Ersin Gülsoy, *Girit'in Fethi ve Osmanlı İdaresinin Kurulması, 1645–1670* (İstanbul, 2004), 150–7.

*Endymion*, and without a word of warning the ship set sail away from Galata towards the Dardanelles. In a foreshadowing of the Gallipoli Campaign of 1915, a British fleet under the command of Admiral Duckworth attempted to force its way through the Dardanelles and onwards to bombard Istanbul; in 1807 the British managed to smash through the straits, but were beaten back by Ottoman fortifications and naval forces two months later without being able to cross the Sea of Marmara.

The conflict that broke out in 1807 marked the end of over two hundred years of peaceful relations between the Ottoman Empire and Britain. This was a crucial period in the political and economic history of both states, and the story of British–Ottoman relations in this period has not received the attention it deserves. This study will therefore examine British diplomacy in the Ottoman Empire in a 'long' eighteenth century, defined by the re-establishment of relations between the British monarchy and the Ottoman state in 1661, and the outbreak of the first British–Ottoman war in 1807. The period is also marked by the history of the Levant Company, the commercial monopoly that funded the embassy between 1580 and 1804, which was granted a new charter in 1661, and ceased to finance the embassy in 1804. The main purpose of my research was to uncover the diplomatic practices of the ambassador based in Istanbul, as the role and duties of ambassadors, in this case and more generally, are often not understood as well as those exercising specifically consular functions. My intention in a broader sense is to demonstrate the centrality and interconnectivity of finance, law, and culture in early modern diplomatic practice in the Ottoman Empire, and the utility of those categories in wider studies of historical diplomacy, and intercultural relations in particular. On another level, this is also the story of how, throughout the eighteenth century, increasing British violence in and around the Ottoman realms fundamentally changed the nature of relations. The processes that took the British from their peaceful arrival in 1661 to their violent retreat in 1807 is indicative of a disentangling of commercial interest and diplomatic practice as part of the journey towards imperialism; commerce and diplomacy did not cease to be linked, but they ceased to be the same thing.

At the beginning, in thinking about how to write this history of diplomacy between the British and the Ottomans, a number of key themes quickly emerged. The first is finance, that is, an examination of how diplomacy was funded, and on what sorts of goods and activities the money was spent. The second is cultural accommodation, which views the interaction of ambassadors with host states not simply through the abstract notion of a meeting of polities personified, but as an engagement of two different cultural conventions. The third, and by no means the least, is the diplomacy of daily interactions, meaning an examination of the impact of diplomacy on the lives of the expatriate communities of (almost exclusively in this period) merchants living in foreign lands. In seeking to develop these themes, financial and legal records, as well as the diplomatic and state correspondence, have been crucial in constructing a more inclusive history of diplomacy based around the experiences of historical actors, rather than abstract states and nations.

As this book neared completion, I took some time to reflect on how different the final product is to how I had imagined my history of British–Ottoman relations would look like. In part this is because I found sources in London and Istanbul that guided me away from the narrative road set out by the letters of the ambassadors and state officials, and off along paths leading to the stories of individuals engaging in and relying on different forms of diplomacy, thoroughly rooted in commercial interest and practice. Aside from these unplanned but ultimately fruitful diversions, a particular passage in a printed source provided much of the initial inspiration in rethinking how to approach this diplomatic history. In his treatise on the art of negotiating, the French diplomat François de Callières gave a rather striking piece of advice on how an ambassador should conduct himself during his posting abroad:

> He ought to accommodate himself to the manners and customs of the country where he is, without showing any aversion to them, or despising them, as many ministers do, who are constantly praising the ways of living in their own country, that they may have occasion to find fault with those of others. A minister ought to persuade himself once for all, that he has not authority enough to reduce a whole country to conform themselves to his way of living, and that it is much more reasonable that he should conform himself to that of the country where he is, for the little time he is to remain in it.[3]

For much of the period under examination, the British conformed to Ottoman diplomatic expectations and practices. Although de Callières was speaking to his contemporaries, his words remain relevant, as notions of cultural accommodation and conformity were clearly central to the development and smooth practice of diplomatic interactions. This was not, however, out of some cultural sensitivity, but rather cultural necessity. In order to ensure the ultimate aim of British relations with the Ottoman Empire – profitable commerce – the British ambassadors conformed to Ottoman diplomatic practices, but also used them as an opportunity to further those commercial aims. On the part of the Ottomans, the main purpose of diplomatic relations was the establishment and maintenance of friendship – *dostluḳ* – through specific signs and actions – *iẓhār* and *iş ʿār* – such as the presentation of royal letters and gifts. In other words, commercial interest and diplomatic practice were so completely linked that the two could not function without each other. However, as the century wore on, and geopolitical interests became more violently enforced, this system began to rupture. The changes that did finally separate diplomacy and commerce are crucial in explaining why relations were so different at the end of the eighteenth century from its beginning.

The British historian G.M. Young famously claimed that 'the greater part of what passes for diplomatic history is little more than the record of what one

[3] François de Callières, *The Art of Negotiating with Sovereign Princes*, trans. anonymous (London, 1716), 164.

clerk said to another clerk'.[4] True as that might have been for the nineteenth and early twentieth centuries – although it was more of a 'casual insult', as Raymond Jones described it, rather than a solid critique – the subfield of diplomatic history remains a source of some contention in historical discourse.[5] It is undeniable that, for a long time, a Rankean *Primat der Außenpolitik* prevailed across British diplomatic history in particular, so that the great critic of 'Whiggish' writing, Sir Herbert Butterfield, wrote in 1955 that British historians of his age had 'gone far beyond Ranke in the exclusiveness of their devotion to diplomatic history'.[6] Such a discipline that relied, as Thomas Smith put it, on 'event-centred history as implied in state documents and other "high" political artefacts', was seen to have gone into decline following the rise of new histories in the 1960s, but remained in various guises.[7]

In the United States of America, in reaction to criticisms from scholars such as Charles Maier, who argued that the field was characterised by an 'intrinsic resistance to new techniques', there was a move towards a so-called 'new' diplomatic history.[8] A few years ago, Thomas Zeiler entered into an impassioned defence of his discipline, claiming that, although Maier's warnings and criticisms had been valid in the 1980s, diplomatic history in the USA had since entered 'the stream of cutting-edge scholarship'.[9] Yet, as Jessica Gienow-Hecht pointed out in a thorough response to that article, Zeiler had simply entrenched the state as the principal category of analysis, with little or no regard for recent trends in cultural or social history; in Zeiler's own words, he wanted to pull 'the mainstream a bit back toward considerations of the state', the study of which he called a 'time-honoured tradition'.[10] It was, perhaps, such persisting state-focused and largely American/Eurocentric positions that led to a notable call to arms in 2008 from John Watkins in *The Journal of Medieval and Early Modern Studies*. 'The time has come,' he declared, 'for a multidisciplinary re-evaluation of one of the oldest, and traditionally one of the most conservative subfields in the modern discipline of history: the study of pre-modern diplomacy.'[11] For Watkins, the 'new' diplomatic history had not, as

4 G.M. Young, *Victorian England: Portrait of an Age* (Oxford, 1936), 103.

5 Raymond Jones, *The British Diplomatic Service, 1815–1914* (Gerrards Cross, 1983), 1.

6 Sir Herbert Butterfield, *Man on his Past: The Study of the History of Historical Scholarship* (Cambridge, 1955), 122.

7 Thomas W. Smith, *History and International Relations* (London, 1999), 16; Karina Urbach, 'Diplomatic history since the cultural turn', *The Historical Journal* 46:4 (2003), 991–7.

8 Charles S. Maier, 'Marking time: The historiography of international relations' in Michael Kammen (ed.), *The Past Before Us: Contemporary Historical Writing in the United States* (Ithaca NY, 1980), 355–87. See also: Edward P. Crapol, 'Coming to terms with Empire: The historiography of late nineteenth-century American foreign relations' in Michael J. Hogan (ed.), *Paths to Power: The Historiography of American Foreign Relations to 1941* (Cambridge, 2000), 79–116.

9 Thomas W. Zeiler, 'The diplomatic history bandwagon: A state of the field', *The Journal of American History* 95:4 (2009), 1053–73.

10 Ibid., 1056; Jessica C.E. Gienow-Hecht, 'What bandwagon? Diplomatic history today', *The Journal of American History* 94:5 (2009), 1083–6.

11 John Watkins, 'Toward a new diplomatic history of medieval and early modern Europe', *The Journal of Medieval and Early Modern Studies* 38:1 (2008), 1–14 at 1.

yet, succeeded in changing the parameters and lenses of study for diplomacy before the nineteenth century.

Many of the problems in approaching diplomatic history are due to a conflation of 'foreign policy' and 'diplomacy'. This is particularly important when thinking about pre-nineteenth-century diplomacy. To borrow Daniela Frigo's way of describing this, diplomacy was not an abstract institution, but an *institutio*, a group of defined functions and roles.[12] Diplomacy was a set of practices through which states and other actors interacted with each other. The American diplomat Charles Freeman described the three elements of statecraft, where military force forms the 'fists' of a state, espionage its 'sixth sense', and diplomacy is described as 'the profession of persuasion'.[13] Yet, in thinking of diplomacy solely in terms of anthropomorphised states rather than of groups of peoples, the difference between diplomacy as a practice of negotiation between individuals and groups on matters of mutual concern, and foreign policy as an articulation of the state's relationship with other states, gets lost.[14] This difference is particularly important in the context of the European ambassadors who lived in the Ottoman Empire in the eighteenth century. Such resident diplomats may have been largely dispatched by states for the purpose of political negotiation, but their duties and daily practices tended to focus on overseeing and mediating the interactions between different groups of subjects. That is, protecting and managing commercial concerns was of far greater importance in practical terms than alliance negotiations and political intrigues. Diplomats were not simply mouthpieces of the state, but mediating actors within specific economic and cultural environments.

One damning critique of the contemporary historical approach came from an historian of modern American diplomatic history, Stephen Pelz, who argued that diplomatic history was lagging behind other historical disciplines because diplomatic historians were lacking in methodology.[15] He called for dialogue between social scientists and historians on the basis that historians could learn much from the analysis of specific case studies to test their hypotheses arising from repeating patterns in their research data, whilst social scientists would benefit greatly from appreciating that 'causal variables' had different effects in different historical periods, cultures, and with different individual historical actors.[16] In recent years, diplomatic history has indeed begun to respond to the

12 Daniela Frigo, 'Prudence and experience: Ambassadors and political cultures in early modern Italy', *The Journal of Medieval and Early Modern Studies* 38:1 (2008), 35–55.

13 Chas. W. Freeman Jr., *Arts of Power: Statecraft and Diplomacy* (Washington DC, 1997), 3–4.

14 See, for instance: Wilfried Bolewski, *Diplomacy and International Law in Globalized Relations* (New York, 2007), 15; Robert Oresko, G.C. Gibbs, & I.M. Scott, 'Introduction' in Robert Oresko, G.C. Gibbs, & I.M. Scott (eds), *Royal and Republican Sovereignty in Early Modern Europe* (Cambridge, 1997), 1–42 at 15.

15 Stephen Pelz, 'Toward a new diplomatic history: Two and a half cheers for international relations methods' in Colin Elman & Mirian Fendius Elman (eds), *Bridges and Boundaries: Historians, Political Scientists, and the Study of International Relations* (Cambridge MA, 2001), 85–110 at 87. See also: Stephen Pelz, 'Essay and reflection: On systematic explanation in international history', *The International History Review* 12:4 (1990), 762–81.

16 Pelz, 'Toward a new diplomatic history', 86–7.

wider changes in historical investigation, resulting in a new wave of studies and scholarly networks that seek to build on and re-evaluate older scholarship using a range of different intellectual tools and approaches.

The 'new' diplomatic history is a result of the increasing interdisciplinary nature of the field, what the historian of early modern France John Rule called 'an intricate and sensitive blending of social and international history with the history of ideas'.[17] In David Onnekink and Gijs Rommelse's thoughtful introduction to a volume on the relationship between ideology and foreign policy in early modern Europe, they charted the development of diplomatic historiography from one of power struggles between states to more nuanced approaches, particularly a constructivist approach that, in their words, 'argued that most aspects of international relations are subject to social and intellectual construction'.[18] This study tends to follow that line of argument, viewing diplomatic practice in terms of cultural convention arising from intellectual and elite construction on the one hand, and from social and economic expediencies on the other.

Such methodological considerations are important in the case of foreign diplomats in the Ottoman Empire, as the role of that polity in the wider story of interactions between states and peoples in the pre-nineteenth-century world has often been misinterpreted. For instance, one of the textbooks on the history of international relations, M.S. Anderson's *The Rise of Modern Diplomacy, 1450–1919* (1993), relies on an anachronistic division between a civilised 'core of western states' and a 'primitive' periphery, but claims that the (peripheral) Ottoman Empire was burdened with 'all the weight of Islamic religious conservatism', precluding any possibility of 'developed' diplomatic practice.[19] Such misrepresentations led Gerald MacLean to dryly observe that, 'for some time now there has been a rumour going about that, during the early modern period at least, the Ottoman Empire did not engage in diplomacy'.[20]

Thankfully, through the work of a number of Ottomanists, such notions have been entirely and convincingly disproved, along with other long-standing assumptions about the Ottomans.[21] Moreover, a deeper understanding of Ottoman state and society before the nineteenth century has led to a reclassification of Ottoman periodisations and notions of modernity, which had previously followed a thoroughly unsatisfying rise-and-decline paradigm. As Dana Sajdi argued in her critical overview of Ottoman historiography for the

17 John C. Rule, 'Review article: Gathering intelligence in the age of Louis XIV', *The International History Review* 14:4 (1992), 732–52 at 732.

18 David Onnekink & Gijs Rommelse, 'Introduction' in David Onnekink & Gijs Rommelse (eds), *Ideology and Foreign Policy in Early Modern Europe, 1650–1750* (Farnham, 2011), 1–10 at 3–4.

19 M.S. Anderson, *The Rise of Modern Diplomacy, 1450–1919* (Harlow, 1993), 27–8, 70–1.

20 Gerald MacLean, 'Courting the Porte: Early Anglo-Ottoman diplomacy', *University of Bucharest Review* 10:2 (2008), 80–8 at 80.

21 One important although problematic departure point was the edited collection of A. Nuri Yurdusev (ed.), *Ottoman Diplomacy: Conventional or Unconventional?* (Basingstoke & New York, 2004), which has provided several points for discussion. See also: Daniel Goffman, *The Ottoman Empire and Early Modern Europe* (Cambridge, 2002), 1–6.

eighteenth century, '[a] Middle Eastern modernity marked by the Napoleonic moment or the Tanzimat [reform] effort is now a questionable equation, and "Ottoman early modernity", not a "post-classical age" has become tenable'.[22] That is, recent historiography places the Ottomans in a wider and more interlinked geographical and conceptual context, not monolithic descriptions of golden classical eras and dark days of political decline.[23] Ottomanists have since pursued a variety of paths in their examinations of the Empire and its interactions with the wider world.[24]

As a result, Ottoman historiography is now strongly interdisciplinary, increasingly engages comparatively with other regions, and has made use of a vast amount of evidence, from the millions of documents held in archives across the former Ottoman dominions and beyond, to a wide variety of material sources. The ever-increasing amount of literature on social, economic, and cultural history is a testament to a refocusing of historical interest in the Ottoman realms from state-dominated metanarratives to examinations of fluid and interconnected institutions, localities, professions, ideas, societies, and cultures. It is also characterised by a remarkable maturity in dealing with some of the thornier questions of historical interpretation. This is perhaps best articulated in a forceful piece of history writing by Gabriel Piterberg in his examination of the interplay between history and historiography, in which he called for a methodological 'middle ground' that would counter 'the absolute dominance of the documentary paradigm that stifles the historical imagination'.[25] This expresses a profound tension in tackling both Ottoman and diplomatic (and Ottoman diplomatic) history: what do we do with the gaps in the sources? What do we do when we *know* that a certain practice *must* be going on, but there is simply no explicit record of it? What are the limits of historical interpretation? And how do we ensure that our historical imaginations do not run into the realms of fantasy?[26]

In attempting to explain the history of British–Ottoman diplomacy in the eighteenth century, I have tried to avoid a Rankean fetishisation of certain kinds of historical evidence that would have led to a grand-narrative and state-centred history. Diplomatic history, if we see it instead as a history of negotiations, does not have to be a story of high political dramas. This does

22 Dana Sajdi, 'Decline, its discontents, and Ottoman cultural history: By way of introduction' in Dana Sajdi (ed.), *Ottoman Tulips, Ottoman Coffee: Leisure and Lifestyle in the Eighteenth Century* (London & New York, 2007), 1–40 at 27. See also: Jane Hathaway, 'Rewriting eighteenth-century Ottoman history', *Mediterranean Historical Review* 19:1 (2004), 29–53.

23 A notable recent example demonstrating the growing sophistication of our understanding of Ottoman links with the wider world can be found in Pascal W. Firges, Tobias P. Graf, Christian Roth, and Gülay Tulasoğlu (eds), *Well-Connected Domains: Towards an Entangled Ottoman History* (Leiden, 2014).

24 The vibrancy of contemporary Ottoman studies was highlighted thoroughly and eloquently in Virginia Aksan, 'What's up in Ottoman studies', *Journal of the Ottoman Turkish Studies Association* 1:1–2 (2014), 3–21.

25 Gabriel Piterberg, *An Ottoman Tragedy: History and Historiography at Play* (Berkeley & Los Angeles, 2003), 1–8 at 5–6.

26 Joseph Esherick, 'Cherishing sources from afar', *Modern China* 24:2 (1998), 135–61.

not mean to say that works on political diplomacy and foreign relations should be discarded. Indeed, some recent histories of eighteenth-century diplomacy have struck a rather beautiful balance between diplomatic and other histories, most notably Jennifer Mori's study of the culture of British diplomacy at the end of the century.[27] Rather, one benefit in moving away from traditional narratives of diplomatic history is to depart from a Eurocentric articulation of diplomatic practice. Above all, the standard refuge of diplomatic history, the ambassadorial and state records, can reveal so much more about diplomatic and wider practices, providing a financial and cultural history of diplomatic interactions. When combined with different sorts of sources, such as financial and legal records, and material evidence, diplomatic history can shed light on the primary reason for diplomatic interaction, that is, the merchants and other expatriates, visitors, and travellers residing in foreign lands.

## The historiographical setting

Reading through the histories of relations between Britain and the Ottoman Empire takes us on an interesting historiographical journey, with varying views of relations but also with a number of running themes. The first account of British–Ottoman relations was a eulogy to the Levant Company, written by an erstwhile Company chaplain, Robert Walsh, on its demise in 1825.[28] Walsh described the history of the Company as one of bold new beginnings and eventual decline, of 'English' nobility in the face of 'Turkish' barbarism, and emphasised that, despite commercial setbacks, its members had enriched British culture through their writings, collections of artefacts, and elucidation of the civilisations of the East. For Walsh, the Ottoman government was despotic, corrupt, and an enemy of progress.[29] This study was, of course, a product of its time, but also came to serve as something of a template for a number of subsequent histories.

For much of the nineteenth century, there was little interest in earlier British–Ottoman relations among British historians, until the traveller James Theodore Bent wrote an article on political and commercial relations between 1580 and 1804.[30] This was followed with an edited collection of early travel accounts from the Ottoman domains, and as such Bent can be considered the first British historian of relations with the Ottomans.[31] Neither the Balkan Wars, nor the Young Turk Revolution produced vastly increased scholarship on earlier relations between London and Istanbul. There were, however, some

[27] Jennifer Mori, *The Culture of Diplomacy: Britain in Europe, 1750–1830* (Manchester, 2011).

[28] Robert Walsh, *Account of the Levant Company: with Some Notices of the Benefits Conferred upon Society by its Officers, in Promoting the Cause of Humanity, Literature, and the Fine Arts* (London, 1825).

[29] Ibid., 5; Robert Walsh, *A Residence at Constantinople, during a period including the Commencement, Progress, and Termination of the Greek and Turkish Revolutions*, 2 vols (London, 1836), vol. I, 1.

[30] J. Theodore Bent, 'The English in the Levant', *The English Historical Review* 5:20 (1890), 654–64.

[31] J. Theodore Bent (ed.), *Early Voyages and Travels in the Levant* (London, 1893).

earnest efforts, with Honyel Rosedale's examination of Elizabethan correspondence on the establishment of relations, and, most importantly, Mordechai Epstein's economic analysis of the Elizabethan and Jacobean periods.[32] The First World War halted such studies, and it was not until the 1920s, for example with Hugh Rawlinson's thoughtful account of the first ambassador from London to Istanbul, William Harborne, that interest resumed.[33] Yet, as with Bent, Rosedale, and Epstein, Rawlinson was not an Ottomanist by trade. He did, however, articulate the duties of the ambassador as agent of the Company and representative of the Crown, and began to explore the functions of this particular embassy.[34]

The 1920s, with the establishment of direct and indirect British imperial hegemony in a number of the former Ottoman lands, seem to have ignited something of an interest in British relations with the recently fallen Ottoman state. Sir Harry Luke's 1921 study on Ottoman Cyprus through the archives of the Levant Company was followed by another article by Rawlinson on the early Levant trade.[35] The trend in the study of early relations continued with Albert Rowland's examination of Elizabethan relations, an edited volume on the sixteenth-century traveller John Sanderson, and, a precursor to Goffman's work, Warner Grenelle Rice's study on early English travellers in the Levant.[36]

A major turning point came in 1925, when a historian called Alfred Cecil Wood published an article discussing the political and structural trends of the British embassy in Istanbul.[37] As with his predecessors, Wood had no background in the study of the Ottoman Empire nor in the Ottoman Turkish language, yet from this article came a book that has remained the standard study for the history of the Levant Company and the study of early modern British–Ottoman interactions, *A History of the Levant Company*, published in 1935.[38] Wood used a vast amount of British archival material, building on the scholarship of Epstein and Rawlinson, and constructed a history of the Levant Company and British–Ottoman relations between the sixteenth and nineteenth centuries using financial and commercial documents, as well as political and diplomatic sources. Since its publication in 1935 and reprint in

32 H.G. Rosedale, *Queen Elizabeth and the Levant Company: A Diplomatic and Literary Episode of the Establishment of our Trade with Turkey* (London, 1904); M. Epstein, *The Early History of the Levant Company* (London, 1908).

33 H.G. Rawlinson, 'The Embassy of William Harborne to Constantinople, 1583–8', *Transactions of the Royal Historical Society* 4:5 (1922), 1–27.

34 Ibid., 10.

35 Harry Luke, *Cyprus under the Turks, 1571–1878* (London, 1921); H.G. Rawlinson, 'Early trade between England and the Levant', *Journal of Indian History* 2 (1922), 107–16.

36 Albert Rowland, *Studies in English Commerce and Exploration in the Reign of Elizabeth* (Philadelphia, 1924); William Foster (ed.), *The Travels of John Sanderson in the Levant, 1584–1602* (London, 1931); Warner Grenelle Rice, 'Early English travellers to Greece and the Levant' in *Essays and Studies in English and Comparative Literature* (Ann Arbor, 1933), 205–60.

37 Alfred C. Wood, 'The English embassy at Constantinople, 1660–1762', *The English Historical Review* 40:160 (1925), 533–61.

38 Alfred C. Wood, *A History of the Levant Company* (Oxford, 1935).

1964, it has been employed, often uncritically, as the textbook on the Levant Company and British–Ottoman relations. Wood also continued a number of themes employed by his predecessors. For instance, his periodisation of the Company's history envisaged a brief rise, a golden age, a protracted decline, partial recovery, and dissolution. This very much echoed an earlier narrative put forward by two historians of the English chartered companies, George Cawston and Augustus Henry Keane, who described the Levant Company's history as one of 'charter, prosperous trade, keen competition, encroachments, decline, debt, difficulties, disappearance'.[39] He echoed both Walsh and Bent by emphasising the supposed cultural endeavours of the Company's members, specifically their contributions to collections of artefacts, cartography, and travel narratives.[40] Moreover, he concluded that although the Levant merchants were '[u]nimportant in their individual lives, collectively they bequeathed a legacy of intrepidity, courage, and endurance which entitles them to an honoured rank among the pioneers of English trade and empire'.[41]

Wood's studies remained the primary work on the Levant Company and British–Ottoman relations for a number of decades, and may continue so for the near future. Subsequent studies have borrowed heavily from his methodology and source base, such as Christine Laidlaw's *The British in the Levant* (2010).[42] A hybrid of Wood's article and book along with other nineteenth-century studies (such as J.B. Pearson's), it examines the development of the Company and its structure (almost entirely sourced from *History of the Levant Company*), with a conclusion borrowing from Walsh, Bent, and Wood by praising the Levant Company merchants and ambassadors for their material and intellectual contributions to British culture.[43] More recently, Despina Vlami's *Trading with the Ottomans* has added some valuable insights into the later history of the Levant Company, but still relies very much on Wood's sources and structure. Other studies have been conscious products of their time, notably James Mather's *Pashas* (2009), which aimed to provide a case study in British–Muslim coexistence, particularly (and explicitly) in the context of the 2003 invasion of Iraq.[44] Arbitrarily deciding to call the Levant Company merchants 'pashas', something equivalent to the East India Company 'nabobs', Mather set his mercantile subjects in a rather ahistorical environment, seeking above all to convey his message that '[t]he pashas [that is, the British merchants] remind us that once upon a time there was a peaceful and mutually enriching encounter between Britain and the still-troubled

39 George Cawston & Augustus Henry Keane, *The Early Chartered Companies, A.D. 1296–1858* (London, 1896), 85. See also: David Hannay, *The Great Chartered Companies* (London, 1926).

40 Wood, *Levant Company*, 248–9.

41 Ibid.

42 Ibid., ix; Christine Laidlaw, *The British in the Levant: Trade and Perceptions of the Ottoman Empire in the Eighteenth Century* (London & New York, 2010), xiii.

43 J.B. Pearson, *A Biographical Sketch of the Chaplains to the Levant Company, Maintained at Constantinople, Aleppo and Smyrna, 1611–1706* (Cambridge, 1883).

44 James Mather, *Pashas: Traders and Travellers in the Islamic World* (New Haven, 2009), 1–14.

Middle East'.[45] None of these studies, Wood's included, used any Ottoman-language material.

Yet with the growth of Turkish scholarship on British–Ottoman relations beginning in the 1930s with studies such as Ahmed Refik Altınay's examination of early relations, the field was about to receive, at last, some input from the Ottoman side of the sources.[46] In 1955, Alfred Horniker, who examined early relations, reviewed a book by a Turkish scholar, Akdes Nimet Kurat, who had published an edited collection of the correspondence of the British ambassador to Istanbul in the early eighteenth century, Sir Robert Sutton.[47] What Horniker had not read was Kurat's earlier Turkish language publications on early British–Ottoman relations using Ottoman sources, and his invaluable documentation of Ottoman-language materials in British archives.[48] It was not until Susan Skilliter's work, first in her PhD thesis on Ottoman documents relating to the embassy of the second ambassador to Istanbul, Edward Barton, and then most notably in her critical volume of British and Ottoman documents from the establishment of relations, published in 1977, that the field of British–Ottoman relations entered an era of multiple archival and linguistic sources.[49] Since the 1960s, there have been a variety of studies of British–Ottoman relations, usually with a commercial focus, using a variety of British and Ottoman sources, although rarely together.[50] This study aims to

45 Ibid., 244. I strongly suspect that Mather got the idea to call them 'pashas' from Wood, *Levant Company*, 248.

46 Arthur Leon Horniker, 'William Harborne and the beginning of Anglo-Turkish diplomatic and commercial relations', *The Journal of Modern History* 14:3 (1942), 289–316; Arthur Leon Horniker, 'Anglo-French rivalry in the Levant from 1583 to 1612', *The Journal of Modern History* 18:4 (1946), 289–305; Ahmet Refik, [Altınay], 'Türkler ve Kraliçe Elizabeth', *Darülfünun Edebiyat Fakültesi Mecmuası* 8:5 (1932), 3–28.

47 Arthur Leon Horniker, 'Review: The despatches of Sir Robert Sutton, ambassador in Constantinople, 1710–1714', *The Journal of Modern History* 27:4 (1955), 421–2; Akdes Nimet Kurat (ed.), *The Despatches of Sir Robert Sutton, Ambassador in Constantinople 1710–1714* (London, 1953).

48 Akdes Nimet Kurat, 'İngiliz devlet arşivinde ve kütüphanelerinde Türkiye tarihine ait bazı malzemeye dair', *Ankara Üniversitesi Dil ve Tarih-Coğrafya Fakültesi Dergisi* 7:1 (1949), 1–18; Akdes Nimet Kurat, *Türk-İngiliz Münâsebetlerinin Başlangıcı ve Gelişmesi (1553–1610)* (Ankara, 1953). See also: Hâmit Dereli, *Kraliçe Elizabeth Devrinde Türkler ve İngilizler: Bir Araştırma* (Istanbul, 1951); Orhan Burian, 'Türk-İngiliz münasebetinin ilk yıllar', *Anakara Üniversitesi Dil ve Tarih-Coğrafya Fakültesi Dergisi* 9:1–2 (1951), 1–41.

49 S.A. Skilliter, 'Turkish documents relating to Edward Barton's embassy to the Porte (1588–1598)', PhD thesis, University of Manchester (1965); S.A. Skilliter, *William Harborne and the Trade with Turkey 1578–1582: A Documentary Study of the First Anglo-Ottoman Relations* (Oxford, 1977).

50 Mübahat Kütükoğlu, *Osmanlı-İngiliz İktisâdi Münasebetleri, I: 1580–1838* (Ankara, 1974); Ralph Davis, *Aleppo and Devonshire Square: English Traders in the Levant in the Eighteenth Century* (London, 1967); Ali İhsan Bağış, *Britain and the Struggle for the Integrity of the Ottoman Empire: Sir Robert Ainslie's Embassy to Istanbul, 1776–1794* (Istanbul, 1984); William Hale & Ali İhsan Bağış (eds), *Four Centuries of Turco-British Relations: Studies in Diplomatic, Economic and Cultural Affairs* (Beverley, 1984); Gerald MacLean, *Looking East: English Writing and the Ottoman Empire before 1800* (Basingstoke, 2007); Aslı *Çırakman, From the 'Terror of the World' to the 'Sick Man of Europe': European Images of the Ottoman Empire and Society from the Sixteenth Century to the Nineteenth* (Oxford, 2002); G.R. Berridge, *British*

build on the work of those scholars, and others from Ottoman studies, particularly the works of Maurits van den Boogert on the capitulations, and Edhem Eldem on French–Ottoman commercial relations.[51] By re-evaluating a number of sources and introducing new ones, including those in Ottoman Turkish, and by approaching the question of diplomacy from the perspective of commercial pressures, financial constraints, cultural conventions, and social interactions, I hope to move the story of British–Ottoman relations further away from Wood's model, and towards a more complex picture of how and why diplomacy was practised by British diplomatic actors in the Ottoman capital.

Just as all of the other studies were products of their time, it would be foolish of me to think that I have written mine in a vacuum. The invasion of Iraq, and more recently the question of British intervention in Syria, has rekindled an interest in the history of British involvement and interference in the Middle East. If we start that story in the twentieth, or even in the nineteenth century, I think that we are missing something. Part of the way that we see diplomatic aims and practices evolving in British–Ottoman relations over the eighteenth century is in the shift from commercial interest to imperial aggression. Violence came to play a far greater role in relations, from privateer attacks against Ottoman subjects and shipping to assistance for Ottoman enemies like Russia, to overt hostility at the opening of the nineteenth century. Increasing rivalry between the European powers for trade, political influence, and prestige meant that conformity to Ottoman practices was no longer acceptable. The gradual changes in the daily diplomatic activities of gift-giving, ceremonial, and dispute resolution, which had been intricately bound with commercial interest, changed or were discarded as the narrative of power entered a new chapter. Although I am interested in practice above all else, it is clear that changes in practice are indicative of the fact that *something* had changed in the political relationship between the British and the Ottomans by the turn of the nineteenth century. We might see this as evidence of a new form of global competition, a new political and commercial order marked by increasing European violence and domination. This has already been charted in a variety of studies, from Christopher Bayly's *The Birth of the Modern World* thinking on the global scale to the debates over the so-called 'Northern Invasion' inspired by Fernand Braudel's *La Méditerranée et le Monde Méditerranéen a l'époque de Philippe II* (The Mediterranean and the Mediterranean World in the Era of Philip II), to discussions over reform and modernity in the Ottoman world.[52] The changes

*Diplomacy in Turkey, 1583 to the Present: A Study in the Evolution of the Resident Embassy* (Leiden, 2009); John-Paul Ghobrial, *Whispers of Cities: Information Flows in Istanbul, London, and Paris in the Age of William Trumbull* (Oxford, 2013).

51 Maurits van den Boogert, *The Capitulations and the Ottoman Legal System: Qadis, Consuls and Beratlıs in the 18th Century* (Leiden, 2005); Edhem Eldem, *French Trade in Istanbul in the Eighteenth Century* (Leiden, 1999).

52 Christopher Bayly, *The Birth of the Modern World 1780–1914: Global Connections and Comparisons* (Oxford, 2004); Fernand Braudel, *La Méditerranée et le Monde Méditerranéen a l'époque de Philippe II* (Paris, 1949); Maria Fusaro, 'After Braudel: A reassessment of Mediterranean history between the Northern Invasion and the *Caravane Maritime*' in Maria

in British–Ottoman relations, and the violence that ended the long eighteenth century, could well be seen as a clear manifestation of a new political era. The rhetoric of the Ottoman state concerning its relations with the British was fixed, as we shall see, on the principles of universal peace and friendship; by the turn of the nineteenth century, the demands of commerce and political power began to remove the British pretence of adhering to those values. Whilst this study will take the British–Ottoman eighteenth century on its own terms, the events that have followed cannot but make the practices of gift-giving, ceremonial, and dispute resolution be seen in a different light.

## Sources and structure

This book relies on both new and previously examined primary sources in an attempt to get a fuller picture of what was going on. As noted earlier, the British embassy in Istanbul was run by the Levant Company between 1580 and 1804, and, as a result, this particular embassy has a very different set of documents to most other historical embassies before the nineteenth century. Large quantities of the Company's records survive, now held largely in The National Archives (TNA) in Kew, primarily correspondence between the Company, the government, and the ambassadors, but also, crucially, detailed financial records of its establishments, including the Istanbul embassy. The accounts ledgers contain minutely detailed figures and descriptions of diplomatic expenditure, largely in the seventeenth and eighteenth centuries, shedding new light on, and giving a quantitative aspect to, a variety of diplomatic practices.

The diplomatic correspondence in the British State Papers is incredibly detailed and almost entirely intact, and includes information on diplomatic practices, financial pressures, and cultural conventions. There are also a large number of French, Italian, Latin, and Ottoman Turkish documents within these files, and the Italian and Ottoman Turkish texts have remained largely unexamined. Similarly, there is a substantial collection of imperial letters, petitions, and reports in a number of different series in TNA, again mainly in Ottoman Turkish and Italian, which provide great insights into a wide variety of practices. When added to similar sorts of documents in the British Library, and the Special Collections of the School of Oriental and African Studies, there is a multilingual corpus of many thousands of documents available to study this period from a variety of perspectives.

Additionally, there are the records of the Ottoman state held in the Başbakanlık Osmanlı Arşivleri (Prime Ministry's Ottoman Archives, BOA) in Istanbul. There are many hundreds of documents relating to various aspects of British–Ottoman relations, and a large number of these have not been

Fusaro, Colin Heywood, & Mohamed-Salah Omri (eds), *Trade and Cultural Exchange in the Early Modern Mediterranean: Braudel's Maritime Legacy* (London, 2010), 1–22; Karen Barkey, *Empire of Difference: The Ottomans in a Comparative Perspective* (Cambridge, 2008), especially part 2; Baki Tezcan, *The Second Ottoman Empire: Political and Social Transformation in the Early Modern World* (Cambridge, 2010), 191–240.

examined in a broader context. The three main series that have been consulted are the *Cevdet Tasnifi* (Cevdet series), mainly for the period after 1750, the İbnülemin Tasnifi (the İbnülemin series) for the earlier period, and the *Düvel-i Ecnebiye Defterleri* (registers of foreign states), which provides huge amounts of detail, mainly from the 1740s, on daily diplomatic practice. The *Cevdet* and *İbnülemin* series contain a number of financial receipts, reports, summaries, and requests, organised thematically, for example *askeriye*, *bahriye*, and *hariciye* (military, naval, and foreign). There are further records in the *Hatt-ı Hümayun* (imperial commands) collection, and a number of the digitised documents from the collection of the Topkapı Sarayı, as well as other collections and series held in the BOA.

The Ottoman sources, along with the non-English-language sources in TNA, offer a new perspective on relations for three reasons. Firstly, examining such sources expands the historical narrative from a British-centred discourse to one that incorporates that of the Ottoman state. Secondly, the Ottoman sources provide a wealth of corroborating and additional commercial and financial information that greatly enhances the understanding of diplomatic practice. Thirdly, and perhaps most significantly, the petitionary, legal, and discursive documentation in the Ottoman archives, especially when used in conjunction with similar and largely unexamined material in the British archives, permits the construction of non-elite, mercantile narratives and case studies within the context of a diplomatic, commercial, cultural, and social history.

There is also a wealth of material evidence, with textiles, paintings, maps, timepieces, armaments, and a variety of other kinds of sources adding a different dimension to the study of diplomatic practice. Not everything can be explained in words or quantified in ledgers, and the productions for and depictions of diplomatic practices should not be ignored; ultimately, they are no more or less open to interpretation than written sources. The collections of the Victoria & Albert Museum and the British Museum in particular have been invaluable, and I have additionally consulted a number of items in other collections, specifically the National Gallery, the National Portrait Gallery, the Museum of London, the National Maritime Museum, the London Metropolitan Archives, and the British Library. In Turkey, in addition to the *Harıta* (map) collection of the BOA, I was able to view the public collections of the Topkapı Sarayı Müzesi (Topkapı Palace Museum), although I was not able to gain access to the storage collections. The non-textual sources not only provide further evidence for themes encountered in the written material, but provide new pieces of information in their own right.

Finally, there are a number of valuable contemporary printed sources that have provided additional evidence of practices and conventions. From the British side, these have included government publications, such as *The London Gazette*, parliamentary records, satirical and polemical pamphlets and tracts, memoirs, histories, travel accounts, and maps. I have also used a number of French, Italian, Latin, and Spanish printed works on subjects such as travel and diplomatic theory. As for Ottoman texts, I have examined a number of histories by writers such as Ahmed Cevdet Paşa and Mehmed Raşid Efendi, as well as printed collections of *fetāvā* (legal rulings) and ceremonial protocols. These publications provide evidence of perceptions of diplomatic practice, and also shed light onto the cultural and legal frameworks in which they operated.

None of these sources, including the financial records, are without their problems and biases: diplomatic letters are full of self-aggrandising narratives and assertions; documentary productions of the state used certain linguistic conventions that promoted a particular image that may not have borne much relation to practice; and financial records were prey to mistakes, omissions, and downright fabrications. This is why using a variety of sources from a variety of perspectives can assist in constructing a more accurate picture, and, whilst acknowledging the limitations of individual types of sources, as a broader corpus they can be used to corroborate or disprove certain features of diplomatic practice. Together, they show the centrality of finance and cultural conventions to diplomatic practice, which in turn points to the importance of conforming to Ottoman values and practices for the benefit of trading subjects, and not simply for state politics. Cultural conventions, law, finance, and commerce, all mixed together into an entangled whole, framed the basis for relations, and the way in which diplomacy was practised and for what purposes.

This study is divided into two parts, with the first establishing those frameworks, and the second examining them in practice. In the first part, three chapters examine the interplay between law, trade, and finance in diplomacy. Chapter 1 summarises the commercial imperatives behind the establishment of British–Ottoman relations in the sixteenth century, before examining the British Capitulations of 1086/1675 as a legal document that nonetheless was subject to change over time, and that in many ways demonstrated the centrality of commerce to the daily business of diplomatic interaction. Chapter 2 initially examines the similarities and differences in the British and Ottoman theoretic conceptions of an ambassador's role. It then looks at the social and political background of the British ambassadors resident in Istanbul between 1661 and 1807, demonstrating how as individuals they were representative of changing patterns of relations and diplomatic practice, before exploring their different duties to the British state and to the Levant Company. A crucial chapter to my argument is Chapter 3, which begins with an in-depth analysis of British–Ottoman trade in the eighteenth century using a variety of customs records, in order to establish and quantify the fortunes of the Company's trade in that period. From that, I provide an audit of the Company's finances in the same period, to demonstrate how the Company was, in the face of shrinking revenues in the middle of the century, increasingly unable to pay its diplomatic bills. The final section of that chapter looks in detail at how a lack of finance squeezed ambassadors' salaries and expense accounts, which in turn hindered the British ability to participate in Ottoman diplomatic conventions.

Having established the legal, commercial, and financial framework, I go on to examine three key elements of daily interactions. I begin in Chapter 4 with a discussion of gift-giving traditions across time and location, demonstrating that the different kinds of Ottoman diplomatic gifts had their roots in a variety of Turkic, Persianate, and Islamic practices, and showing the prevalence of gifts in diplomacy across the world. The analysis then moves on to examining the specific contexts in the Ottoman Empire in which gifts were given or exchanged, focusing on two formal occasions: gifts given on formal audiences with the sultan and grand vizier in exchange for ceremonial robes (*ḫilʿat*); and tributary gifts given to officials on their appointments and on religious festivals (*pīşkeş*). Finally, there is an examination of gifts given to establish and solidify social relationships with Ottoman officials (*hibe*), as a representation of trends in commercial interests and elite consumption. In Chapter 5, focus moves to performative diplomacy, examining how diplomatic practice revolved around a number of ceremonies and rituals between the Ottomans and the British, and among the European ambassadors. Using the initial audiences of the ambassador on his arrival in Istanbul, the chapter explores how ceremonial defined and regulated relations, how the lack of finance affected the British embassy, and additionally how such rituals and practices were viewed back in Britain. The final chapter examines what sorts of situations required ambassadorial intervention, looking specifically at commercial disputes, at the legal and financial implications of British privateering against Ottoman shipping and merchants, and at the pursuit of British foreign policy.

Building on existing scholarship on the Ottoman Empire and beyond, using avariety of sources from different perspectives, I argue that British diplomacy in the Ottoman Empire, practised in forms such as gift-giving, ceremonial, and negotiations, operated within the cultural conventions of the Ottoman state. Moreover, the ambassadors' ability to engage in those conventions relied in a large part on their ability to finance such practices, requiring money for salaries, materials, and provisions. At the heart of relations was commercial interaction, and in this context commerce had a particularly important role, with the embassy being financed by the merchants. That this was the case demonstrated the centrality of commerce to relations between the British and the Ottomans in this period, with the primary duties of the ambassador focusing on maintaining the freedoms and ensuring the welfare of British merchants within the legal bounds of the Capitulations and Ottoman law. Therefore, I propose that there was a specific cycle of relations in British diplomacy in the Ottoman Empire in the long eighteenth century, in which British merchants funded their ambassadors, who were required to spend significant amounts of money in order to participate in Ottoman diplomatic culture – which they also used as an opportunity to market the merchants' wares – thus maintaining the signs of friendship with the Ottoman state, which would in turn ensure that the merchants were able to go about their business and trade, thus beginning the cycle again.

# 1

# The framework of relations

## The development of British–Ottoman relations

Just as the story of British ambassadors in the Ottoman Empire began with a sea voyage, so too did the story of Ottoman ambassadors in London. The nineteenth-century historian Ahmed Cevdet recorded that, 'in the first days of the year [12]07 [1792/3], [Yusuf] Agah Efendi, having been prepared to make his departure, chartered a ship and was dispatched by sea to Britain in order to [present] the imperial gifts'.[1] This was a far more momentous journey than may first appear. The majority of this study presents British–Ottoman relations through the prism of the British embassy in Istanbul, as for most of the period under consideration relations were not bilateral in the sense of an equal Ottoman representation in London. However, as part of a series of reforms of the Ottoman state during the reign of Selim III, collectively known as the 'New Order' (*Niẓām-ı Cedīd*), the Ottoman state began to dispatch resident ambassadors to foreign courts, as opposed to the temporary messengers they had sent up to that time. The first resident ambassador to be sent abroad – Yusuf Agah Efendi – went to London, and this marked a substantial change in the nature of relations.

Why did the Ottomans, after hundreds of years, suddenly decide to employ resident ambassadors? Ahmed Cevdet concluded that the dispatch of these new resident ambassadors was due to increasing political uncertainty in Europe, relating that 'as all the states of Europe were obliged to make cautious preparations with the onset of the French Revolution, so too did the Sublime State prepare to send ambassadors to reside at each of the great European states, each with the appropriate rank for the said states'.[2] And why was London the first destination? Ahmed Cevdet explained that, as an old ally, France would have been the obvious first choice, but the turmoil of revolution ruled it out, along with many other European powers.[3] Therefore, although London was the first destination for an Ottoman resident ambassador, this was not necessarily a

1 Ahmed Cevdet, *Tārīḫ-i Cevdet,* 10 vols (Dersaadet, 1309 [1891/2]), vol. VI, 89.

2 Ibid., 78.

3 Ibid., 78–9.

comment on the political importance of a British alliance to Istanbul. France, although it had been at times a temperamental ally, and even at times an open enemy, had in the past been a key friend in Europe.[4]

Relations with the British, although venturing into the political from time-to-time, had revolved almost entirely around trade. Indeed, relations between the British Isles and the Ottoman realms began as a result of commercial contacts. Certainly, there are documents that attest to an English awareness in a political sense of 'the Turk' before the establishment of formal relations. In addition to the English soldiers who served in the Varangian Guard of Byzantium, from across Britain many had taken part in the various crusades to the Islamic lands, with Richard I (r. 1189–99) and Edward I (r. 1272–1307) among them. English intervention in favour of the Levantine Christians, in the form both of arms and of money, was regularly requested of Edward III (r. 1327–77) by numerous domestic and foreign notables.[5] The courting of northern Europe by Byzantine emperor Manuel II (r. 1391–1425), as part of that monarch's attempt to gather support against the growing Ottoman threat, culminated in his visit to London in 1400, and brought him some money but little else.[6]

There seems to have been almost no political interaction between England and the Ottomans before the sixteenth century. With no regular encounters between the populations of either polity, the English image of that part of the Islamic world was, at best, limited; a number of public houses in towns and villages across the country known as The Saracen's Head or The Turk's Head perhaps provide some clue as to how Muslims were viewed.[7] Following the crusading theme, among the indulgences printed by William Caxton's press in the 1480s were those issued to fight the 'Turks' and to ransom their captives.[8] Nor was there much serious scholarship on the Islamic world; not until the seventeenth century would Oxford and Cambridge establish chairs in Arabic, and Turkish studies were virtually non-existent until the nineteenth century, with linguists such as Elias Gibb and Sir James Redhouse.[9] On the other side, it seems rather unlikely that the Ottoman state would have had anything other than a broad awareness of this minor Frank kingdom before the sixteenth century. The basic form of the British Isles features in the famous *Kitāb-ı Baḥriye* (Book of Navigation, 1521/5) of Piri Reis, and a more

4 Christine Isom-Verhaaren, *Allies with the Infidel: The Ottoman and French Alliance in the Sixteenth Century* (London, 2013), especially 114–40.

5 TNA/SC7/11/5, 18 December 1342; TNA/SC7/13/8, 13 March 1343; TNA/SC7/13/17, 1 February 1345; TNA/SC7/17/3, 23 January 1372; TNA/SC7/34/7, 6 October 1366; TNA/SC7/64/54, 14 May 1400.

6 TNA/E135/25/13, 22 Ric. II (1398/9); E135/25/14, 1399; E135/25/17, 1401; E135/25/18, 1406. For an interesting account, see: D.M. Nicol, 'A Byzantine emperor in England: Manuel II's visit to London in 1400–1401', *University of Birmingham Historical Journal* 12:2 (1971), 204–25.

7 For a discussion on the construction of 'Islam' in Britain later on, see: Nabil Matar, *Islam in Britain, 1558–1685* (Cambridge, 1998).

8 *Indulgences issued to raise money to fight the Turks or to ransom captives* (Westminster, c. 1480).

9 Robert Irwin, *For Lust of Knowing: The Orientalists and their Enemies* (London, 2006), 90–113.

detailed map appears in another anonymous sixteenth-century maritime atlas showing London, Edinburgh, Belfast, and Dublin as idealised mighty cities, but with literally three main islands, with *cezīre-i İsḳoçya*, literally 'the island of Scotland', separated from England.[10] However, those islands do not seem to have attracted much comment from Ottoman writers. What began to encourage political interaction between England and the Ottoman Empire was growing commercial speculation, particularly on the part of English merchants.

How many merchants risked the long and perilous journey from England to the Levant is unclear. The records of the English Chancery Courts show through commercial complaints and disputes that, by the first half of the sixteenth century, there would appear to have been a regular, if not necessarily significant, English commerce to the Eastern Mediterranean. This included indulging both the English sweet tooth and love of alcohol with imports from Venetian-held Crete and Genoese Chios of currants and wine.[11] In addition to trade with the Christian territories there, those merchants also began to interact with the Ottoman Empire. As with any commercial venture, particularly in its infancy, there were failures. One Robert Dobbes had a dispute in around 1510 with a London draper for the quality of cloth delivered for sale in 'Turkey', and Sir John Bruges found himself embroiled in disputes over non-payment of Ottoman duties that led to one of his factors in Syria being imprisoned.[12] Other threats were ever-present; John Cheriton, a merchant from Exeter, made a petition to Henry VIII (r. 1509–47) complaining of an attack on his ship by an Ottoman fleet in the Mediterranean, with dozens of his men killed or enslaved.[13] Indeed, as trade increased, so did the British interaction with the newly gained western extremes of the Ottoman realms, the North African Regencies of Algiers, Tunis, and Tripoli.

By the later sixteenth century, it seems clear that there was sufficient interest, at least from the English side, to pursue commerce in the Ottoman Empire. A summary of the trade between England and the Ottomans in 1588 shows a variety of commodities traded, and this pattern must have been established over the course of the sixteenth century. In a system of trade that would continue for the next two hundred years, the document recorded large quantities of woollen manufactures traded for raw silk, dyes, drugs, cotton wool and yarn, currants, oil, carpets, and many more.[14] Such a trade cannot

[10] A digital copy of the *Kitāb-ı Baḥriye* held at the Walters Art Museum (Ms.W.658) and the anonymous 'Deniz atlası' can be can be found via http://www.thewalters.org/. In the 'Deniz atlası', as well as the three (sic) islands of England, Scotland, and Ireland, the isles of Man and White, and the Scilly Isles, are marked by name.

[11] Almost all of the following documents concerning disputes heard in the Court of Chancery make mention of either currants or some variety of Levantine wine: TNA/C1/31/514, c. 1465–71; TNA/C1/523/35, c. 1518–29; TNA/C1/525/30, c. 1518–29; TNA/C1/572/12, c. 1518–29; TNA/C1/886/57, c. 1533–8; TNA/C1/1037/50 c. 1538–44; TNA/C1/1063/33, c. 1538–44; TNA/C1/1186/51, c. 1544–51.

[12] TNA/C1/310/17, c. 1504–15; TNA/C1/697/39, c. 1532–48, STAC2/19/61, 1509–47.

[13] TNA/SC8/182, c. 1540–2.

[14] TNA/SP97/1 Certaine articles specifieing such comodities as this Realme enjoyeth by the inter-course to the gran S: his dominions, c. 1588.

have sprung up overnight, but would have built on foundations, however small, constructed prior to the establishment of formal relations. As a note on the wider British aspect of relations, after some initial investigations in the Scottish archives, I have yet to find any records showing any significant trade between the still independent Scotland and the Ottoman realms in this period. Scots would become a key part of this story – disproportionately so in some respects – but not in those early days.

A likely encouragement to English trade came from the French, who, by the 1560s, had become the first non-neighbouring Christian power to establish relations with the Ottomans through a resident ambassador. Following the conquest of Constantinople, the only foreign Christians who had had any significant diplomatic or commercial contact with the Ottoman government were the Italian trading states such as the Venetians and Genoese, who in many ways continued the agreements they had reached with the Byzantines. However, the Ottoman expansion into Syria and Egypt in the 1510s and 1520s brought the Empire more directly into the commercial interests of France. Having secured previous trade agreements with the Mamluk rulers of Egypt, in 1535/6 the French government proposed a treaty of alliance with Süleyman I ('the Magnificent', r. 1520–66), which led to Ottoman military involvement on the French side against their mutual enemy, the Habsburgs, including the decisive role of the Ottoman fleet at the siege of Nice in 1543.[15] This was followed by a more detailed commercial treaty in 1569 known in Ottoman Turkish as *ʿahdnāme-i hümāyūn* (imperial covenants) and in English as Capitulations, from the Latin *caput,* referring to the headings which divided the agreement.

It is perhaps not surprising that one should find the English following suit not long afterwards. Initially, English ships would have made use of the protection of the French flag in Ottoman waters. Perhaps the first recorded Englishman to begin the process of establishing direct relations with the Ottoman government was Anthony Jenkinson, a merchant who viewed Süleyman I on the march with his army towards Iran from Aleppo in November 1553.[16] In Richard Hakluyt's invaluable collection of documents concerning English travel up to the 1580s, there is a copy of a translation of a *ḫaṭṭ-ı şerīf* (an imperial command) issued by Süleyman in 1553 giving Jenkinson protection and licence to trade in his realms, the first, if genuine, granted to an English merchant.[17]

[15] See: Isom-Verhaaren, *Allies with the Infidel*, 23–48; Viorel Panaite, 'French Capitulations and consular jurisdiction in Egypt and Aleppo in the late sixteenth and early seventeenth centuries' in Firges et al., *Well-Connected Domains*, 71–87.

[16] 'The manner of the entring of Solyman the Great Turke, with his armie into Aleppo in Syria, marching toward Persia against the Great Sophie, the fourth day of November, 1553, noted by Master Anthonie Jenkison, present at that time' in Richard Hakluyt (ed.), *The Principall Navigations, Voiages and Discoveries of the English nation, made by Sea or over Land, to the most remote and farthest distant Quarters of the earth at any time within the compasse of these 1500 yeeres* (London, 1589), 81–2.

[17] 'The safe conduct or priviledge, given by Sultan Solyman the Great Turke, to Master Anthony Jenkinson at Aleppo in Syria, in the yeere 1553' in Hakluyt, *Principall Navigations*, 82.

Jenkinson was not the only Englishman active in the Ottoman trade, and by the 1570s there was sufficient interest to enable direct contact with the Ottoman state to begin. Merchants could not continue to rely on French protection, and wanted the opportunity to open new markets. In 1578, a group of three merchants dispatched a fellow trader, William Harborne, to Istanbul in order to begin negotiating an official agreement to permit and regulate English commerce to the Ottoman Empire. His efforts were aided by royal correspondence between Elizabeth I (r. 1558–1603) and Sultan Murad III (r. 1574–95). In the first of these letters, Murad noted the arrival of a certain man acting in her name in Istanbul, requesting for himself and two other merchants the licence and liberty to trade in the Ottoman Empire.[18] As noted in the introduction, this Elizabethan opening of relations has received quite a lot of historiographical interest, and at the time the Ottoman historian Feridun Bey recorded much of the official royal correspondence in his *Mecmūʿa-ı münşeʾātüʾs-selāṭīn* (Review of the letters of the sultans, late sixteenth century), marking the first rights granted to the English.[19]

In what essentially constituted the first formal agreement between the English and Ottoman crowns, Murad assured Elizabeth that English merchants would be granted full liberty to trade, free from molestation, and, crucially, that English merchants should be granted the same rights to come and go in their trade as the merchants of the French, Venetians, Poles, and Habsburgs; these were all key elements that will be discussed in more detail later.[20] Elizabeth's reply noted that as Harborne and his fellow merchants had acted of their own free will and without her intercession, the sultan might clarify that he would extend these privileges to all her subjects and not just to those few initial merchants.[21] This was formalised in the privileges accorded to English merchants, constituting the first treaty between the English and the Ottomans.[22]

Along with this came the formal establishment of the Turkey Company, later known as the Levant Company. It was one of several companies of traders granted a charter under the Elizabethan government, including the Muscovy Company (1555), the Eastland Company (to the Baltic, 1579), and the Barbary or Morocco Company (1585). Such ventures were designed to extend English trade outside its northern European heartlands and to secure a regular supply of luxury goods that had previously reached England via the hands of foreign merchants. Just as the Turkey Company's charter was requested of Elizabeth's government by the merchants trading in the Ottoman realms, those same merchants petitioned the queen via Lord Burghley in 1582 to appoint a permanent resident ambassador in Istanbul or, in the parlance

[18] TNA/SP97/1 Murad III to Elizabeth I, 987 [1579].

[19] Feridun Bey, *Mecmūʿa-ı münşeʾātüʾs-selāṭīn*, 2 vols (Istanbul?, 1265 [1849]), vol. II, 380–7.

[20] TNA/SP97/1 Murad III to Elizabeth I, 987 [1579].

[21] TNA/SP97/1 Elizabeth I to Murad III, 25 October 1579.

[22] TNA/SP97/1 Interpretatio Latina Privilegiorum, seu literarum Cæsaris potentissimi Musselmanici Suldan Murad Chan ad postulatum Elizabethæ Deiter Maximi, et Unici Cæli Terræque conditoris gratia Ænglïæ Franciæ et Hiberniæ Reginæ pacem et fedus sanctissimum, 988 [1580].

of the petition, 'an agent there continually resident'.[23] The rationale was that the queen had to send an ambassador to the sultan in order to confirm the newly established agreement and to present gifts, as was customary, in the queen's name. The ambassador proposed was the original negotiator, William Harborne. Whilst not the first ambassador sent by Elizabeth to an Islamic state, that being Edmund Hogan to Sultan Abu Marwan ʿAbd al-Malik I (r. 1576–8) of Morocco in 1577, the way in which Harborne was appointed was to have a profound impact on future relations.[24]

In the petition, the Turkey Company made very clear that the ambassador, although acting in their interest, was the queen's ambassador, and not the Company's. However, when it came to the rather delicate question of finance, the Company offered the government a deal:

> And for the supporting by us (as abovesaid) of all charges to any such ambassador or agent incident, it may please Her Majesty to rent us the custom of our goods in and out for the same trade of Turkey only, at some reasonable rate for these seven years.[25]

In other words, the Company agreed to finance the running of the embassy in return for favourable concessions in customs and duties due to the Crown. This arrangement made the Turkey Company unique; in the case of the Muscovy Company, for instance, the Company helped to fund some of the initial contacts, but by the seventeenth century the Crown paid for the ambassador and the embassy.[26] The ambassador, necessary to protect the merchants of the Turkey Company, could only claim diplomatic authority by virtue of his commission from the English court, but in recognition of his role in protecting the Company's trade, the Company footed the bill. This set a pattern that was to last for the best part of two hundred years, and that would solidify relations not only between the ambassador and the merchants, but between commerce and diplomatic practice.

The original Turkey Company operated as a joint-stock company. That is, it was a venture in which a number of individuals combined their capital into purchasing shares of stock in the company, with returns and liabilities shared according to the percentage of their investment. Rather than going to faraway and dangerous places in person, these investors would appoint agents, called factors, to trade on behalf of the Company, residing in mercantile communities known as factories. This had the benefit of allowing a number of merchants to combine their goods or cash in order to be able to provide the necessary

23 TNA/SP97/1 Petition of the Levant Company merchants, *c.* 1582.

24 'The ambassage of Master Edmund Hogan, one of the sworne Esquires of her Majesties person, from her Highnes, to Mully Abdelmelech, Emperour of Maroccus, and King of Fes, and Sus: in the yeere 1577 written by himselfe' in Hakluyt, *Principall Navigations*, 156–9.

25 TNA/SP97/1 Petition of the Levant Company merchants, c. 1582.

26 *The Origin and Early History of the Russia or Muscvoy Company* (London, 1830); Maija Jansson & Nikolai Rogozhin, *England and the North: The Russian Embassy of 1613–1614*, trans. Paul Bushkovitch (Philadelphia, 1994), 6, 196–8.

volume of goods or specie necessary to enable a large and potentially risky venture, of which the early trade to the Ottoman Empire was a good example.

This model did not last long, however. Over the course of the 1580s, the Turkey Company began to seek a merger with the Venice Company, which had control over the valuable trade to the Venetian-held Ionian Islands, and by 1592 the two entities had merged to form the Levant Company. With the provision of Royal Charters to the new company, by 1595 at the latest the Levant Company was operating as a regulated company.[27] This meant that instead of the members of the Company jointly owning stock and sharing profits and liabilities, they paid a membership fee to the Company and carried on their own trade at their own risk and expense, subject to the Company's regulations of trade. The Company was managed by a director who was elected by the members, and through him and the 'husband', or accountant, the affairs of the Company were coordinated. The membership fees were used to pay for the upkeep of the diplomatic establishments that protected the Levant trade. In short, to use the words of a nineteenth-century writer, '[a] regulated company is, in fact, a device for making those engaged in a particular branch of trade bear the public expenses incident to it, at the same time that it leaves them to conduct their own business with their own capital, and in their own way'.[28] This late sixteenth-century model helped in many ways to influence the Company's structure, and the transition to regulated company so early on also solidified the dual obligations of the ambassador to the merchants and to the state. The eight ambassadors who followed Harborne until the restoration of the monarchy in 1660 were all very able diplomats in their own right, and certainly pursued any political agendas they found compatible with policy communicated to them from London. However, they were above all resident in Istanbul to serve and protect the merchants and their commerce.

The position of ambassador to Istanbul was on paper one of great importance, despite the post's distance from London and the fact that it was a non-Christian court. The ambassador from England, and later Britain, to the Sublime Porte was one of only a small number of English/British diplomatic posts that always held the high rank of ambassador, as opposed to envoy or resident (others being politically important positions such as in Paris or Madrid).[29] As per the convention established in 1582, the ordinary costs of the embassy, including the ambassador's pay, were provided by the Company,

[27] Wood, *Levant Company*, 21–3; T.S. Willan, 'Some aspects of English trade with the Levant in the sixteenth century', *The English Historical Review* 70:276 (1955), 399–410 at 405–10; Robert Brenner, *Merchants and Revolution: Commercial Change, Political Conflict, and London's Overseas Traders, 1550–1653* (Princeton NJ, 1993), 63–72.

[28] J.R. McCulloch, *A Dictionary, Practical, Theoretical, and Historical, of Commerce and Commercial Navigation* (London, 1850), 387.

[29] The term 'Sublime Porte' came from a common Ottoman denomination of their state, *Devlet-i ʿAliye*, 'the Sublime State', and this particularly refers to the Bāb-ı ʿĀlī, 'the sublime or lofty gate', due to the location of the grand vizier's offices in the complex behind the *Bāb-ı ʿĀlī* opposite the head of the Sultanic government in the imperial palace of Topkapı. It is therefore at once representative of the high language the Ottomans employed when referring to themselves, and also acknowledged the idea that the centre of power was the grand vizier, and not the sultan.

which had a great say in who the ambassador would be. All British ambassadors were commanded to protect British merchants and promote their trade, but only the ambassador in Istanbul was so formally linked to the merchants he was bound to protect.

This situation remained in the same basic form until the beginning of the nineteenth century. Where matters began to diverge from that early diplomatic model was the re-establishment of the Levant Company in 1661.[30] From that point, the British government began to assert more of a right over the appointment and conduct of the ambassador in Istanbul, although still graciously permitting the Company to issue him instructions and pay all the embassy's expenses. Despite this, the model that had been developed under Elizabeth I and William Harborne remained the norm for British diplomatic representation in the Ottoman Empire until 1804, when the Crown formally assumed control of the embassy. This could be seen in the context of a changed political landscape: the wars with France, growing geopolitical interests in the Mediterranean, and a professionalising diplomatic corps were all contributing factors. At the same time, this transfer of control seems to have occurred largely because of the Company's inability to pay the high costs of the embassy in the face of commercial difficulty, and it was only with a growing financial stake in the embassy on the part of the British state that the Company was sidelined in 1804.

What difference should it make whether the ambassador was an agent of a company or a government? It does not mean that before 1804 political matters figured little, or that after 1804 commercial concerns disappeared. This question does, however, have the potential to give us a focus on matters of diplomatic practice and infrastructure that are difficult to establish in other embassies. In other words, having a commercial venture so closely linked with a diplomatic establishment, with the ambassadorial model set as it was in the sixteenth century, it is possible to examine a diplomatic establishment not just from the perspective of central government, but to examine it from a whole variety of perspectives and see it in action. The bond between the ambassador and the merchants gives us crucial insights into the foundations of British–Ottoman relations, and blurs the lines between diplomacy and commerce, something that would become more fixed after 1804. Diplomacy is never simply the story of foreign policy, of royal alliances, or of grand treaties. It is, above all, the story of interaction and negotiation between different groups of people and how, through a variety of methods, they negotiated a common understanding and intercourse. British–Ottoman relations developed in the way they did almost entirely because of trading subjects, rather than political common ground. This is entirely evident in the treaty that governed relations between the two, a document the British frequently referred to as sacred: the Capitulations.

[30] LMA/MS.3325, 1661.

## *ʿAhdnāme-i hümāyūn* – The imperial capitulations

So far I have presented one narrative of the history of the earliest British–Ottoman relations, largely from the British perspective, yet the treaty between those two states contains its own, rather different version of events as narrated by the Ottoman state:

> In the past, the chief of the nobles of the queen of the said province [*vilāyet*] [of England] came to and arrived at our threshold of the workings of felicity – which is the refuge of asylum of the sultans of the world and the place of retreat of the sovereigns of the globe – with her gentlemen and her ships with her tribute, and the gifts that she had sent were gladly accepted. In the time of my ancestor who dwells in heaven in the paradise of the mercy of the merciful protector of all things, Sultan Murad Khan (may his tomb be pleasant to him), a man was sent to our Threshold of Felicity manifesting friendly, sincere, and agreeable affection, asking that their gentlemen might come and go at the Porte, [and] a positive response was given. In the time of the same aforementioned [sultan], noble commands were given, saying that 'at the stopping places and stations, at the crossings and at the gateways, at sea and on land, no one should trouble them'.[31]

This passage describes the same story in a sense, of the British coming to the Ottoman realms seeking to trade and then to formalise that commercial relationship. However, through the language used here it is clear that the Ottomans did not view this as an equal partnership. The queen had to send her best men, with presents as tribute, and only when they were accepted would the sultan graciously agree that they should have the right to come and go in his realms. The ambassador had to make demonstrations of friendship at the Ottoman court, in this case through presenting the queen's letter. One might be tempted to dismiss this as mere political rhetoric, yet here we find clear evidence of how the Ottoman state chose to record their first encounters with the British. The fact that this is the opening passage of the formal treaty says much about the Ottoman world-view, and the treaty itself; it is as much a record of history as a treaty.

As well as being historical documents themselves, the treaties that emerged between the British and Ottomans from the late sixteenth century owe their existence in a large part to the corpus of agreements that had been entered into between Christian and Islamic powers from the very first Islamic states, as well as to the heritage of the ancient Mediterranean world inherited via the Byzantine Empire. The first of these treaties were between the Ottomans

[31] BOA/TS.MA.d 7018/002 fols 7r–7l. For further detail on the Capitulations as historical narrative, see: Michael Talbot, 'A treaty of narratives: Friendship, gifts, and diplomatic history in the British Capitulations of 1641', *Osmanlı Araştırmaları / The Journal of Ottoman Studies* 48 (2016), 357–398. My research in that article concludes that this narrative was probably written first during the 1620s, then added to in subsequent additions to the Capitulations up to 1675.

and commercial states such as Genoa. The trading colonies established by the Genoese, Pisans, Florentines, and Venetians under the Byzantines in Constantinople, the Aegean, and the Black Sea were largely retained and encouraged by the Ottomans, for the purposes of both commercial and economic links, most notably in the commercial colony at Galata. The Byzantines, having adopted the principle of unilateral treaties following the re-establishment of imperial authority in Constantinople in the 1260s, saw that model in turn used and adapted by the growing Ottoman state.[32] At the same time, the Mamluks granted commercial privileges to the same Italian states that bear important similarities to those of the Ottomans.[33] The question of trade was rarely far from the contracting parties' minds.[34]

Historians examining diplomacy from a European perspective, even up to the most current textbooks on the subject, always highlight supposed dichotomies present in 'classical' Islamic thought, in which there were two major divisions: *dār al-Islām*, the 'abode of Islam' where Islamic law was in full force; and *dār al-ḥarb*, or the 'abode of war' that formed the non-Islamic world.[35] Finally, during periods of threat to the Islamic lands, jurists developed the notion of *dār al-ṣulḥ*, 'the abode of peace or truce', with peace via treaty permissible with non-Muslim polities.[36] There is a danger, perhaps, in giving such legal theories and classification undue weighting when it comes to practice. States with Muslim rulers did not make or refuse treaties with non-Muslim states based on rigid ideas of some 'orthodox' or 'classical' set of laws; certainly, senior members of the *ʿulemāʾ* (religious scholars) were consulted, but political and economic imperatives were also key. Despite the theoretical constructions of the various *dūr* (abodes), evidence shows

32 See: Alexander H. de Groot, 'The historical development of the capitulatory regime in the Ottoman Middle East from the fifteenth to the nineteenth centuries', *Oriente Moderno* 22(83):3 (2003), 575–694; Eric R. Dursteler, *Venetians in Constantinople: Nation, Identity, and Coexistence in the Early Modern Mediterranean* (Baltimore, 2006), 23–40, 151–86; Kate Fleet, *European and Islamic Trade in the Early Ottoman State: The Merchants of Genoa and Turkey* (Cambridge, 2006); Louis Mitler, 'The Genoese in Galata: 1453–1682', *International Journal of Middle East Studies* 10:1 (1979), 71–91; Donald M. Nicol, *Byzantium and Venice: A Study in Diplomatic and Cultural Relations* (Cambridge, 1988); Angeliki E. Laiou, 'Byzantine Trade with Christians and Muslims and the Crusades' in Angeliki E. Laiou & Roy Parviz Mottahedeh, *The Crusades from the Perspective of Byzantium and the Muslim World* (Washington DC, 2001), 157–96.

33 John Wansbrough, 'Venice and Florence in the Mamluk commercial privileges', *Bulletin of the School of Oriental and African Studies* 28:3 (1965), 483–523.

34 Catherine Holmes, 'Treaties between Byzantium and the Islamic world' in Philip da Souza & John France (eds), *War and Peace in Ancient and Medieval History* (Cambridge, 2008), 141–57.

35 A prime example of this notion of Islamic diplomacy can be found in Keith Hamilton & Richard Langhorne, *The Practice of Diplomacy: Its Evolution, Theory and Administration*, 2nd edn (Abingdon & New York, 2011), 25–7.

36 Ibid. A variety of studies have also discussed this idea in terms of political theory: Ralph H. Salmi, Cesar Adib Majul, & George K. Tanham, *Islam and Conflict Resolution: Theories and Practices* (Lanham MD, 1998), 72–4; Hadia Dajani-Shakeel, 'Diplomatic relations between Muslim and Frankish rulers, 1097–1153 A.D.' in Maya Shatzmiller (ed.), *Crusaders and Muslims in Twelfth-Century Syria* (Leiden, 1993), 190–215 at 209–11.

significant diplomatic activity between Islamic and European Christian polities from the very earliest times, along with practices designed to facilitate such contacts. More than this, and to borrow from Palmira Brummett's recent study, the dichotomy between abodes of war and of Islam 'fails to express the scope of Ottoman conceptualisations of space'.[37] The question of Islamic theory cannot be entirely discounted; neither can it produce from its limited palette the entire picture. When one considers the nature of trade routes that passed through the western Islamic lands, and the demand for luxury commodities from Christian Europe, commerce must have been central to relations. From such concerns arose the treaties between peripheral kingdoms like England and great empires like that of the Ottomans.

What the Ottoman Capitulations with the mercantile states of France, Britain, and Holland shared with earlier treaties was the fact that they were unilateral, in that they were decreed rather than formally negotiated, and that they embodied the principle of *amān*, safe passage and good treatment of non-Muslims in Muslim lands; such protected foreigners were often referred to as *müste'min*.[38] Moreover, as Maurits van den Boogert has argued, these treaties need to be seen as part of a singular group, and by examining the Capitulations in the eighteenth century from a legal perspective, focusing on case studies and assessing the question of theory over practice, he has demonstrated the importance of supplementary documents, particularly imperial commands known as *fermān*s, as well as the inter-referential nature of the separate Capitulations granted to different European states.[39] He also emphasised the importance of local qadis (judges) in dealing with disputes in the provinces.[40] Beyond the technicalities, one of the most interesting points he raised related to a question of terminology. The British often referred in an official context to their Capitulations as 'sacred', or '*sacra*' in Italian translations. However the Ottomans only ever described them as '*hümāyūn*', 'imperial'.[41] This clearly demonstrates the differing interpretations of the Capitulations between European powers like the British and Ottomans. This sort of commercial treaty was above all fluid, constantly being altered, if not by a formal amendment of or addition to the extant articles, then by the numerous *fermān*s issued and the development of legal practices in individual cases, rather than a fixed convention.

As such, the articles of the Capitulations that will be examined in some detail shortly were important in setting and addressing the parameters of

[37] Palmira Brummett, *Mapping the Ottomans: Sovereignty, Territory, and Identity in the Early Modern Mediterranean* (New York, 2015), 77.

[38] J. Wansbrough, Halil İnalcık, A.K.S. Lambton, & G. Baer, 'Imtiyāzāt' in P. Bearman et al., *Encyclopaedia of Islam 2*, vol. III, 1178; J. Schacht, 'Amān' in P. Bearman et al., *Encyclopaedia of Islam 2*, vol. I, 429–30; Edhem Eldem, 'Capitulations and Western trade' in Suraiya Faroqhi (ed.), *Cambridge History of Turkey, Volume 3: The Later Ottoman Empire, 1603–1839* (Cambridge, 2006), 283–335 at 292–6.

[39] Van den Boogert, *Capitulations*, 34–62. For an important study on a large body of capitulatory texts see: Dariusz Kołodziejczyk, *Ottoman-Polish Diplomatic Relations, 15th–18th Century: An Annotated Edition of 'Ahdnames and Other Documents* (Leiden, 2000).

[40] Van den Boogert, *Capitulations*, 34–62.

[41] Ibid., 19–23.

relations, which were overwhelmingly commercial. In terms of overall commerce, British–Ottoman trade, for the entirety of the period under examination, formed a fairly small portion of the total volume of both states' trade income. Despite this, for much of this period, the British were able to benefit from the favourable terms granted in the Capitulations through the import of raw silk and other luxury commodities into their domestic markets. Indeed, the relatively low tariffs enjoyed by British merchants in the Ottoman realms often disguised the fact that the 'Turkey trade' formed a negligible portion of both imports and exports in the wider British foreign commerce. How far the provisions of the Capitulations were implemented in practice on a daily commercial basis varied from place to place and in different times, as did the ability of the British to utilise the inter-referential nature of the Capitulations. At a more fundamental level, even the basic aspects of *amān* required almost constant reaffirming, and disputes between British and Ottoman merchants were common.

The Capitulations granted to the British by the Ottoman state were not, therefore, anything particularly special. The basic rights and freedoms granted to British merchants were essentially the same as those granted to the French and the Dutch. They were not concessionary in the same way that treaties and commercial agreements made with the Ottomans and Qajar Iran would be in the nineteenth century. They were still very much privileges granted by the benevolence of the Ottoman government, rather than terms demanded by the British. In accordance with the language and tone of earlier treaties, regardless of commercial benefit, the Ottoman state engaged to treat British subjects and emissaries in an appropriately friendly manner, depending entirely on Britain maintaining peaceful relations with the Ottomans. Freedom of movement and of trade were key in the British and other Capitulations. Taking their lineage from earlier treaties, these were fairly pragmatic documents, justified from the Ottoman perspective by the precepts of Islamic legal practice, especially in the treatment of British subjects as *müste᾿mīn*, and were linked to all the other Capitulations and *fermān*s granted by the Ottoman government. They provided the historical and legal framework for relations; to take the narrative of the Ottoman text, the British monarch sent their ambassadors with their gifts, and once accepted the Ottoman sultan granted them their commercial freedoms through the document of the treaty. It is important, therefore, to establish exactly what the Capitulations granted to the British contained, and how those grants reflected the daily practice of relations.

## Privileges, taxes, and debts: The British capitulations of 1086/1675

The English received their first Capitulations from the Ottoman government in 1580, and it was this document that remained at the heart of British–Ottoman relations. After the initial grant, the Capitulations were renewed, confirmed, and added to fairly regularly, with the text of the treaty itself recording renewals and additions in 1601, 1607, 1612, 1618, 1621, 1641, 1647, and 1662.

The 1675 version, secured by Sir John Finch, was essentially the final draft of the Capitulations between Britain and the Ottoman Empire. Occasionally amended by the proclamations of a *ḫaṭṭ-ı şerīf* or other imperial commands, they were added to by a defensive treaty in 1799, and again confirmed following the British–Ottoman War (1807–9) by the Treaty of the Dardanelles, and a number of articles were amended and added in the Treaty of Baltalimanı in 1838.[42] The basic treaty remained in force until the abolition of the Ottoman Capitulations under the provisions of Article 28 of the Treaty of Lausanne, ratified by the United Kingdom and the new Republic of Turkey in 1924.[43] Examining the basic content of those Capitulations, from both the English- and Ottoman-language texts, therefore helps us to understand how they were used and abused, and how they helped to define British–Ottoman relations.[44]

The 1675 treaty was a cumulative text that was the end product of at least half-a-dozen other documents, and, as a historical document, these reflect the different needs of specific historical moments. The articles received under Elizabeth I in 1580 and 1601 concentrated on securing privileges for and enshrining the security of English merchants, so that twelve out of the twenty articles granted at that time considered privileges, seven concerned protection and due process, and only one covered duties and taxes. Under James I (r. 1603–25), there were three different sets of Capitulations secured, in 1607, 1612, and 1621, with the 1607 and 1621 additions under Thomas Glover and Thomas Roe being the most significant, clarifying the privileges of the ambassador and the nation, dealing with issues of lawsuits, debts, and abuses, confirming the rates and manner of collection of customs and duties. After the renewal by Sir Sackville Crowe in 1641, Thomas Bendish in 1647, the Earl of Winchilsea in 1662, and finally Sir John Finch in 1675. This final period of renewals and additions concentrated heavily on clarifying and delineating

42 *Treaties &c. between Turkey and Foreign Powers, 1535–1855* (London, 1855), 269–73, 276–83.

43 *The Treaties of Peace, 1919–1923*, 2 vols (New York, 1924), vol. II, 970.

44 For comparison of the English-language version the following three documents have been used, with preference for the first: *The Capitulations and Articles of Peace between the Majesty of the King of Great Britain, France, and Ireland &c. and the Sultan of the Ottoman Empire* (London, 1679); TNA/FO881/80, *The Capitulations and Articles of Peace between Great Britain and The Ottoman Empire, as agreed upon, augmented and altered at different periods, and finally confirmed by the Treaty of Peace, concluded at the Dardanelles in 1809* (London, 1809); *Treaties &c. between Turkey and Foreign Powers*, 247–73. There are two Ottoman-language versions in the İngiltere Nişan Defteri, BOA/A.(DVNSDVE.d) 35/1, 1086 [1675], the first in a very neat scribal hand at fols 2–28, the second penned by a more frenetic quill at fols 42–55. They are both copies of the 1675 Capitulations, being dated 'avāsiṭ-i şehr-i Cemāẕīü'l-āḫire sene sitt ve semānīn ve elf' and 'avāsiṭ C 1086' respectively, that is, the middle of the month of Cemāẕīü'l-āḫire of 1086. The reason for the existence of two texts in the same *defter* can be explained by a note above the start of the second text dated 1224/1809, indicating that it relates to the confirmation of the Capitulations following the British–Ottoman War. The content and wording of the articles are the same, although the second document includes the full preamble. I have also consulted a copy book of the Capitulations from 1086 in a collection dated 1187 (1773/4) that contains a full and very clearly transcribed version: BOA/TS.MA.d 7018/002 fols 7–18. In Talbot, 'A treaty of narratives', I examined a hitherto unexamined Ottoman Turkish and English version of the capitulatory text dating to 1641, at TNA/SP108/540.

the rate of and practices of collecting customs and duties. Winchilsea's renewal had three dealing with privileges, two on debts, and four on customs; and Finch's negotiations contained one article on privileges, two on legal disputes, and six on customs. Alexander de Groot summarised this final result nicely, in that '[t]he capitulation of 1675 … contains an accurate summary of the previously granted privileges and mentions the names of the ambassadors involved. Precedent, old custom and sultanic law (*ḳānūn*) are stressed throughout. The text amalgamates all privileges ever granted. No obsolete ones are omitted.'[45] This evolutionary process shows clearly a chronological split in the development of the Capitulations, in that the majority of privileges and rules concerning disputes were settled by the 1620s, and the majority of articles concerning customs and duties were granted after the British trade was consolidated and expanded in the early seventeenth century.

The British seem on the whole to have been very conscious of the fact that they had been granted favourable terms by the Ottomans; '[t]he advantages given by the Capitulations to the trade of Great Britain', wrote Privy Council clerk William Fawkener in 1790, 'are exceedingly extensive'.[46] What privileges, then, did this document grant? The most basic privileges were provided by the four initial articles. The first is the most important, and deserves to be quoted in full, with both the English and Ottoman Turkish texts provided to show the differences in content and tone:

> *English text:*
> That the said [English] nation, and the English merchants, and any other nation or merchants which are or shall come under the English banner and protection, with their ships small and great, merchandise, faculties, and all other their goods, may always pass safe in our seas, and freely and in all security may come and go into any part of our dominions in such sort, that neither any of the nation, their goods and faculties shall receive any hindrance or molestation from any person whatsoever.[47]

> *Ottoman Turkish text:*
> The British nation and merchants, and groups of merchants coming with the British flag by sea with their various goods, ships, and galleons, may come and go in peace and security to the Well-Protected Domains. Let no person ever meddle and infringe upon their men, goods, and possessions. There should not be offered any ignorance, embarrassments, or troubles as they proceed in their business and trade.[48]

Freedom of movement in order to trade without hindrance: this was the essence of the Capitulations, for the British and all the other European powers. Added

45 De Groot, 'The historical development of the capitulatory regime', 602.
46 TNA/FO78/11 William Fawkener to the Duke of Leeds, 19 October 1790.
47 *The Capitulations and Articles of Peace*, 7.
48 BOA/A.(DVNSDVE.d) 35/1 fol. 2.

to this was the more general promise by the sultan to observe the rules of peace and friendship (*ḳavvāʿid-i ṣulḥ ve ṣalāḥ ve müṣāfāt*). All that was expected in return from the British monarch was a firm and enduring (*s̱ābit-ḳadem ve rāssiḫ*) sincerity of observance (*iḥtirām-ı müşāhede*) of their friendship (*ṣadāḳat*) towards the Ottoman Empire.[49] All these words and phrases formed the staple vocabulary of the business of conducting relations, from royal letters to commercial petitions.

As well as laying down the framework for diplomatic friendship, these Capitulations were above all a commercial document designed to ensure that, because of the basic freedoms of movement granted, British merchants could engage in trade, ultimately to the benefit of the Ottoman treasury in customs and duties gained. These Capitulations were not directly reciprocal in the sense that they explicitly granted similar rights to any Ottoman subjects who might wish to venture to British ports, although that could inferred as part of the mutual commitment to friendly relations. Moreover, they were not simply a granting of privileges, but a statement of obligations of British subjects whilst residing or sojourning in the Ottoman realms. The articles of the 1675 Capitulations – made of seventy-six numbered articles in the English version and sixty-four in the Ottoman text – can be broken down into three broad categories.[50] The first consists of the privileges granted to the British nation and their ambassador and consuls; the second concerns customs and duties liable to be paid by British merchants; and the third relates to resolving disputes and administering civil matters such as bankruptcies and wills.

The first category, made up of twenty-eight articles, has been already briefly touched upon. These guarded the freedom of movement of British merchants and other subjects within the Ottoman Empire, both on land and at sea, assuring that they could come or go without any unnecessary let or hindrance anywhere in the Ottoman Empire, with the specific exception of the port of Caffa (modern Feodosiya) and other Black Sea ports that were out of bounds to foreign merchants to protect an Ottoman monopoly on the valuable trade

[49] The most common word used to refer to this friendship was *dostluḳ* but it had a variety of other terms, particularly *muṣāfāt* and *muvālāt*.

[50] Reference to the Capitulation Articles will be given with specific attention to the copy of the Capitulations in *The Capitulations of Articles and Peace* printed in 1679 and the two copies in the İngiltere Nişan Defteri. The printed text has numbered the articles of the first Capitulations until those gained by the Earl of Winchilsea from I to LXVII, and those secured by Sir John Finch in 1675 from I to IX. I have simply combined the two sets to give a total of LXXVI. Although the content of the articles is the same, the Ottoman copies have been numbered differently, with a total sixty-four articles given by placing together some that were separated in the English version. The separate articles, where not differentiated by the start of a new line, are sometimes clearly identified with a tabular space in the text, and several articles that appear as separate in the English version appear as one in the Ottoman. The scribal hand that noted the numbers has also given a short descriptor for each article (*mādde*), much in the same way that the 1679 printed English version did. For clarity and consistency, all Capitulation Articles referred to will be numbered from I to LXXVI in accordance with the combined total of the 1679 printed English version, followed by the Ottoman equivalent from the aforementioned manuscript in Arabic numerals from 1 to 64, e.g. Article IV/2.

there.[51] These freedoms were backed with promises of support from Ottoman officials, both administrative and military, and strict commands that those officials should always permit freedom of movement.[52] Specific examples given were promises that the imperial fleet would not molest British ships, nor would the ships of the North African Regencies – the so-called Barbary pirates – attack them.[53] Particular attention was paid to the problem of pirates operating in Ottoman waters, with the Ottoman government promising to hunt them down and restore any goods taken.[54] Moreover, Ottoman officials and subjects were commanded to help British ships in distress, to assist in salvage efforts following shipwrecks, and to return any goods that might go astray in such circumstances.[55] Something that was of special concern to the British government was the enslavement of British subjects or dependents, and the Capitulations expressly forbade this practice and made provision for the release of those already in captivity.[56] Crucially, it was guaranteed that all of these basic freedoms, and other articles, would be always interpreted in a manner favourable to the British, and that no commands would be made that might contradict the articles of that agreement.[57]

Considering that the first English merchants had traded under the protection of the French in the absence of a treaty between London and Istanbul, it is interesting to note that in the 1607 additions to the Capitulations, the British were granted jurisdiction over Dutch merchants in the Ottoman realms, this of course being prior to the issuing of the Dutch Capitulations in 1612.[58] On the subject of articles granted to other European states, the final of these basic privileges granted would be the basis for numerous disputes between the Ottomans and British, and among the other European nations in Istanbul:

[51] Articles I/1, II/1, III/2, IV/2, VII/3, XXXVI/29, XXXVIII/30.

[52] Article XX/13.

[53] Articles XVII/11, XLVIII/38, LV/41, LIX/46.

[54] Article XIX/12.

[55] Articles V/2, VI/2.

[56] Article XII/7. This very important article has near complete textual accuracy in both the English and Ottoman versions. The English text reads: 'All English men, or subjects of England, which shall be found slaves in our state, or shall be demanded by the ambassador, or consul, the cause shall be duly examined, and such persons as are found truly to be subjects of England shall be set free, and delivered to the ambassador, or consul.' For comparison, and to demonstrate the lack of ambiguity, the Ottoman text says: 'Any person found [to be a] slave from among the British nation [or] from among their dependents, if the British ambassadors and consuls make their request and solicitation [*murād ve ṭaleb*], there shall be a diligent investigation and enquiry [*teftīş ve tefaḥüṣ*], and if it is clear and evident [*ẓahir ve ma'lūm*] that they are British, let them be freed and delivered to their ambassador or consul.' In essence, the slave had to be asked for by a British official, following which an examination was undertaken to confirm whether or not they were British. Only after this would they would be delivered to a British official if they were deemed to be under British protection. The examination was crucial, and in practice required the presence of a British translator and consular official.

[57] Articles XXVII/20, XXXIV/26, XLV/37.

[58] Article XXXIII/25. The Ottoman text calls them 'Flāndralu tüccār', 'Flemish merchants'.

*English text:*
All those particular privileges and capitulations, which in former times have been granted to the French, Venetians, or any other Christian Nation, whose King is in peace and friendship with this Porte, in like manner, the same were granted and given to the said English Nation; to the end, that in time to come, the tenor of this our Imperial Capitulations may be always observed by all men; and that none may, in any manner, upon any pretence, presume to contradict, or violate it.

*Ottoman Turkish text:*
The imperial covenants, provisions, and articles given to the kings of Venice, France, and others in friendship with our Threshold of Felicity are also decreed and confirmed [*fermān ve muḳarer*] to the British. Let the requisites of this present imperial covenant always be performed, and henceforth no person should interfere in or dispute implementation and enacting of these our imperial covenants.[59]

This article in particular, with quite a close relationship between the two translations of the text, gives strong support to the idea of the Capitulations as an interlinked body of texts; whatever is granted for one is applicable to the others.

There were other more specific privileges granted to the British regarding jurisdiction. The British ambassador was given permission to appoint consuls in Aleppo, Alexandria, Tripoli in Syria, Algiers, Tunis, Tripoli in the Maghreb, Chios (not listed by name in the English version), Izmir, and in the ports of Egypt (*Mışır iskelelerinde*), with the allowance that consulates might be set up in other ports in the Ottoman realms not mentioned in that list.[60] This reflected imperial sovereignty, but also the importance of those commercial centres in Ottoman internal and overseas trade, and in many cases probably simply confirmed an existing situation where a local agent may have been acting on behalf of British merchants, or where a French or Venetian consul had taken them under their protection. The Capitulations additionally set a limit of anchorage to be paid whilst British ships were docked in those Ottoman ports, mentioning specifically Istanbul, İskenderun, Izmir, and Cyprus.[61]

These articles therefore confirmed the basic geography of the Levant Company's settlement in the Ottoman realms, with the open-endedness of the article allowing the addition of consuls in other places where British merchants required their presence, particularly Salonica, Patras, Larnaca, Ankara, İskenderun, and Latakia. An additional agent was maintained by the Company in Livorno, a Tuscan free port that was a crucial link in the Levant trade. The eastern parts of the Ottoman Empire, in particular Basra and Baghdad, hosted agents and consuls of the East India Company, and did

[59] Article XVIII/11.
[60] Article XIV/9.
[61] Article LXXI/60.

not fall under the remit of the Levant Company's jurisdiction. Moreover, the consuls stationed in the North African Regencies of Algiers, Tunis, and Tripoli also did not fall under the Levant Company's control, being directly appointed by the Crown with a salary from the Civil List similar to other Crown agents, primarily because the British state had separate treaties with the Regencies that developed over the course of the seventeenth and eighteenth centuries. The inclusion of those ports in the Capitulations was mainly an assertion of Ottoman dominion over them, even if that assertion had a limited ability to effect any practical implementations in influencing the policies of the beys and deys.

The remaining general privileges concerned the ambassador and his household. Two related to food and drink, the first, and very much utilised, granted permission for the ambassador (and British subjects in general), 'for the use of their own persons and families [to make] must or wine in their own houses', although according to the Ottoman text they were allowed only to make non-alcoholic must for their own consumption (*kefāf-ı nefsler içün şıra şıḳub*).[62] The importation of alcohol, although not specifically covered in the Capitulations, was generally permitted provided it was for personal consumption and not for sale, something set down in imperial *fermān*s throughout the period, such as the command to the Earl of Kinnoull in 1730 using the very words of the Capitulations in permitting an incredible 7,000 *medre*s (around 71,750 litres or 126,300 pints) 'for the personal consumption of the ambassador and his men' (*elçiniñ ve adamlarınıñ kefāf-ı nefsler içün*).[63] Even as late as 1796, this practice remained in force, with a command of Selim III ruling that a shipment of wine, arak, and beer (*ḫamr ve ʿaraḳ ve arpa ṣuyu*) was permissible in accordance with that provision.[64] The other consumption privilege, a remnant of the currant craze that gripped fashionable cuisine in the sixteenth and seventeenth centuries, granted the British monarch the right to purchase two ships full of 'figs and grapes' (*incir ve üzüm*) for the royal kitchen if there was enough to spare, phrased as a reward for the monarch 'being in a firm friendship with our Sublime state' (*Devlet-i ʿAliyemiz ile dostluḳda s̱ābit-ḳadem olmağla*).[65]

62 Article XXX/23. For an interesting discussion of wine and wine production, see: Oleksander Halenko, 'Wine production, marketing, and consumption in the Ottoman Crimea, 1520–1542', *Journal of the Economic and Social History of the Orient* 47:4 (2004), 507–47.

63 BOA/AE.SAMD.III 202/19530, middle of Muharrem 1143 (mid-July 1730).

64 BOA/HAT 203/10512, end of Zilhicce 1210 (beginning of July 1796).

65 Article LXXV/63. For a discussion on the 'currant craze' see: Maria Fusaro, *Uva Passa: Una guerra comerciale tra Venezia e l'Inghilterra, 1540–1640* (Venice, 1997), passim; Maria Fusaro, 'Les Anglais et les Grecs: Un réseau de coopération commerciale en Méditerranée vénitienne', *Annales HSS* 58:3 (2003), 605–25; Pagano de Divitiis, *English Merchants in Seventeenth-Century Italy* (Cambridge, 1997), 141–6. The British really did put currants into a huge variety of savoury and sweet dishes. Almost every recipe given in one particular seventeenth-century book, from custards to bone marrow pies, featured currants as a key ingredient: Gervase Markham & William Lawson, *A Way to get Wealth: containing Six Principall Vocations, or Callings, in which every good Husband or House-wife may lawfully imploy themselves*, book 2 (London, 1668), 49–101. Even as late as the middle of the nineteenth century, politician John Dunn Gardner

In terms of the personnel of diplomatic administration, the ambassador and the consuls were free to choose and appoint their own janissaries for their security, and translators for use in official business, rather than have individuals imposed upon them by the Ottoman government.[66] Furthermore, the embassy interpreters were to be exempt from taxes collected by the imperial government in both life and on their estates, and a maximum of ten servants (*yalñız on nefer ḫidmetkārı*) of the ambassador's choosing would be exempt from taxes.[67] The Ottoman text says simply that they would be exempted from taxes (*tekālīfden müʿāf olub*), which presumably refers to the *tekālīf-i ḳefere* (taxes on unbelievers) as the English text refers specifically to the 'harach' (from the Ottoman *ḫarāç*), a particular kind of poll tax levied on Ottoman non-Muslims.

This leads to the second major group of articles granted in the Capitulations, which are those relating to customs, duties, and taxes. As a cumulative document, new terms were added as time went on. In one of the later articles, the Ottomans listed a set of commodities and the customs due on them for both import and export. Imports into the Ottoman Empire from Britain according to this list included London broadcloth (*Londra çūḳası*), kersey coarse cloth (*ḳerzīye çūḳası*), coney furs (*ṭavşān kürkü*), tin (*ḳalāy*), and lead (*ḳūrşūn*). For exports, the Capitulations listed raw linen cloth (*ḫām bez*), leather (*saḫtiyān*), Iranian textiles (*ḫorasān*), Indian textiles (*Hindī*), cotton yarn (*penbe ipliği*), galls (*māzi*), silk (*ḥarīr*), rhubarb and other 'drugs' (*rāvend ve saʾīr ve ġayrī eczā*), and spices (*bahār*).[68] Additional articles dealt with goods passing via Ankara, specifically camlet (*ṣūf*), mohair (*moḫīr*), and grogram yarn (*tüfek ipliği*).[69] These goods formed the majority of British trade with the Ottoman Empire from the sixteenth until the end of the eighteenth century. As the number of commodities traded between the British and the Ottomans multiplied over time, rather than amending the Capitulations, a separate catalogue was kept by the British and the *gümrük emini* (chief customs officer), which by the 1790s listed between 300 and 400 individual commodities and their applicable rates.[70] In addition to that extensive list, there were also prohibited commodities, specifically the exportation of gunpowder (*bārūt*) and weapons of war (*ālet-i ḥarb*), although by the end of the eighteenth century, as we will see in Chapter 6, British merchants imported significant quantities of naval material and arms for the use of the Ottoman navy.[71]

gave currants as a reason for Britain to retain the Ionian Islands: '[t]here is another, smaller, but not contemptible, ground for our keeping the islands, and that is the currant trade; in England currants are almost a necessary of life'. John Dunn Gardner, *The Ionian Islands in Relation to Greece, with suggestions for advancing our trade with the Turkish countries of the Adriatic, and the Danube* (London, 1859), 23–4.

66 Article XXIX/22.

67 Articles LXV/51, LXVI/52.

68 Articles LIV/41, LXVIII/54, LXIX/55.

69 Article LXXIII/62. A detailed study of this trade can be found in: Gülay Webb Yıldırmak, *XVIII. Yüzyılda Osmanlı-İngiliz Tiftik Ticareti* (Ankara, 2011),

70 TNA/FO78/15, Robert Liston to Lord Grenville, 25 October 1794.

71 Article XXII/15.

As well as tariffs on individual commodities, British merchants were required to pay three per cent custom (*yüzde üç aḳçe gümrük*) on all their transactions in the Ottoman Empire.[72] This generally worked as a base level without much trouble, but on occasion the inter-referential nature of the Capitulations came into play. In the early seventeenth century, the British seem to have been overcharged on silk duties at Aleppo, as one article specifically emphasised that they should pay the same as the French and Venetians, 'and not one asper or farthing more'.[73] This is restated in a later article, where it is also revealed that the French and Venetians were being charged only two-and-a-half per cent.[74] The inclusion of such disputes in the Capitulations is symptomatic of wider problems concerning customs levels, so that although in theory the same rates applied to all foreign traders, in practice some nations received a better deal than others at different times. Overall, the Europeans received a better deal in trade than local Ottoman merchants, something that would become a greater point of contention towards the later eighteenth century.[75]

One customs problem that was evidently commonplace during the formation of the articles of the Capitulations, and that would remain an issue throughout the eighteenth century, was the double charging of customs on goods moved from one place to another in the Ottoman Empire. That is, sometimes merchants would be told to pay customs again in ports en route, even if the goods were not unloaded for sale. No fewer than eight articles dealt with this issue, a good indication that the Capitulations had little effect on this practice.[76] The first article to address this shows the extent of the abuse, ordering that if British merchants had loaded goods in Istanbul, Aleppo, İskenderun, Chios, Izmir, or any other ports and paid the correct customs there, it was forbidden for Ottoman customs officials or any others to take a second set of customs from the said goods if they then stopped in another port.[77] One reason given was that officials refused to accept or issue customs certificates (*teẕkere*, in the English version 'teschere'), the main document for proving ownership of goods or payment of duties.[78] There was also a prohibition against charging customs on goods not intended to be sold in Ottoman ports, an article designed to protect the goods of British merchants, but also those of Ottoman subjects, specifically Muslim pilgrims freighting British ships en route to Mecca and Medina.[79]

In addition to attempting to regulate the behaviour of Ottoman officials, certain articles tried to stop bad practices among British merchants. There had

72 Articles XXXVII/29, LXII/47.

73 Article XLIII/34. In the Ottoman version: 'Giving three akçe in customs let them not give one akçe more.'

74 Article XLIX/39.

75 Mehmet Genç, *Osmanlı İmparatorluğunda Devlet ve Ekonomi* (Istanbul, 2000), 44–6; Mehmet Bulut, 'XVII yüzyılda Osmanlılar ve merkantilistler', *Ekonomik Yaklaşım Dergisi* 39 (2007), 23–36.

76 Articles XXXI//24, L/40, LI/40, LII/40, LVI/41, LX/46, LXI/47.

77 Article XXXI/24.

78 Article LX/46.

79 Articles XXXIX/30, XL/31. Both texts for Article XL/31 specifically mentioned 'ehl-i İslām'/'Mahometans' and 'ḥücāc'/'pilgrims'.

been a widespread practice among European merchants, in the seventeenth century in particular, of importing specie – often of poor quality – to pay for goods in the Ottoman realms.[80] This had caused so many disputes that, by the time of the refounding of the Levant Company in 1661, the practice was specifically forbidden from the British side, and a command to enforce this prohibition was issued in the instructions to new ambassadors well into the nineteenth century. The problems of importing coinage are also reflected in the Capitulations, with two articles dealing specifically with the issue of customs officials taking percentages of the coinage as custom, which was forbidden by imperial command.[81]

Perhaps a rather surprising entry is an article specifically referring to the duties owed to the Company by British merchants, making it clear that, in addition to paying customs (*gümrük*) to the Ottoman government, merchants trading under British protection also had to pay consulage (*ḳonsolosluḳ*) to the British consul or ambassador in the port in which they were trading.[82] The duty to pay consulage extended to any 'Muslim, Sciot, protected foreign Christian, or enemy merchants' (*Müsülmanları tüccārı ve Sāḳızlu ve müstemʿin ve ḥarbī*) lading goods on British ships.[83] The collection of consulage was the main source of financing the British embassy and consulates in the Levant, and its importance is highlighted by its formal inclusion in the Capitulations despite it having no direct financial impact on the Ottoman treasury. Presumably the purpose of including it in the Capitulations was not to cement the importance of the Elizabethan funding model, but to ensure that any merchants trading under British protection would be subject to British authority, thus avoiding any legal confusion.

Finally, British subjects and dependents (*tābiʿ*) were exempted from taxes normally paid by Ottoman non-Muslims. The specific examples given were exemption from the *ḫarāç* poll tax, and the 'meat tax' levied on non-Muslim communities (*ḳaṣāb aḳçesi*, literally butchery money, which the English text renders as 'Hassapie').[84] This was important because it exempted British dependents who were also Ottoman subjects, such as translators who held

80 Şevket Pamuk, 'In the absence of domestic currency: Debased European coinage in the seventeenth-century Ottoman Empire', *The Journal of Economic History* 57:2 (1997), 345–66; Elizabeth Frangakis-Syrett, 'Monetary shortage and the Ottoman economy: Late seventeenth to late eighteenth centuries' in Walid Arbid, Salgur Kancal, Jean-David Mizrahi, & Samir Saul (eds), *Méditerranée, Moyen-Orient: Deux siècles de relations internationales* (Paris, 2003), 109–31.

81 Articles XXI/14, LVIII/43. The denominations mentioned in the English-language text are 'chequeens' and 'dollars', which correspond to the Ottoman 'āltūn' and 'ġurūş'.

82 Article XXXV/28.

83 Article XLII/33. Note the distinction in the Ottoman text between merchants who were 'müstemʿin', that is those Christians whose nations were at peace with the Ottomans and so protected by *amān*, and 'ḥarbī', those who were from the *dār ül-ḥarb*, the Christian nations without peace agreement with the Ottomans.

84 Articles XIII/8, XXXII/24. For a discussion of this, see: Daniel Goffman, 'Negotiating with the Renaissance state: The Ottoman Empire and the new diplomacy' in Virginia Aksan & Daniel Goffman, *The Early Modern Ottomans: Remapping the Empire* (Cambridge, 2007), 61–74 at 65–8.

*berāt*s (a licence that gave them the same legal rights as Europeans), from taxes they would otherwise have been liable to pay. This set them aside, therefore, from the majority of Ottoman non-Muslims, and this privilege would, later in the Empire's history, become a great point of contention in relations between the Ottomans and the Christian powers as it became increasingly abused.[85]

With privileges granted and customs duties set, the third category of articles covered by the Capitulations related to what happened when things went wrong or when the various legal systems needed to come into play, specifically in terms of commercial disputes, bankruptcies, wills, and the legal process. Debt and its non-payment was a major source of commercial disputes.[86] The Capitulations, implicitly acknowledging the inevitability of such occurrences in routine commerce, attempted to set up some bounds to ensure that all parties would be assured of regulated process. The first guaranteed that internal British disputes should be settled by the ambassador and consuls without Ottoman interference, and therefore without reference to any Ottoman legal system: to quote from the Ottoman text, 'if any of the British nation have a legal dispute with one another [*birbirler ile nizā'ları oldukda*], they shall be seen by their ambassadors and consuls, and the judges and the other officials from among my slaves may not interfere'.[87] This article therefore gave the British diplomats the right to implement their own judicial process over British disputes without reference to the Ottoman authorities or legal systems.

However, with so much trade between Ottoman and British merchants, the Capitulations also had to set some form of process to deal with mixed cases. A key article ensured that if a British subject ran away in order to escape his debt or surety, his Ottoman creditors could not simply demand the debt from another British subject in lieu without a formal proof – a document known as a *ḥüccet* – that the third party had guaranteed the debt.[88] In other words, no British subject could be held accountable for the debt of another without documented legal proof. This was extended by another article to any offences in general, with emphasis on the pursuit of the guilty party (*müttehim*).[89] The importance of the *ḥüccet* was established very firmly and comprehensively:

> *English text:*
> In all causes, businesses, and occasions, which shall occur between the said nation, their merchants, interpreters and brokers, or servants, and any other

[85] İsmail Hakkı Kadı, *Ottoman and Dutch Merchants in the Eighteenth Century: Competition and Cooperation in Ankara, Izmir, and Amsterdam* (Leiden, 2012), 299–315; Ali İhsan Bağış, *Osmanlı Ticaretinde Gayri-Müslimler: Kapitülasyonlar-Beratlı Tüccarlar Avrupa ve Hayriye Tüccarları, 1750–1839* (Ankara, 1983), passim.

[86] See: Van den Boogert, *Capitulations*, 159–262. He has convincingly argued that whilst Europeans were broadly able to enjoy legal autonomy when disputes occurred between Europeans, when disputes over wills or debts involved Ottoman subjects, the Ottoman government attempted to assert its own legal systems over European debtors or executors.

[87] Article XVI/10.

[88] Article VIII/4.

[89] Article XI/6.

> whatsoever, that is to say, in selling or buying, in paying or receiving, in giving or taking security, or pledge, debt or credit, and all other such things which appertain to the ministers of the law and justice, they must always (if they please) in such occasions go to the caddee [*ḳāżī*], who is the judge of the law, and there make a hoget [*ḥüccet*], or public authentic act with witness, and register the same, and take a copy of the same to keep by them, to the end that if in the future any difference or pretence shall arise between the said parties, they may both have a recourse to the said hoget and act.
>
> *Ottoman Turkish text:*
> The British and [their] dependents being resident in the Well-Protected Domains with their merchants, gentlemen, translators, and brokers desiring to buy and sell, give and trade, in the event of particular sureties and other legal matters, may go to the judge [who] can give a proof [and] write it in the register [*sebt-i sicil eyderüb*]. If there are any subsequent disputes, the proof and register will be examined. If their claim is conformable to the proof, let action be taken in accordance with the legal proof [*daʿvāları ḥüccete muvāfiḳ ise mūceb-i ḥüccet-i şerʿiye ile ʿamel oluna*], and if there is no proof from the judges, only the producing of a false witness [*şāhid-i zūr*], the claims may not be heard. The enforcement of the law will always be in accordance with the legal proof [*dāʾimā hüccet-i şerʿiye muḳtażāsınca icrā-yı ḥaḳḳ oluna*].[90]

Despite this careful wording and clear definitions, particularly in the Ottoman Turkish version of the text, the *ḥüccet* was a document that was often the focus of disputes between the British ambassador and the Ottoman government, with accusations put forward of false witnesses and forgeries.

The Capitulations attempted to ensure that such suspicions might be raised directly with the local judges or Ottoman officials by legislating that cases could only be heard against British subjects in Ottoman courts in the presence of a British translator, consul, or the ambassador himself. No fewer than five articles of the Capitulations emphasised that right for British subjects, including one that extended it even to cases involving the shedding of blood.[91] To provide further protection it was decreed that in cases involving debts above 4,000 aspers/*akçe*s, the case would be heard at the very highest level, described in the English text as the 'Imperial Porte' and in the Ottoman text as Āsitāne-i Saʿādet, both referring to the imperial *divan* situated at 'the Threshold of Felicity'.[92] As I will demonstrate in chapter 6, this became a way for complex provincial disputes to be sent for arbitration in Istanbul; the real value of 4,000 *akçe*s decreased significantly between the seventeenth and eighteenth centuries, making it impractical to have every case of that value

[90] Article IX/5.

[91] Articles X/5, XV/10, XXIII/16, XLI/32, LVII. Referring to criminal offences, the Ottoman text refers specifically to 'ḳān ve sāʾir ḳabāḥat eydüb' ('committing blood crimes and other atrocious crimes').

[92] Articles XXVII/16, LXX/58.

heard in Istanbul. As an alternative to such recourse to imperial justice, it was later agreed that if the local British consul could provide security on the debt, then the case could be heard by the local qadi instead. How far these rules were enforced and observed depended very much on the attitude of the British merchants on one side, and Ottoman creditors and judges on the other, together with the involvement of the consuls and the ambassador.

## Conclusion

There are a number of ways in which the history of first relations between these two states can be constructed. One could look at the wider geopolitical picture, and think of early British–Ottoman relations in terms of an attempt to outflank their mutual enemies in European politics. Doubtless, some significant political consideration went into the final decision to formalise relations in the context of what Akdes Nimet Kurat called 'the Spanish question' (*İspanya meselesi*).[93] Yet the evidence from both sides tells an overwhelmingly commercial story, best demonstrated by the Capitulations granted to the British, a complex series of texts that show us in great detail how British–Ottoman relations developed in historical, legal, and commercial terms. This was not a treaty of political alliance, but a commercial agreement. The articles of this treaty were not fixed, but ever-changing as the economic situation demanded. Even after the Capitulations were finally set in 1675, a large number of imperial commands were issued ruling on all different sorts of disputes and abuses brought forward by the British ambassador, generally on behalf of the merchants. Many of these decrees were subsequently clarified, replaced, or annulled, again demonstrating the constantly changing set of laws that sought to regulate British–Ottoman relations. In addition to this, the textual framework of relations included imperial letters sent to the British monarch, the rulings of local qadis, and ceremonial and commercial registers. The sheer mass of paperwork available to both Ottoman and British officials had the potential to give both parties written proofs of often contrary positions. Crucially, the Capitulations were insufficient on their own either to prevent or to resolve disputes. They provided a framework for relations based on historical need, reflected in changing customs regulations and the reissuing of previous articles. But the framework was fleshed out by oral and other written practices, by legal negotiation, and by additional commands and practices. It would only be with the changing focus on political and commercial domination going into the nineteenth century that this 'ancient' text would see extensive modification, particularly after 1838.

However, the Capitulations also give a sense of what the basic business of diplomacy in the Ottoman Empire in the eighteenth century was all about. They provide a narration of the beginning of relations, and subsequent developments, based around the commercial privileges the British sought and gained from the Ottoman state. Rather than negotiating grand alliances, the

93 Kurat, *Türk-İngiliz Münasebetleri*, 118–73.

daily bread of an ambassador was earned by constantly trying to persuade the Ottomans to interpret the Capitulations in a way that favoured British subjects, and to protest against violations when they were considered to have occurred. The document itself shows how the Ottomans viewed relations, not as a partnership between equal sovereigns, but as a sort of contract between the sultan and a lesser ruler in order to ensure the maintenance of friendship, the key theme of the cycle that drove British–Ottoman interactions. Indeed, it is telling that when they finally sent an ambassador to London at the end of the eighteenth century, there was not even a suggestion that a new form of bilateral treaty should be established, but rather his key aim was to strengthen the bonds of amity.

Beyond their symbolic value, the Capitulations did provide strong evidence for the British to argue for favourable terms and treatment from the Ottoman government. Additionally, many other factors influenced the practice of diplomatic relations other than this agreement. Other conventions and institutions, such as gift-giving and ceremonial, and practices such as oral and written petitions, along with constraints of finance, helped or hindered the implementation of the Capitulations. The ambassadors who represented the interests of their merchants with the Ottoman government had therefore to balance a number of commercial, financial, and cultural factors in pursuing their business in Istanbul. This leads us to consider the nature of ambassadorial duties in the Ottoman context, and to examine who the ambassadors were, and how their social and professional backgrounds were indicative of changing trends in relations within the historical and legal frameworks set by early encounters and the texts of the Capitulations.

# 2

# The office of ambassador

## 'A deviant ambassador is a prey to misfortune': The ambassador and his duties

In 1797, after almost four years of service, the first Ottoman resident ambassador in London, Yusuf Agah Efendi, received his recall from Istanbul. In an Ottoman translation of a letter from George III (r. 1760–1820) to Selim III, the British government requested that the Ottomans continue to send ambassadors to the Court of St James's. The letter also spoke highly of Yusuf Agah and his abilities:

> We came to know from your imperial letter sent to us that the resident official at our court from the Crown-holder, the excellent and wise Yusuf Agah Efendi, is to make his return in accordance with your exalted order. During his residence, the said ambassador strengthened and reinforced beyond all expression the complete concord of love and affection that has happily and blessedly endured and persisted of old between your Sublime State and the state of Britain.[1]

Here, one role of the ambassador, as expressed in an Ottoman translation of a British letter, is clear. Yusuf Agah, 'excellent and wise' (*izzetlü recāḥetlü*), had solidified the bonds of friendship between the two states. This idea of the ambassador was one that was easily translated between the two cultures. It also emphasised that he was part of a historical narrative; this was not just any friendship, but one 'of old' (*ez-ḳadīm*). This echoes the narrative of the Capitulations, where friendship and its maintenance were paramount.

Despite these noble aims in rhetoric, the art of diplomacy has held, at least in the Anglophone world, rather negative connotations. The acerbic wit of Ambrose Bierce's *Cynic's Word Book* defined diplomacy as 'the patriotic art of lying for one's country'.[2] Taking things even further, the first Secretary-General of the United Nations, Trygve Lie, suggested that a good diplomat

1 BOA/C.HR/164/8183, 28 Rebiülahir 1212 (19 October 1797).

2 Ambrose Bierce, *The Cynic's Word Book* (London & New York, 1906), 76.

should be able to 'cut his neighbour's throat without having his neighbour notice'.[3] Negative connotations came early in the word's history, with Edmund Burke, one of the first public figures to make use of the term, employing it several times in his tirade against the prospect of peace with the French Republic in 1796, using expressions such as 'diplomacy of humiliation', 'double diplomacy', and 'mendicant diplomacy'.[4] Diplomacy was something distinct from the duties of an ambassador. Whilst Johnson's *Dictionary* did not give a definition for 'diplomacy', it defined 'ambassadour' as being '[a] person sent in a public manner from one sovereign to another', on an 'embassy', which was 'a public message or any solemn message'.[5] As such, the ambassadors featured understood their job as a specific event or a negotiation. This is also the case in the Ottoman language, where ambassadors were engaged in an embassy (*elçilik*). The Ottomans had two terms for ambassador, the first being *sefīr*, which has its origin in the Arabic root *s-f-r*, relating to travel. The second term was *elçi*, derived from two words, *el* meaning a land or a polity, and *-çi*, the suffix denoting employment, so that an *elçi* was literally someone working for their country.

Long-standing conventions and traditions informed both the European and Ottoman understanding of the ambassador and his role, and we can get some sense of how these were shaped from texts on the subject of ambassadorship. Writings and publications on the ambassador and his office in Europe began to appear in any appreciable quantity from the very end of the fifteenth century with the increasingly intricate system of alliances and conflicts among the northern Italian city-states, but it was the seventeenth century that saw a flourishing of diplomatic writing.[6] Among the first of this particular kind of diplomatic manual-cum-history originated, perhaps unsurprisingly for the early part of the seventeenth century, in Spain. Juan Antonio de Vera's *El Enbaxador* (The Ambassador, 1620) began to articulate some of the most fundamental ideas about the role of ambassadors. To de Vera, an ambassador was a mediator between two princes (*un conciliador de las voluntades de dos principes*), and selecting an unsuitable person as an ambassador was more detrimental to a ruler's interests than the appointment of an inappropriate person as minister of state (*desdichadissimo el que ierra la [elecion] de los enbaxadores*).[7]

3 Charles W. Freeman, *The Diplomat's Dictionary* (Washington DC, 1994), 112.

4 Edmund Burke, *Two Letters addressed to a Member of the Present Parliament on the Proposals for Peace with the Regicide Directory of France* (Dublin, 1796), 19, 121; Edmund Burke, *A Third Letter to a Member of the Present Parliament on the Proposals for Peace with the Regicide Directory of France* (Dublin, 1796), 19.

5 Samuel Johnson, *A Dictionary of the English Language*, 3rd edn (Dublin, 1768).

6 José Calvet de Magalhães, *The Pure Concept of Diplomacy*, trans. Bernardo Futcher Pereira (London & New York 1988), 38–40; Hamish Scott, 'Diplomatic culture in old regime Europe' in Hamish Scott & Brendan Simms (eds), *Cultures of Power in Europe during the Long Eighteenth Century* (Cambridge, 2007), 58–8 at 60–5; William James Roosen, *Daniel Defoe and Diplomacy* (London, 1986), 68–9.

7 Juan Antonio de Vera y Figueroa Ávila y Zúñiga, *El Enbaxador* (Seville, 1620), 10, 18. This work was translated into French in both France and the United Provinces, with editions appearing

Perhaps the most influential of those early texts was by the Dutch philosopher Huig de Groot, better known as Hugo Grotius. Grotius was more famous as a theologian than a political theorist, a catalogue of the Levant Company's library in the British embassy in Istanbul showing a holding of his *Opera Omnia Theologica* (Complete Theological Works, 1679) but none of his political studies.[8] Yet, his seminal *De Jure Belli ac Pacis Libri Tres* (On the Law of War and Peace in Three Books, 1625) was a major attempt to codify 'the law of nations' (*jus gentium*). Using biblical, classical, and contemporary examples, Grotius argued that the office of the ambassador was sacred and inviolable (the *sanctimoniam legatorum*) and that ambassadors should, without exception, always be received and never suffer their persons to be violated (*prius ut admittantur, deinde ne volientur*).[9] The inviolability of the person of an ambassador, and the guarantee of his free movement, became a cornerstone of an increasingly universalist European 'law of nations'. Two influential works strongly advocated the inviolability of the office of ambassador, the first being *Discours sur l'Art de Negocier* by French diplomat Antoine Pecquet (Discussion on the Art of Negotiating, 1737), the other by the Swiss philosopher Emerich de Vattel in his *Le Droit des Gens* (The Law of Nations, 1758).[10]

Other works considered the ambassador's role and duties in more depth. The first of these texts was penned by the Dutch diplomat Abraham de Wicquefort, *L'Ambassadeur et Ses Fonctions* (The Ambassador and his Functions, 1682). He concurred with de Vera's assessment that an ambassador was primarily a mediator between rulers, but added:

> It may be said in general, that his chief function consists in his entertaining a good correspondence between the two princes. In his delivering the letters his master writes to the prince with whom he resides; in soliciting an answer thereto; in his observing all that passes at the court where he negotiates; in protecting the subjects, and in preserving the interest of his master; he serves as an interpreter to the two Princes and as a broker in the commerce that is

into the eighteenth century: *Le Parfait Ambassadeur*, trans. Sieur Lancelot (Paris, 1635); *Le Parfait Ambassadeur*, trans. anonymous (Leiden, 1709).

8 TNA/SP105/179 fols 300–2. A large proportion of the volumes (numbering over one hundred) catalogued in 1711 were theological works; this particular copy would appear to be a version printed in London in 1679: Hugo Grotius, *Opera Omnia Theologica in Tres Tomos Divisa*, 4 vols (London, 1679).

9 Hugo Grotius, *De Jure Belli ac Pacis* (Amsterdam, 1631), 269–70. Other editions consulted in this study include: *The Most Excellent Hugo Grotius His Three Books Treating the Rights of War & Peace*, trans. William Evats, 3 vols (London, 1682); *Of the Rights of War and Peace, In Three Volumes*, trans. anonymous, 3 vols (London, 1715); *Le Droit de la Guerre et de la Paix*, trans. Jean Barbeyrac, 2 vols (Amsterdam, 1729).

10 Antoine Pecquet, *Discours sur l'Art de Negocier* (Paris, 1737); Emerich de Vattel, *Le Droit des Gens ou Principes de la Loi Naturelle Appliqués à la Conduite aux Affaires des Nations & des Souverains*, 2 vols (Leiden, 1758). An English translation of de Vattel's work appeared right at the end of the eighteenth century: *The Law of Nations, or, Principles of the Law of Nature, Applied to the Conduct and Affairs of Nations and Sovereigns*, trans. anonymous (Dublin, 1792).

> between them … an ambassador … is … a messenger of peace on one side, and an honourable spy on the other.[11]

The second text, *De la Manière de Negocier avec les Souverains* (On the Method of Negotiating with Sovereigns, 1716) by the French diplomat François de Callières, concurred that the ambassador was a mediator, a resolver of conflicts and disputes, and encourager of trade, always aiming to preserve his ruler's honour and advance his interests.[12] Fundamentally, however, he gave the ambassador two primary functions: 'the one is, to negotiate there the affairs of his own Prince; and the other is, to discover those of others'.[13] The office of the ambassador in eighteenth-century Europe, therefore, from the perspective of the state, can be summed up, using de Callières's definition, as a negotiator and a spy.

Whilst the Ottoman notion of the ambassador and his office was not radically different from that of Christian Europe, it is perhaps harder to define because the Ottomans did not write about ambassadors in the same volume or specificity as did the French or Dutch. Additionally, historiographical assumptions about Ottoman diplomacy have presented a rather distorted narrative that has only recently begun to be revised. In a collection of articles entitled *Ottoman Diplomacy: Conventional or Unconventional?* A. Nuri Yurdusev put forward a strong and persuasive case that the overemphasis on the Ottoman Empire as an 'Islamic' empire was distorting understandings of Ottoman diplomacy.[14] The kind of historiography Yurdusev sought to challenge put forward the idea that the Ottoman Empire avoided the 'conventional' bilateral diplomacy of Christian Europe due to an 'orthodox' Islamic approach that forbade peaceful contact with the *dār al-ḥarb*, and a lack of shared diplomatic culture.[15] Rather, what Yurdusev and his co-contributors proposed was that the Ottomans went by pragmatism rather than orthodoxy. Bülent Arı's discussion of the 'ad hoc' nature of early Ottoman diplomacy summed up this position: 'it is more accurate to characterize Ottoman practice as a synthesis of abstract Islamic principles with Ottoman Realpolitik. In other words, the Ottomans created their own method of diplomacy while respecting the pillars of Islam.'[16] Moving beyond dichotomies of Islamic versus non-Islamic requires looking at individual case studies of embassies, and particularly at the writings of Ottoman ambassadors.

11 Abraham de Wicquefort, *The Ambassador and His Functions*, trans. Mr. Digby (London, 1716), 296.

12 François de Callières, *De la Manière de Negocier avec les Souverains* (Amsterdam, 1716), 89–90; François de Callières, *The Art of Negotiating with Sovereign Princes*, trans. anonymous (London, 1738), 84–6. See also de Magalhães, *The Pure Concept of Diplomacy*, 39.

13 de Callières, *De la Manière*, 85; de Callières, *The Art of Negotiating*, 80. 'L'une est d'y traiter les affaires de son Prince, & l'autre est de découvrir celles d'autrui.'

14 A. Nuri Yurdusev, 'The Ottoman attitude toward diplomacy' in Yurdusev (ed.), *Ottoman Diplomacy*, 5–35.

15 Anderson, *Modern Diplomacy*, 71–3.

16 Bülent Arı, 'Early Ottoman diplomacy: Ad hoc period' in Yurdusev, *Ottoman Diplomacy*, 36–65 at 37.

What did the ambassadors themselves have to say about their role? The answer is, relatively little directly, but we can get a very good idea of what the job entailed from the corpus of writings they have left us. The main sources for the missions of the Ottoman ambassadors to foreign courts in the eighteenth century are the *sefāretnāme*s, the travel books that documented their journeys and time abroad. Often they described their duties in simple terms. That of Yirmisekiz Mehmed Çelebi, ambassador to France in 1720, merely stated that 'in this present year 1132 [1720], this humble person, full of short-comings [*ḥaḳīr-i pürr-taḳṣīr*], was appointed ambassador from the Eternal Sublime State to the emperor of France [*Devlet-i ʿAliye-i ebed-peyvend cānibinden Françe pādişāhına elçi taʿyīn olunmağla*]'.[17] From his account, the purpose of his visiting embassy is made very clear, and is similar to the ideas put forward in European texts: to present the imperial letters with which he had been entrusted; and to report on what he saw and experienced in France and on his journeys. As to the first, his narrative of his audience with Louis XV explains:

> We took the majestic imperial letter before us. We put our hands to our chest, and then, coming closer and taking the imperial letter, we made our salutation, saying, 'This is the majestic letter of the great, mighty, and powerful Padishah of Islam, my generous master, my lord, His Majesty Sultan Ahmed Khan son of Sultan Mehmed Khan.' We gave it to the hands of the vizier. Then we took the letter of His Highness the Master of the State, saying: 'And this is the splendid letter of the illustrious and felicitous Grand Vizier, His Highness the esteemed bridegroom İbrahim Pasha.' We gave it into the hands of the vizier. I then said, '[The sultan] has sent me with this embassy [*elçilik ile beni irsāl eylediler*] in order to strengthen the bonds of friendship that have been observed from ancient times between these two states [*bu iki devlet beyninde ḳadīmden merʿī olan*], and in order to clearly convey to His Majesty the illustrious and respected Padishah of France his affection, amity, regard, and esteem [*muḥabbet ve müveddet ve iʿtibār ve rağbetlerini*].[18]

This ceremonial presentation of letters and articulation of a friendship was at the heart of the mission of an Ottoman ambassador, playing out the rhetoric found in the Capitulations of strengthening the bonds between the two monarchs.

Despite employing some literary humility, Yirmisekiz Mehmed was an educated member of the Ottoman elite, with experience in both the military and the state administration.[19] Although there was no diplomatic corps until much later, Ottoman ambassadors were therefore drawn from a particular

17 Yirmisekiz Mehmed Çelebi, *Relation de l'ambassade de Mohammed Effendi, texte turc* (Paris, 1841), 1.

18 Ibid., 29.

19 On the importance of ambassadors' backgrounds, see: Fatma Müge Göçek, *East Encounters West: France and the Ottoman Empire in the Eighteenth Century* (New York & Oxford, 1987), 90–4.

section of the state elite. As with European ambassadors, these diplomats were intent on maintaining the honour of their state during their missions. Ahmed Vasıf Efendi was the non-resident ambassador to Spain in 1787–8 following the establishment of peace with that nation in 1786.[20] He insisted on lodging with the gifts with which he was entrusted by the sultan and this, along with other minor points, was opposed by the Russian ambassador on the grounds of established protocol. At the hottest point of this dispute, Ahmed Vasıf reported in his *sefāretnāme* that he declared: 'We may hold the title of minister plenipotentiary [*orta elçilik*], but we are not like the others. We are appointed for the inauguration of this friendship, and the embassy is a symbol of this [*müceddeden-i muṣāfāta me'mūruz ve elçilik bir 'arażnesnedir*]. Moreover, we are [a] powerful individual in the Sublime State, and, what is more, every state has protocols that are particular to itself.'[21] Clearly, although his mission was to cement friendship between the sultan and foreign monarchs, he did not feel bound to conform entirely to the protocols of European diplomatic practice in the same ways European diplomats did in Istanbul.

The symbolic elements of the embassies aside, the majority of the narratives of ambassadors like Ahmed Vasıf and Mehmed Çelebi detailed their observations and served as intelligence-gathering documents. For instance, the record of Mahmud Raif Efendi, the chief secretary accompanying Yusuf Agah's embassy to London, barely mentions the ceremonial aspects of diplomacy, instead focusing on recording his observations on politics, the military, and British society.[22] As with many of these sorts of accounts, they might be seen not just as a record of the ambassadors' observations, but also as a critical reflection on Ottoman institutions and society.[23] As well as being reflective pieces, the fact that the immediate task of delivering letters and gifts was accompanied by the observations (perhaps even spying) and information-gathering found in Ahmed Vasıf's and most other *sefāretnāme*s, makes their task very similar to the ideal of the ambassador's role put forward in European writings like that of Wicquefort.[24]

[20] On Ottoman–Spanish relations in this period, see: Hüseyin Serdar Tabakoğlu, 'The re-establishment of Ottoman–Spanish relations in 1782', *Turkish Studies / Türkoloji Araştırmaları* 2/3 (2007), 496–524.

[21] Cevdet, *Tārīḫ-i Cevdet*, vol. IV, 350.

[22] Mehmet Alaaddin Yalçınkaya, 'Mahmud Raif Efendi as the chief secretary of Yusuf Agah Efendi, the first pemanent Ottoman-Turkish ambassador to London (1793–1797)', *Ankara Üniversitesi Osmanlı Tarihi Araştırma ve Uygulama Dergisi* 5 (1994), 385–434 at 422–34.

[23] This idea was put foward convincingly by Henning Sievert at a paper presented at the 'Well-Connected Domains: Intersections of Asia and Europe in the Ottoman Empire' conference held at the University of Heidelberg, 10–12 November 2011, entitled 'Post-Safavid Iran and Habsburg Austria as seen by Ottoman diplomats'.

[24] For an important discussion on spying, see: Emrah Safah Gürkan, 'Espionage in the 16th century Mediterranean: Secret diplomacy, Mediterranean go-betweens, and the Ottoman–Habsburg rivalry', PhD thesis, Georgetown University (2012); Gürkan, 'Mediating boundaries: Mediterranean go-betweens and cross-confessional diplomacy in Constantinople, 1560–1600', *Journal of Early Modern History* 19 (2015), 107–28.

Ahmed Vasıf went to Spain as an ad hoc ambassador just five years before Yusuf Agah went to London and changed the Ottoman model forever. As Virginia Aksan has suggested in her analysis of Ottoman political writing in the late eighteenth century, and in her study on Ahmed Resmi Efendi, a major Ottoman official and ambassador to Prussia, there was a clear change in Ottoman diplomatic discourse following the defeat to the Russians in the war of 1768–74.[25] The change was not necessarily to do with notions of 'Europeanisation', although 'modernisation' played a part, particularly with the diplomatic reforms under Selim III.[26] Those reforms established the first Ottoman resident embassies, with the dispatch of Yusuf Agah Efendi to London in 1793 marking not only the first visit of an Ottoman ambassador to London, but the first official of this kind to be dispatched in Ottoman history. Just as the Capitulations were defined by unilateralism on the Ottoman part, so the dispatch and receiving of embassies had further demonstrated this one-sided approach, until these later innovations.

There are several reasons as to why the Ottomans did not adopt the model of bilateral diplomacy until, in a very limited way, the last years of the eighteenth century.[27] One might be tempted to use the argument of Islam, in that it simply would not do for the Ottoman sultan, also holding the office of caliph, to dispatch ambassadors to reside in the courts of infidels. Yet such religious scruples clearly did not extend to the sending of embassies in general. Dozens of Ottoman officials were dispatched across Europe and Asia before the 1790s. In his fairly comprehensive study of Ottoman ambassadors and their *sefāretnāme*s, Faik Reşit Unat listed some thirty examples of Ottoman ambassadors sent across Europe, Asia, and Africa between 1655 and the arrival of Yusuf Agah Efendi in London in 1793.[28] Although a number of European countries had received Ottoman ambassadors, the British were none too keen at the prospect, primarily because of the expense entailed in entertaining him, and because of the cost of transport and upkeep for the Levant Company. Sir William Trumbull managed to stop one being sent on the accession of Süleyman II (r. 1687–91); that embassy was so far advanced that an ambassador had actually been appointed, equipped, and was on the point of departure, and great expenditure was required to halt its departure.[29] When

[25] Virginia Aksan, 'Ottoman political writing, 1768–1808', *International Journal of Middle East Studies* 25:1 (1993), 53–69 at 56–7; Aksan, *An Ottoman Statesman in War and Peace: Ahmed Resmi Efendi, 1700–1783* (Leiden, 1995), 42–6. Other similar analyses can be found in: J.C. Hurewitz, 'The Europeanization of Ottoman diplomacy: The conversion from unilateralism to reciprocity in the nineteenth century', *Belleten* 25:99 (1961), 455–66.

[26] Carter Vaughn Findley, *Bureaucratic Reform in the Ottoman Empire: The Sublime Porte, 1789–1922* (Princeton, 1980), 126–39.

[27] For a discussion of the evolution of Ottoman diplomatic practices, see: Güneş Işıksel, 'Méandres d'une pratique peu institutionalisée: La diplomatie ottomane, Xve–XVIIIe siècle', *Revue Monde(s)* 5:1 (2014), 43–55.

[28] For a thorough discussion, see: Faik Reşit Unat, *Osmanlı Serfirleri ve Sefaretnâmeleri* (Ankara, 1968).

[29] BL, Add. 34799, fols 30–3. This is from Trumbull's unpublished 'Memorials of my embassy in Constantinople'. It is also briefly mentioned in TNA/SP97/20 Sir William Trumbull to the Earl

the Ottoman government planned to send an ambassador to London on the accession of Mahmud I (r. 1730–54), the Earl of Kinnoull lobbied frantically and spent a significant amount of money to hinder it.[30] These two embassies were planned at key political moments, the first in the midst of a major conflict when the Ottomans were looking for potential allies, particularly the British, French, and Dutch, and the second following the tumultuous end of the reign of Ahmed III (r. 1703–30) and the wars with Iran.

The sending of royal letters was an important part of the performance of the narrative of friendship, and so the idea of sending a friendly letter to London was not an unusual one.[31] Yet, as we have already seen, it was not until 1793 that an Ottoman ambassador finally arrived on British soil carrying the sultan's letters, and going even further by staying as a resident ambassador. As Sir Robert Ainslie reported in a letter to London, this was an 'altogether unexpected appointment', and one that was followed by an Ottoman assurance that 'commencing with Great Britain, it has been resolved to appoint ministers to all the European powers at amity with the Porte'.[32] The Ottomans did not initially consult Ainslie, but simply informed him that an ambassador was being sent, and that he would not accept any financial assistance from the British government.[33] By this time, however, there was a greater reason for justifying a resident ambassador in London, not just on the grounds of growing political interests and the need for intelligence, but also because of a growing number of Ottoman subjects – mainly Greeks, but increasingly others too – seeking to trade and live in London. This population increased following the suspension of the Navigation Act in 1797 that allowed Ottoman ships and merchants to play a greater role in British–Ottoman trade.[34] An interesting insight into this growing Ottoman community can be found in a survey of London in 1805, which features a portrait of a 'Turk' selling rhubarb in the streets around Russell Square, accompanied by text explaining that 'he has sold rhubarb in the streets of the metropolis during many years. He constantly appears in his turban, trousers, and mustachios, and deals in no other article.'[35] Ottoman ambassadors, therefore, had a new and important reason to reside in the British capital, to protect their subjects as well as to gather information for and represent the political interests of the Ottoman government.

of Sunderland, 29 October 1687. I have yet to find a reference for this embassy in the Ottoman sources.

30 TNA/S97/26 Earl of Kinnoull to the Duke of Newcastle, 3 January 1730/1.

31 For an example of such a letter, see: TNA/SP97/26, Sultan Mahmud I to George II, Reibülahir 1143 (end of December 1730 OS), Italian translation by Giusppe Pisani.

32 TNA/FO78/14 Sir Robert Ainslie to Lord Grenville, 10 August 1793.

33 TNA/FO78/14 Sir Robert Ainslie to Lord Grenville, 10 July 1793; 25 August 1793.

34 David McPherson, *Annals of Commerce, Manufactures, Fisheries, and Navigation*, 4 vols (London, 1803), vol. IV, 420–1; Gelina Harlaftis, 'The "Eastern invasion": Greeks in the Mediterranean trade and shipping in the eighteenth and nineteenth centuries' in Fusaro et al., *Trade and Cultural Exchange*, 223–52.

35 Richard Phillips, *Modern London, Being the History and Present State of the British Metropolis* (London, 1804); MOL, 35.96/3.

There was a lot in common between how the European states and the Ottomans saw the role of the ambassador, and what this meant in practice. However, the Ottomans differed in one major respect from the other European states concerning the inviolability of the ambassador's office. It was an Ottoman custom that the ambassador of a belligerent power should be locked in the infamous fortress of the Seven Towers (Yedikule), an imposing castle constructed some five miles from the imperial centre of Istanbul on the old city walls of Constantinople by Mehmed II ('the Conqueror', r. 1444–6, 1451–81) overlooking the Sea of Marmara. There are numerous examples of such imprisonments in the British diplomatic correspondence: the French ambassador Jean de la Haye was confined for two months following a row with the grand vizier in 1660; the Dutch ambassador Justinus Colyer was threatened with incarceration during his negotiations for new Capitulations in 1680; and on the outbreak of war in 1710, 1768, and 1787, the Russian ambassadors were locked up.[36] The Ottomans seem to have adopted a more gentle approach later in the century to the Habsburg ambassadors, for instance giving Baron Herbert permission to leave for Livorno in 1788 rather than remain and be imprisoned.[37]

The Russians, however, were not so lucky. In the official Ottoman declaration to the British government on the outbreak of war with Russia in 1768, it was explained that:

> The great scholars issued as their answer a noble decree, unanimous of opinion, that it was necessary to make an expedition against Russia, and that, due to the great ignorance of the [Russian] agent [*ḳapıketḫüdāsı*], it was necessary to imprison him in the Seven Towers according to the ancient custom of the Sublime State [*ʿādet-i ḳadīme-i Devlet-i ʿAliye üzere*].[38]

The imprisoned Russian ambassadors were not mistreated, and were permitted some degree of comfort and company. Such an action was nonetheless completely unacceptable to the rest of the European diplomats, who spent the majority of those wars lobbying for the release of the Russians held in the Seven Towers. The incarcerations could be lengthy, as with Pyotr Tolstoy's imprisonment between November 1710 and April 1713, and that of Yakov Bulgakov between August 1787 and November 1789. According to Ainslie, Selim III himself ordered Bulgakov's release in the imperial *divan*, calling the detention 'a conduct equally inconsistent with justice, with the formal

[36] TNA/SP97/17 Earl of Winchilsea to Sir Edward Nicholas, 4 March 1660/1; TNA/SP97/19 Sir John Finch to the Earl of Sunderland, 6 November 1680; TNA/SP97/22 Sir Robert Sutton to the Earl of Sunderland, 20 November 1710; BOA/AE.SAMD.III/62/6320, end of Zilhicce 1124 (mid-January 1713); TNA/SP97/44 John Murray to the Earl of Shelburne, 7 October 1768; TNA/SP97/44 Devlet-i ʿAliye dāʾimüʾl-ḳarār, 1182 (1768); TNA/FO78/8 Sir Robert Ainslie to the Marquess of Carmarthen, 17 August 1787; BOA/C.DH/67/3315, end of Zilkade 1201 (1788].

[37] TNA/FO78/9 Sir Robert Ainslie to the Marquess of Carmarthen, 14 February 1788.

[38] TNA/SP97/44 Devlet-i ʿAliye dāʾimüʾl-ḳarār, 1182 (1768).

engagements of the Porte, and with his own sentiments of humanity'.[39] Pavel Levashov and Alexei Obreskov were only briefly imprisoned from October until December 1768 thanks to strenuous lobbying from John Murray, who reported that 'the Porte has been so indulgent to change their lodgings and give them the aga's [*ağa*'s] house with all conveniences'.[40] Not long after, with growing rumours of Britain's financial and military support of the Russians in that conflict, Murray confided to the secretary of state in London 'that it is now said, that I shall be sent to the Seven Towers. It is a bad residence.'[41]

The Ottomans, on the whole, held the office of ambassador in as high regard as states of Western Europe. Just as de Vera considered appointing a bad ambassador to be worse than appointing a bad minister of state, so an Ottoman advice book on good social behaviour in the nineteenth century proposed that whilst 'a deviant ambassador is a prey to misfortune [lit. plague], a dependable ambassador is sound [lit. healthy] [*fāṣıḳ elçi belāya dūçār olub muʿtemed elçi ṣıḥḥatda olur*]'.[42] Or, in less poetic terms, a suitable ambassador must be sufficiently respectable and trustworthy to carry out the mission at hand, as someone of lesser morals or of an unreliable character would bring great trouble to the office, with potentially grave results for the state. Sir Robert Ainslie's description of Yusuf Agah Efendi exemplified this shared notion: '[he] is a native of Morea, about fifty years of age, of a middling stature, and homely countenance, but lively, affable, and upon the whole rather agreeable … frank and open in manner and dispositions, nay he is accounted unusually (for a Turk) detached from vulgar prejudices'.[43]

The Ottomans did not adopt the model of permanent resident ambassadors until the very end of the eighteenth century simply because they did not see a need. With all the friendly European nations residing in Istanbul, the Ottomans had a regular source of information and scope for intrigue. Yurdusev's volume posed the question, was Ottoman diplomacy conventional or unconventional? Of course, that entirely depends on what one considers the 'convention' to have been, and that book posits two possible sources, one in the Islamic world, and the other in Christian Europe. Ottoman diplomacy may have taken some aspects of its diplomatic theory and practice from both, but it fundamentally created its own conventions to which European ambassadors were obliged to conform, even when the Ottomans seemed themselves to be conforming to European practice in establishing resident embassies. Aside from imprisoning ambassadors during wartime, the Ottomans did not hinder the free movement of ambassadors, nor did they physically harm them or their embassies. They treated them as representatives from other – if distant and less significant – monarchs, and when deemed necessary, dispatched their own ambassadors for specific purposes. The Ottoman concept of diplomacy did not strictly conform

39 TNA/FO78/10 Sir Robert Ainslie to the Duke of Leeds, 8 November 1789.

40 TNA/SP97/44 John Murray to the Earl of Shelburne, 1 December 1768.

41 TNA/SP97/45 John Murray to Viscount Weymouth, 3 March 1769.

42 *Kitāb-ı ʿilm-i ādeb ve merāsīm-i ülfet ve ünsiyet* (Beirut, 1850?), 143.

43 TNA/FO78/14 Sir Robert Ainslie to Lord Grenville, 10 August 1793.

to any idealised homogeneous 'Islamic' or 'European' diplomacy, but operated on pragmatic terms for the benefit and prestige of the Ottoman state. The British ambassadors in Istanbul may have brought their own ideas about their role from their differing backgrounds and experience; yet once in residence they swiftly appreciated that, whether they approved of the methods or not, they had to do things the Ottoman way.

## Barons, barristers, and businessmen

From the re-establishment of relations from 1661 until the outbreak of the Anglo-Ottoman War in 1807, a total of twenty-two ambassadors were dispatched to the Sublime Porte. They had different backgrounds and attitudes towards their employment, and the way in which they conducted the duties they were dispatched to undertake, for both the Company and the Crown, depended often quite significantly on the ambassador's character and abilities. That said, I do not intend to provide in-depth biographies or any sort of character analysis. Certainly their personalities would have been important in determining their ability to perform the tasks required of them; this was not a job for the timid. Alfred Wood concluded that the British had largely failed in their diplomatic aims in the Ottoman Empire, positing that this failure 'was not due to any personal deficiencies in her representatives. Four of them at least ... were men of outstanding ability, and of the remainder none was below the normal level of competency.'[44] In his *History of the Levant Company* he considered that the ambassadors between 1660 and 1718 'deserve[d] a brief notice', and those in office between 1718 and 1793 called 'for little comment' as they were 'men of average ability, most of whom filled the office efficiently if not with distinction; none of them showed outstanding talent or rose to greater fame in later life'.[45] How fair that assessment is is another matter, and I do not intend to pass any such judgement on these long-dead individuals. Rather, in examining the ambassadors before and after their posting to Istanbul, it is possible to reveal something about trends in the appointment, and the history of the embassy itself.

One way to examine these gentlemen without going into problematic questions of personality is to examine what we do know about them and their experience. That is, by comparing them as a group in terms of age, status, education, and previous and subsequent employment, it is possible to examine the ambassadors in qualitative terms. This does not seek to displace individual personality and agency in looking to explain how they fared in Istanbul, but will analyse the role of education and prior experience, and the importance of the position based on its ability to provide social advancement. Of particular interest is the previous employment of the ambassadors, to see how important it was for them to have held previous diplomatic or administrative positions, and what role other professions or trades appear to have played in

[44] Wood, 'The English embassy', 560.

[45] Wood, *Levant Company*, 128, 174.

the appointment. For easier reference, table 1 gives the names, titles, dates, and appointment period of the British ambassadors to the Ottoman Empire between 1660 and 1807. The information that has been collected on these ambassadors is then divided into seven sections: place of birth; social status; education; employment and honours before going to Istanbul; age at the time of appointment; duration of appointment in Istanbul; and employment and honours after returning from Istanbul.[46] Approaching the embassy in this way allows us to move the focus away from narrow periods or individual embassies to view changes in the nature of the appointment over a longer period of time.

The first category of analysis is geography, the ambassadors' place of origin. With the seat of government and Levant Company both located in London, it is interesting to see how far the origins of the ambassadors determined their appointment, and to what extent they represented Britain rather than just England. There was a heavy bias towards those born in London and the south-east of England, accounting for a third of the ambassador group in total. There was a good representation from the Midlands, in this case Chandos from Herefordshire, Hussey from Lincolnshire, Sutton from Nottinghamshire, and Paget from Staffordshire. This can be largely explained by the social position of Chandos, Sutton, and Paget as landowning gentry. The rest of

[46] A large number of the ambassadors (fifteen out of twenty-two) have entries in the *Oxford Dictionary of National Biography* (Oxford, 2004), online edn, [http://www.oxforddnb.com/view/]. A further amount of detailed information is available from *The History of Parliament* project, which has created an online database from earlier publications of all Members of the House of Commons and is currently working on a similar database for the House of Lords. The database is *History of Parliament Online*, [http://www.historyofparliamentonline.org/]. Six ambassadors have no biography in *ODNB* or *THP* at time of writing, namely Baron Chandos, Sir William Soame, Henry Grenville, and John Murray. The information on their lives, and supplemental evidence for those included in the *ODNB* and *THP*, has been gathered from a number of sources: Gary M. Bell, *A Handlist of British Diplomatic Representatives, 1509–1688* (London, 1990); D.B. Horn, *British Diplomatic Representatives, 1689–1789* (London, 1932); S.T. Bindoff et al., *British Diplomatic Representatives, 1789–1852* (London, 1934); Wood, *Levant Company*, 128–35, 174–8, 181–5, 250–2; P.G.M. Dickson & J.V. Beckett, 'The finances of the Dukes of Chandos: Aristocratic inheritance, marriage and debt in eighteenth-century England', *The Huntington Library Quarterly* 64:3/4 (2001), 309–35; Susan Jenkins, *Portrait of a Patron: The Patronage and Collecting of James Brydges, 1st Duke of Chandos (1674–1744)* (Aldershot & Burlington VT, 2007); Rosemary O'Day (ed.), *Cassandra Brydges, Duchess of Chandos, 1670–1735: Life and Letters* (Woodbridge, 2007); John Burke & John Bernard Burke, *A Genealogical and Heraldic History of the Extinct and Dormant Baronetcies of England, Ireland, and Scotland*, 2nd edn (London, 1844); John Burke & John Bernard Burke, *A Genealogical and Heraldic Dictionary of the Landed Gentry of Great Britain and Ireland*, 2 vols (London, 1847); Bernard Burke, *A Genealogical History of the Dormant, Abeyant, Forfeited, and Extinct Peerages of the British Empire* (London, 1866); John Burke, *A Genealogical and Heraldic History of the Commoners of Great Britain and Ireland*, 4 vols (London, 1836); Joseph Foster, *Alumni Oxoniensis: The Members of the University of Oxford, 1500–1714* (Oxford, 1892); John Venn & J.A. Venn, *Alumni Cantabrigienses*, 2 Parts, 10 vols (Cambridge, 1922–7); William Tooke, *A New and General Biographical Dictionary*, 15 vols (London, 1798); *The Biographical Dictionary of the Society for the Diffusion of Useful Knowledge*, 4 vols (London, 1842); John Beckett, *The Rise and Fall of the Grenvilles: The Dukes of Buckingham and Chandos, 1710 to 1921* (Manchester, 1994), 35–57; Laidlaw, *British in the Levant*, 49–72; Arthur William Moore, *Manx Worthies* (Douglas, 1901).

Table 1: *British ambassadors to the Ottoman Empire, 1660–1807*

| Name | Title | Appointed | Arrived | Recalled | Departed |
|---|---|---|---|---|---|
| Heneage Finch | Earl of Winchelsea | 1660 | 1661 | 1667 | 1669 |
| Daniel Harvey | Sir | 1667 | 1668 | † | † |
| John Finch | Sir | 1672 | 1674 | 1680 | 1681 |
| James Brydges | Baron Chandos | 1680 | 1681 | 1684, 1686 | 1687 |
| William Soame | Sir | 1684 | † | † | † |
| William Trumbull | Sir | 1686 | 1687 | 1690 | 1691 |
| William Hussey | Sir | 1690 | 1691 | † | † |
| William Harboard | Sir | 1691 | 1692 | † | † |
| William Paget | Baron Paget | 1692 | 1693 | 1701 | 1702 |
| Robert Sutton | Sir | 1701 | 1702 | 1716 | 1717 |
| Edward Wortley Montagu | Mr | 1716 | 1717 | 1717 | 1718 |
| Abraham Stanyan | Mr | 1717 | 1718 | 1729 | 1730 |
| George Hay | Earl of Kinnoull | 1729 | 1730 | 1735 | 1737 |
| Everard Fawkener | Sir | 1735 | 1735 | 1742 | 1742 |
| James Porter | Mr | 1746 | 1747 | 1761 | 1762 |
| Henry Grenville | Mr | 1761 | 1762 | 1765 | 1765 |
| John Murray | Mr | 1766 | 1766 | 1775 | 1775 |
| Robert Ainslie | Sir | 1776 | 1776 | 1793 | 1794 |
| Robert Liston | Mr | 1793 | 1794 | 1795 | 1795 |
| Thomas Bruce | Earl of Elgin | 1798 | 1799 | 1802 | 1803 |
| William Drummond | Laird of Logiealmond | 1802 | 1803 | 1803 | 1803 |
| Charles Arbuthnot | Mr | 1804 | 1805 | 1807 | 1807 |

England was barely represented, but there were two ambassadors from Ireland (Porter from Dublin and Arbuthnot from County Mayo), another from the Isle of Man (Murray), and almost a quarter came from Scotland. Of these, Kinnoull came from Edinburgh, Ainslie and Elgin from Fife, Liston from West Lothian, and Drummond from Perthshire; only one served before 1750, the rest of them being appointed after 1775. The demographic shift from the Midlands and south-east England to Scotland and Ireland from the 1740s demonstrates not only the increasing integration of other British subjects into administrative and diplomatic structures following the Jacobite turmoil of the first half of the century, but also increased social mobility away from the traditional administrative fodder of the landed gentry. As a group, they fit in quite nicely with the overall statistics compiled by Jennifer Mori, who showed 65.5% of diplomats coming from England (in the Istanbul case 68.2%) and a slightly higher representation of Scots and Irish (22.7% and 9.1% vs Mori's 13.3% and 4.3%).[47]

More than place of origin, a crucial indicator of changes and continuities in the group of British ambassadors to the Ottoman Empire was social status. There was a fairly even division between ambassadors who held noble titles, knighthoods, or no honours. What may be surprising, perhaps, is that so many of these ambassadors held no form of official honour. This overall breakdown again masks a distinct chronological split. For the first half of the period, almost a third of the ambassadors sent to the Ottoman Porte were noblemen (Winchilsea, Chandos, Paget, and Kinnoull), and a further half were knights (Harvey, Finch, Soame, Trumbull, Hussey, Harbord, and Sutton). This balance changed completely from the 1740s, with two-thirds of the ambassadors having no official titles or honours. Considering that the position of ambassador to the Ottoman Empire was, as previously noted, one of the few diplomatic positions to always host the high rank of ambassador, it is perhaps surprising that so many of the embassy's occupants in the eighteenth century should be ordinary merchants as well as diplomats. It was not unique, as the envoys and ministers to Russia display a similar trend, but the ambassadors to France, for example, were almost entirely title-holders.

A clear division from the middle of the 1730s emerges, with a move away from the titled, southern gentry to a more diverse group of merchants and diplomats. This division further extends in terms of the educational background these ambassadors had received. In the absence of formal state education, or indeed any sort of qualification to enter the business of government, the education received by these gentlemen was varied.[48] Unfortunately, particularly for their earliest education, the concrete data is lacking, with evidence only for the early schooling of eight of the ambassadors. Five of those went to formal schools, with three attending Westminster (Wortley Montagu, Elgin, and Arbuthnot), one at Eton (Finch), and one at Wokingham (Trumbull); the

[47] Mori, *Culture of Diplomacy*, Appendix A: Male Diplomats, 1750–1830. This difference can be explained by the absence of ambassadors of German origin dispatched to Istanbul, compared with other diplomatic posts.

[48] For a discussion of the education of diplomats, see ibid., 41–61.

other two (Harvey and Fawkener) were noted as being tutored at home. As all of the ambassadors were literate, and almost all displayed some knowledge of at least one foreign language, it is reasonable to assume that they all had some formal early schooling, either in a school or at home. In terms of further education, the division before and after 1735 again is clear. Until 1735, a majority of the ambassadors were educated at either Oxford or Cambridge, with two ambassadors attending both. Two had even attended university outside Britain during the Interregnum, Finch in Padua and Harbord in Leiden. A significant number also received legal training at the Middle and Inner Temples in London (Finch, Harbord, Sutton, Wortley Montagu, and Stanyan). After the 1730s, the educational background changed dramatically. There were no trained lawyers, and relatively few at the old English universities, with none from Cambridge. Considering the changing demographic in this period in favour of Scots, it is unsurprising to see the proportion of those educated there increase, with Elgin and Drummond attending St Andrews and Liston at Edinburgh.

As evidenced by the diversity of the ambassadors in their geography, social status, and education, there was a definite split in the type of person employed in the embassy from the 1730s, something further demonstrated by their employment history. Most striking is the relative lack of diplomatic experience there was among this group before 1735. Only five out of thirteen ambassadors before 1735 had prior diplomatic experience, and only Abraham Stanyan as envoy to Switzerland and envoy-extraordinary to Vienna had held more than one posting above the rank of embassy secretary. In the post-1735 group, seven out of nine in total had diplomatic experience, with three of them having held more than one posting above the rank of embassy secretary (Liston in Spain and Sweden, Elgin in Vienna and Prussia, and Arbuthnot in Württemberg and Sweden). The lack of experience of the Istanbul embassy's residents prior to 1735 could indicate it being used as a place for diplomats to gain experience, or simply a reflection of a position held in low regard by the London bureaucrats. What is clearer from this breakdown is that as the century wore on, the career diplomat held an increasingly important role in this story.

In context, this all makes a lot of sense. In the earlier period, the ambassador was likely to have been born within 100 miles of London, been of noble birth or knighted, educated at Cambridge, Oxford, or the Inns of Court, and employed as a high official in government or as a Member of Parliament. After 1735, the ambassadors were more often born at a great distance from London, with no official honours, educated at home and other universities, and had been previously employed as either merchants or diplomats. If the early decades of this study show a preponderance of nobles and government favourites in the embassy, there was a subsequent and marked increase in the number of merchants taking office, with a straight run of them between 1735 and 1775. This was largely a reaction to the desperate financial crisis facing the Levant Company, just as their subsequent replacement by career diplomats showed an increasingly methodical approach to the business of foreign affairs and the growing role of politics over commercial interest.

To round off this examination of these ambassadors, it is important to see how they fared after their employment in Istanbul. One rather sombre set of figures relates to the number of ambassadors who died in office or five years or less after being recalled. A significant proportion of the ambassadors suffered from some sort of illness during their embassy, and a total of seven ambassadors died after being appointed to the embassy, of whom one died en route to Istanbul, three in office, and one on the journey home, the remaining two dying within a few years of their return to Britain. For those who survived long enough to re-establish themselves back in Britain, their employment prospects were varied. The determining factor was probably their professional background. For the pre-1735 group, many of them had their own lands and parliamentary seats to return to, and, if they found themselves in favour, could generally expect to be given a relatively high government posting. It is interesting to note that two them became involved in other chartered trading companies after their posting in Istanbul (Trumbull in the Hudson's Bay Company, and Sutton with the Royal Africa Company), evidence perhaps that this position had the potential to open commercial doors. The merchant ambassadors between 1735 and 1775 found themselves elevated into the realms of government and favour, with two receiving knighthoods (Fawkener and Porter). As for the career diplomats, two embarked on subsequent postings abroad (Drummond to Naples, and Liston to Denmark, the United States, the Batavian Republic, and back to Istanbul), three were given high government positions, and Ainslie entered Parliament. Increased social mobility and the advent of career paths based on salaried employment within a growing bureaucracy had in many ways replaced the old patronage networks among the landed and commercial elites.

The information gathered by this analysis of the British ambassadors to the Ottoman Empire can give some sense of the type of men who occupied the embassy. However, the variables involved in judging how suitable and successful an ambassador was at his job are too numerous and, in many cases, completely unquantifiable. Some situations required wit and charm, others firm logic and commercial sense; with meeting any of these long-deceased gentlemen an impossibility, how far any of them can reasonably be said to have possessed either of those types of quality is impossible to confidently surmise. In their correspondence they often spoke ill of each other; Trumbull accused Chandos of being addicted to 'his pipe and bottle', and Kinnoull reported of Stanyan that 'his whole life here for these 12 years past, as I am informed, has been upon a sofa with the women'. [49] Even with a strength of character, the success of their embassies was dependent on so many other factors outside their control such as disease, the weather, global trade, distant and local wars, not to mention friendly, cold, corrupt or intransigent officials in London or Istanbul.

All of these variables combined to provide a sometimes challenging working environment for the ambassadors, but one constant was that they operated

[49] BL, Add. 34799, fol. 3; TNA/SP97/26 Earl of Kinnoull to Charles Delafaye, 19 August 1730.

within an Ottoman diplomatic framework. The constraints of distance, communications, and finance meant that in this period the pursuit of policy dictated by London was problematic, regardless of the pedigree or abilities of the ambassadors themselves. The peculiar aspect of this employment was the double duty the ambassador owed to monarchy and government on the one hand, and the Levant Company on the other. One of the main ways of explaining the difference in the type of ambassador appointed after the mid-1730s was the evolving relationship between the Crown and the embassy, due in part to a gradual professionalisation of British diplomacy as the eighteenth century wore on, and also to the changing fortunes of the Levant Company and the British Levant trade itself. It was not practical in such an embassy to have an ambassador who did not understand commerce. Before 1737, only Harvey, Hussey, and Trumbull had such insights, and it is telling that the ambassadors appointed after that time were either experienced merchants or, as the government began to have more of a say in financing and running the embassy, professional diplomats.

As we have already seen, the end of the eighteenth century saw the appointment of Ottoman ambassadors to London. What can be said of their background and character, and how did they compare with their British counterparts? Being the first of their kind, the first two Ottoman ambassadors, Yusuf Agah Efendi and İsmail Ferruh Efendi, had no previous experience as resident ambassadors.[50] They came from the Ottoman bureaucracy, and so had substantial experience in the business of state, if not in the business of diplomacy abroad. Yusuf Agah had served in the provincial administration, and then as a *kalyonlar katibi* (a naval clerk) for the central government. Similarly, İsmail Ferruh came from a mercantile family and had been Istanbul's *arpa emini* (superintendent of grain). Both came from the provinces, with Yusuf Agah from Tripoli in Greece and İsmail Ferruh from Özi (Ochakow) in Crimea. Carter Vaughn Findley described İsmail Ferruh and the other early Ottoman diplomats as 'marginal types', that is, officials who did not quite fit the usual bureaucratic mould.[51] Perhaps the same was true of the British ambassadors, who came from a variety of backgrounds, but who could draw on a variety of skills and experience, be they in government, diplomacy, or commerce.

## The ambassador between crown and company

Some six months after his arrival in Istanbul in 1661, Heneage Finch, Earl of Winchilsea, wrote to the secretary of state, Sir Edward Nicholas, with a frank assessment of his new appointment:

[50] For a more detailed discussion of these two individuals, see: Findley, *Bureaucratic Reform*, 130–3; Mehmet Alaaddin Yalçınkaya, 'III. Selim Döneminde Dış Temsilciliklerin Kurulması' in Seyfi Kenan (ed.), *Nizâm-ı* Kadîm'den Nizâm-ı Cedîd'e*: Üçüncü Selim ve Dönemi* (Istanbul, 2010), 593–624 at 607–13; Mehmet Alaaddin Yalçınkaya, *The First Permanent Ottoman Embassy in Europe: The Embassy of Yusuf Agâh Efendi, 1793–1797* (Istanbul, 2010), esp. chapter 2; Yalçınkaya, 'Mahmud Raif Efendi', 401–5.

[51] Findley, *Bureaucratic Reform*, 131.

> Though perhaps you may reckon the information of affairs here (by reason of the distance of the place, the little correspondence and intercourse between the two crowns, and the negotiation of former ambassadors, which was nothing anciently but the support of merchandise and traffic) to be impertinent to the matters of state in England; yet I can assure you, it was always a gross mistake, and the interest of His Majesty might as well have been active and not gone on a false principle, supposing they had discharged all points of their duty, and satisfied all expectations, did they only protect the merchants, and keep the trade free, and open from avanias, or other oppressions.[52]

Perhaps it was the fear of being branded a mere commercial agent that led the young earl to pursue a more politically oriented embassy in Istanbul. After all, de Vera in his treatise on ambassadors, doubtless swiping at the English, wondered 'who judges it prudent that merchants can be elevated to be ambassadors, whilst at the same time they secretly go about some business?'[53] It simply would not do in terms of Britain's reputation with their European rivals, and the Ottoman government, that their ambassador in Istanbul should be simply a Company man.

Indeed, a number of diplomats remarked that the Ottomans were very much aware of questions of background and title. Following the departure of Sir Everard Fawkener, who had been a prominent Levant Company trader, from the embassy in 1742 on leave, the position of ambassador remained unoccupied for five and a half years, in part because Fawkener may have intended to return had he not got a better offer in London, and in part because the British government did not seem in a hurry to appoint a replacement. When the chargé d'affaires, Stanhope Aspinwall, informed the grand vizier 'Hacı Mehmed Paşa in 1747 of the impending arrival of a new ambassador, James Porter, formerly a businessman in the City of London, he reported the vizier as saying:

> I hope he is not a person of such low rank as the other ambassador was, who thought of nothing, I believe, but his own interest, like a true merchant, without showing any attention since his departure either to the sultan, to this Empire, the honour of his embassy, or the affairs of his nation settled here.[54]

Having assured Hacı Mehmed that Porter was 'a gentleman of rank, and of worth and talents', the vizier continued:

> We are not here always satisfied with having a mercantile ambassador. Affairs and conjunctures often occur, in which we are glad to have men of another stamp, and higher way of thinking than such persons can be of. If we have a man of rank sent us, we know our duty in showing him proportionable honours to it. And if the Christian courts think we make no difference and

52 TNA/SP97/17 Earl of Winchilsea to Sir Edward Nicholas, 12 June 1661.

53 De Vera, *El Enbaxador*, 25.

54 TNA/SP97/32 Stanhope Aspinwall to the Duke of Newcastle, 26 January 1747.

> are not inquisitive, as to the rank of persons they send to reside amongst us, they are much mistaken.[55]

This may well reflect the vizier's actual sentiments; after all, the narrative text of the Capitulations had emphasised that Elizabeth I sent her high-ranking noblemen and gentlemen to secure relations. As these thoughts were transmitted orally, and with no note of the conversation on the Ottoman side, it is hard to tell. The Ottomans may well have expected ambassadors to be of a certain social rank, just as their ad hoc ambassadors were senior members of the state administration. Things were, of course, rather more complicated with the British embassy in Istanbul, with the Levant Company structurally intertwined with the various duties of the ambassador, not least through paying his salary.

As the ambassador derived his authority – from the perspective of the Ottomans and the other Europeans resident in Istanbul – from being the representative of the British monarch, the practice over the later seventeenth and eighteenth centuries was that the ambassador was nominated by the sovereign and approved by the Company. The ambassador was issued with a set of instructions that, although occasionally including directives specific to one particular crisis or other, contained the same basic points between 1661 and 1804. To take the example of those issued by Queen Caroline (in George II's absence in Hanover) to Sir Everard Fawkener in 1735, he was instructed on arrival to inform himself of the state of the Ottoman Empire, to learn the manner in which he was to make his initial visit to present the king's letters of credence, to ensure that he was treated with respect and with the same ceremonies as the ambassadors of other states, and to profess the king's friendship for the sultan at that audience.[56] Next, he was told to cultivate a friendship with all Christian ambassadors whose states were friendly with Britain, and to offer protection when necessary to all Christians of whatever creed, but 'more particularly those of the reformed religion'. He was further instructed to join with the other Christian ambassadors to complain against harmful initiatives by the Ottoman government, and most importantly 'to be truly informed of all negotiations and practices in that court, which may disturb the peace of Christendom, in any part of it'.[57]

The rest of the instructions almost entirely concerned British commerce. He was to protect all the privileges and immunities of the Levant Company by insisting on the implementation and protection of the Capitulations, soliciting for additional provisions to that treaty if necessary. 'If any attempt be made to violate and infringe the Capitulations, or any part thereof,' Fawkener was told, 'you are to appear in person before the vizier, in the defence of them.'[58] He

[55] Ibid.

[56] TNA/SP97/27 By Her Majesty the Queen, Guardian of the Kingdom &ca Caroline R.C.R Instructions for Everard Fawkener Esq whom His Majesty has appointed his Ambassador to reside at the Court of the Grand Signior, 21 August 1735.

[57] Ibid.

[58] Ibid.

was particularly enjoined to reinforce to the sultan and the grand vizier that, in any case of misfortunes of piracy or accident befalling Ottoman subjects freighting or travelling on board British ships, the British government would be in no way liable to pay any compensation, an instruction that would become a point of contention during periods of intense British privateering across the century. Another specific instruction that appeared from the instructions to Sir Daniel Harvey in 1668 concerned the problems that had arisen from the importation of underweight Dutch, Spanish, or French specie, because of which the Levant Company had forbidden their merchants to import such coinage or use them in their transactions; the ambassador was obliged to enforce that rule, and ensure the Ottoman government was aware of its implementation.[59] Aside from these royal instructions, the ambassador also received instructions and additional directions from the Levant Company, and was instructed to put himself at their complete service; in the words of Article 5 of Fawkener's instructions, he 'must, in the best and most effectual manner, proceed towards the protection of all the privileges and immunities of His Majesty's subjects of the Turkey Company, for whose good and benefit you are most especially to reside there'.[60] The royal instructions therefore made clear that above all the ambassador's job was to protect the Levant Company and its trade.

How far, then, were these ambassadors servants of the Crown, and how far were they servants of the Company? Perhaps the clue in answering this question is to examine further the split observed in the statistical analysis between those ambassadors dispatched before 1735 and those sent after that time. It is possible to divide the history of the embassy between 1660 and 1807 into four distinct periods. The first, between 1661 and 1692 saw a tussle for control of the embassy between the Crown and the Company; the second period between 1692 and 1735 saw the occupants given this position largely because of their political connections in Britain; the third period was between 1735 and 1775, during which time the embassy was occupied by merchants; and the fourth period of 1775 to 1807 was dominated by career diplomats.

To begin with the thirty-or-so years following the restoration of both the monarchy in Britain and that monarch's relations with the Ottoman sultan, it is clear from the beginning that Charles II attempted to assert his control over the embassy by appointing the Earl of Winchilsea, who had been one of the first peers to welcome the king back to England at Dover, as ambassador. He was succeeded by Sir Daniel Harvey, who was related to Winchilsea by marriage, and who was also a successful and prominent Levant Company merchant.[61]

[59] TNA/SP97/19 Instructions for Your Trusty & Wellbeloved Servant Sr Daniell Harvey Knt goeing to reside in quality of Our Ambassador att the Court of the Grand Signor, 3 August 1668. The actual royal command is at TNA/SP97/19 By the Kings most Excelent Matie and the Rt Honbl the Lords of his Matys most Honble Privy Councill, 31 July 1668.

[60] TNA/SP97/27 By Her Majesty the Queen, Guardian of the Kingdom &ca Caroline R.C.R Instructions for Everard Fawkener Esq whom His Majesty has appointed his Ambassador to reside at the Court of the Grand Signior, 21 August 1735.

[61] Harvey's father, also Daniel, had run a very successful trading house in the Levant: LMA/CLC/B/227-059, 1623–46.

Upon his death in Istanbul in 1672, the king appointed Sir John Finch, another relative of Winchilsea, an experienced diplomat who had resided for a number of years in Florence. However, royal authority was again challenged when the Company determined to replace Finch with Baron Chandos, a City merchant, Company member, and son-in-law of the notable Levant trader Sir Henry Bernard. Although the king approved the appointment, Chandos was in poor standing due to his support for excluding the overtly Catholic James, Duke of York from the succession, and this lack of favour was compounded by disputes with the French in Istanbul and with his own merchants, so that one of the last diplomatic decrees of Charles II, and one of the first of James II (r. 1685–8) was to recall him.[62]

The first replacement suggested was Sir William Soame, about whom little is known except that he was a friend of Dryden, and that he died en route to Istanbul in Malta in 1686. Following that, James II appointed Sir William Trumbull, a man of good education, diplomatic experience from his embassy to France, and knowledge of dealing with merchants and Muslims from his time as the attorney general of the British colony in Tangier. However, Trumbull, a staunch Protestant, saw his appointment to Istanbul as something of a voluntary exile, and breathed a very audible sigh of relief following the accession of William III (r. 1688–1702) and Mary II (r. 1688–94), 'for as I willingly entered into this banishment for the sake of my religion, as things stood then in England', he explained to the secretary of state, 'so whether His Majesty shall be pleased to continue me here, or to recall me, I shall always most readily obey'.[63] The Company were wary of the expense of dispatching a new ambassador, and petitioned the king to keep Trumbull in his post, resulting in letters of credence being reissued, but William III was keen to have the talented Trumbull as secretary of state, and recalled him a year later.[64] His replacement was a Levant merchant, Sir William Hussey, who, having arrived in Edirne in June 1691, soon died of 'fevers and agues'.[65] In his place came Sir William Harbord in May 1692. A royal favourite, he had accompanied William's invasion fleet in 1688; he too succumbed to illness and died at Belgrade in October 1692.[66]

It was from this point that the Crown successfully asserted itself over the Company in the choice of ambassador. Having seen a fair alternation between Company and Crown choices up to 1692, strategic aims came to the fore. As he was at war with France, William needed his ally, the Habsburgs, free to attack on the other front. However, the Habsburgs were currently engaged in a

62 TNA/SP105/109 Charles II to the Levant Company, 15 December 1684; TNA/SP105/109 James II to the Levant Company, 22 February 1684/5.

63 TNA/SP97/20 Sir William Trumbull to the Earl of Shrewsbury, 16 May 1689.

64 BL, Add. 72550 Petition of ye Gov. & Compa. of Mercht.s of England Trading into ye Levant Seas, 5 July 1689; BL, Add. 72550 William III to Sir William Trumbull, 5 August 1689.

65 TNA/SP97/20 Sir William Hussey to the Earl of Nottingham, 3/13 June 1691; TNA/SP97/20 Thomas Coke to the Earl of Nottingham, 17 September 1691.

66 SOAS/SC.PP/15/65 William III to Sir William Harbord, 12 May 1692; TNA/SP97/20 Thomas Coke to the Earl of Nottingham, 2/29 October 1692.

long and bitter war against the Ottomans, so that ensuring peace between the Habsburgs and Ottomans became a key aim of British foreign policy, and as such a political and diplomatic appointment to the embassy was of paramount importance. The year 1692 therefore initiated the second phase in the history of the embassy in this period with the appointment of Baron Paget, who had gained significant diplomatic experience as envoy to Vienna. It was from there that he was sent to negotiate peace between the Ottomans and the Habsburgs, an objective which he achieved at Carlowitz in 1699. Paget solicited and received his recall in 1701, and was replaced by a young gentleman, Sir Robert Sutton. Sutton, too, had diplomatic experience in the Habsburg Empire, having been embassy secretary in Vienna.

Sutton served in Istanbul for fifteen years before being sent on a mission to mediate peace between the Ottomans and the Habsburgs at Passarowitz in 1717. He was replaced by Edward Wortley Montagu, husband of the famous Mary Wortley Montagu. He had been a career politician, and was particularly close to the Whig establishment and the Kit-Cat Club, who regularly toasted the beauty of his wife. Wortley Montagu was recalled some five months after his arrival due to various political shuffles in London.[67] He was replaced by another favourite and member of the Kit-Cat Club, Sutton's co-mediator at Passarowitz, Abraham Stanyan, who had diplomatic experience in Venice, France, the Swiss Cantons, and Vienna. After almost thirteen years in Istanbul, Stanyan was recalled to London, and replaced by the Earl of Kinnoull. Kinnoull had a questionable past. Having come from a prominent Jacobite family, he was arrested for suspected Jacobite activity during the rebellion of 1715, was investigated on the uncovering of plots in the 1720s, and seems to have kept up some links with Catholic recusant groups even in Istanbul.[68] However, his links to the Whig establishment including the Duke of Devonshire and Sir Robert Walpole secured his appointment. After several warnings over his conduct, he was recalled in some disgrace in 1735, accused of aiding the French. This second phase of ambassadorial history was characterised by the appointment initially of favourites of the Crown, and then by gentlemen with close connections to or membership of Whig governments during that early phase of 'Whig Supremacy'. However well this might have served political interest in the context of peace mediations and attempting to influence the foreign policy of the Ottoman government, this had done little for the merchants, and in the commercial context of a crisis of trade in the 1720s and 1730s, it was clear that mercantile minds were needed.

The third phase therefore saw the appointment of four merchants to the embassy between 1735 and 1775. The first was a Levant Company merchant who had spent a significant amount of time in the Ottoman Empire as a factor

67 Ophelia Field, *The Kit-Cat Club: Friends Who Imagined a Nation* (London, 2008), 95, 125–6, 264–9.

68 Ibid., 362; Nigel Webb & Caroline Webb, *The Earl and His Butler in Constantinople: Introducing the Diary of Mr Samuel Medley, Butler, 1733–36* (Oakham, 2006), 21–3; Michael Talbot, 'A Jacobite lady in Constantinople: The story of Lady Mary Gerard of Gerard's Bromley', *Staffordshire History* 53 (2011), 3–14.

in Aleppo, Everard Fawkener. He returned to London, during which time he befriended and hosted Voltaire.[69] Knighted by George II en route to Istanbul, he analysed and attempted to solve the commercial problems of the merchants, but was hampered by the outbreak of the War of the Austrian Succession that saw both French and British privateering severely disrupt trade. He solicited temporary leave to Britain in 1742, which was granted. He never returned to Istanbul, being offered a more lucrative position, and the embassy was left vacant in the charge of the secretary Stanhope Aspinwall for five years, during which time British privateers caused severe tensions between the Ottoman government and the British.

Finally a new appointment was made, and James Porter arrived in 1747. Porter had been a London businessman who had risen to some prominence in the City of London Corporation, and so had good connections with both British politicians and Levant Company merchants. He resided in Istanbul for fifteen years, and spent much of his time on commercial matters. Soliciting his recall, he was replaced in 1762 by Henry Grenville, a member of the powerful Grenville political family. He had been apprenticed to a business in the City, but eventually followed his kin into politics, being governor of Barbados before his appointment to Istanbul. He stayed there for only three years: he was recalled in 1765 to take a new job in the customs department. The British government did not immediately nominate a successor, so that the embassy was once again vacant, this time under the charge of the consul at Aleppo, William Kinloch. The successor appointed a year later was John Murray, a former merchant from York, who had diplomatic experience as the resident in Venice. Murray presided over a difficult period of British support for the Russians against the Ottomans, but aided the general rise in British trade through improvements to some of the customs duties of the Capitulations. He solicited a leave of absence to tend to his private affairs in London, appointing the consul at Izmir, Anthony Hayes, as chargé d'affaires, but died en route home in quarantine at Venice.[70]

This ended the period of mercantile ambassadors, and between 1775 and the assumption of Crown control over the embassy in 1804 the remaining appointments were professional diplomats. This period coincided with increased financial contributions from the Crown to the embassy, marking the beginning of the end for the Elizabethan funding model, and also a more active political agenda being pursued by the British state in the region. The first of these appointments was Sir Robert Ainslie, the first knight to hold the embassy since Fawkener's departure forty years earlier. Ainslie's past is shrouded in some mystery, but his father was a Scottish merchant trading to France, and Sir Robert was largely raised in Bordeaux.[71] By the 1770s he was involved in espionage, focusing on French and Spanish foreign policy, following which

69 See: Norma Perry, *Sir Everard Fawkener, Friend and Correspondent of Voltaire* (Banbury, 1975).

70 TNA/SP97/51 John Murray to the Earl of Rochford, 18 March 1775; TNA/SP97/51 Anthony Hayes to the Earl of Rochford, 3 October 1775.

71 Arthur Collins, *The Baronetage of England* (London, 1806), 532–3.

he was appointed to Istanbul where he resided for almost twenty years. He managed to secure extra funding from the British government to undertake an increasing number of political missions, and although commerce hit an all-time low during the American War of Independence, he worked tirelessly for the betterment of trade, including arranging the lifting of several Ottoman duties. He was recalled in 1793, and was succeeded by Robert Liston, a career diplomat with secretary experience in Munich, Regensburg, Berlin, and Madrid, and full diplomatic experience as envoy to Sweden. In the midst of the French Revolutionary Wars, and with the added pressures that placed on diplomacy in Istanbul, Liston was offered leave of absence back to Britain, which he accepted after just two years in the post. He left John Spencer Smith, brother of the admiral Sir Sidney Smith, as chargé d'affaires for three years.

In the final year of the eighteenth century, Spencer Smith was relieved by the arrival of the Earl of Elgin, famous now of course for the antiquities he brought back from the Ottoman Empire. The British had supported the Ottomans in expelling the French from Egypt, and Elgin's background as an officer in the Scots Guards, together with his political connections and diplomatic experience in Vienna, Brussels, and Berlin, made him seemingly ideal for the post. Demonstrating the total political rather than commercial importance of Elgin's embassy, it was almost two years after his arrival in Istanbul that the Company actually elected him ambassador.[72] At the same time, the responsibilities of Company business began to drift from the embassy. Although he was not happy with the situation, Spencer Smith remained as secretary, with the added duty of minister plenipotentiary in charge of Company business. This, then, signified the first division in the embassy's history of the ambassador's responsibilities between commerce and politics.[73]

The peace with France in 1803 gave an opportunity for Elgin's recall, and he left his secretary Alexander Straton in charge until the arrival of William Drummond in May 1803. Drummond also had political connections, but was above all a career diplomat, with experience as embassy secretary in Copenhagen, and as envoy to the Two Sicilies. He remained in Istanbul only until the end of the year, going on leave on grounds of ill-health, and once again Straton became chargé d'affaires.[74] The final appointment related to this study was another career diplomat, Charles Arbuthnot. A former under-secretary in the Foreign Office, Arbuthnot had served as embassy secretary in Stockholm, consul at Lisbon, and envoy to Württemberg and Sweden. On his appointment, the government notified the Company that the embassy would for the future attend to political matters, and that they should appoint

[72] TNA/SP105/109 George III to the Levant Company, 20 January 1801; TNA/SP105/109 Levant Company to Lord Grenville, 23 January 1801; TNA/SP105/109 Levant Company to the Earl of Elgin, 30 January 1801.

[73] TNA/FO78/24 Circular to Levant Consuls, 2 December 1799; TNA/FO78/24 Earl of Elgin to Lord Grenville, 11 December 1799 [No.12]; TNA/FO78/24 Earl of Elgin to Lord Grenville, 11 December 1799 [No.14]; TNA/FO78/24 Earl of Elgin to Lord Grenville, 29 December 1799.

[74] FO78/40 Lord Hawkesbury to William Drummond, 9 September 1803.

a consul-general to guard their commercial interests.[75] This finally ended the unique relationship between the embassy and the Company that had been first instigated under William Harborne in the late sixteenth century, and, perhaps not coincidently, Arbuthnot's embassy saw at its end the first direct conflict between Britain and the Ottoman Empire.

These four phases of the occupants of the embassy show that whilst there might have been some tension in the role, the fact was that the Crown held control over the embassy from the 1660s onwards, and even the appointment of the mercantile ambassadors between the 1730s and 1770s was linked to political concern over the fortunes of British trade in the Levant. The ambassador, no matter how tied up he might have been in errands for the British government, was always mindful of his obligation to the merchants, and the day-to-day activity of the embassy was governed by commercial matters. It does not seem that the changes in the type of gentleman appointed as analysed here and in the preceding section were coincidental, but were clearly linked to the perception of the British government concerning the changing needs of British interests in the Ottoman Empire. Having established control by the 1690s, a series of politically motivated appointments were made in a time where diplomatic concerns in terms of peace mediations seemed more pressing than a seemingly flourishing trade. With the evident decline in commercial fortunes from the 1730s, there seems to have been a conscious effort to send gentlemen with mercantile backgrounds, not as a slight to the Ottoman government, but to try and improve British commerce. The final decades of the eighteenth century saw the appointment of more experienced and professional diplomats, as the British government itself professionalised and responded to a series of foreign policy challenges. The division of the political and commercial arms of the embassy also marked something rather more profound, with the British pursuing a more aggressive foreign policy in the Ottoman realms and wider Mediterranean.

## Conclusion

Despite some differences, the British and the Ottomans largely shared a common notion of diplomacy and the role of an ambassador, as a messenger of his monarch to the court of another, engaging in information gathering alongside formal conventions of presenting letters and gifts. The Ottomans, far from pursuing some supposed 'Islamic' diplomacy, took a pragmatic approach towards foreign relations, and so developed their own form of ad hoc diplomacy. The British, too, due to the relationship between the embassy and the Levant Company, did not conform to many of the ideals put forward in the numerous studies on that subject in the seventeenth and eighteenth centuries. The focus in this chapter has mainly been on the British side of things, and this is in itself a reflection of the unbalanced nature of relations. Only at the very end of the eighteenth century would the Ottomans appoint a

[75] TNA/SP105/109 George III to the Levant Company, 6 June 1804.

resident ambassador to London, so that for the majority of the period under examination relations were carried out in Istanbul alone. In many ways, British diplomacy in the Ottoman Empire demonstrates an embassy governed by commercial interests, at least until the beginnings of separation of commercial and political responsibilities in the late eighteenth century. The background of the ambassadors shows that appointments were at some times influenced by political imperatives, and at other times by commercial necessity. Appointments to the embassy were a balancing act between government favourites, experienced merchants, and career diplomats, depending on the needs of the British subjects in Istanbul as well as policy formulated in London and the expectations of the Sublime Porte. From all of this, it is reasonable to add that the interests of the Crown did not necessarily conflict with those of the Company until the period's end. Certainly, the ambassadors' time might have been more diverted towards political intrigues as the century wore on, but none of what was being asked in that regard was, in principle, against the interest of a trade that was esteemed so important to Britain. However, as will be seen, many of the manifestations of British foreign policy, such as privateering, were very damaging to the Company and the British merchants, and when the British government finally took full control of the embassy in the early years of the nineteenth century, the merchants soon suffered.

In tracing the embassy across a century-and-a-half, the different phases – struggle for control, dominance of political favourites, mercantile ambassadors, and career diplomats – emerge to show that this was a changing institution. The way in which the embassy was financed until the end of the period meant that the ambassadors had to pay as much heed to their Company masters as they did to the government. Working within the commercial framework of the Capitulations, this position needed ambassadors who could be more than courtiers and intriguers, who could really put in the work to ensure the trade of the British merchants. This had changed by the late eighteenth century, and by the time Yusuf Agah arrived in London, the embassy was already shifting towards state control. This, however, ended a long period when a large number of the ambassadors, in one way or another, had been involved or interested in the Levant trade. This link with the Company, which would end finally in 1804, was rather nicely summed up by Baron Chandos not long after his arrival in Istanbul in 1681. In the midst of a huge commercial dispute, Chandos wrote to William Raye, the consul in Izmir, declaring that 'I promise you all, I neither will fear danger, nor spare pains in doing the duty of my place, that the searcher of all hearts may bless my faithful endeavours with success suitable to the zeal and integrity of my heart to serve the king and his Levant Company, whose bread I eat.'[76]

However, that bread could be hard to come by. Just as commerce provided the framework of relations, and in many ways determined the occupants of the embassy, finance shaped the ability of the ambassador to engage in the diplomatic practices necessary to ensure commercial freedoms and success.

[76] BL, Stowe 219, Baron Chandos to William Raye, 12 November 1681.

Regardless of their rank or background, the British ambassadors experienced trouble with finance, and this provides a key explanation for the need to professionalise the Istanbul embassy as the job became more politically demanding in the later eighteenth century. Such problems were not limited to the British. The Ottoman chargé d'affaires (and later ambassador) in London in the early nineteenth century was Sıdkı Efendi, who was described, as with Yusuf Agah Efendi and İsmail Ferruh Efendi, as being 'one of the scholars of the imperial council' (*ḫacegān-ı dīvān-ı hümāyūndan*). The one thing he shared with all the other British and Ottoman diplomats was the necessity of adequate finance, and the archives are full of evidence pointing to that concern, such as this request for his salary from December 1805 to June 1806:

> The yearly allowance and allocation of salary of ten thousand *guruş* to Mehmed Sıdkı Efendi, one of the scholars of the imperial council, resident in Britain with the rank of chargé d'affaires [*maṣlaḥatgüzārlıḳ*] from the Sublime State, is required for the period from the beginning of Şevval 1220 to the end of Rebiülevvel 1221. The six-monthly salary of ten thousand *guruş* is to be provided from the imperial mint.[77]

From such unremarkable and rather dry documents a fundamental truth emerges. Without the provision of finance, even the most able ambassadors would be unable to fulfil their duties. In this, the early Ottoman resident embassies had the hindrance of distance and inexperience, but the British embassy throughout the eighteenth century had the complication of a commercially financed embassy.

[77] BOA/C.HR 50/2476, 17 Şevval 1220 [7 January 1806].

# 3

# Trade and diplomatic finances

## British trade with the Ottoman empire

In January 1806, about a year before he evacuated the British merchants from Istanbul as the start of the British–Ottoman War, ambassador Charles Arbuthnot concluded a major customs agreement with the *reisülküttab*, Ahmed Vasıf Efendi.[1] This agreement reiterated the fixed customs rates (*resm-i gümrük*) due from British merchants at three per cent as per the Capitulations, and detailed the tariffs for dozens of types of commodities subject to import duty (*eşyā-yı āmedīye*) and export duty (*eşyā-yı deftiye*). This is one document of many that saw the British ambassador attempt to secure and maintain favourable trading rights for the Levant Company merchants from the Ottoman government. Such records are not only excellent indicators of trade, but can tell us much about the nature of British–Ottoman relations, at the heart of which, as we have seen, was commerce. The merchants, the Levant Company, and the ambassador operated within a particular diplomatic framework, a key part of which saw the merchants relying on the ambassador's efforts to protect their trade, the Company relying on the merchants to pay their dues, and the ambassador relying on the Company to pay his expenses for maintaining British friendship with the Ottoman Empire. A key component of this cycle was diplomatic finance, and this chapter will examine the relationship between trade levels and ambassadorial finance to understand how the British embassy in Istanbul functioned.

Compiling statistics for British–Ottoman trade in the eighteenth century has its problems. Whilst the Ottoman archives hold valuable information on commercial interactions, that information can be less useful when compiling long-term trends due to the organisation of the archive's collections, and nature of the documentation. As Edhem Eldem argued in his study of French–Ottoman trade in the same period, the European archives in this regard are far more accessible and coherently organised, and so the statistics here are based largely on British data.[2] There is an invaluable source for trade statistics

[1] BOA/C.HR 19/930, 21 Şevval 1220 [12 December 1806].

[2] Eldem, French Trade, 7.

in the British government's customs ledgers from 1697 to 1803, which list the quantity and value of every commodity traded between England and the rest of the world.[3] They are crucial for the study of the Ottoman trade, as the Levant Company's imposition books are very incomplete, and although we lose the information on revenue collected by the Ottoman state from British trade, problematic as that would be to gather, they give an excellent sense of the overall scale of commerce.[4] As John McCusker highlighted, rather than reflecting the market value of goods, the clerks stopped adjusting commodity prices in the first years of the eighteenth century, and so the ledgers provide a constant value series.[5] This is very useful for looking at the volume of different kinds of commodities and regions in British trade over a long period. However, the ledgers cannot account for smuggled goods, which by their nature have proved particularly difficult to quantify, but accounted for as much as one-fifth of imported commodities.[6] Moreover, they cannot account for trade between non-English ports, so that, for instance, goods purchased in Aleppo by a British merchant and sold in Livorno were not included, and this may also have distorted the regional figures. Those problems noted, the customs series still offer a valuable insight into British–Ottoman trade to get the overall picture necessary for the purposes of this study.

In the global context of British trade, as table 2 shows, the direct trade between Britain and the Ottoman Empire, including the North African Regencies, was small, and decreased as a percentage of total trade across the century. The volume of the Levant trade itself remained relatively stable, with a noticeable decrease during the 1730s and a small recovery from the 1780s. For the majority of the period, Britain relied on a favourable balance of trade with its continental neighbours, particularly the Netherlands, the specie gained from these exports permitting the purchase of luxury goods from more distant destinations such as Russia and the East Indies. The colonies and plantations in North America and the Caribbean provided huge amounts of raw materials and, by the 1780s, consumed great quantities of British manufactures. Globally there was a decent trade surplus for Britain, but the Ottoman trade played only the most minor of roles; this does not mean that Levant merchants did not conduct a sizeable trade, but simply that in macro trends they were meagre. As shown in table 2, as well as being a small part of British commerce, the Levant trade declined in absolute terms throughout the century, from 7.19% of

3 TNA/CUST3 1–80, 1697–1780; TNA/CUST17 7–25, 1781–1803; E. Minchinton & C.J. French, *Customs 3 (1696–1780) in the Public Record Office, London* (East Ardsley, 1964). The ledgers for 1705 and 1712 are missing.

4 TNA/SP105 166–73, 1669–1813.

5 John J. McCusker, 'The current value of English exports, 1697–1800', *The William and Mary Quarterly* 28:4 (1978), 607–28, especially 607–17.

6 For a discussion over the quantity of smuggled goods using the example of tea, see: W.A. Cole, 'Trends in eighteenth-century smuggling', *The Economic History Review* 10:3 (1985), 395–410; Hoh-Cheung & Lorna H. Mui, '"Trends in Eighteenth-Century Smuggling" Reconsidered', *The Economic History Review* 28:1 (1975), 28–43; W.A. Cole, 'The arithmetic of eighteenth-century smuggling: Rejoinder', *The Economic History Review* 28:1 (1975), 44–9.

Table 2: *British imports from and exports to the Ottoman Empire, 1704–1803 (decadal figures)*

| **Period** | **Ottoman imports (£000s)** | **Total imports (£000s)** | **Ottoman exports (£000s)** | **Total exports (£000s)** | **Ottoman imports %** | **Ottoman exports %** |
|---|---|---|---|---|---|---|
| 1704–13 | 2,691 | 37,414 | 1,316 | 50,925 | 7.19 | 2.58 |
| 1714–23 | 2,905 | 60,263 | 2,137 | 71,367 | 4.82 | 2.99 |
| 1724–33 | 2,788 | 72,954 | 2,123 | 83,131 | 3.82 | 2.55 |
| 1734–43 | 1,819 | 73,898 | 1,518 | 95,446 | 2.46 | 1.59 |
| 1744–53 | 1,701 | 73,572 | 1,214 | 109,404 | 2.31 | 1.11 |
| 1754–63 | 1,278 | 86,433 | 721 | 123,907 | 1.48 | 0.58 |
| 1764–73 | 1,351 | 119,949 | 764 | 149,827 | 1.13 | 0.51 |
| 1774–83 | 1,013 | 101,537 | 886 | 115,712 | 1.00 | 0.77 |
| 1784–93 | 1,845 | 179,195 | 1,144 | 187,567 | 1.03 | 0.61 |
| 1794–1803 | 1,438 | 256,583 | 1,409 | 337,549 | 0.56 | 0.42 |

*Source*: TNA/CUST3 1–80, 1697–1780; TNA/CUST17 7–25, 1781–1803

British imports and 2.58% of British exports in the period 1703–14, to 0.56% and 0.42% respectively by the period 1794–1803.

Table 2 illustrates that British trade with the Ottoman Empire decreased across the century as a trade in itself, and declined in relative terms with regard to overall British overseas trade. This demonstrates that the Levant Company's commerce was not only becoming less significant in terms of its own income, something that, as we will see, impacted on the embassy, but also, crucially, that trade with the Ottoman Empire was far less significant at the end of the eighteenth century than at its beginning. In terms of the trends in the volume and type of commodities traded between the two states (figures 1 and 2), in addition to a number of changes in trade routes and commodity demands, overall trends were greatly affected by war, with noticeable dips caused by captures and shipping restrictions during the War of the Spanish Succession (1701–14), the Austrian Succession (1740–8), the Seven Years' War (1754–63), and particularly during the American War of Independence (1775–83) and the French Revolutionary Wars (1793–1802). The general decrease that can be observed between the 1720s and 1770s will be explained in detail below. Moreover, the balance of trade was firmly in the Ottomans' favour, with the value of goods exported from the Ottoman realms by the British exceeding the amount they were able to sell in Ottoman ports.

With an overall balance of trade in favour of imports from the Ottoman Empire, those imported commodities will be analysed first. They can be broken down into five major categories: miscellaneous goods; food, drink, and drugs; textiles and dyes; cotton and mohair; and silk. Starting with the miscellaneous

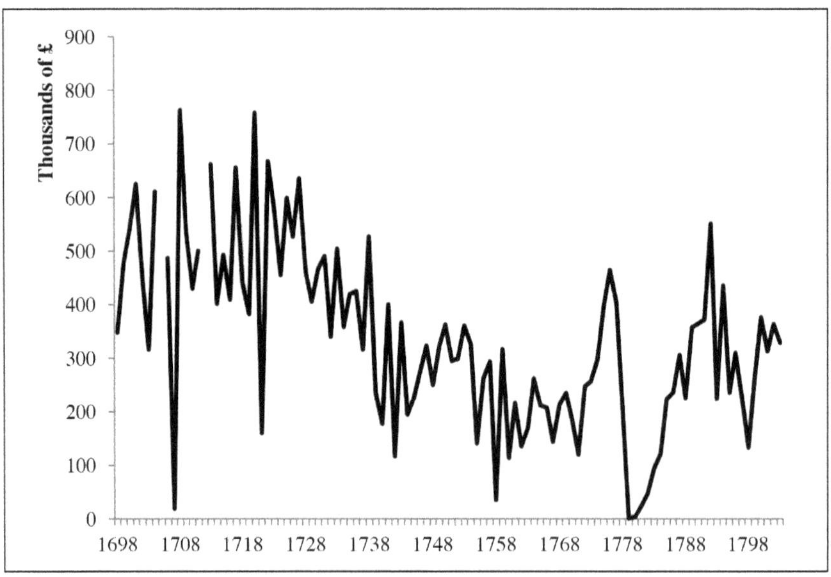


Figure 1: *Total volume of British trade with the Ottoman Empire, 1698–1803*
*Source*: TNA/CUST3 1–80, 1697–1780; TNA/CUST17 7–25, 1781–1803

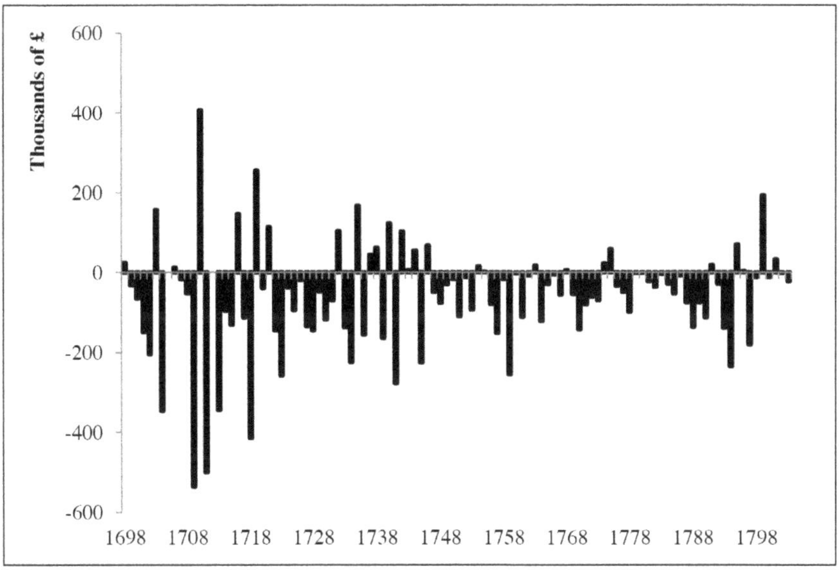


Figure 2: *The balance of the British Levant trade, 1698–1803*
*Source*: TNA/CUST3 1–80, 1697–1780; TNA/CUST17 7–25, 1781–1803

goods, around 1% of total imports, these included animals such as birds and horses, books, paintings and paint, ivory (referred to as 'elephants' teeth'), human hair, feathers, candles, earthenware, flax, glassware, paper, sponges, millstones, wax, soap, and dozens of other assorted provisions. The majority of the second group, food and drugs, were labelled as 'groceries', mainly the currants and raisins with which the British were so obsessed, along with spices, figs, dates, and almonds, accounting for 44% of this group. Coffee was an Ottoman staple, to the extent that shortages caused civil unrest, and foreign export was often forbidden, but after the opening of Britain's first coffee shop by an Ottoman subject in St Michael's Alley off Cornhill in 1652, it became an incredibly popular beverage in Britain, and accounted for 17% of consumables imported from the Ottoman Empire in this period.[7] Ottoman coffee was subject to a duty called *resm-i bid'at* (tax on un-Islamic 'innovations') that could be increased to raise funds in wartime, as Hüseyin Paşa did in 1697; the French managed to gain exemption from these taxes in 1738 and the British in 1772.[8]

[7] TNA SP97/35 James Porter to the Earl of Holdernesse, 19 November 1752; TNA/SP97/46 John Murray to Viscount Weymouth, 3 August 1770; TNA/SP97/47 John Murray to the Earl of Rochford, 18 February 1771; TNA/SP97/55 Sir Robert Ainslie to Viscount Weymouth, 4 October 1779; TNA/FO78/02 Sir Robert Ainslie to the Earl of Hillsborough, 26 May 1781; TNA/FO78/4 Sir Robert Ainslie to Lord Grantham, 10 January 1783; TNA/FO78/6 Sir Robert Ainslie to the Marquess of Camarthen, 10 December 1785; TNA/FO78/13 Sir Robert Ainslie to Lord Grenville, 25 September 1792; Pasqua Rósee, *The Vertue of the Coffee Drink, First publiquely made and sold in England by Pasqua Rosee* (London, 1666).

[8] Mehmed Raşid Efendi, *Tārīḫ-i Rāşid*, 6 vols (Istanbul, 1282 [1865]), vol. II, 425–6; TNA/

Despite growing production in British plantations, a Board of Trade report in 1790 sought to gain the same privileges that the French had already acquired in the late 1730s to legally import coffee.[9] Cooking oils such as olive oil enjoyed a small level of trade until the mid-1720s, with brief rises in the 1740s, 1780s, and 1790s, and Levantine wine, particularly from Cyprus and Izmir, also proved a popular import, with a noticeable peak between 1710 and 1740. There was an attempt to encourage a salt trade between 1790 and 1792, before the pressure to consume (and pay duties on) British salt ended this traffic.[10] Drugs constituted 33% of consumables, and included rhubarb, amber, sulphur ('brimstone'), senna and scammony (both powerful laxatives), frankincense, different kinds of medicinal and industrial gums, and opium, which was widely cultivated and consumed in the Ottoman Empire.

Food, drink, drugs, and miscellaneous items accounted for just 10% of British imports from the Ottoman Empire. The remaining 90% related to the manufacture of clothing and other materials, specifically silks, textiles, and dyes. Dyes accounted for 7% of British imports from the Levant and provide an interesting insight into changing British tastes and demands.[11] Tiny quantities of cochineal, indigo, and valonia were imported, as well as chemicals used in the dyeing process such as argol, weed-ashes, and barilla, but the main dyes imported were galls, safflower, and madder. Galls, providing a high-quality black dye and ink, were imported at a high level between 1700 and 1730, with a long stagnation, probably due in part to the successful importation of the Aleppo oak into Britain in 1735, until the trade began to return to earlier levels from the mid-1780s.[12] Safflower, growing in Egypt and elsewhere in the Levant, produced a yellow dye that was imported into Britain in a fair volume in the 1730s. Finally, madder was imported in great quantities from the mid-1770s following the French discovery of the 'secrets' of the

SP97/48 John Murray to the Earl of Rochford, 3 January 1772; Eldem, *French Trade*, 240; Ariel Salzmann, *Tocqueville in the Ottoman Empire: Rival Paths to the Modern State* (Leiden, 2004), 91; Kadı, *Ottoman and Dutch Merchants*, 283.

9 TNA/FO78/11 William Fawkener to the Duke of Leeds, 19 October 1790; TNA/SP97/30 Sir Everard Fawkener to the Duke of Newcastle, 15 March 1739; TNA/SP97/31 Sir Everard Fawkener to the Duke of Newcastle, 7 January 1740 (Separate); TNA/FO78/16 Robert Liston to Lord Grenville, 25 June 1795; Gavin Fridell, *Fair Trade Coffee: The Prospects and Pitfalls of Market-Driven Social Justice* (Toronto, 2007), 105–8; Clive Y. Thomas, 'Coffee production in Jamaica', *Social and Economic Studies* 13:1 (1964), 188–217 at 189–91.

10 E. Ashtor, A.Y. al-Hassan, R. Murphey & Eva Baer, 'Ma'din' in P. Bearman et al. (eds), *Encyclopaedia of Islam 2*, vol. V, 963–93; Halil İnalcık, *An Economic and Social History of the Ottoman Empire, 1300–1914* (Cambridge, 1994), 58–64; K.L. Wallwork, 'The mid-Cheshire salt industry', *Geography* 44:3 (1959), 171–86; Andrew Fielding & Annelise Fielding, *The Salt Industry* (Princes Risborough, 2006), 49–50; Mark Kurlansky, *Salt: A World History* (London, 2003), 337–42.

11 Some of the more obscure terms and products in the eighteenth-century textile industry are defined in *The Dictionary of Merchandize and Nomenclature in All Languages* (London, 1803). For an interesting account of dyeing in this period, see: John Edmonds, *The History and Practice of Eighteenth Century Dyeing* (Little Chalfont, 1999).

12 Margaret M. Fagan, 'The uses of insect galls', *The American Naturalist* 52:614 (1918), 155–76; John H. Harvey, 'Turkey as a source of garden plants', *Garden History* 4:3 (1976), 21–42 at 22.

Ottoman dyeing processes, so that the madder roots were imported to stimulate domestic dyeing industries as mass production of red garments was necessary for British military dress.[13]

An assorted range of manufactured textiles was imported, including small amounts of leather goods, linen, dimity, calico, and camblet. Most popular were carpets, imported in fair quantities across the period and in particularly great volume between 1725 and 1750 at the height of *Turquerie* fashion. However, most textile goods were raw materials. Smaller types included 'cordevant skins', a prized kind of leather produced from tanned goats' hides, most imported in the 1710s and 1790s.[14] Of particular note was mohair, made from the wool of the wonderful Angora goat, with its hair 'of dazzling white ... almost as fine as silk' according to one nineteenth-century author.[15] There is evidence that William Harborne intended to dispatch James Towerson, the first consul at Aleppo, to Ankara to establish trade in mohair in 1583.[16] Bought mainly as yarn, it was a hugely successful Ottoman commodity in the seventeenth century, and the British customs figures show that it remained so until the end of the 1730s, when the volume imported dropped by around two-thirds.[17] An Ottoman document from 1740 noted the decline of this trade to foreign states in general, suggesting customs breaks to stimulate trade.[18] But, as the Duke of Bedford explained in a parliamentary debate on the declining Levant trade in 1744, much of this fall in demand was due to changing fashions, giving the example that mohair was previously used in the manufacture of buttons and buttonholes; such fashion trends influenced consumption of mohair in the Ottoman lands too.[19]

Another commodity that evidenced changing consumption trends and demands was raw cotton, known at the time as 'cotton wool'. Aside from a brief period in the early 1750s when its volume exceeded that of mohair, cotton was at a fair but stable level until the 1770s, from when it began to be

13 Susan Fairlie, 'Dyestuffs in the eighteenth century', *The Economic History Review* 17:3 (1965), 488–510 at 491–2; Robert Chencier, *Madder Red: A History of Luxury and Trade* (London, 2005), 202–90; Donald Quataert, *Ottoman Manufacturing in the Age of Industrial Revolution* (Cambridge, 1993), 34.

14 *The Art of Tanning and of Currying Leather, With the Processes for Dying Leather Red and Yellow, As Practiced in Turkey* (Dublin, 1773).

15 For a detailed analysis see: Webb Yıldırmak, *Osmanlı-İngiliz Tiftik Ticareti*, passim; *Dictionary of Merchandize*, 148.

16 David French, 'A sixteenth century English merchant in Ankara?', *Anatolian Studies* 22 (1972), 241–7.

17 Bruce McGowan, *Economic Life in Ottoman Europe: Taxation, Trade and the Struggle for Land, 1600–1800* (Cambridge, 1981), 39–40; Suraiya Faroqhi, 'Mohair manufacture and mohair workshops in seventeenth century Ankara', *İstanbul Üniversitesi İktisat Fakültesi Mecmuası* 41:1–4 (1982–3), 211–36.

18 BOA/C.İKTS 24/1181, 14 Rebiülahir 1153 (9 July 1740).

19 W. Cobbett (ed.), *The Parliamentary History of England from the Earliest Period to the Year 1803*, 12 vols (London, 1812), vol. X, 903; Quataert, *Ottoman Manufacturing*, 92–3; Jonathan I. Israel, *Dutch Primacy in World Trade, 1585–1740* (Oxford, 1989), 382–3; Davis, *Aleppo and Devonshire Square*, 28–9, 93. Davis and McGowan noted the shift in button fashions in the first half of the eighteenth century that damaged mohair returns.

imported at a greatly increasing rate. The quantity of raw cotton imported into Britain from the Ottoman Empire increased tenfold between 1765 and 1775, and had tripled again by 1795, before falling back to the 1775 level at the beginning of the nineteenth century. The increasing interest in raw cotton had much to do with a slowly changing economic balance, with cotton manufactures playing an increasing role in British production from the 1770s through gradual mechanical improvements, great quantities of raw material available from the American and Caribbean plantations, and appalling attitudes towards labour, leading to British manufactures undercutting Ottoman and eventually Indian cotton goods.[20] In total these dyes and textile goods formed 30% of imports from the Ottoman Empire.

The main commodity imported by the British was raw silk, accounting for 60% of all goods brought from Ottoman ports to Britain.[21] There were two main sources of silk in the Ottoman Empire, with imported silk coming from Iran, and a domestic sort produced primarily in the province of Syria but also in Bursa, Istanbul, and Cyprus.[22] The great emporium of Aleppo was a centre of the silk trade, with caravan goods arriving from Iran to the east, and from Damascus in the south. However, silk imports from the Ottoman Empire by British merchants decreased dramatically across the century, with a 97% drop between 1704 and 1803. This can in part be explained by the wars between the Ottomans and Iran (1722–36) following the Afghan invasions, the biggest drop in British silk imports coming after 1727; Davis considered this to be a major but not overriding factor in the decrease of British silk imports from the Ottoman Empire.[23] Another potential explanation comes from changing fashions. As with mohair, silk played a key role in the making of buttons and buttonholes, yet fashions changed from the 1730s. So important, in fact, was button and buttonhole manufacturing to the Levant trade that it was the subject of several Acts of Parliament until the 1720s, intended to guarantee the continuing use of mohair, and above all silk, in that industry.[24] It can also

20 As Donald Quataert demonstrated, the Ottomans had a positively enlightened attitude towards even child labour in the eighteenth century compared to the horrors of the British factories. Quataert, *Ottoman Manufacturing*, 33–5; Halil İnalcık, 'When and how British cotton goods invaded the Levant markets' in Huri İslamoğlu-İnan (ed.), *The Ottoman Empire and the World-Economy* (Cambridge, 1987), 374–83 at 374–8; Wolf-Dieter Hütteroth, 'Ecology of the Ottoman lands' in Faroqhi (ed.), *Cambridge History of Turkey 3*, 18–43 at 40–1; Şevket Pamuk, *The Ottoman Empire and European Capitalism, 1820–1913* (Cambridge, 1987), 109–12.

21 Davis, *Aleppo and Devonshire Square*, 134–71.

22 Ronal Ferrier, 'Trade from the mid-14th century to the end of the Safavid period' in Peter Jackson & Laurence Lockhart (eds), *The Cambridge History of Iran 6* (Cambridge, 1986), 412–90; Eldem, 'Capitulations and Western trade', 299–305; Suraiya Faroqhi, 'Declines and revivals in textile production' in Suraiya Faroqhi (ed.), *The Cambridge History of Turkey 3*, 356–75 at 371–3.

23 Ralph Davis, 'English imports from the Middle East, 1580–1780' in M.A. Cook (ed.), *Studies in the Economic History of the Middle East from the Rise of Islam to the Present Day* (Oxford, 1970), 193–206 at 197–8.

24 I have traced the Acts that mention the encouragement of the 'Turkey' trade as the main reason of their being enacted: *An act prohibiting the importation of foreign bone-lace, cut-work, imbroidery, fringe, band-strings, buttons and needle-work* (13&14 Cha. 2 c. 8 [1662]) in Danby

be explained, in the work of both Ralph Davis and Edhem Eldem, by the increasing dominance in the market in terms of cost and quality of Italian silk, mainly from manufacturing centres such as Lucca and Florence, and Indian silk, especially from Bengal.[25] The increasing British consumption of silk and other goods from India and Italy was such that whereas the three regional volumes were at roughly the same level in the 1720s, Ottoman trade was left far behind by the start of the 1750s. Thus, disruption of trade routes, changing fashion and consumption trends, and cheaper alternatives contributed to the decline of the British–Ottoman silk trade.

If silk were simply a standard import commodity then the decrease in the volume of trade might not necessarily have been a problem. However, the nature of British commerce in the Ottoman Empire made the decline in silk especially detrimental due to its relationship to Britain's primary export, woollen manufactures. The relationship between Britain, Aleppo, woollen goods, and raw silk was something like a simple electrical circuit. Company merchants in London purchased a quantity of woollen manufactures that were then exported to the Ottoman Empire. The vast majority of those goods ended up in Aleppo where they were often bartered for raw silk, that is, with little or no specie involved in the transaction.[26] With periodic prohibitions on the export of Ottoman coinage, as well as a depreciating rate of exchange of the *guruş* against the pound, British returns were made in kind rather than cash, so that raw silk was received as payment for woollen manufactures.[27] The benefit of this to the British economy is clear; in exchange for British-made manufactures, raw materials were procured that could be turned into more British-made goods for internal consumption or export for specie to neighbouring European markets. Over the period 1698 to 1803, the annual mean ratio of silk to woollen goods in the Ottoman trade was 2:1, showing that the British merchants were on average able to barter a high volume of raw silk for the woollen goods they exported.

The problem with simple electrical circuits is that if they are broken at any point the current cannot flow anywhere at all. Such was the case with the Aleppo–London silk–wool trade. A lack of demand for British cloth

Pickering (ed.), *The Statutes at Large*, 46 vols (Cambridge, 1762–1807), vol. VIII, 103–5; *An act for prohibiting the importation of all foreign hair buttons* (4&5 Will. & Mar. c. 10 [1692]) in ibid., vol. IX, 196–7; *An act to prevent the making or selling buttons made of cloth, serge, drugget, or other stuffs* (10 Will. 3 c. 2 [1698]) in ibid., vol. X, 237–8; *An act for employing the manufacturers by encouraging the consumption of raw silk and mohair yarn* (8 Ann. c. 6 [1709]) in ibid., vol. XI, 9–10; *An act for making effectual an act made in the eighth year of the reign of the late Queen Anne, intituled, An act for employing the manufacturers, by encouraging the consumption of raw silk and mohair yarn* (4 Geo. I c. 7 [1717]) in ibid., vol. XIII, 466–8; *An act for imploying the manufacturers and encouraging the consumption of raw silk and mohair yarn, by prohibiting the wearing of buttons and button-holes made of cloth, serge or other stuffs* (7 Geo. I c. 12 [1720]) in ibid., vol. XIV, 322–5.

[25] Davis, 'English imports', 198–200; Eldem, 'Capitulations and Western trade', 300; Brenda M. King, *Silk and Empire* (Manchester, 2005), 68–72.

[26] See: Davis, *Aleppo and Devonshire Square*, 33–5.

[27] Şevket Pamuk, *A Monetary History of the Ottoman Empire* (Cambridge, 1999), 71–3.

would render the British merchants unable to purchase raw silk; similarly if the demand for raw silk fell at home, the merchants might find themselves landed with an unsalable amount of raw materials. Just as wars, fashion, and competition diminished the demand for raw silk from the Ottoman realms to Britain across the eighteenth century, changes in demand decreased the export of British woollen manufactures. Trying to figure out whether it was an imbalance on the part of wool exports or silk imports that first broke the circuit is difficult as they fell at very similar rates, although there is a clear decrease in demand for British woollen goods at the end of the 1740s. Overall, this was a gradual decline, with a decrease in the volume of exported woollen manufactures from the 1730s at an average drop of 20% per decade, culminating in a 74% drop between the 1770s and 1780s. Silk also declined at a mean decadal rate of about 18% from the 1730s, falling by 69% between the 1770s and 1780s, almost collapsing by the 1790s.

The primary reason for the decline in Ottoman consumption of British woollen goods was the increase in the French share of the cloth trade throughout the eighteenth century.[28] In comparative terms with British trade, Robert Paris's analysis reveals that similar sorts of commodities, specifically silks, cottons towards the end of the century, dyes, food, and drugs, were being imported by the French from the Levant. There was a similar switch as the cloth-for-silk trade pattern changed, with cotton imports to Marseilles overtaking silk imports by the 1750s.[29] The French exported the same sorts of commodities as the British, notably cloth (*draps*), and later sugar and dyes, with French-sold indigo and cochineal being very popular.[30] Moreover, Paris's examination of French exports to the Ottoman Empire from Marseilles demonstrates that French textiles became increasingly popular in the Ottoman market, with the number of pieces of cloth sent to the Levant and North Africa doubling from 10,300 pieces in 1700–5 to 21,800 pieces in the period 1708–15, doubling again to 41,400 pieces for the period 1726–30, and reaching 85,300 pieces by 1763–73.[31] Paris opined that French success in

[28] Eldem, *French Trade*, 34–67; Davis, *Aleppo and Devonshire Square*, 127–33; Daniel Panzac, *Commerce et navigation dans l'Empire Ottoman au XViiie siècle* (Istanbul, 1996), especially 195–216; Panzac, 'Les échanges maritimes dans l'Empire ottoman au XVIIIe siècle', *Revue de l'Occident Musulman et de la Méditerranée* 39:1 (1985), 177–88 at 177; Panzac, *La caravane maritime: marins européens et marchands ottomans en Méditerranée, 1680–1830* (Paris, 2004); Junko Thérèse Takeda, *Between Crown and Commerce: Marseille and the Early Modern Mediterranean* (Baltimore, 2011). See also: Paul Mason, *Histoire du commerce français dans le Levant au XVIIe siècle* (Paris, 1896); *Histoire du commerce français dans le Levant au XVIIIe siècle* (Paris, 1911). For useful statistics and data: Gaston Rambert (ed.), *Histoire du commerce de Marseille*, 8 vols (1949–66); Robert Paris, *Histoire du commerce de Marseille*, vol. V, 'De 1660 à 1789, le Levant' (Paris, 1957), 499–503. For an early treatise on French success, see: *Reasons Humbly Offered to the Consideration of Both Houses of Parliament against the Exportation of Wooll out of England and Ireland* (London, 1700).

[29] Paris, *Histoire du commerce de Marseille*, vol. V, 504–41.

[30] Ibid., 542–66.

[31] Ibid., 545.

the export of their cloth manufactures was due to an increase in quality, and a better understanding of the Ottoman market.[32]

British cloth had proved popular in the seventeenth century, and was an integral part of diplomatic relations in the form of ceremonial garments (as discussed in the next chapter). Numerous Ottoman receipts attest to purchases of two particular kinds of British cloth, *Londra çuḳası* (London cloth) and *isḳarlaṭ çuḳası* (scarlet cloth), for various occasions, usually relating to the ceremonial of the imperial palace.[33] However, there is direct correlation between the beginning of British commercial decline from the 1720s and the rise of the French share. Abraham Stanyan gave his opinion to the secretary of state in 1721:

> The French trade of late was very great in the Levant, and even grew upon ours, particularly in the vent of their cloth, which though much slighter than English, yet is preferred by many, because it is cheaper, has a brighter colour, and at first sight looks as fine.[34]

At the beginning of the collapse that occurred in the 1750s, James Porter lamented that the French had completely overtaken British commerce in the Levant:

> To trace this revolution from its origin, it is only necessary to observe the gradual increase of the imports of French cloth, as these continued augmenting in the sales, ours became proportionally depressed ... by various essays, and trials, they have at last brought their cloth into reputation with the Turks, it is in general thinner, softer wool, and consequently brighter colours than ours. And one principal misfortune with us is, that instead of keeping up to the former goodness of our cloth it falls infinitely short of the quality of that imported twenty years past. Whether this arises from the fault of the manufacturer, or some difference in the growth of our wools is what I cannot determine, but in supposing the quality of the French middling and coarser cloth called Londrinas, and Londras, only equal to ours, the French find means to undersell us about ten per cent.[35]

In essence, the French produced cloth that was more appealing to the Ottoman market, and at a better price, than the British.

32 Ibid., 546.

33 Various examples of orders include: BOA/İE.SM 4/338, Zilhicce 1098 [1687]; BOA/AE.SAMD. II 4/326, 15 Şaban 1106 [30 March 1695]; BOA/AE.SAMD.II 4/337, 11 Ramazan 1106 [24 April 1695]; BOA/İE.SM 24/2488, 14 Zilhicce 1113 [11 May 1702]; BOA/İE.SM 31/3268, 1 Rebiülahir 1121 [9 June 1709]; BOA/C.BH 80/3850, Muharrem 1135 [1722]; BOA/C.SM 159/7986, Ramazan 1145 [1733]; BOA/C.SM 15/762, 8 Ramazan 1156 [25 October 1743]; BOA/C.ML 483/19711, Zilkade 1166 [1753]; BOA/C.SM 8/389, 29 Rebiülevvel 1176 [1762]; BOA/C.SM 175/8791, 27 Safer 1199 [8 January 1785]; BOA/C.SM 68/3418, 21 Safer 1224 [6 April 1809].

34 TNA/SP97/24(4), Abraham Stanyan to Lord Carteret, 16 September 1721.

35 TNA/SP97/34 James Porter to the Duke of Bedford, 22 February 1749.

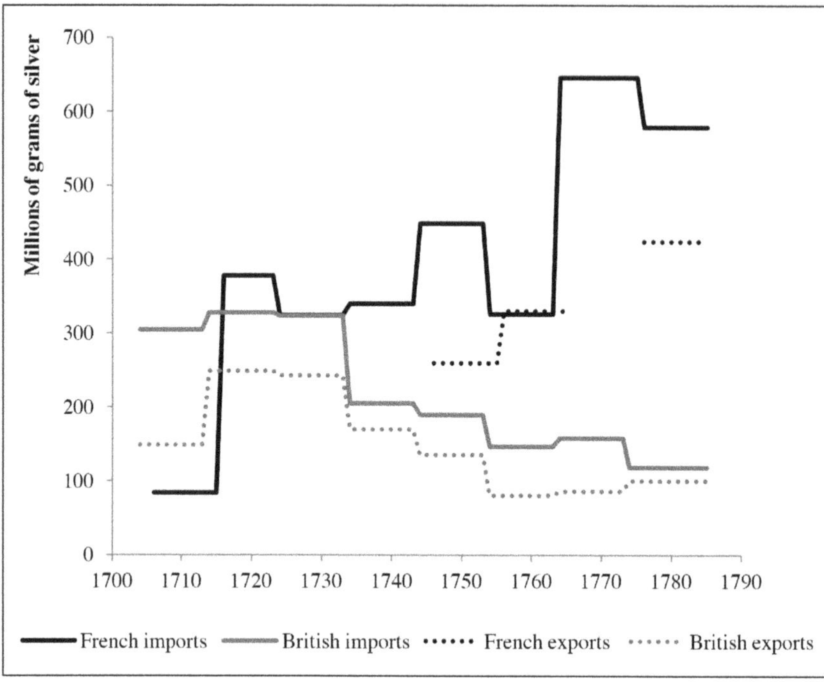


Figure 3: *French and British trade with the Ottoman Empire, 1700–89 (decadal figures)*
*Source*: French figures from Paris, *Histoire du commerce de Marseille*, vol. V, 545, 600–1. British figures from TNA/CUST3 1–80, 1697–1780; TNA/CUST17 7–25, 1781–1803. French silver figures from A.B. McCullough, *Money and Exchange in Canada to 1900* (Toronto, 1984), 44; Michel Morineau, 'Les frappes monétaires français de 1726 à 1793: premières considérations' in John Day (ed.), É*tudes d'histoire monétaire, XIIe–XIXe siècles* (Lille, 1984), 69–141. British silver figures from: John McCusker, *Money and Exchange in Europe and America, 1600–1775* (London, 1978), 9–17; Albert Feavearyear, *The Pound Sterling: A History of English Money*, 2nd edn (Oxford, 1963), 453.

Such developments are illustrated by figure 3, which combines the British customs figures and those of the Bureau du Commerce de Marseille, showing the dramatic increase in the French share of imports from and exports to the Ottoman Empire from the 1730s, and the concurrent and consequent decrease of the British trade. One of the primary reasons for the substantial increase in French–Ottoman trade in the eighteenth century was the growing demand for French cloth manufactures. This data shows quite clearly that there is a symmetry between the decreasing share of British trade and the increasing French trade, and moreover that the value of French trade at its height in the eighteenth century far exceeded that of the Levant Company merchants.

Unlike the diplomatic framework that required the British merchants to contribute to the Levant Company to fund the British embassy in order to maintain diplomatic relations through signs of friendship, changes in French trade did not effect French diplomatic finances, as the French ambassador received significant finance from the French state. Therefore, although the collapse of the silk–wool trade system and the ascendancy of French textiles had the effect of severely curtailing the revenue provided by merchants to the Company to support the embassy, no such constraint existed for the French, although Takeda's study of the Marseilles merchants has done much to improve our understanding of the pressures faced by such merchants.[36] These changes in commercial patterns certainly dealt a great blow to the British trade in the Levant; it did not destroy it. This is because the trade diversified from specialisation in cloth and silk to trade in a variety of goods. This was particularly true of British goods exported to the Ottoman Empire from the 1770s, as products traded for specie were now necessary in order to satisfy the rapidly increasing demand for cotton and dyes from the Levant.

In addition to woollen manufactures, which accounted for 74% of exports, there were four main groups of British exports: miscellaneous; food and drugs; textiles and dyes; and metals. The miscellaneous group included small quantities of goods for the consumption of resident European merchants. Such goods included bridles, saddles, coaches, sedans, hats, belts, quills, candles, pipes, furniture, and bedding. The miscellaneous group does include one article of commercial and diplomatic significance in the import of timepieces, specifically silver and gold pocket watches. As will be seen, watches formed an important part of British diplomatic gift-giving. As a result of the necessity of provisioning the European mercantile community with a variety of products, and with increasing numbers of merchants resident in the Ottoman Empire from the 1770s, exported miscellany accounted for 2.6% of total exports.

The second category was food, drink, and drugs. Until the end of the 1760s, these were exported in insignificant quantities, with the exception of pepper. From the 1770s the rate of pepper exported to the Ottoman realms increased greatly, along with growing amounts of pimento, ginger, nutmeg, and cloves. The majority of the foodstuffs traded by British merchants were either from the East Indies as the spices were, or from the West Indies, such as sugar exported from the 1770s, which came with an increase in the amount of rum sent to the Levant in the same period. A small amount of beef, cheese, butter, beer, and cider was brought in to satisfy mercantile tastes, although some of these items made their way to the tables of Ottoman officials. Increasing demand in the Ottoman market led to Britain becoming a net exporter of coffee in its Levant trade from the 1760s, with the produce coming from colonial plantations. Foodstuffs comprised 6% of British exports to the Ottoman Empire, largely accounted for by the surge in coffee, sugar, and spices in the last quarter of the eighteenth century.

The same model is true for textiles and dyes exported from Britain. For most of the eighteenth century, the main items exported in this category were dyes from the Americas, specifically indigo and cochineal, although the

[36] Takeda, *Between Crown and Commerce*, 78–105.

French held the lion's share of the relatively small European market (Indian dyes still being very prominent).[37] As Eldem has argued, the increasing quantity of these dyes imported by Ottoman merchants, from the French, British, and others, could be indicative of expanding textiles industries in the Ottoman Empire.[38] Linked to this change was the great increase from the 1770s of the export of calicoes and other cotton linens to the Ottoman Empire. Largely a product of India, calicoes had been seen as a threat to the British wool industry and so were banned by an Act of Parliament in 1720, at almost the same time as protectionist legislation was made concerning the use of silk in the button industry; the regulations on cotton wool and yarn were relaxed in 1736, but calicoes remained theoretically proscribed.[39] Indeed, a number of the entries for the export of calicoes to the Ottoman Empire noted that they were 'prohibited', although clearly as fashions and production methods changed such legislation was ignored, and the Act was finally repealed in a parliamentary spring-cleaning session in 1825.[40] The export of British cotton to the Ottoman Empire went from virtually zero in the first part of the 1760s to matching those of the (admittedly vastly decreased) wool exports in the 1780s, overtaking them in the first years of the nineteenth century. This increase in cotton exports permitted the overall level of British trade to recover in the 1780s to roughly the volume it had been half a century earlier.[41]

The third category, also rising to prominence in the last quarter of the eighteenth century, was metal goods and military equipment, accounting for 9% of overall British exports to the Ottoman Empire. A small quantity of brassware,

[37] Eldem, *French Trade*, 81–6; Jenny Balfour-Paul, *Indigo in the Arab World* (London, 1997), 30–41. On the relationship between Indian dyes and Ottoman textiles, see: Gilles Veinstein, 'Commercial relations between India and the Ottoman Empire (late fifteenth to late eighteenth centuries): A few notes and hypotheses' in Sushil Chaudhury & Michel Morineau (eds), *Merchants, Companies and Trade: Europe and Asia in the Early Modern Era* (Cambridge, 1999), 95–115 at 102–3.

[38] Eldem, 'Capitulations and Western trade', 322.

[39] *An act to preserve and encourage the woollen and silk manufactures of this kingdom, and for more effectual employing the poor, by prohibiting the use and wear of all printed, painted, stained or dyed callicoes in apparel, household stuff, furniture, or otherwise, after the twenty fifth day of December one thousand seven hundred and twenty two (except as therein is excepted)* (7 Geo. 1 stat. 1. c. 7 [1720]) in Pickering, *Statutes at Large*, vol. XIV, 318–21; *An act to amend an act passed in the seventh year of the reign of his late majesty King George the First, intituled, An act to preserve and encourage the woollen and silk manufactures of this kingdom, and for more effectual employing the poor, by prohibiting the use and wear of all printed, painted, stained or dyed callicoes in apparel, household stuff, furniture, or otherwise, after the twenty fifth day of December one thousand seven hundred and twenty two (except as therein is excepted), so far as relates to goods made of linen yarn, and cotton wooll, manufactured in Great Britain* (9 Geo. 2 c. 4 [1736]) in ibid., vol. XIV, 1–3; Woodruff D. Smith, *Consumption and the Making of Respectability, 1600–1800* (London & New York, 2002), 49–63; Espen Moe, *Governance, Growth and Global Leadership: The Role of the State in Technological Progress, 1750–2000* (Aldershot & Burlington VT, 2007), 61–3

[40] *An act to repeal the several Laws relating to Customs* (6 Geo. 4 c. 105 [1825]) in *The Statutes of the United Kingdom of Great Britain and Ireland, 6 George IV 1825* (London, 1825), 614–76.

[41] For a polemic on this cotton trade: *A Treatise on the Cotton Trade in Twelve Letters Addressed to the Levant Company, West-India Planters, and Merchants* (London, 1789).

copperware, pewter, and silver plate was exported, presumably for mercantile or elite consumption, and the majority of metal and military goods were in the form of tin, iron, lead, and gunpowder. The most prominent metal commodity sent to the Ottoman realms was tin. Tin exports experienced a period of prosperity in the first quarter of the eighteenth century, followed by something of a slump, and then with a great increase from the 1770s onwards. Both tin and (in a small quantity) tinplate had long been prized in the armaments industry, being used with copper to make bronze cannons.[42] The Ottomans made great efforts to increase and improve their armaments, particularly naval armaments, following their defeat to the Russians in 1774. A new war with St Petersburg and Vienna from 1787 increased demand, which explains the increase of British tin in that later period.

Britain sided with the Ottomans following the Russian annexation of the Crimea in 1786, and trade in military stores flourished. The Ottoman government contracted British merchants in 1787 on a deal worth one million *guruş* (perhaps £130 million today) for naval stores including ropes, anchors, nails, tin, tar, gunpowder, iron cannon and munitions; in separate agreements, they also purchased British frigates.[43] As a result, exports of iron and lead also grew substantially, with iron exports 55 times greater in 1787 than they had been in 1767, and lead goods increased 27 times in the same period. These were goods the British were comfortable with exporting, as it took trade away from European rivals, particularly the Swedes and French, and they continued to be exported at a high volume following peace with Russia in 1792.

There was a prohibition on the export of gunpowder from the Ottoman Empire, and for the most part consumption was provided by an extensive domestic industry that employed the latest production techniques, particularly the process of English glazed gunpowder (*İngiliz perdāḫtı bārūt*) practised, for instance, at the Gallipoli powder-mill from 1717 onwards.[44] Although the Ottomans had made use of British gunpowder imported in the earlier part of the seventeenth century, in the latter half of the century the supply dried up,

[42] Suraiya Faroqhi, *The Ottoman Empire and the World Around It* (London, 2006), 14; V.J. Parry, 'Materials of war in the Ottoman Empire' in Cook (ed.), *Studies in the Economic History*, 219–29 at 225–7; Gábor Ágoston, *Guns for the Sultan: Military Power and the Weapons Industry in the Ottoman Empire* (Cambridge, 2005), 166–89.

[43] TNA/FO78/8 Sir Robert Ainslie to the Marquess of Carmarthen, 25 September 1787; BOA/C.HR 32/1567, 1 Rebiülevvel 1208 [6 October 1793]. I have used my own figures of the exchange rate of the *guruş* to the pound to calculate the eighteenth-century equivalent. Converting eighteenth-century prices to modern ones is incredibly problematic and inaccurate. However, for a guide I have used the datasets of MeasuringWorth.com. Laurence H. Officer & Samuel H. Williamson, 'Purchasing power of British pounds from 1245 to present', *MeasuringWorth* [http://www.measuringworth.com/ppoweruk/].

[44] Some of the Gallipoli mill files that specifically mention the production of British-style glazed powder include: BOA/KK.d 6687, 1129 [1716/1717]; BOA/KK.d 6690, 1166 [1752/1753]; BOA/KK.d 6692, 1199 [1784/1785]; BOA/KK.d 6693, 1200 [1785/1786]; BOA/KK.d 6695, 1201 [1786/1787]; BOA/KK.d 6697, 1208 [1793/1794]. For a general discussion on the Ottoman gunpowder industry, see: Ágoston, *Guns for the Sultan*, 128–63, with an examination of the Gallipoli powder-mills at 141–3.

not least in the context of an attempt to mediate peace between the Ottomans and the Habsburgs prior to Carlowitz in 1699.[45] Gunpowder continued to be exported in small quantities throughout the century; changing methods in Ottoman manufacturing of gunpowder, and a more relaxed attitude by the British, saw a boom in the import of British gunpowder between 1783 and 1792, and although the British government refused to grant an unlimited trade to the Ottomans, as had been requested in a new contract issued to British merchants in 1793, British gunpowder continued to be imported in fairly high volumes.[46]

This resurgence of the British gunpowder trade to the Ottoman Empire is indicative of a trend towards diversification that allowed merchants on both sides to adapt to changing demands despite the overall decline in British–Ottoman trade during the eighteenth century. The transition from a commerce almost completely reliant on the wool-for-silk exchange to a diverse trade based on a variety of products took time, and the constant warfare that both states found themselves engaged in provided fairly regular disruptions. It is unsurprising that Alfred Wood looked at the Levant trade in the seventeenth and eighteenth centuries and saw the latter as a period of decline until a resurgence at its very end. Broadly the story was one of high volume of trade until the 1720s, a gradual decline until the 1770s, after which time it began to rise again rapidly towards its former levels. The changing patterns of British–Ottoman trade in the eighteenth century did not simply have an effect on manufacturers, suppliers, and merchants, but on the very nature of British diplomacy in the Ottoman Empire, which relied on income from the Company for its finances. After all, the diplomatic framework saw the money the Company raised from its merchants used to support the embassy that protected their interests, and so the peaks and troughs of commerce were to have a profound impact on the relationship between the Company and the embassy.

45 BOA/İE.BH 10/865, 28 Zilhicce 1109 (6 July 1698); BOA/C.AS 102/4627, 25 Rebiülevvel 1115 (8 August 1703).

46 Ágoston, *Guns for the Sultan*, 143–53. Between 1787 and 1792 the British gunpowder trade to the Ottoman Empire was conducted from the Edmund Hill's Gunpowder Office in Savage Gardens (next to the Tower of London) via the brokers Barbe and Greene 200 yards away in Seething Lane, to two major houses of British traders in Istanbul and Izmir. TNA/FO78/10 Barbe & Green to the Duke of Leeds, 23 October 1789; TNA/FO78/10 Messrs Lee & Sons (Izmir) to Messrs Lee & Sons (London), 22 August 1787; TNA/FO78/8 Sir Robert Ainslie to the Duke of Leeds, 22 November 1789; TNA/FO78/11 Sir Robert Ainslie to the Duke of Leeds, 22 October 1790; TNA/FO78/12A Edmund Hill to Lord Grenville, 4 August 1791; TNA/FO78/12A Messrs James Barbaud & Co. (Istanbul) to Edmund Hill, 15 June 1791; TNA/FO78/12A Messrs James Barbaud & Co. (Istanbul) to John Fish, undated [1791]; TNA/FO78/14 Sir Robert Ainslie to Lord Grenville, 31 March 1793; TNA/FO78/14 Edmund Hill to Lord Grenville, 7 June 1793; TNA/FO78/14 Extract from the Council Office Minutes of 15 August 1793 TNA/FO78/14 Edmund Hill to Lord Grenville, August 1793; BOA/C.HR 180/8966, 25 Safer 1203 [24 November 1788]. An example of import records can be found at: BOA/C.AS. 958/41657, 29 Safer 1204 (17 November 1789), detailing 350 barrels delivered in Istanbul. For a discussion on British–Ottoman naval cooperation in this period, see: Tuncay Zorlu, *Innovation and Empire in Turkey: Sultan Selim III and the Modernisation of the Ottoman Navy* (London & New York, 2008), 62–73.

## An audit of the Levant Company

The relationship between the merchants and the Company was fairly straightforward. The Company took membership fees and duties from the merchants, who appointed the Company's governor, deputy, treasurer, and assistants by election. The Company was not a settled entity, holding its meetings in a number of locations among the livery companies in the City of London before acquiring its own premises off Bishopsgate in 1802.[47] It comprised several distinct trading houses that held their own stock and traded at their own risk. Because of the monopoly granted to the original Turkey Company in the late sixteenth century, all those merchants had to be members of the Levant Company, which meant paying a membership fee to enjoy the freedom of the Company. The 1661 charter gave this fee at the level of £25 for those under 26 years of age, and £50 for those over that age.[48] The level of fees was decreased by an Act of Parliament in 1753 to £20, and other conditions, such as the requirement to be a freeman of London, were abolished in an attempt to open up the Levant trade to remedy its decreasing levels. Eventually the trade was thrown open to all British subjects on the condition that they received licence from the Company.[49]

Until 1744, the Company had required goods to be freighted in Company ships known as general ships, which went out rather sporadically and often in insufficient numbers.[50] Moreover, the Company attempted to regulate the trade through its by-laws, and the existence of a monopoly on the Ottoman trade came under increasing attack during the course of the eighteenth century.[51]

47 These were all geographically close: the Fishmongers' Hall on the Thames off Upper Thames Street; the Ironmongers' Hall on Fenchurch Street; the Pewterers' Hall on Lime Street; and the Salters' Hall at St Swithin's Church. The premises acquired in 1802 were on Little St Helen's off Bishopsgate, further north almost on the London Wall.

48 LMA/CLC/B/145 Charter incorporating the Governor and Company of Merchants of England trading to the Levant Seas, 2 April 13 Car. 2 [1661], fols 8–9.

49 Ibid., fols 42–3; Cobbett, *Parliamentary History*, vol. XIII, 895–963; *An Act for Enlarging and Regulating the Trade into the Levant Seas* (26 Geo. 2 c. 18 [1753]) in Pickering, *Statutes of the Realm*, vol. XXI, 49–53; Wood, *Levant Company*, 156–8.

50 Davis, *Aleppo and Devonshire Square*, 49–57; Wood, *Levant Company*, 153–7.

51 Wood, *Levant Company*, 152–3; *The Levant Company's Orders and By-Laws* (London, 1800). A selection of pamphlets attacking and defending the Levant Company include: *Observations on the late Management of the Levant-Company, with Extracts of Letters from Constantinople and Smirna* (London, 1719); *Paragraphs of some Letters, among many others, from Aleppo, Smyrna, Constantinople, to prove the Reasonableness of the Levant Company's late Orders to carry on their Trade by General Ships* (London, 1719); *Considerations on the Dispute Between the Levant Company and the Italian Merchants, Relating to the Importation of Raw Silk from Leghorn* (London, 1720); *Reasons Offer'd by the Merchants Trading to Italy, against the Bill desired by the Levant-Company, for Repealing a Clause in the Act of Navigation* (London, 1720); *The Case Fairly Stated between the Turky Company and the Italian Merchants* (London, 1720); *The Turkey Merchants and their Trade Vindicated From the Aspersions and unjust Reproaches cast on them, In several Cases and Pamphlets Published in the Names of the Italian Merchants* (London, 1720); *Reasons Against The Bill now depending in Parliament, Intitutled, A Bill for Inlarging and Regulating the Trade to the Levant Seas* (London, 1744); Jonas Hanway, *An Answer, to the Appendix of a Pamphlet, entitled Reflextions upon Naturalization, Corporations*

The majority of the Company's by-laws regulated the conduct of the factors in the Ottoman realms, the rates of impositions due to the Company in London and consulage due to the factories in the Levant, and the role and conduct of the Company's treasurers. Other articles defined the rules for assemblies, freedoms, entries, quarantine, consuls, and 'avanias' (the supposed imposition of extraordinary duties on British merchants that caused great disputes, discussed in a later chapter).

A number of these by-laws regulated the fees due to the Company from trade, the impositions and consulage.[52] Goods were classified as rated *ad valorem* or unrated, *ad valorem* being goods taxed on their value (noted in the customs ledgers as 'at value' goods). On being exported to Ottoman ports from Britain, merchants paid a 'leviation' of consulage at 0.25% *ad valorem* or 0.5% unrated on goods shipped from foreign ships to foreign ports, 0.5% or 1% on goods shipped in British ships to foreign ports, and 1% or 2% on goods shipped to ports under British dominion. Goods imported to Britain were charged at 7% unrated or 1% *ad valorem*, an exception made in the 1800 Orders for cotton wool, charged at 5%. These charges paid for the expenses of the factories, and were thus central to the funding of diplomatic affairs, and were also supplemented with remittances sent from London when necessary. As for the income generated by the Company in London, in addition to fees from its members, it came primarily from the 'impositions' paid on Levant goods imported into Britain. These were paid in pounds sterling at differing rates on goods by their weight, size, or value, so that, for instance, currants were liable to 5 shillings for every ton, hare skins at 2 shillings for every 120 skins, and large carpets at 1 shilling per 100 cubits. The Company's establishments in the Levant therefore received fair but potentially lucrative rates on imports and exports to support the diplomatic staff there to protect the trade, and the Company in London took its share on imported goods for its administrative costs.

However, as we have just seen, the Levant Company came into financial trouble in the middle of the eighteenth century due to French competition and the decline of the silk-for-wool trade. Using the ledgers from the London treasurer, it has been possible to examine the profit-and-loss account of the Levant Company between 1710 and 1803.[53] As with the customs ledgers, these

*and Companies, &c Relating to the Levant Trade and Turkey Company, As this Subject is occasionally mentioned in Hanway's Travels* (London, 1753); *Reflections on the Expediency of Opening the Trade to Turkey* (London, 1753); *Some Remarks on a Late Pamphlet, Intituled, Reflections on the Expediency of Opening the Trade to Turky* (London, 1753); William Eton, *A Survey of the Turkish Empire* (London, 1798), 463–94; *A Letter to Mr. Eton, from A Merchant in Turkey, in Answer to a Chapter in His Survey of the Turkish Empire, to prove the necessity of Abolishing the Levant Company* (London, 1799); *A Short Reply to Mr. Eaton's Observations Respecting the Establishment of The Levant Company* (London, 1799).

52 *The Levant Company's Orders and By-Laws*, 1–6.

53 TNA/SP105 164–5, 1710–1803. For contemporary discussions on accounts, see: John Collins, *An Introduction to Merchants-Accompts: containing Seven distinct Questions or Accompts* (London, 1675); John Mair, *Book-keeping Methodised: or, a Methodical Treatise of Merchant-Accompts, According to the Italian Form* (Dublin, 1772).

Table 3: *Expenditure, income, and profit-and-loss of the Levant Company, 1714–1803 (decadal figures)*

| Period | Expenditure (£000s) | Income (£000s) | Profit-and-loss (£000s) |
|---|---|---|---|
| 1714–23 | 123 | 165 | 42 |
| 1724–33 | 112 | 118 | 6 |
| 1734–43 | 98 | 81 | -17 |
| 1744–53 | 114 | 130 | 16 |
| 1754–63 | 119 | 110 | -9 |
| 1764–73 | 112 | 122 | 10 |
| 1774–83 | 112 | 94 | -18 |
| 1784–93 | 107 | 109 | -2 |
| 1794–1803 | 131 | 129 | -2 |

accounts do not reflect the real value of the goods noted, but provide a fictive currency of account that permits an analysis of the trends of this period. Table 3 shows the decadal expenditure and income entries for the Company, and shows that although in some periods the Company's expenditure exceeded its income resulting in a loss, overall income appears to have covered expenditure, and, indeed, after a dip in the 1730s, income remained at a relatively stable level along with expenditure. However, as with the accounts of any commercial enterprise, it is necessary to examine some of the entries in more detail to see how accurate a picture those figures present.

The Company's income and expenditure featured in these accounts ledgers can be divided between that generated in London, and that in the Ottoman Empire. London accounted for 39% of the Company's income, and 15% of its expenditure. The expenditure was largely on salaries for the husband (accountant), rent for meeting premises, and other administrative expenses. Income derived from two sources, the first being the impositions collected on goods imported from the Levant by the customs officials, and the second through the collections made by the London treasurer. For most of this period, the income gained by that treasurer was from various fines and admissions fees, yet, as figure 4 shows, income through his books rose sharply from the period 1764 to 1773. This is due to the decreasing income from impositions – duties paid from Levant goods imported into Britain – from the 1730s as a result of the decrease in British imports from the Ottoman Empire. Coupled with other losses, this meant that the Company was struggling to support the diplomatic establishments in the Levant, and consequently it sought help from Parliament to pay for the expenses of the ambassador and consuls. The monies from these parliamentary grants explain the huge jump in the amounts received by the treasurer from the 1760s.

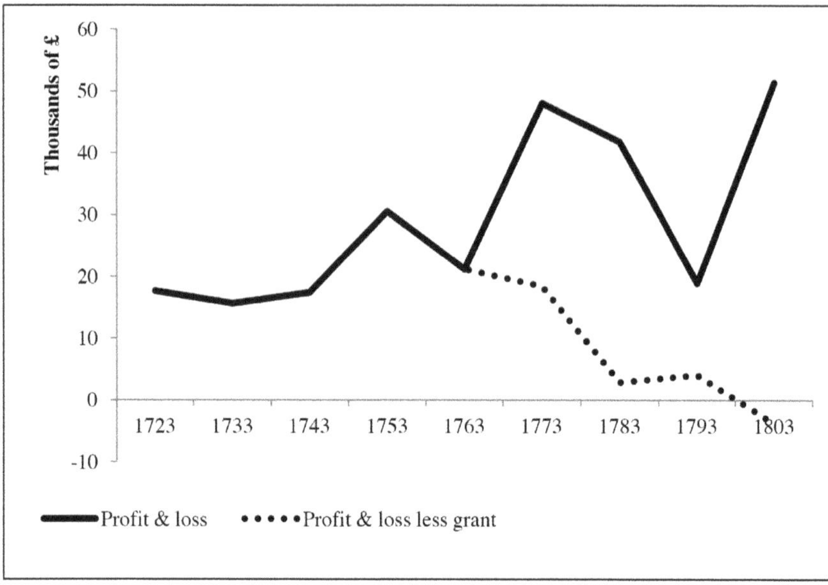


Figure 4: *The London income and expenditure of the Levant Company, 1714–1803 (decadal figures)*

In the forty years between 1728 and 1767 the Company saw its total annual profit-and-loss slip into negative figures twenty-four times, with seven out of ten years between 1758 and 1767 resulting in a loss. This led the Company to present a petition to Parliament on 31 January 1767 pleading that:

> The petitioners are sensible, that they should not discharge the duty incumbent upon them by Charter, nor the justice they owe to the public, if they did not declare their inability to proceed any further, unless relieved by Parliament, as on account of their declining trade, they have unavoidably incurred considerable debts, and are now under the necessity of levying very high duties (more than their trade can support) in order to raise supplies equal to their expenses.[54]

As a result, in 1768 the Company was granted the sum of £5,000 to cover its expenses.[55] This being insufficient, further petitions were presented in 1769 and 1770 claiming that the diplomatic burden amounted to £10,000 per annum, and Parliament again granted £5,000 in both years.[56] This recourse to parliamentary grants continued fairly consistently for the remainder of the Company's charge over the diplomatic establishments in the Ottoman Empire,

[54] *Journals of the House of Commons*, online edn, [http://parlipapers.chadwyck.co.uk/] vol. XXXI, 96.

[55] Ibid., 640, 645, 648, 652.

[56] Ibid., vol. XXXII, 360, 369, 379, 592, 883–4, 889.

with grants on petition made of £5,000 in 1772, 1773, 1775, 1779 (plus an additional £10,000), and 1783, £4,000 in 1784, and £3,000 in 1785.[57] After this, the volume of trade increased greatly, and it was only with the disruption of the wars with France in the 1790s that the Company was again forced to apply to Parliament, receiving £5,000 in 1794 and 1796, £10,000 in 1798, and £5,000 per annum between 1799 and 1802.[58] Although much of this money was paid in arrears of months or even years, without it the Company was unable to meet its expenses. Without the parliamentary grants, the Levant Company would have made a loss in thirty-two years out of forty between 1764 and 1803, including a run of eleven years of straight losses between 1793 and 1803.

The reason for the chasm that had opened up in the Company's finances cannot be found in London, but rather in its factories in the Ottoman Empire. The diplomatic establishments that the Company was expected to support, particularly the embassy in Istanbul, relied entirely on the income from

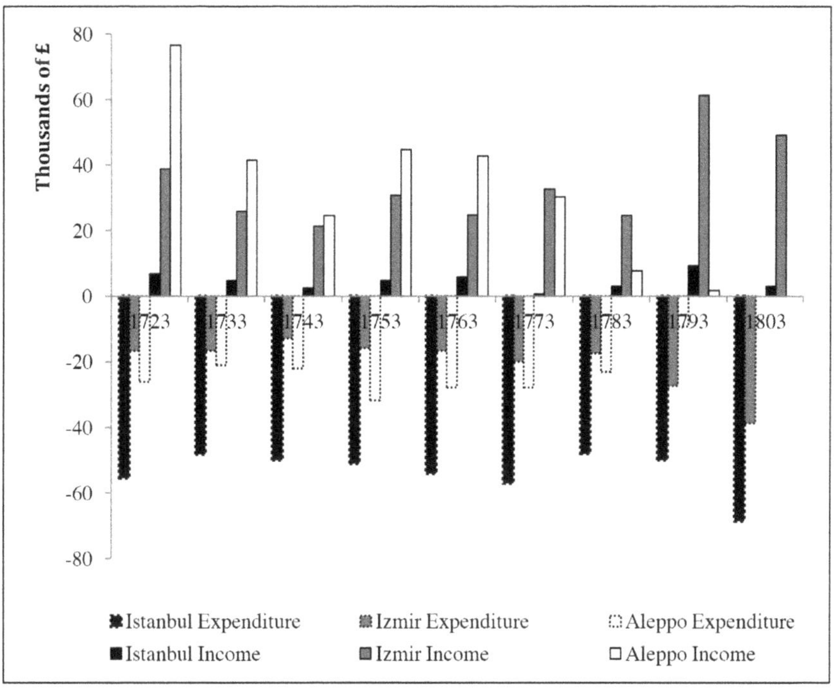


Figure 5: *Income, expenditure, and balance of the British factories in Istanbul, Izmir, and Aleppo, 1714–1803 (decadal figures)*

[57] Ibid., vol. XXXIII, 272, 322, 644, 689, 694; vol. XXXIV, 148, 182; vol. XXXV, 230, 305, 307; vol. XXXVII, 130–1, 148, 150, 498, 514; vol. XXXVIII, 114; vol. XXXIX, 19, 283, 412, 416, 651, 1040; vol. XL, 111, 197, 587, 623; vol. XLI, 426.

[58] Ibid., vol. XLIX, 176, 391, 399; vol. LI, 371, 647, 654; vol. LIII, 151, 276, 352; vol. LIV, 92, 372, 373, 440, 483, 492; vol. LV, 193, 351–2, 767–8; vol. LVI, 379–80, 535, 540; vol. LVII, 149–50, 571, 577.

consulage and other fees collected, all of which relied on a successful trade. The balances of the three major British establishments in the Ottoman Empire – Istanbul, Izmir, and Aleppo – show that the Company was unable to cover its expenditure with its income from the factories due to the heavy costs of diplomacy and problems caused by declining fortunes in trade, as demonstrated in figure 5.

The decline of the Aleppo trade with the shift from wool–silk commerce is evident, with huge drops from the 1760s onwards. At the same time, the diversification of British–Ottoman trade can be seen in the increasingly high share of income being taken at Izmir from the 1780s. The expenditures of those factories remained relatively stable throughout the period, with the Aleppo figures (for both income and expenditure) disappearing with the closure of the factory in 1792, and the Izmir expenditure rising proportionally to its increasing commercial significance. However, the figures for Istanbul are the most striking. Despite being a huge centre of Ottoman trade, the Ottoman capital accounted for only 6.6% of the income of the British Levant factories. At the same time, the embassy at Istanbul consumed 56.5% of total expenditure. This was the main problem with the Levant Company's finances. From the middle of the 1720s, the mean annual income from Istanbul, Izmir, and Aleppo was between £5,000 and £7,000, whereas the expenditure at the same establishments was between £8,000 and £10,000 mean per annum, leading to a mean annual loss of £2,000 to £5,000.

Under the original Elizabethan agreement, the Company was responsible for maintaining the British diplomatic establishments in the Ottoman Empire in return for the right of its members to trade to the Levant. It was inconceivable that Britain should not maintain a diplomatic presence in the Ottoman realms. However, by the beginning of the nineteenth century, despite an increasing volume of trade, the Company was still unable to support those diplomatic establishments without help from Parliament, which contributed at least £97,000 between 1769 and 1802. Considering that Civil List expenditure on all other British diplomatic establishments totalled £2.6 million in the same period, Parliament's bailout of the Levant Company equated to 3.6% of expenditure on diplomatic affairs. It was undoubtedly the fact that this burden was placed upon government that prompted the separation of the embassy from the Company in 1804 with the appointment of Charles Arbuthnot as ambassador, and the royal instruction that the Company should appoint its own consul-general in Istanbul whilst retaining temporary control of the consular establishments.[59]

The great expense of the embassy in Istanbul, as clearly demonstrated by figure 5, saw the Levant Company unable to balance its books without the continual support of Parliament until it was relieved of that burden in 1804. This, however, called into question the very purpose of the Company's incorporation. The Company's *raison d'être* had been to fund the establishments that protected the trade that it regulated to the Ottoman Empire. Although it

[59] TNA/SP105/109 George III to the Levant Company, 6 June 1804.

retained control over the consul at the main commercial centre of Izmir, the fact that a private company continued to fund diplomatic establishments that were almost everywhere else under the control of the British government seemed rather anachronistic, and it was no surprise that just over twenty years after surrendering the Istanbul embassy to the Crown, the Company voted to dissolve itself in 1825.

Over the course of the eighteenth century, changing trends in British–Ottoman trade influenced by supply, conflict, and fashion, had dealt a severe blow to the Levant Company's finances, so that whereas before the 1720s the Company had been fairly profitable as an entity, by the end of that decade it was incurring significant annual losses. Those losses can largely be attributed to the expense of the embassy in Istanbul, which although not necessarily increasing over the century, remained a constant burden that the Company's decreasing income was unable to support. It was unable and unwilling to raise its leviations or consulage as that would have discouraged trade, and so was forced to rely on the benevolence of Parliament. This led in time to the Crown taking over the embassy as a result of its increasing contributions. Given the intimate link between trade and diplomatic practices and finances, the changing fortunes of British trade and declining income of the Levant Company had a direct impact on the pursuit of British diplomacy in the Ottoman Empire through the finance – or lack thereof – available to the ambassador in Istanbul.

## 'How very inadequate this sum is to the expenses of an embassy': Issues of diplomatic finance

Finance, or lack thereof, is something that was a concern for the majority of early modern diplomats. When the Ottoman Empire dispatched its first resident ambassadors to London at the end of the eighteenth century, large parts of their correspondence with Istanbul concerned questions of pay. A typical example is a note concerning the second Ottoman ambassador in London, İsmail Ferruh Efendi, on the eve of his vacating the embassy in 1800:

> As the resident ambassador from the Sublime State in Britain, your servant İsmail Ferruh Efendi, is about to complete his term of residence, it was to be ordered that he be given an additional allowance. However, the replacement for the said [ambassador] has not yet departed from the Abode of Felicity, and in [İsmail Ferruh's] petition it is evident that he will be hard-up [*muḥtāc*] during the time that it will take between [the replacement] leaving here and arriving there. In order to manage the matter until that time, it is necessary to send more money to your servant the said efendi.[60]

Underneath that text is a set of figures that summarise the salary expenses for the embassy from the previous three years, given to provide the relevant minister with the necessary financial information in considering this matter.

[60] BOA/C.H. 27/1330, 8 Muharrem 1215 (1 June 1800).

It records that İsmail Ferruh Efendi received a six-monthly salary of 25,000 *guruş*; his chief secretary 5,000 *guruş* and his assistant 1,500 *guruş*; and his chief translator 4,000 *guruş* and the second translator 3,000 *guruş*. This meant that the embassy in London, in salaries alone, cost the Ottoman government 77,000 *guruş* per year. Deciding whether or not to send İsmail Ferruh Efendi these extra allowances therefore required investigation and consideration, and although it seems that he was indeed sent some funds, ambassadors were not simply able to withdraw from a limitless account. This scenario would have been a common one for ambassadors: unexpected circumstances or pressures, plus distance from home, plus a budget-conscious government, equalled financial pressure and debt.

It is possible to read much of the British diplomatic correspondence dispatched from Istanbul between 1661 and around 1800 as an extended dirge lamenting the lack of finances for the necessary expenses of diplomacy in the Ottoman Empire. The question of finances, in the Ottoman and British case, and in general, is one that remains to be addressed methodically, and more comparative studies are needed to really get an insight into wider trends. Moreover, it is not sufficient to see how much diplomatic establishments cost from the side of the state, but it is also necessary to examine how the money was spent, where that money came from, and how it reached the ambassador. The Istanbul embassy allows a particularly detailed analysis because of the Levant Company's accounts and the expense accounts provided in the ambassadors' correspondence, but, as the note about İsmail Ferruh's salary shows, it is possible to do this from a variety of sources.

As has been seen, the Levant Company underwent significant periods of commercial decline and crisis in the eighteenth century, and, as a result of the intimate link between the fortunes of the Company and the financing of the embassy, commercial constraints equalled diplomatic constraints, in a way not experienced by other European embassies in Istanbul, nor by the Ottoman diplomats in London. In examining the British ambassador's salary, I have used two major sets of accounts ledgers, the first being the records of the Civil List between 1727 and 1802, since as many expenditures around foreign policy, including ambassadors' salaries, fell under the royal prerogative, it was paid for from the royal purse.[61] The second set are the accounts of the embassy in Istanbul, which are somewhat incomplete, but broadly cover the finance the ambassadors received via the Levant Company in the period 1693 to 1803, contained in the surviving accounts ledgers and otherwise in the registers of the factory.[62]

The basic annual salary of the ambassador was paid by the Levant Company in Istanbul in Ottoman *guruş*, known as 'piastres' or 'dollars' in English. The smallest subdivision of the *guruş*, the *akçe*, was known as the 'asper'. Alfred Wood assumed that these eighteenth-century payments were

[61] TNA/T38/156–71, 1727–1802.

[62] TNA/SP105/202–6, 1730–1816; TNA/SP105/177–91, 1693–1804. The years missing are: 1694, 1699–1701, 1705–7, 1718–22, 1725–9, and 1745–65.

made in either Spanish *real de a ocho* (*real*s for short, commonly known as 'pieces-of-eight') or Dutch *leeuwendaalder* (L$, 'the lion dollar'), but from analysing the accounts it is evident that payments were computed and paid in Ottoman *guruş* from the 1690s onwards.[63] On his arrival in Istanbul in 1661, the Earl of Winchilsea noted that he received an annual salary of 10,000 *real*s plus a gratuity of 2,000 *real*s (the gratuity equating to £500) in consideration of his relinquishing the right to a percentage of consulage collected.[64] The basic salary level remained at 10,000 *real*s until the arrival of Baron Chandos in 1681, when it decreased to 8,000 *real*s. By the time the Istanbul embassy accounts begin in 1693, payments are being noted as being made in *guruş*, doubtless due to the dispute over the importation of foreign currencies, but at the same amount, that is, 8,000 *guruş* salary with a gratuity of 2,000 *guruş*. It would remain at this level until the Company lost control of the embassy.

In response to Ottoman currency reforms in the mid-1710s, there was a slight augmentation known as an '*agio*' (from the Italian *aggio*, a premium) of 12.5% from the 1720s.[65] The narrative in the salary entries of the accounts at that time noted that each quarterly payment of 2,000 *guruş* was adjusted by *agio*, resulting in '2,500 p[iastres] to 12½ percent on the above salaries and being the difference between zalotes [*zolota*s] at ¾ p[iastres] as they are received and ⅔ p[iastres] as they are paid by Their Worships' order'.[66] This complicated calculation requires some unpacking. Ottoman currency reforms in the 1690s had begun to fix, and by the 1720s had largely standardised, the *guruş* at 120 *akçe*s, one denomination of which was a coin called the *zolota* worth 90 *akçe*s. As the Levant Company continued to compute its salaries based on the old system of coinage, where the *zolota* was worth 80 *akçe*s, it was necessary for the treasurer to apply an *agio* in order to bring the salary up to the new level, so that to the Levant Company the ambassador continued to receive 8,000 *guruş* per annum on paper, when in reality, with the *agio* applied, he was paid 9,000 *guruş*. The annual gratuity introduced under Winchilsea seems to have remained, and was also adjusted by *agio* to 2,500 *guruş*.

Already we can get a sense of the complicated nature of record-keeping, and adjusting for changing circumstances. Establishing a reasonable trend in prices and wages in the eighteenth-century Ottoman Empire is problematic. As well as the intrinsic value of coinage in its precious metal content, its purchasing power was influenced by wars, famine, and other disasters, leading to price increases, particularly in a city like Istanbul that was so vulnerable to shortages when a passing army required feeding or unseasonable weather resulted in a bad harvest. Prices for items such as meat and fruit seem to have risen first, with bread and rice not far behind, and such scarcity could see prices double

63 Wood, *Levant Company*, 134. He states explicitly that the Company ordered its payments to be made in *leeuwendaalder*s, when the accounts clearly show that they were made in *guruş*. Using Wood as their source, this error was repeated in Webb & Webb, *The Earl and His Butler*, 219–22.

64 TNA/SP97/17 Earl of Winchilsea to Sir Edward Nicholas, 28 November 1661.

65 Pamuk, *Monetary History*, 159–60; Eldem, *French Trade*, 159–63.

66 This particular example is taken from the salary entries for 1730/1 in TNA/SP105/202, 1730–1744.

or even triple on certain commodities. For instance, a long conflict with the Habsburgs saw the price of provisions double by 1686, the war with Iran in the 1720s and 1730s caused the price of meat and corn to double, and likewise in the 1768–74 war with Russia the price of bread doubled by 1771. A series of hard winters saw the cost of provisions double between 1738 and 1740, and in the great freeze of 1778–9 Sir Robert Ainslie reported that the price of meat had risen by 80%.[67] The framework I have used to understand price changes comes from the work of Şevket Pamuk on long-term trends in Ottoman currency, prices, and wages that demonstrated the impact of the depreciating precious metal content in Ottoman silver coins on price inflation in Istanbul in particular, along with comparisons to other parts of the Empire and the world.[68] According to Pamuk, the worth of Ottoman currency was largely dependent on its silver content, so if the silver content of Ottoman coinage decreased, prices would adjust accordingly. Pamuk has made use of a range of sources to determine changes in prices on the one hand, and changing silver content of Ottoman coinage on the other. Although this cannot take into account the changes in prices occasioned by wars and so forth mentioned above, Pamuk's figures for the silver content of the Ottoman *guruş* expressed in grams along with the coin's weight show that the currency remained at a relatively stable rate from the minting of the first batch of the new *guruş* in the 1690s until the more detrimental debasements that began at the end of the century. At the same time, the main British silver coin, the shilling, was strictly regulated from around 1705, its weight of 6g comprising 92.5% silver, or a 5.5g silver content, so that £1 (of 20 shillings) had a total silver content of 110g.

What did this all mean for the ambassador's salary, which remained at the same level for most of the eighteenth century? The accounts ledgers of the Levant Company in London present two possible conclusions in terms of how this was justified financially by the Company. On the one hand, the Company may have used a fictive version of the *guruş* that bore no relation to actual diminutions in the currency's value. On the other, it could be that the Company in London did not calculate its exchange figures in *guruş* at all, but in *leeuwendaalder*, which had been a popular alternative coin before the Ottoman currency reforms. The use of the piastre symbol (₰) in the accounts would point to the former, but the correlation with the *leeuwendaalder* rate is striking. Table 4 illustrates the exchange rate as calculated by the Levant Company in London, and a silver content-based exchange rate I have constructed that

67 TNA/SP97/20 Baron Chandos to the Earl of Sunderland, 29 September 1686; TNA/SP97/26 Earl of Kinnoull to the Duke of Newcastle, 4 June 1731; TNA/SP97/47 John Murray to the Earl of Rochford, 3 December 1771; TNA/SP97/30 William Fawkener to the Duke of Newcastle, 23 January 1738/9; TNA/SP97/31 Sir Everard Fawkener to the Duke of Newcastle, 17 April 1740; TNA/SP97/55 Sir Robert Ainslie to Viscount Weymouth, 3 February 1779.

68 Pamuk, *Monetary History*, 1–20, 170–1; Şevket Pamuk, 'Prices in the Ottoman Empire', *International Journal of Middle East Studies* 36:3 (2004), 451–68; Süleyman Özmucur & Şevket Pamuk, 'Real wages and standards of living in the Ottoman Empire, 1489–1914', *The Journal of Economic History* 62:2 (2002), 293–321; Şevket Pamuk, İstanbul ve Diğer Kentlerde 500 Yıllık Fiyatlar ve Ücretler, *1469–1998* (Ankara, 2000).

tallies more with the figures mentioned in the diplomatic correspondence. Therefore, the Levant Company in London calculated a fixed salary for the ambassador based on a currency situation that no longer existed by the 1720s, and that did not reflect the depreciating value of the *guruş*, particularly from the 1750s when price inflation would prove devastating to the ambassador's salary. Figure 6 displays the sharp difference between the nominal value of the salary as paid by the Company, and the real value that salary held based on its silver content. It demonstrates that whilst the real value of the salary remained at a stable level until the middle of the century, following the debasements of the 1750s its value decreased initially by around 25%, followed by a sharp drop to 64% of its nominal value in the 1780s, and with the great debasements under Selim III it fell to around 40% of its nominal value.

Ottoman currency reforms, inflation, and a lack of response by the Levant Company did not go unnoticed by the ambassadors. In 1702, Sir Robert Sutton complained that the real value of his salary had been cut by 40% since the Company switched to paying in the new Ottoman coinage, and in 1716 he

Table 4: *The exchange rate of the pound sterling, guruş, and leeuwendaalder*

| Year | Levant Company exchange rate (*guruş* in the £) | Silver-based exchange rate (L$ in the £) | Silver-based exchange rate (*guruş* in the £) |
|---|---|---|---|
| 1683 | 4.61 | - | - |
| 1693 | - | 6.12 | 4.66 |
| 1703 | - | 5.84 | 7.20 |
| 1713 | 5.00 | 5.88 | 7.16 |
| 1723 | 6.00 | 6.06 | 7.32 |
| 1733 | 6.00 | 6.04 | 7.50 |
| 1743 | 6.00 | 5.83 | 7.52 |
| 1753 | 6.00 | 5.80 | 7.69 |
| 1763 | 6.00 | 5.88 | 9.91 |
| 1773 | 6.00 | 6.09 | 10.17 |
| 1783 | 6.00 | 5.88 | 10.38 |
| 1793 | 6.00 | 5.88 | 11.31 |
| 1803 | 6.04 | 5.88 | 19.17 |

*Source*: For the Levant Company exchange rate: TNA/SP105/164–5, 1710–1803. The Company noted figures from the Levantine factories in both pounds and 'dollars', using the sign for the guruş, and to arrive at the exchange rate simply divided one against the other. For the silver-based exchange rates, calculations have included data from: Pamuk, *Monetary History*, 163; McCusker, *Money and Exchange*, 9–17; Feavearyear, *Pound Sterling*, 453.

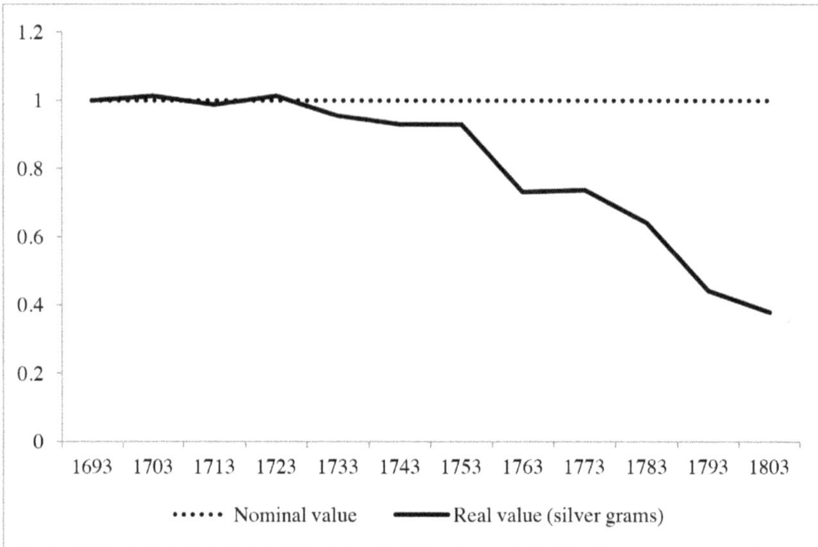


Figure 6: *The nominal and real value of ambassadorial salary, 1693–1803*

complained that his annual salary of 10,000 *guruş* from which he was expected to pay for all the costs of his embassy was 'not really worth much more than £700 sterling intrinsic value, and all things are risen in price proportionably to the debasement of the Grand Signior's coin'.[69] Sutton may have been exaggerating the worthlessness of Ottoman currency in his attempt to procure funds from the British government, the exchange rate he gave being at over 14 *guruş* to £1 and out of keeping with other contemporary assessments. However, the start of drastic debasement in the later century was noted by Sir Robert Ainslie with some concern in 1780, when he wrote about the Ottoman resolution to diminish the silver content of its coinage by 8.3% of its weight. Despite calculating that the real value would only be decreased by about 4.6%, he described the problems this move caused: 'Credit is at a stand, as the alterations of the coin must proportionally influence the exchanges, the price of every article in trade, the necessaries of life, and the price of labour.'[70] Ten years later, he opined that 'the alteration of the coin has not had a little influence on the price of goods, as well as of all necessaries, much beyond what is credited by the rise of the exchange'.[71]

Under Ainslie's successor, Robert Liston, the situation became truly desperate. In 1795, he wrote to London at length explaining that his position required him to pay for 'the entertainment of a large household, and a certain

[69] TNA/SP97/23 Sir Robert Sutton to James Stanhope, 4 April 1716.

[70] TNA/FO78/1 Sir Robert Ainslie to the Earl of Hillsborough, 16 November 1780.

[71] TNA/FO78/11 Sir Robert Ainslie to the Duke of Leeds, 22 June 1790.

display of magnificence', including a country house, boats, a chaplain, a private secretary, the Levant Company's cancellier, and interpreters. His income, he explained, came in part from the Company's salary, and in part from some perks of the job, such as consulage collected from foreigners under British protection and the appointment of new interpreters by a charter called a *berāt*; Ainslie claimed that the sale and renewal of *berāt*s brought 3,000 *guruş* per *ber*āt, although the Ottoman government began to limit the number permitted for each embassy in order to curb abuses from 1786 onwards.[72] Robert Liston calculated that in the earlier part of the century, ambassadors had received around 12,000 *guruş* (£2–3,000 by his reckoning) per year from *berāt*s. However, most of his income came from the Company's salary, also known as his 'entertainment', and Liston's opinion of this was scathing:

> The entertainment granted by the Turkey merchants appears to have been calculated with a view to what was during the last century ... The annual allowance was fixed at 8,000 piasters, which at the then course of exchange, was equivalent to £2,000. The remaining £2,500 was left to be supplied by the ordinary emoluments of the embassy here. The state of matters is not strikingly altered. The Company's allowance is paid in piasters of the country, and the value of that coin, besides the common causes of diminution, has been so rapidly degraded ... [that] the disproportion between the real and supposed value of the piasters has of late years become so enormous, that the present ambassador can hardly be said to receive from Their Worships about half of what used to be paid to his predecessor.[73]

Having emphasised that his salary was half the level it had been in James Porter's time just thirty to forty years earlier, something that tallies with my calculations, Liston concluded: 'Your Lordship cannot avoid being sensible how very inadequate this sum is to the necessary expenses of an embassy. The answer to this letter will determine whether I may flatter myself with the hopes of an augmentation of salary, or must resolve on a diminution of my establishment.'[74] With the Company unwilling – largely because it was, by this point, unable – to raise the ambassador's salary, Liston had warned that without support, he would be unable to meet the expenses of his position.

What role, then, did government play in supporting the ambassador who was, at least nominally, the representative of the Crown? The answer is, until the second half of the eighteenth century, very little, due to the Elizabethan funding arrangement. There were only certain occasions upon which the ambassador could draw on state funds, and that depended upon the British government's interpretation of what constituted the business of Crown or

[72] TNA/SP97/55 Sir Robert Ainslie to Viscount Weymouth, 17 March 1779; TNA/FO78/7 Sir Robert Ainslie to the Marquess of Carmarthen, 24 May 1786; TNA/FO78/7 Translation of a Turkish Paper delivered to the chief Interpreters of the foreign Ministers at the Ottoman Porte, 12 May 1786.

[73] TNAFO78/16 Robert Liston to Lord Grenville, 11 April 1795.

[74] Ibid.

Company. Prior to his departure to Istanbul in 1660, the Earl of Winchilsea petitioned the secretary of state in vain for an allowance of £2 per day to permit his embassy to be kept in a suitable manner, citing the precedent of that allowance being given to the ambassadors to Venice. All that he was managed to procure, however, based on a warrant issued by Charles I in January 1648, was the provision of a bed at the king's expense.[75] Despite numerous requests by almost all the ambassadors, the British government was only willing to pay an allowance when the ambassador was involved in trying to procure, or actually engaged in, British mediation in Ottoman treaties, which will be examined in Chapter 6. Similarly, despite Wood's assumption that the ambassador was entitled to an allowance from the Ottoman government, known as a *taʿyīn* (lit. ration/allowance), such imperial benevolence was only bestowed on exceptional occasions, such as on the renewal of the Capitulations or engagement in peace mediation.[76]

It was only with the appointment of James Porter to the embassy in 1746 that the British government began to take some share of the embassy's expense. Putting forward his case prior to his departure for Istanbul for an allowance from the Civil List as an ambassador, he argued:

> The vast increase of expense [the embassy] is accompanied with, arising not only from the great luxury and figure which has been of late years introduced by other ambassadors at Constantinople, and now required by the Turks as essentially annexed to that character, but also from the real advance in price of the most common commodities of life, which at this time exceed by a full third what they were worth ten years ago, so that the old pay must fall very short of what is actually sufficient to subsist there, and consequently expose me to inconveniences.[77]

Porter, who at the time of his appointment was the envoy-extraordinary in Vienna, persuaded the British government that they should continue the £3 he received per day in allowance there, and he succeeded in his request to continue to receive it following his arrival at Istanbul in 1747.[78] This government contribution of £3 per day to the ambassador to Istanbul, equal to £1,095 per annum, continued at the same level until the Crown took full control of the embassy in 1804.

The increasing contributions of the Crown towards the ordinary expenses of the Istanbul embassy were not part of a wider trend in increased diplomatic expenditure. The accounts of the Civil List are quite enlightening in this respect. The Civil List took its income from Parliament and crown lands, and was spent on the upkeep of the royal family, its household, and the salaries of senior bureaucrats, judges, and ambassadors. That basic arrangement lasted

[75] TNA/SP97/17 Earl of Winchilsea to Sir Edward Nicholas, 27 June 1660; 1 March 1660/1.

[76] Wood, *Levant Company*, 134.

[77] TNA/SP97/33 James Porter to the Duke of Newcastle, 7 September 1746.

[78] TNA/SP97/33 James Porter to the Duke of Newcastle, 1 October 1746.

Table 5: *Civil List expenditure, 1733–1802*

| Period | Istanbul allowance (£000s) | Total diplomatic expenditure (£000s) | Total expenditure (£000s) |
|---|---|---|---|
| 1733–42 | - | 547 | 8,971 |
| 1743–52 | 7 | 572 | 8,778 |
| 1753–62 | 11 | 592 | 8,861 |
| 1763–72 | 12 | 853 | 8,641 |
| 1773–82 | 12 | 738 | 9,808 |
| 1783–92 | 10 | 808 | 11,371 |
| 1793–1802 | 17 | 705 | 11,434 |

until the beginning of William IV's reign in 1830, when Parliament assumed total control over civil expenditure. The accounts show that the expenditure of the Civil List rose by 27% between the 1733 and 1802, with a pronounced increase from the 1770s. This is probably linked to a change in the established arrangement in 1760, when Parliament guaranteed to pay the Civil List in total in return for the income from the crown lands. In Table 5, the figures show that, from the perspective of the British state, the allowance to the Istanbul embassy was an easy burden to bear, accounting for between 1 and 2% of total diplomatic expenditure, and around 0.1% of total expenditure. Moreover, the decision to contribute from the 1740s was not part of a general increase in diplomatic expenditure on the part of the state, which averaged about 7% of Civil List expenditure across the period, and diplomatic expenditure rose by only 29% between 1733 and 1802.

Nonetheless, the government did begin, for the first time, to contribute to the general expenses of the Istanbul embassy. The ambassador did not take on a greater 'political' burden after the introduction of the government allowance in 1747 in terms of mediation or other services directly for foreign policy interests. The most compelling reason was summed up in 1741 by the chargé d'affaires, Stanhope Aspinwall, on the departure of Sir Everard Fawkener:

> The appointments for the support of this embassy being at present entirely from the Company, and their affairs not flourishing so as to add anything to the present allowance, I see plainly that His Excellency spends annually out of his own pocket near double that, only to support his family with decency. £1,300 a year (which is the appointment) is a small matter to support an embassy.[79]

This observation, that the ambassador was forced to pay for embassy expenditure out of his own pocket due to the poor level of his salary, was not limited to

[79] TNA/SP97/31 Stanhope Aspinwall to the Earl of Harrington, 5 July 1741.

Aspinwall. When Henry Grenville was granted a continuation of the government allowance previously permitted to James Porter, the secretary of state said that the money was 'to enable you to maintain the dignity of your character'.[80] Robert Liston complained that he found himself 'reduced nearly to the pay of an envoy extraordinary, with a very extensive and costly establishment, which long received custom, and perhaps the advancement of the king's service, makes it necessary to keep up'.[81] Maintaining that dignity and that establishment meant not only being able to support the basic expenses of the embassy household, but also having access to sufficient funds to conform to the diplomatic culture of the Ottoman Empire, which, as will be seen, was necessarily an expensive endeavour. The Levant Company, by the later eighteenth century, in the face of a difficult trade, was not able or willing to raise the ambassador's salary, and so the ambassador was forced to use his own finances and seek money from the government in order to cover the basic functions of his embassy. Because of this, the Elizabethan model of finance, where the Company paid for the diplomatic establishments necessary to protect their merchants, broke down, leading to the government assuming responsibility for the ambassador's salary and expenditure, severing the link between Company and embassy.

## Conclusion

As the petition of İsmail Ferruh Efendi showed, ambassadors were often concerned about the question of finance. In order for a resident embassy to function, the ambassador had to have a source of money or credit from which to pay his retinue, and to keep himself and his embassy in a sufficiently grand, or at least comfortable, manner. İsmail Ferruh's money troubles perhaps represent the common model of an ambassador relying on his (often penny-pinching) state for finance. The case of the British ambassadors in Istanbul, however, is rather different due to the intertwined relationship between commerce, finance, and diplomacy. The embassy existed to support, encourage, and protect British commerce in the Levant. That was reflected in the dual role of the ambassador as representative of the Crown and employee of the Company, and in the way that the embassy was financed until the beginning of the nineteenth century. However, the close relationship between the merchants, the Company, and the embassy meant that they were, as a group, subject to the changing fortunes of commerce. As trade routes, fashions, and technology changed, the Levant Company's trade to the Ottoman Empire, so dependent as it was on the exchange of British woollen manufactures for Ottoman raw silk, was caught out. In early 1739, Sir Everard Fawkener reported back to London that 'the affairs of the Company are at such a low ebb from the decay of their trade that they are not really in a condition to bear the expense they are already at'.[82] The sole purpose of the Company was to collect customs and dues from

80 TNA/SP97/41 Earl of Egremont to Henry Grenville, 25 June 1762.

81 TNA/FO78/15 Robert Liston to Lord Grenville, 9 June 1794.

82 TNA/SP97/30 Sir Everard Fawkener to the Duke of Newcastle, 15 March 1738/9.

the merchants who operated under its regulations in order to support the diplomatic establishments that protected their trade. As the income from that trade dropped, the Company found itself increasingly unable to balance the books, particularly given the large expenses of the embassy in Istanbul.

This situation was aggravated by the meagre salary the Company paid to the ambassador, a salary that remained largely unadjusted across the eighteenth century. With rising inflation in the Ottoman Empire due in part to depreciation of coinage, it became increasingly clear that the salary was inadequate. The ambassador needed a ready source of money in order to pay for the expenses required of the diplomatic culture of the Ottoman Empire, and it was a matter of pride as well as interest that the British should not be seen to be wanting in conforming to those norms for lack of finance. Consequently, the depression in trade in the middle of the century that hurt the Company's finances, together with the growing complaints of the ambassadors, led to increasing state intervention in the second half of the century. This intervention took the form of an allowance to the ambassador from 1746, and the grants given to fill in the holes in the Company's finances from 1768. By 1804 these government contributions led to the Crown assuming responsibility over the embassy, and by 1825 the Company, without a reason to continue as an entity, dissolved itself.

The question of the funding of diplomacy is often a neglected one, yet how much money an ambassador had available to him was crucial in determining his ability to conduct his embassy to the satisfaction of his superiors, and of the trading subjects who relied on his protection and mediation. In the case of the Istanbul embassy, it is clear that very often the ambassadors had to operate on a tight budget. With the Levantine factories operating at a loss from the 1730s, the Company became less and less willing to approve the payments for gifts, ceremonies, and journeys that were a necessary part of diplomatic practice. As the responsibility of supporting the embassy was that of the Company by charter and tradition, the government was not obliged to contribute to those expenses except in extraordinary circumstances such as mediations. This resulted in the situation of Sir Everard Fawkener having paid twice as much from his own purse towards the upkeep of the embassy and diplomacy than he had received from the Company in salary. This underscores the link between commerce and finance in the story of British diplomacy in the Ottoman Empire, and helps to explain how diplomacy was practised in British–Ottoman relations. In the text of the Capitulations, born from early commercial encounters, we saw how the unique employment of the ambassador developed as an agent of both Crown and Company, something further evidenced in the close relationship between commercial income and diplomatic finance. The way in which the embassy was funded was complex and often unreliable, and this created pressures on the running of the embassy and the implementation of the ambassador's instructions from his two employers. All of this affected how the embassy functioned on a daily basis in the framework of diplomatic practice established in the Ottoman Empire in the eighteenth century.

# 4

# Gift-giving

## Cultures of gift-exchange

When the Ottoman government appointed ambassadors to reside in London, a number of important and unprecedented questions arose. One of the most pressing was, what gifts should the sultan send to the king? This generated a number of discussions, one of which concerned cultural appropriateness. In 1799, during the ambassadorship of İsmail Ferruh Efendi, the Ottoman government dispatched a gift to George III. The grand vizier, Yusuf Ziyaüddin Paşa, wrote a note to Selim III requesting his approval for the design of this latest present:

> It was petitioned to the dust at the imperial feet for your consideration that a number of aigrettes with the base made from diamonds, by God's will, were fashioned as a gift to go to Britain [*İngiltere'ye gidecek hedīye*]. The image of the Great Word [i.e. Allah] was deemed to be contrary to the [British religious] community [*ḫilāf-ı millet*], and, although appropriate to some extent, the requirements of making a portrait from diamonds instead made it too expensive to set. Therefore, if each will have an image of the radiant *tuğra* [the sultan's caligraphic monogram] made from a reasonable number of diamonds, the value will not be compromised, the radiant *tuğra* will be honoured, [and] the top of the aigrettes will be headed with the distinction of your imperial name.[1]

This idea met with the approval of the sultan, who wrote, 'my vizier: very beautiful [*pek güzel*]! The matter has been considered well. The image of the *tuğra* is appropriate.'[2] Here we see a concern not only for the financial value of the gift (*mālīyet*) but above all for its suitability (*münāsib*). A religious image was not appropriate, but one that was a symbol of the sultan's authority, the *tuğra*, was seen as a fit decoration for the aigrette. Here, we can see the Ottoman state, at the highest level, giving careful consideration to the form

1 BOA/HAT 257/14769, Zilhicce 1213 (May 1799).

2 Ibid.

and meaning of diplomatic gifts to be sent to foreign courts. For the British embassy in Istanbul, gifts were a key link in the cycle of friendship. So far, we have seen how British–Ottoman relations were largely geared towards supporting trade, and how the British ambassadors relied on that trade for their finance. However, in order to protect the merchants, they needed to represent those merchants' interests at the Ottoman court, and the first step in that was gift-giving, one of the key practices of diplomacy in the Ottoman Empire.[3] The centrality of gifts to relations is indicated in the Ottoman narrative of the Capitulations, where the queen sent her tributary gifts (*pīşkeşleri*), and only when those gifts had been accepted (*hedāyā ḫayr-ı ḳabūlda*) could formal relations begin.

Ottoman practices were often associated with bribery and corruption, with the Earl of Winchilsea claiming that 'here a man may procure a friendship, and by corruptions create many confidents'.[4] Baron Paget noted that 'if we can't find money to give the ministers their usual presents … we who have ever passed with an esteem superior to all other nations shall make ourselves the most contemptible'. The Earl of Kinnoull lamented that 'it is impossible to succeed with the Turks without money, especially when all other nations bribe them so high'.[5] Likewise, Henry Grenville claimed that 'money is the supreme mover of all measures in this corrupt, irregular, ill-conducted government; however that might reflect upon a Christian state, it carries no infamy with it here'.[6] This attitude was popularised in publications such as Paul Rycaut's history of the Ottoman Empire. He noted that ambassadors from neighbouring (that is, often belligerent) states had their gifts reciprocated as they represented the bonds of peace, but painted a very different picture of the Ottoman attitude to other states:

> Ambassadors and representatives from other princes, whose principal design is esteemed for the promotion of trade and commerce, as the English, French, and Dutch, are always admitted with their presents, which the Turk by custom calls his right, and judges not himself obliged to return the like, esteeming his Capitulations and articles he makes with those princes, privileges and immunities granted their subjects.[7]

Similarly, James Porter's memoirs described the symbolic submission of foreign ambassadors:

3 Hedda Reindl-Kiel, 'East is East and West is West, and sometimes the twain did meet: Diplomatic gift-exchange in the Ottoman Empire' in Colin Imber, Keiko Kiyotaki & Rhoads Murphey (eds), *Frontiers of Ottoman Studies: State, Province, and the West*, 2 vols (London & New York, 2004), vol. II, 113–24.

4 TNA/SP97/17 Earl of Winchilsea to Sir Edward Nicholas, 13 September 1661.

5 SOAS/SC.PP/1/6 Baron Paget to the Consul and Gentlemen of the Factory at Smyrna, 14 October 1693; TNA/SP97/27 TNA/SP97/43 Earl of Kinnoull to the Duke of Newcastle, 12 October 1734.

6 TNA/SP97/42 Henry Grenville to the Earl of Egremont, 31 January 1763.

7 Paul Rycaut, *The History of the Present State of the Ottoman Empire* (London, 1675), 150–1.

> [Some ambassadors] have gone so far as even to pretend, that the presents they carry, and which they are obliged to give at every audience, reflect honour on themselves as the givers, but not on the Turks as receivers. Whoever is acquainted with the Oriental practice, and knows the ostentation, pride, and haughtiness of Turkish government, must know that they look upon, and consider such presents as actual tributes.[8]

Although creating exaggerated and distorted conceptions of Ottoman practices, such texts contained kernels of truth.

The Ottoman state held what Mehmet Sinan Birdal has described as 'a world-view based on a universal empire' that, at least in official and ceremonial terms, viewed the rest of the world through a very particular prism.[9] Royal correspondence was a key medium of conveying an imperial message. In a letter from the grand vizier Mehmed Emin Paşa to George III in 1769, Ottoman self-representation was expressed in what John Murray called 'a great deal of oriental bombast':

> Your friendly letter … was delivered to the exalted throne (the refuge of the mightiest princes and the shelter of the monarchs of the universe) of the most august, most venerated, most formidable, most potent, and most magnificent emperor, my master, who is the sun of the sublime empire, the splendour of august monarchy, the greatest of the great princes, the head of the sublime monarchs, specimen of superiority, hero of sovereignty, executor of justice … benefactor of equity to all the world.[10]

This was a clear statement of the Ottoman world-view, within which a distant kingdom such as Britain was only a very insignificant entity. In a later letter on the accession of Abdülhamid I (r. 1774–89), the sultan's titles were used to emphasise that fact. As well as being sultan, he was 'servant and master of honoured Mecca, resplendent Medina, and noble Jerusalem, ruler of the three great cities longed-for of the kings, that is of Istanbul, Edirne, and Bursa, of heaven-scented Damascus and peerless Cairo rare-of-ages, of all Arabia and Africa … of the Mediterranean Sea and the Black Sea, of the islands and of the shores, of the countries of Anatolia and the kingdoms of the land of the Romans', as well as naming a further forty towns, provinces, and territories.[11] The grandest titles the British sovereign could muster were nothing

8 James Porter, *Observations on the Religion, Law, Government, and Manners, of the Turks*, 2 vols (London, 1768), vol. I, 41–2.

9 Mehmet Sinan Birdal, *The Holy Roman Empire and the Ottomans: From Global Imperial Power to Absolutist States* (London & New York, 2011), 139, and for the broader discussion on Ottoman self-conception, 135–51; Robert Dankoff, *An Ottoman Mentality: The World of Evliya Çelebi* (Leiden, 2004), 7, 230–45. For a discussion on the idea of universal monarchy, see: Carina L. Johnson, *Cultural Hierarchy in Sixteenth-Century Europe: The Ottomans and Mexicans* (Cambridge, 2011), especially 74–8; Giancarlo Casale, *The Ottoman Age of Exploration* (Oxford, 2010), 29–30, 105–20.

10 TNA/SP97/45 Italian translation of a letter from Halil Paşa to George III, January 1769.

11 TNA/SP97/50 Translation of Abdülhamid I to George III, 17 Zilkade 1187 [30 January 1774]

in comparison, and this was exactly the intention of a diplomatic technique designed to put lesser rulers firmly in their place.[12] For instance, the British monarchs always employed the title 'King of Great Britain, France, and Ireland' (*Magnæ Britanniæ, Franciæ et Hiberniæ Rex*) in formal correspondence, but, outside of the text of the Capitulations, the Ottomans made no mention of 'Great Britain', using the short-hand *İngiltere* to refer to the entire polity, and when they did employ that name they assumed that *Britanya-ı Kebīr* was just another one of the king's provinces; only with some fairly persistent badgering did the ambassadors persuade the Ottomans to make any mention of the ancient British claim to the French throne, usually referring to the monarch simply as '*İngiltere ve İsḳoçya ve İrlanda ḳralı*' (king of England, Scotland, and Ireland).[13]

The aim of Ottoman diplomatic rhetoric was to demonstrate their superiority, and this was complemented by gift-exchange. The role of gifts in Ottoman diplomacy is particularly apparent from the following quote from the translation of a letter from Mehmed IV (r. 1648–87) to Charles II on the arrival in Istanbul of Sir Daniel Harvey: 'We received also your presents with satisfaction and [the ambassador's] requests and demands, whilst they are conform unto our noble laws and correspond to the friendship between us, shall be considered.'[14] This link between gifts and official business is as clear a statement of purpose as might be found in the sources on Ottoman gift-exchange. Gifts, as the narrative of the Capitulations showed, were the initial foundations upon which relations were built, and the maintenance of friendship required further gifts. Without discounting the economic role and value of gifts, their rhetorical and political importance should not be discounted.

Before examining the occasions of gift-giving, it will be useful to briefly consider the concept of gift-giving. The classic text on this subject, certainly in anthropology and sociology, is Marcel Mauss's 'Essai sur le don: forme et raison de l'échange dans les sociétés archaïques' ('Essay on the gift: form and reason for exchange in archaic societies', 1925).[15] Using examples primarily from Polynesia, Melanesia, and the Pacific Northwest, Mauss argued that gift-exchange in 'archaic' societies was a 'system of total benefits' (*système des prestations totales*). Rather than exchanges of purely economic utility, he contended, 'exchanges and contracts are made in the form of gifts, in theory

(Italian translation); TNA/EXT7/10 Abdülhamid I to George III, 17 Zilkade 1187 [30 January 1774], (Ottoman original, labelled as 'The Grand Signior's Letter to The King Received 25 June 1774 by Sigr Pisani').

12 One example of a British royal title from a letter from George II to the grand vizier is as follows: 'Giorgios-u s̱ānī ki bi-ʿināyet-i Allah taʿāla İngiltere ve Françya ve İrlandya'nıñ ḳrālı ve ṭarīḳ-ı naṣārānıñ ḥāmī ve Bruncvik ve Luneborġ duḳası ve Roma İmparāṭorluġunuñ arḫītezāryūs' ('George II by the grace of almighty God king of England, France, and Ireland, and protector of the Christian faith, Duke of Brunswick and Luneburg, and arch-treasurer of the Roman Empire'). BOA/HAT/1427/58446, 1732. See also: BOA/A.DVN.DVE.(3)/81/8, 15 Safer 1160 [25 February 1747].

13 For example see: TNA/SP97/19 Charles II to Mehmed IV, 1668.

14 TNA/SP97/19 Translation of Mehmed IV to Charles II, 1669.

15 Marcel Mauss, 'Essai sur le don: forme et raison de l'échange dans les sociétés archaïques', *L'Année Sociologique* 1 (1925), 30–86.

voluntary, but in reality given and received obligatorily'.[16] Mauss's theory remains useful in thinking about what gifts were and what they meant, and in the Ottoman context the giving of gifts was certainly more on the obligatory side of things. However, the attitudes between the Europeans who gave them and the Ottomans who received them could be quite different. One important example of this can be found in a treaty signed at Zitvatoruk in 1606 between the Ottomans and the Habsburgs. The Latin text of the Habsburg copy of the treaty read:

> 10. That for our part an ambassador is to be sent with gifts to the Turkish Emperor and the great Murat Pasha Zerdar, and he is also to send his ambassador to our most esteemed Archduke Matthias, our most gracious lord, with gifts. And when our ambassador arrives at Constantinople in order to ratify the peace, as well as the ambassador sent thence by the Turkish Emperor to our [city of] Prague, he will be with a greater number of gifts than has been the usual custom.
> 11. That now the ambassador of His Caesarean Majesty promises to bring to Constantinople a gift with the value of two-hundred thousand florins, once and for all.
> 12. That the peace will last for twenty years, calculated from the first of January to future years, and after three years both [parties] will reciprocally [send] ambassadors with gifts, without obligation, and nominate gifts of their own volition and choice.[17]

The emphasis here was on the reciprocity of gifts, but also on the fact that they would be given 'without obligation' (*sine obligatione*). The Ottoman Turkish text, however, takes a very different tone:

> And after sending tributary presents to our Lofty Porte, nothing further may be demanded for three years after the writing [of the treaty at] the River Žitava. Three years afterwards, tributary presents are to be dispatched corresponding to the requirements of friendship between the two [parties], with suitable presents to be sent together with a letter-bearing ambassador to our Exalted Footstool.[18]

Here, tributary presents were a central part of the establishment and maintenance of friendship (*pīşkeş olageldiği üzere mābeynde olan dostluḳ muḳteżāsınca münāsib olan*), and thus were non-negotiable and certainly not without obligation as the Habsburg texts suggest.

From my research into diplomatic gifts between the British and the Ottomans, I have divided them into three basic categories, and given them names that I think best reflect their function based on terms found in the

[16] Ibid., 32.

[17] *Treaties between Turkey and Foreign Powers*, 3–4.

[18] BOA, A.DVN.DVE.d 57/1, fol. 6.

sources. The Ottomans themselves used a variety of terms for gifts, but for the objects themselves usually referred to them as *hediye* (pl. *hedāyā*). The categories I have delineated are: reciprocal gift-exchange involving ceremonial robes (*ḫilʿat*); tributary gifts given at particular formal occasions or established times (*pīşkeş*); and more informal gifts aimed at relationship-building (*hibe*). The roots of these practices can found in the Turkic, Persian, Byzantine, and Islamic heritages of Ottoman elite society, but are difficult to pin down precisely. Not all gift-giving practices were recorded in the Ottoman sources, and what was there was largely to do with gifts to the sultans, and so I have had to rely more than I would have liked on the British side of the records in order to explore wider practices. With more research being done into Ottoman ideas of gifts, I hope that soon we will have a better sense of what was going on from the Ottoman records.

The lines between these forms of gift that I have delineated were often blurred, and the fluidity of type seems to have partly arisen from interpretations in Islamic jurisprudence on the subject of gifts. The main concern of Islamic jurists had been to define what constituted a permissible gift (*hiba*), or a bribe (*rashwah*, also referred to as *akl al-suḥt*, 'eating of forbidden things'). Franz Rosenthal's study into gift-giving in Islamic jurisprudence emphasised that gifts accepted by supposedly impartial figures such as judges were *suḥt*, or unwarranted gains.[19] One of Rosenthal's sources, an eleventh-century scholar, considered that 'a bribe is what a person gives in order obtain help, whereas a gift is something to which no condition is attached'.[20] However, such a ruling was by no means practical, as gifts are only in very exceptional cases given with no conditions attached. Another example given by Rosenthal was Jamal al-Din al-Qazwini's *Kitāb mufīd al-ʿulūm wa mubīd al-humūm* (*A book of useful knowledge and the eradication of concerns*). Al-Qazwini gave four kinds of permissible gifts: giving a gift in order to receive a gift in return; to honour someone of noble birth or scholarly reputation; to gain access to the ruler by giving gifts to the palace doorkeepers or officials; and in the course of official duties.[21] Essentially, a gift would be permitted if it were returned in the form of another gift or a favour; but if the occasion were used purely for personal gain on the part of the recipient, then it would be considered prohibited. Al-Qazwini noted that the attempt to define what might be considered a legitimate gift and what should be termed a bribe was a difficult issue that had been discussed by scholars at length.[22] Further work needs to be done on Ottoman ideas of corruption in the context of diplomacy and gift-giving, but a number of cases appear in the Ottoman archives, such as an extended argument over the permissibility of a portion of barley given by the treasurer Hüseyin Hüsnü Efendi to the governor of Tırhala (Trikala), Mehmed

19 Franz Rosenthal, 'Gifts and bribes: The Muslim view', *Proceedings of the American Philosophical Society* 108:2 (1964), 135–44.

20 Attributed to Abu Nasr al-Bagdadi, cited in ibid., 136.

21 Ibid., 139–40; Jamal al-Din abu Bakr al-Qazwini [attributed as al-Khawarizmi], *Kitāb mufīd al-ʿulūm wa mubīd al-humūm* (Damascus, 1906/1333), 213–14.

22 al-Qazwini, *Kitāb mufīd al-ʿulūm*, 213.

Paşa, in 1776: if it was offered as a bribe (*rüşvet*) then the governor should not accept it; if, however, it was simply a present (*hediye*), then he could take it.[23] Given the wide-ranging practices of gift-giving, discerning corruption was never an easy task, and each case had to be considered on a variety of factors.

Of the main types of gift given between the British and the Ottomans, the sort that attracted the least criticism from the British ambassadors was the exchange of official robes. The ceremonial giving of a robe, called a *ḫilʿat*, by a social superior to an inferior had a long lineage. The presentation of clothing as a sign of social and political bonds was prevalent in pre-Islamic societies, and the symbolic clothing of a subordinate emphasised dependence on the ruler even for basic necessities; presenting the gift demonstrated the ruler's power and generosity, and the act of receiving confirmed the recipient in the bonds of dependence.[24] The practice of bestowing *ḫilʿat*s became more formalised during the ʿAbbasid Caliphate, when Iranian court practices were integrated with existing traditions into a more concrete set of conventions, and the association of robe-giving with the Prophet Muhammad was established with Imam al-Busiri's influential thirteenth-century poem *Qaṣīdat al-Burda* (*Poem of the Cloak*).[25] A set of diplomatic conventions also developed more fully at this time, demonstrated in the *Kitāb al-hadāyā wa al-tuḥaf* (*Book of gifts and treasures,* ninth to fifteenth centuries), which documented gift-giving from the last days of the Sassanid Empire until the Fatimid rulers in Egypt.[26] Such sources provide wonderful evidence for diplomatic contacts involving gift-exchange between, for instance, the ʿAbbasid Caliph Harun al-Rashid (r. 786–809) and Charlemagne, and the Cordovan Umayyad Caliphate of 'Abd al-Rahman III (r. 912–29) and Iberian Franks. Textiles, animals, jewels, precious stones and metals, and expensive foodstuffs were exchanged to cement relations between different rulers, just as such gifts were used to confirm social bonds within the courts themselves.

The Ottomans also inherited gift-giving practices from the Byzantines. A tenth-century mosaic at one of the entrances to the great imperial church of Hagía Sofía (later the mosque – and now the museum – of Aya Sofya) depicts the emperors Constantine (r. 306–37) and Justinian I (r. 527–65) presenting models of the city and the church as gifts to the Virgin Mary. Such images presented an ethereal reciprocity of gift-exchange for divine protection and heavenly reward.[27] Gifts formed an important part of official Byzantine life,

[23] BOA/C.DH/147/7336, 10 Ramazan 1190 (23 October 1776).

[24] N.A. Stillman, 'K̲hila" in *Encyclopaedia of Islam 2*, vol. V, 6–7.

[25] Yedida Kalfon Stillman, *Arab Dress from the Dawn of Islam to Modern Times: A Short History*, ed. Norman A. Stillman (Leiden, 2000), 40–9, 71–5; Suzanne Pinckney Stetkevych, *The Mantle Odes: Arabic Praise Poems to the Prophet Muḥammad* (Bloomington, 2010).

[26] *Book of Gifts and Rarities: Kitāb al-Hadāyā wa al-Tuḥaf*, trans. Ghada al-Hijawi al-Qaddumi (Cambridge MA, 1996). See also: Ann Christys, 'The queen of the Franks offers gifts to the caliph al-Muktafiʾ' in Wendy Davies & Paul Fouracre (eds), *The Languages of Gift in the Early Middle Ages* (Cambridge, 2010), 149–70.

[27] Leslie Brubaker, 'The visualisation of gift giving in Byzantium and the mosaics at Hagia Sophia' in Davis & Fouracre (eds), *Languages of the Gift in the Early Middle Ages* (Cambridge, 2010), 33–61.

with a reliance on patronage networks to disseminate wealth and favour, particularly at the higher official levels where, as in the ʿAbbasid, Umayyad, and Fatimid cases, gifts would be exchanged between ruler and official on appointment.[28] The Byzantines and their Muslim neighbours engaged with each other's cultures of gift-giving. There had been a long tradition of gift-exchange between Byzantium and the Sassanid Empire, including of precious textiles, and this formed a sort of competition of superiority between the two.[29] Much as the Byzantines used gifts to display imperial wealth and power to neighbouring Christian peoples, propagandistic use of gifts was clear in the practice of the ʿAbbasid Caliphate, particularly in the reign of al-Muqtadir (r. 908–32), so that robes, horse furniture, weapons, jewellery, and coinage were used in precise ways to denote rank and favour in an imperial context.[30] Diplomatic interaction between the Byzantines and the Fatimids in Egypt demonstrates that the Byzantines conformed to the ceremonial protocol of the Fatimid court, giving gifts of precious materials, slaves (non-Christian), and animals not only to the caliph, but to members of his court that they deemed to be influential.[31]

Thus, in a number of ways, the Ottomans inherited notions of gift-giving from their Islamic and Christian predecessors, and Elias Muhanna's study on Ottoman–Mamluk gift-exchange has demonstrated how such conventions developed based on older practices.[32] Yet, it is important also to examine the Turkic heritage, which influenced so many Asian polities. Diplomatic gift-exchange occurred between Turkic tribes and settled states early on, for instance on the occasions of marriages between Türk or Uyghur nomads and their Han neighbours.[33] The aim was to demonstrate respect, so that one eighth-century T'ang envoy to a Turkic tribe who arrived without gifts was given a hostile reception; the ambassador hurriedly sent for textiles and wine, following which horses were presented in return.[34] Such conventions remained over time, with Qing rulers conforming to Kirghiz notions of gift-exchange to maintain peace on the frontiers. As Nicola Di Cosmo has argued, using gifts in

[28] Anne McClanan, *Representations of Early Byzantine Empresses: Image and Empire* (Basingstoke & New York, 2002), 96–102, 150–2; Angeliki E. Laiou & Cécile Morrison, *The Byzantine Economy* (Cambridge, 2007), 133–9, 230–40.

[29] Matthew P. Canepa, *The Two Eyes of the Earth: Art and Ritual of Kingship between Rome and Sassanian Iran* (Berkeley & Los Angeles, 2009), 154–66.

[30] Lynn Jones, 'ʿAbbasid suzerainty in the medieval Caucasus: Appropriation and adaptation of iconography and ideology', *Gesta* 43:2 (2004), 143–50.

[31] Y. Lev, 'Charity and gift giving in medieval Islam' in Miriam Fenkel & Yaacov Lev (eds), *Charity and Giving in Monotheistic Religions* (Berlin, 2009), 235–64 at 250–2.

[32] Elias I. Muhanna, 'The sultan's new clothes: Ottoman–Mamluk gift exchange in the fifteenth century', *Muqarnas* 27 (2010), 189–206.

[33] Carter V. Findley, *The Turks in World History* (Oxford, 2005), 52–4.

[34] Edward H. Schafer, *The Golden Peaches of Samarkand: A Study of T'ang Exotics* (Berkeley & Los Angeles, 1963), 63–4 and passim. For later examples between the Ulus of Djochi and Mamluk Egypt, see: Alsu A. Arslanova, 'Notes on the history of political relations between the Ulus of Djochi and the Uluses of the Khulaguyids' in Elena V. Boikova & Rostislav B. Rybakov (eds), *Kinship in the Altaic World: Proceedings of the 48th PIAC* (Wiesbaden, 2006), 25–42 especially 28–9.

defining such relations 'filtered' notions of subordination through conventions of equal reciprocity.[35] Textiles were central in the solidifying of political and social bonds, particularly in Mongol society, where silks and brocades were given by the ruler to his officials on special occasions, and where belts and hats were exchanged between rival rulers to demonstrate friendship. The giving of clothing to social inferiors solidified the symbolism of ruler as provider, and acceptance of the gift meant acceptance of his authority.[36] In the Seljuk context, the importance of furs was established from the eleventh century, particularly sable furs, a commodity that would assume great significance in Ottoman gift-giving.[37] In a later example, from eighteenth-century Uzbekistan, one of the high praises given to Eltüzer Khan of Khwarezm was that 'there is no poor man who would not be distinguished by a robe of honour from the wardrobe of his gifts'.[38]

This fusion of traditions within Ottoman practice is also apparent in the other major Islamic powers of the early modern period, the Mughals and the Safavids.[39] The one overriding concept common in both Iran and India was that of *pīshkash* (in the Ottoman context, *pīşkeş*). This term relates to gifts in the form of tribute from a social inferior to a superior, and had its origins in Mongol levies.[40] Anne Lambton's study demonstrated the economic importance of *pīshkash* gifts, and the practice's lineage in Persian, Islamic, and Turkic customs.[41] *Pīshkash* could form a regular sort of tribute, or would be given on formal events, such as a visit by the shah to a minister, the appointment of a new minister, a royal birth or circumcision, or large public festivals, in the Iranian case particularly the New Year celebration of *Nawrūz*. Such *pīshkash* ensured continuing royal generosity in the form of continued land grants or official positions, and of course ensured an annual income from

35 Nicola Di Cosmo, 'Kirghiz nomads on the Qing frontier: Tribute, trade, or gift-exchange?' in Nicola Di Cosma & Don J. Wyatt (eds), *Political Frontiers, Ethnic Boundaries, and Human Geographies in Chinese History* (London & New York, 2003), 351–72 especially 365–6.

36 Thomas T. Allsen, *Commodity and Exchange in the Mongol Empire: A Cultural History of Islamic Textiles* (Cambridge, 1997), 46–70. See also D.G. Tor, 'The Islamization of Central Asia in the Sāmānid era and the reshaping of the Muslim world', *Bulletin of the School of Oriental and African Studies* 72:2 (2009), 279–99; Edward A. Allworth, *The Modern Uzbeks: From the Fourteenth Century to the Present: A Cultural History* (Stanford CA, 1999), 24, 39, 69, 80–95.

37 Janet Martin, *Treasure of the Land of Darkness: The Fur Trade and its Significance for Medieval Russia* (Cambridge, 1986), 17–18, 103–6.

38 Shir Muhamad Mirab Munis & Muhammad Riza Mirab Agahi, *Firdaws al-Iqbāl: History of Khorezm*, trans. Yuri Bregel (Leiden, 1999), 9–12.

39 Stewart Gordon, 'Introduction: Ibn Battuta and a region of robing' in Stewart Gordon (ed.), *Robes of Honour: Khil'at in Pre-Colonial and Colonial India* (Oxford, 2003), 1–30; Bernardo A. Michael, 'When soldiers and statesmen meet: "Ethnographic moments" on the frontiers of empire, 1800–15' in Gordon, *Robes of Honour*, 80–94 at 80–5; Finbarr B. Flood, *Objects of Translation: Material Culture and Medieval 'Hindu-Muslim' Encounter* (Princeton NJ, 2009), 74–9; Gavin R.G. Hambly, 'The emperor's clothes: Robing and "robes of honour" in Mughal India' in Gordon (ed.), *Robes of Honour*, 31–49.

40 Ann K.S. Lambton, *Continuity and Change in Medieval Persia* (Albany NY, 1988), 185–220.

41 Anne Lambton, ' "Pīshkash": Present or tribute?', *Bulletin of the School of Oriental and African Studies* 57:1 (1994), 145–58.

the shah's wealthier subjects. *Pīshkash* was therefore more than a present, but a formalised presentation that linked the ruler with his subjects, and this system was a key part of relations between the Ottoman state and its provincial subjects and foreign residents.

Ottoman conventions of gift-giving, therefore, had a mixed heritage, sharing much in common with other contemporary polities. It is also notable that in these economies, which functioned without great amounts of specie, gift-exchange could be a major source of material wealth. Cash salaries, including salaries paid by the Ottoman government, usually only formed a part, and possibly a rather meagre part, of an individual's total income.[42] Higher officials might gain revenue from land ownership, but these incomes were not always guaranteed with frequent famines and rebellions. Therefore, even into the nineteenth century, gifts from the sultan to his subjects remained a prominent feature of Ottoman elite society, so that occasional imperial benevolence (*ʿaṭiye-i seniye*) continued to be the basis of many officials' income and was even formally entered into the state accounts from the 1840s.[43] Gifts were a central function of economic exchange, and diplomatic gifts in particular could be a lucrative source of income for different levels of Ottoman elite society.

The significance of gifts in British–Ottoman relations makes more sense given this wider political and social context. They were a means of conveying messages of power and circulating wealth, but also, as we have seen from the Capitulations, served as a benchmark for and facilitator of ideas of inter-state friendship. Therefore, on the whole, the British were obliged to conform to the conventions of Ottoman gift-giving, much as the Habsburgs were obliged to give gifts in a certain form set in the Treaty of Zitvatoruk. Moreover, the British would have been familiar with different forms of gift-giving in their own and other societies.[44] There has been a recent set of studies made into early modern European gift-exchange, including with other cultural traditions, and there is increasing scholarship on cultures of gift-giving by European states, including with the Ottomans.[45] That gifts were a feature of British

[42] Jane Hathaway, *The Arab Lands Under Ottoman Rule, 1516–1800* (Harlow, 2008), 63–5.

[43] Candan Badem, *The Ottoman Crimean War (1853–1856)* (Leiden, 2010), 399; Carter V. Findley, 'The legacy of tradition to reform: Origins of the Ottoman foreign ministry', *International Journal of Middle East Studies* 1:4 (1970), 334–57 at 348; Linda Darling, *Revenue-Raising and Legitimacy: Tax Collection and Finance Administration in the Ottoman Empire, 1560–1660* (Leiden, 1996).

[44] Natalie Zemon Davis, *The Gift in Sixteenth Century France* (Oxford, 2000), especially 173-109, 142–66; Irma Thoen, *Strategic Affection? Gift-Exchange in Seventeenth Century Holland* (Amsterdam, 2007), especially 97–150; Ilana Krausman Ben-Amos, *The Culture of Giving: Informal Support and Gift-Exchange in Early Modern England* (Cambridge, 2008), especially 45–81, 145–241.

[45] Christian Windler, *La diplomatie comme expérience de l'autre: consuls français au Maghreb (1700–1840)* (Geneva, 2002), 170–8; Christian Windler, 'Diplomatie et interculturalité: les consuls français à Tunis, 1700–1840', *Revue d'Historie Moderne et Contemporaine* 50:4 (2003), 63–91; Christian Windler, 'Diplomatic history as a field for cultural analysis: Muslim–Christian relations in Tunis, 1700–1840', *The Historical Journal* 44:1 (2001), 79–106; Maureen Cassidy-Geiger (ed.), *Fragile Diplomacy: Meissen Porcelain for European Courts ca. 1710–63* (New Haven CT, 2007); Michael Elia Yonan, *Empress Maria Theresa and the Politics of Habsburg*

diplomacy is clear from the Civil List accounts, with a total of 2.8% of British diplomatic expenditure between 1728 and 1802 spent on gifts to ambassadors resident in London, on the conclusion of treaties, or on embassies to and from the North African Regencies and Morocco. These accounts barely covered a fraction of the real expenditure on diplomatic gifts, particularly on relations with non-European polities.

Further examples can be found from the expanding European commercial sphere, and from missionary groups. For instance, the Jesuit mission of Matteo Ricci to the Wànlì Emperor in the late sixteenth century presented gifts such as polyglot bibles, astrolabes, maps, and clocks to establish social relationships.[46] Ricci believed in accommodating local customs, but British diplomats often resented such practices as foreign impositions, because of the inferior status British envoys were placed in as a result. The embassy of George Macartney to the Qiánlóng Emperor, two centuries after Ricci, was obliged to conform to Qing court ritual, and the British were put in their place by the emperor's letter to George III, which thanked the king for showing his humble devotion by sending 'offerings of your country's produce'.[47] This has many echoes of Ottoman practice and rhetoric. In colonial and imperial contexts, European states encountered a variety of gift-giving conventions. Across North America, the British and French adopted local gift-giving practices to encourage trade and form alliances; these gifts were crucial in spreading wealth and prestige, and there was competition between the British and French colonists to provide the best gifts, particularly to access the lucrative fur trade.[48] Across the Atlantic, on the trading outposts of West Africa, Portuguese, British, French, and Dutch merchants found themselves only able to deal with the powerful slaving polities through large amounts of gift-giving. On the one hand, this

*Imperial Art* (University Park, 2011), 45–64; Diana Carrió-Invernizzi, 'Gift and diplomacy in seventeenth-century Spanish Italy', *The Historical Journal* 51:4 (2008), 881–99; Harriet Rudolph, 'The material culture of diplomacy: The impact of objects on the dynamics of Habsburg–Ottoman negotiations at the Sublime Porte (1530–1650)' in Gunda Barth-Scalmani, Harriet Rudolph, & Christian Steppan (eds), *Politische Kommunkation zwischen Imperien: Der diplomatische Aktionsraum Südost- und Osteuropa* (Innsbruck, 2013), 211–37.

46 Jonathan D. Spence, *The Memory Palace of Matteo Ricci* (London, 1985), 179–95; Mary Laven, *Mission to China: Matteo Ricci and the Jesuit Encounter with the East* (London, 2011), 69–98, 151–60.

47 James L. Hevia, *Cherishing Men from Afar: Qing Guest Ritual and the Macartney Embassy of 1793* (Durham NC, 2002); Mark C. Elliott, *Emperor Qianlong: Son of Heaven, Man of the World* (Harlow & New York, 2009), 138–42.

48 Elisabeth Tooker, *An Ethnography of the Huron Indians, 1615–1649* (Syracuse NY, 1991); John C. Ewers, *Indian Life on the Upper Missouri* (Norman, 1968); Richard White, *The Middle Ground: Indians, Empires, and Republics in the Great Lakes Region, 1650–1815* (Cambridge, 2011), especially 94–141; Wilbur R. Jacobs, *Diplomacy and Indian Gifts: Anglo-French Rivalry Along the Ohio and Northwest Frontiers, 1748–1763* (Stanford CA, 1950); Arthur J. Ray, *Indians in the Fur Trade* (Toronto, 1998), especially 65–87; John Smolenski, 'The death of Sawantaeny and the problem of justice on the frontier' in William A. Pencak & Daniel K. Richter (eds), *Friends and Enemies in Penn's Woods: Indians, Colonists, and the Racial Reconstruction of Pennsylvania* (University Park, 2004), 104–28; Joseph M. Hall, *Zamumo's Gifts: Indian–European Exchange in the Colonial Southeast* (University Park, 2009).

formed part of a discourse of Europeans honouring local rulers upon whom their commerce depended, and on the other constituted a sort of tributary tax, common to polities such as Asante, Benin, Fante, and Dahomey.[49] The British encountered also gift-giving conventions throughout the Islamic world. From their earliest contacts with the Mughals, the British had conformed to their court etiquette. Both the English East India Company (EIC) and the Dutch Vereenigde Oost-Indische Compagnie conformed to Mughal gift-exchange, receiving *khilʿat* and giving tribute (*nazr*), as well as to the conventions of smaller polities across South and South-East Asia.[50] In the EIC's heartland of Bengal, gifts of cash, firearms, clocks, telescopes, and other luxury products were essential in maintaining alliances.[51] Ania Loomba, in her fascinating assessment of early gift-exchange between the British and Mughals, beautifully summarised the British position: '[t]he English became gift-givers in an attempt to secure trading privileges in the East, but their "pearls" were treated as glass beads by Eastern emperors'.[52] Things began to change from

49 Ivana Elbl, 'Cross-cultural trade and diplomacy: Portuguese relations with West Africa, 1441–1521', *Journal of World History* 3:2 (1992), 165–204; Kawsi Konadu, *The Akan Diaspora in the Americas* (Oxford, 2010), 85–8, 121–3; Joseph K. Adjaye, 'Indigenous African diplomacy: An Asante case study', *The International Journal of African Historical Studies* 18:3 (1985), 487–503; Larry W. Yarak, 'A Dutch embassy to Asante in 1857: The journal of David Mill Graves', *History in Africa* 24 (1997), 363–80; Charles Piot, 'Of slaves and the gift: Jabre sale of kin during the era of the slave trade', *The Journal of African History* 37:1 (1996), 31–49; Harvey M. Feinberg, 'Africans and Europeans in West Africa: Elminans and Dutchmen on the Gold Coast during the eighteenth century', *Transactions of the American Philosophical Society* 79:7 (1989), 1–186; Robert B. Edgerton, *The Fall of the Asante Empire* (London & New York, 1995), 19–28, 45–7, 75–6, 125–32; T.C. McCaskie, *State and Society in Pre-Colonial Asante* (Cambridge, 1995); G. Ugo Nowkeji, *The Slave Trade and Culture in the Bight of Biafra: An African Society in the Atlantic World* (Cambridge, 2010); P.C. Emmer, *The Dutch Slave Trade, 1500–1850* (New York, 2006), 48–9; Rebecca Shumway, *The Fante and the Transatlantic Slave Trade* (Rochester NY, 2011); Elishée Soumonni, 'The compatibility of the slave and palm oil trades in Dahomey, 1818–1858' in Robin Law (ed.) *From Slave Trade to 'Legitimate' Commerce: The Commercial Transition in Nineteenth-Century West Africa* (Cambridge, 1995), 78–92.

50 Sudipta Sen, *Empire of Free Trade: The East India Company and the Making of the Colonial Market Place* (Philadelphia, 1998), 16, 70–2; Douglas E. Haynes, *Rhetoric and Ritual in Colonial India: The Shaping of a Public Culture in Surat City, 1852–1928* (Berkeley & Los Angeles, 1991), 86–91; Wil O. Dijk, *Seventeenth-Century Burma and the Dutch East India Company, 1634–1680* (Singapore, 2006), 105–6 and passim; Sanjay Subramanyam, 'Frank submissions: The Company and the Mughals between Sir Thomas Roe and Sir William Norris' in H.V. Bowen, Margarette Lincoln, & Nigel Rigby (eds), *The Worlds of the East India Company* (Woodbridge & Rochester NY, 2002), 69–96; Els M. Jacobs, *Merchant in Asia: The Trade of the Dutch East Company during the Eighteenth Century* (Leiden, 2006), 42–66 and passim.

51 Kathleen Gough, *Rural Society in Southeast India* (Cambridge, 1981); H.B. Vashishta, *Land Revenue and Public Finance in Maratha Administration* (Delhi, 1975); C.A. Bayly, *Rulers, Townsmen and Bazaars: North Indian Society in the Age of British Expansion, 1770–1870* (Cambridge, 1983); K.N. Chitnis, *Glimpses of Maratha Socio-Economic History* (New Delhi, 1994); Norbert Peabody, *Hindu Kingship and Polity in Precolonial India* (Cambridge, 2003); John R. McLane, *Land and Local Kingship in Eighteenth-Century Bengal* (Cambridge, 1993).

52 Ania Loomba, 'Of gifts, ambassadors, and copy-cats: Diplomacy, exchange, and difference in early modern India' in Brinda Charry & Gitanjali Shahni (eds), *Emissaries in Early Modern Literature and Culture: Mediation, Transmission, Traffic, 1550–1700* (Farnham, 2009), 41–76 at 41.

the 1770s, as Natasha Eaton has convincingly argued, with a tightening of the EIC's finances following near-financial collapse.[53] The EIC 1773 Regulating Act aimed to remove British subjects from local gift-giving conventions, and, indeed, stop British abuse of such practices, but it was not until the 1840s that the British ceased to give *nazr* and receive *khil'ats*.[54]

In the wider Ottoman context, the British gave gifts on numerous occasions to the North African Regencies. These were given and received equally as part of a formal court structure, but were viewed by the British as tributary gifts to maintain peace treaties and protect British shipping.[55] A number of North African ambassadors came to Britain on various missions in the eighteenth century, including Khwajah Hassan from Tripoli (1729), al-Hajji al-Sayyid Muhammad from Algiers (1731), Yusuf Khwajah from Tripoli (1735), al-Sayyid Muhammad Mustafa from Tunis (1736), Abd al-Qadir Perez from Morocco (1742), and İbrahim Ağa from Tripoli (1750). They and their retinue received gifts paid from the Civil List, and other gifts were paid for by other means, the British consuls in North Africa having generous allowances to pay for gifts. This situation changed over time, and regular Royal Navy patrols in that part of the Mediterranean from the 1770s seem to have negated the perceived necessity of continuing former *pīşkeş*-like gifts from the British state, which had averaged £550 on each occasion.

The British engaged in gift-giving practices throughout the world, be it with local rulers in Canada and North Africa or with great imperial figures in West Africa, East Asia, and South Asia. That they had to give gifts in order to receive and maintain diplomatic relations with the Ottomans was, therefore, not unusual. The Ottoman conventions of gift-exchange, inherited and developed from earlier Islamic, Byzantine, and Turkic practices, were also not particularly alien; gifts defined and developed social bonds, played an important role in economic exchange in an economy with limited specie, and formed a central function of the ceremonial of state power. The British ambassadors in Istanbul were therefore not encountering an arbitrary or inherently corrupt system designed to cheat unwitting foreigners, but a sophisticated and long-established set of conventions. Moreover, with the detailed records of the Levant Company, it is possible to see just how far the British did conform to those conventions, and in what ways British–Ottoman diplomatic gift-exchange is indicative of the nature of their relations. In the diplomatic framework, gifts formed a junction that saw the fees gathered from the British Levant merchants transformed into silk and brocade robes, watches, and foodstuffs in order to make the displays of amity required by the Ottoman idea of diplomatic friendship.

53 Natasha Eaton, 'Between mimesis and alterity: Art, gift and diplomacy in colonial India, 1770–1800', *Comparative Studies in Society and History* 46:4 (2004), 816–44.

54 Thomas R. Metcalf, *Ideologies of the Raj* (Cambridge, 1995), 49–51.

55 G.E. Aylmer, 'Slavery under Charles II: The Mediterranean and Tangier', *The English Historical Review* 114:456 (1999), 378–88; Nabil Matar, *Turks, Moors and Englishmen in the Age of Discovery* (New York & Chichester, 1999); Nabil Matar, *Britain and Barbary, 1589–1689* (Gainesville, 1998).

## 'Presents are so necessary in carrying on business in the east': Occasions of gift-giving

The accounts of the British embassy in Istanbul contain a huge amount of information on gifts given throughout the eighteenth century by British ambassadors at the imperial court.[56] Through analysing well over ten thousand gifts, I have attempted to reconstruct the nature of this sort of gift-giving, and to discern patterns across the century. Where possible, I have consulted Ottoman sources as well, but the level of detail and consistency of record-keeping make the British records the most accessible for what I wanted to achieve. The results show the variety of gifts given and the occasions on which they were presented, but also give insights into the workings of the imperial court and consumption trends, as well as political developments.

It seems apt to begin with the most formal and ancient sort of diplomatic gift-giving occasions in the Ottoman Empire, those related to the receiving of *ḫilʿat*s. Those robes, in their very design as signs of patronage and benevolence, were only given in the diplomatic context by the sultan and grand vizier, and therefore on such occasions involved the ambassador coming formally into the imperial presence. In practice this usually only took place on the arrival of a new ambassador. The information in the embassy's accounts provides figures in terms of quality, that is, what sort of gift was given, and quantity, how much of each kind. Details survive for the gifts presented on the arrival of nine of the ambassadors in the period of the accounts (1693–803), representing two-thirds of the ambassadors: Baron Paget (1693); Sir Robert Sutton (1702); the Earl of Kinnoull (partial, 1730); Sir Everard Fawkener (1736); John Murray (1766); Sir Robert Ainslie (1776); Robert Liston (1794); the Earl of Elgin (1798); and William Drummond (1803). Together, these figures give a useful insight into the sort of gifts given on this occasion. The ceremonial of the ambassador's arrival will be discussed in detail in the next chapter, but in brief it consisted of two official audiences, the first with the grand vizier, and the second with the sultan. The gifts that were given by the British on both occasions consisted primarily of kaftans, essentially the Persian equivalent of the Arabic *ḫilʿat*, and the British received in return a number of *ḫilʿat*s presented by the sultan. In the first audience with the grand vizier and the members of the *divan*, a large number of officials received gifts of kaftans. At the top of the list, perhaps unsurprisingly, was the grand vizier himself, who received an average of twenty kaftans of varying qualities. Beneath him were three great officers of state present on these occasions: the grand vizier's *kahya*; the *reisülküttab* (commonly shortened in the English texts to *reis efendi*); and the *çavuşbaşı*.

The *kahya* was nominally the grand vizier's steward who became something like an interior minister as the century wore on, and in reflection of his growing importance went from receiving an average of five kaftans in the first part of the century to an average of eight in the second half. The *reisülküttab*

[56] TNA/SP105/202–6, 1730–1816; TNA/SP105/177–91, 1693–1804. The years missing are: 1694, 1699–1701, 1705–7, 1718–22, 1725–9, and 1745–65.

developed into a kind of a foreign minister, and was often the official with whom the ambassadors would have the most regular contact; the average number of kaftans he received also increased from an average of five before 1750 to nine afterwards. The çavuşbaşı was head of the imperial ushers, and played a very important role in court ceremonial, as well as being an influential figure in government circles, and he received an average of five kaftans throughout the period. The grand vizier and those three major officials also received the richest qualities of silk and satin kaftans (the details of which are discussed below), so that the value of their gifts was not simply in the quantity but also in the quality.

On a tier below those high-ranking men were four other officials associated with government administration. The first was the *mektubcu*, a senior secretary of the governmental administration of the Bab-ı Ali, and he received four kaftans on each occasion following the first gifts given to a holder of that particular office in 1736. The second senior administrator was the *beylikci*, one of the heads of the imperial chancery who generally received a cloth and a satin kaftan. A third and crucial official in the diplomat context was the *baş tercüman*, the head translator. As with the *mektubcu*, he only began receiving gifts from 1736 onwards, and the number of kaftans presented to him alternated between four and five. The final two were senior administrative secretaries known as the *büyük tezkereci* and the *küçük tezkereci*, the more senior *büyük tezkereci* receiving three kaftans in the earlier period, and five in the later period; the *küçük tezkereci* received only two kaftans before 1750 and an average of four in the second half of the century.

A number of lower-ranking officials who regularly received gifts on the occasion of the ambassador's first audience with the grand vizier were generally from the retinue of the higher-ranking officers. For example, the secretary, treasurer, and intendant of the ushers (the *çavuşlar katibi*, *çavuşbaşı haznadarı*, and the *çavuşlar emini*) who accompanied the çavuşbaşı each received a cloth kaftan. Other officials present were involved in the ceremonial protocol of the imperial court, such as the *kapıcılar kahyası* (intendant of the doorkeepers) and the *selam ağası* (master of ceremonies), and its security, such as the *odabaşı* and the *muhzir ağası*, the first two receiving one satin and one cloth kaftan, the last two receiving just one cloth kaftan each. Until 1776 the *mir-i ahor* (master of the horse) also received a cloth kaftan, along with an official in charge of the imperial wardrobe, the *kaftancı*, who suitably received a cloth and a satin kaftan. Overall, the total number of officials of the grand vizier's court who received kaftans from the British stood at between fifteen and twenty before 1750, and between twenty and twenty-three in the second part of the century, an average of sixty-five kaftans being distributed on this occasion.

The second part of that ceremony involved the ambassador presenting himself to the sultan. The sultan, naturally, was the largest recipient of kaftans, being presented with no less than fifty of the finest cloth and silk on each of the six occasions noted in the accounts between 1693 and 1776, and subsequently received a slightly lower total of forty kaftans. The imperial clerks made a careful note of the quality of fabric of the kaftans given to the sultan, so that, for example, in the note of the gifts given on Sir William Trumbull's audience in 1688, the Topkapı Palace registers record fifty kaftans comprising ten each of brocade (*dībā*), velvet (*ḳaṭīfe*), tabby (*ḫāre*), broadcloth (*çūḳa*), and satin (*aṭlāṣ*).[57] The year 1776 would appear to be a date of some cutbacks in this respect, as two major court officials, the *teşrifatcı* (master of protocol) and the *pişkeşci* (collector of *pīşkeş*), who had previously each received a satin and wool kaftan, stopped being presented gifts after that point, although the sultan's *kaftancı*, who began receiving the same gifts from 1730, did not lose his share. Aside from the *asesbaşı* (head of the watchmen) who received a cloth kaftan in the second half of the century, only an average of five officials received kaftans from the British ambassador. Although an average of fifty-one kaftans were distributed at this ceremonial 82% of them went to the sultan himself.

In return for the gifts presented to the sultan, that monarch in turn distributed a number of garments to the British ambassador and his retinue as *ḫilʿat*. The Ottoman ceremonial and accounting records provide details of the quality and quantity of the *ḫilʿat*s given to the ambassador himself, and the bulk was for distribution among his attending officers. For instance, the entry for John Murray's audience in Muharrem 1180 (June 1766) noted that the ambassador was presented with the gift of a new (as in specially made) *ḫilʿat* that was a most particular and personal gift of the sultan (*ḫilʿat-ı ḫaṣṣü'l-ḫaṣṣ-ı cedīd*), and that his gentlemen (*erkān*), translator (*tercümān*), and retinue (*etbāʿ*) were presented with a variety of robes (*ḫilʿat-ı mutenevviʿa*) consisting of twenty garments.[58] These would be distributed at the audiences, and the British ambassadors were always careful to ensure that they received as near as possible the same number as their political rivals, the Dutch and French. The symbolism of this giving is clear in the Ottoman narratives. For instance, at the audience of leave (*vedāʿ*) of Henry Grenville in 1765, the record reads 'the ambassador of Britain … came to the Sublime Porte into the presence of the grand vizier [and] the esteemed ambassador and his dependents were clothed [*ilbās olunan*]'.[59] The clothing of the ambassador and his retinue was a symbol of their dependence on the benevolence of the Ottoman state.

In the earlier part of the period under examination, the ambassadors reported back to London on how many *ḫilʿat*s had been bestowed. Seventeen were given at the Earl of Winchilsea's audience, which he proudly noted was one more than usual, and the same number was given at Baron Chandos's audience twenty years later.[60] Trumbull and his retinue were honoured with twenty-five kaftans at his audience with the grand vizier and a further thirty

57 BOA/TS.MA.d 22, 1099 [1687], fol. 7.

58 BOA/A.)d 352, 1210–12 [1795/6–1797/8], fol. 12.

59 Ibid.

60 TNA/SP97/17 A narrative of ye sucksesse of my Voyage from Smirna to Constantinople, my arrivall there, ye manner of my entry to Pera, and my audience with ye Grand Vizier and Grand Seignour, March 1661; BL, Stowe 219 Baron Chandos to the Levant Company, 23 September 1681.

when he met with the sultan.[61] These large numbers seem to have become commonplace; Sir Robert Sutton and his gentlemen received thirty-two (which he noted to be more than customary) from the grand vizier, and thirty-five from the sultan, with a similar number of thirty being received on the first occasion in the Earl of Kinnoull's time (he only specified 'several' being given at his audience with the sultan which may suggest the number was less than usual).[62] After the 1730s, the ambassadors seem to have become less concerned with the number of ordinary kaftans given as *ḫilʿat* to their retinue, and instead aimed to ensure that they received a particular honour known as the *semmūr*. The *semmūr* was a kaftan of particularly rich material lined with a sable fur trimming.[63] This sort of kaftan was hugely valuable, due to its symbolic value and the monetary value of the fur itself, the sable being a species of marten found only in the depths of Siberia. Describing the seizure of the assets of a deposed *reisülküttab* in 1663, Winchilsea noted how the ninety sable kaftans in his possession were worth the same as sixty of his finest horses.[64] Until the middle of the eighteenth century, the practice of giving sable kaftans in a diplomatic context had been almost entirely limited to the signing of peace treaties.[65] Baron Paget received forty sable skins from the Russian ambassador at Carlowitz in 1699, and a Russian ambassador brought 800 sable skins as a gift for Mustafa II in 1701 following the conclusion of peace.[66]

It was therefore with some surprise that Sir Everard Fawkener learned in March 1737 that the new Dutch ambassador had been gifted a sable kaftan at the presentation of new credential letters relating to a proposed mediation of peace. This was, Fawkener wrote to London, an honour 'never shown, but on the arrival after a war of a minister with that character, or on some very uncommon occasion', and he insisted very strongly to the Ottoman government that he should receive the same honour.[67] This set a precedent, so that even the new ambassador from the Two Sicilies in 1741 insisted on being presented a

[61] TNA/SP97/20 A Relation of what passed at the Audience which His Excellency Sir William Trumbull Lord Ambassadour for His Matie of Great Britain residing at Constantinople had of the Vizier, December 1687; BL, Add. 72554 An Acct of his Excys Aud:ce of ye G. Sigr, August 1688.

[62] TNA/SP97/21 A Relation of the Publick Audience wch Sir Robert Sutton Ambassadr from his Majesty of Great Brittaine to the Ottoman Port had of the Grand Vizir March 1702; TNA/SP97/21 A Relation of the Publick Audience wch Sr Robt Sutton Ambassdr from his Majty of Great Brittaine to ye Ottoman Port had of ye Grand Sigr, 10 March x1701/2, March 1702; TNA/SP97/26 Account of His Excellency the Earl of Kinnouls Visits to the Grand Vizir and Grand Signior, May 1730.

[63] For an illustration, see: NPG, PC/3797 Francis Smith, *An Audience of the Grand Signor* (c. 1755–65).

[64] See Martin, *Treasure of the Land of Darkness*, 166–8. Winchilsea gave the value of the ninety sable kaftans as at least 90,000 'dollars', and that seventeen of the deposed official's finest horses had been valued at 1,500 'dollars' each.

[65] See, for example: BOA/İE.HR/6/586, 9 Ramazan 1111 [27 February 1700]; BOA/C.HR 59/2901, 11 Receb 1153 [1 October 1740].

[66] SOAS/SC.PP/3/19 Baron Paget to Robert Sutton, 31 January 1698/9; SOAS/SC.PP/4/21 Baron Paget to George Stepney, 4/15 July 1701.

[67] TNA/SP97/29 Sir Everard Fawkener to the Duke of Newcastle, 31 March 1737.

sable *ḫilʿat*.[68] The Ottoman government was wary of the expense this might entail, and in 1751 attempted to officially abandon this new practice, but both the French and Venetian ambassadors were subsequently given sable kaftans and, so strong was the rule of precedent, that William Pitt specifically ordered Porter to put a stop to any proposed changes.[69]

The exchange of kaftans between the British and Ottomans as part of the gift process of *ḫilʿat* was only slightly unequal, so that the 77 kaftans Sir Robert Sutton received from the sultan and grand vizier in 1702 were in exchange for 106 given to Ottoman officials; this ratio decreased slightly over time in part due to the decreased size of the ambassador's retinue, so that John Murray in 1766 received 42 kaftans at his two audiences for which he gave 148 to the courts of the grand vizier and sultan. Murray's audiences also show a change in that an increasing amount of non-textile gifts were being presented by the British. It is frustrating that the period between 1744 and 1765 is missing in the accounts, as it would have been helpful to see exactly when this practice began. A whole new convention of gift-giving in the *ḫilʿat* context was being developed in the second half of the eighteenth century. Unlike the case of the EIC's 1773 Regulating Act, such non-textile gifts did not replace but supplemented the Ottoman conventions of *ḫilʿat*. These gifts were few in number, but of a great expense, such as bejewelled boxes of gold and silver, rare medicines, intricate table clocks, and watches cased in precious metals. This reflects a change in the role of gifts at the Ottoman court. If before it was important that a wide range of the imperial retinue would receive valuable gifts on these formal occasions, the growing professionalisation of the Ottoman bureaucracy in the later eighteenth century meant that less emphasis was placed on this sort of moveable capital.

Such were the gifts given at the occasions on which the British ambassador and his officers received *ḫilʿat*s from the sultan and grand vizier. There was, at least in this case, an element of material reciprocity in that the British received almost (but not quite) as good as they got. More importantly, this was still part of imperial theatre, with the British having to present their gifts before the sultan would bestow and renew his friendship, and they would be ushered into his presence donning the gifts he had bestowed as a sign of their acceptance of the sultan's authority and proof of the maintenance of friendly relations. These particular occasions were – with the rare exception of successful peace mediations – the only occasions that might be reasonably referred to as ones of gift-exchange. As the second major form of gift, *pīşkeş*, demonstrates, it was usually more a case of British gift-giving.

*Pīşkeş* might be referred to as a tributary gift, an official gift, but it categorically was not a bribe. This is despite the assertions of several modern histories

68 TNA/SP97/31 Sir Everard Fawkener to the Duke of Newcastle, 4 May 1741. The same honour was granted to the Danish ambassador on the establishment of relations in 1758: BOA/C.HR 24/1188, 13 Cemaziülahir 1171 [21 February 1758].

69 TNA/SP97/35 James Porter to the Duke of Bedford, 22 April 1751; TNA/SP97/35 James Porter to the Earl of Holdernesse, 23 November 1751; TNA/SP97/40 James Porter to William Pitt, 2 March 1758; TNA/SP97/40 William Pitt to James Porter, 26 May 1758.

of the Balkans, as it was generally associated with the annual fee paid by the heads of the various non-Muslim communities to renew their *berāts*.[70] Indeed, the giving and receiving of *ḫilʿat*s was a particular form of *pīşkeş*, in a sense the official gifts of the British monarch that placed them within the Ottoman hierarchical framework. There were more regular occasions, however, in which we can see the idea of *pīşkeş* more clearly at work. In the case of the British, and indeed other European ambassadors resident in Istanbul, the time for their annual tribute to the Ottoman state was on the festival of *Ramazan Bayramı* (Eid al-Fitr), called the 'Great Bairam' by the British. The three-day celebration at the end of the holy month of Ramadan was an occasion of public feasting and celebration. For the majority of the eighteenth century, it was the time of year that the British had to provide a large number of gifts to various members of the Ottoman court, and was a major part of British gift expenditure, averaging at about 29% of those expenses across the century.

As in the case of the occasions of giving *ḫilʿat*, textile goods dominated British gift-giving at the Great Bairam, and the recipients were largely the same as on the occasion of the ambassador's arrival. One major difference was that the sultan only received a token gift, at least comparatively, being presented with just a single broadcloth kaftan. The same was given on this occasion to the *bostancıbaşı*, in theory the head of the palace gardeners, but in fact leader of the palace guard. Otherwise, the quality and quantity of gift-giving on that festival remained generally consistent between 1695 (the first complete record of the *bayram* gifts in the accounts) and 1773. The officials receiving kaftans and measures of cloth were almost identical to those who received such gifts at the ambassador's arrival, but the amounts, at least for the higher officials, tended to be less than on that occasion. The grand vizier, for instance, received twelve cloth kaftans and other richer fabrics of brocade, silk, and satin. In addition, in the event of the grand vizier's absence from Istanbul, his appointed deputy, an official known as the *kaymakam*, tended to receive three-quarters of what the grand vizier received, that is, eight kaftans. Sometimes gifts would be presented to the *kaymakam* (and his *kahya*) in lieu of those to the grand vizier, sometimes in addition to them, so that, for instance, the *reisülküttab* would receive an extra set of kaftans, two as part of the court of the *kaymakam* and four as part of that of the grand vizier.

70 Sima M. Ćirković, *The Serbs* (Oxford, 2004), 131; Walter F. Weiker, *Ottomans, Turks and the Jewish Polity: A History of the Jews of Turkey* (Jerusalem, 1992), 133; Richard Clogg, *A Concise History of Greece* (Cambridge, 1992), 13; Marios Philippides & Walter K. Hanak, *The Siege and the Fall of Constantinople in 1453: Historiography, Topography, and Military Studies* (Farnham, 2011), 71, 84–5; Anthony J. Papalas, *Rebels and Radicals: Icaria 1600–2000* (Wauconda IL, 2005), 50, 95. For a more Ottoman-focused view, see: Minna Rozen, *A History of the Jewish Community in Istanbul: The Formative Years, 1453–1566* (Leiden, 2002), 30–3; Phokion P. Kotzageorgis, 'About the fiscal status of the Greek Orthodox Church in the 17th century', *Turcica* 40 (2008), 67–80; Sabire Arık, 'Polonya kralı Jan Sobıeski'nin eşine yazdığı mektuplarında Türk olgusu' in Ekrem Causevic, Nenad Moacanin, & Vjeran Kursar (eds), *Perspectives on Ottoman Studies: Papers from the 18th Symposium of the International Committee of Pre-Ottoman and Ottoman Studies (CIEPO)* (Münster, 2010), 81–97.

The high officials – the *kahya*, *reisülküttab,* and *çavuşbaşı* – received a similar amount as they did in the arrival ceremonies, between two and four kaftans of cloth and satin, and the second-tier officials generally received one each of cloth and satin. At *bayram*, the British also gave out lengths of scarlet cloth to lower administrative and supporting officials. Higher-ranking officials such as the *selam ağası*, *odabaşı*, and *muhzir ağası* received five cubits, as did lower officials such as the *keysedar*s (lit. purse-bearers) of the great officials, and military men like the *bölükbaşı*. One set of officials who were presented with gifts at *bayram* who did not receive such tokens on the ambassador's arrival were the Ottoman governors located in *Frengistan* (lit. the abode of the Franks), the area on the opposite side of the Golden Horn to the imperial heart of Istanbul where the Europeans and many Ottoman non-Muslims lived in the neighbourhoods of Galata and Beyoğlu (Pera). Thus the *Galata Sarayı ağası*, chief of the Galata palace, and the *Beyoğlu voyvodası*, governor of Beyoğlu, each received gifts, generally one or two cloth kaftans, and their secretaries and chief doorkeepers would receive some lengths of cloth.

The second occasion of annual *pīşkeş* began in 1723 and continued until 1801, and was noted in the embassy's accounts as gifts 'for confirming the tariffs at Constantinople and Smyrna'. There is nothing written about this particular type of *pīşkeş* in the diplomatic or commercial correspondence, and so these accounts would appear to be the only reference to what must have been a purely customary practice. The basic premise was that in order to maintain the customs and duties at a favourable level, the British were expected to present an annual renewal fee in the form of a set amount of *pīşkeş* to several customs officials, much in the way that the Christian priests and Jewish rabbis paid a certain amount to the Ottoman government each year to ensure the maintenance of their privileges. Before 1750, the primary recipient was the 'head customer', the *gümrük emini*, who each year received 500 *guruş* and a gold watch. Other officials also benefited, such as the customs collector of Galata, and the *mühürdar* (seal-keeper), who would receive silver watches. When the embassy accounts resume in the mid-1760s, the number of officials receiving this *pīşkeş* had expanded. The *gümrük emini* received 900 *guruş* (the extra 400 *guruş* apparently being in lieu of the gold watch) and a cloth kaftan, the *mühürdar* and Galata customs collector received silver watches, joined now by the *yazıcı* (scribe) and *nazir* (head administrator), as well as one official noted as 'the Jew stimador' (probably from the Ladino word *estimádor*, valuer/appraiser), who appraised unrated goods for customs. Similarly, between 1716 and the mid-1740s, gifts were given to numerous officials, usually a pair of kaftans to the *kahya* and *bostancıbaşı*, and fabric rolls to lower officials, on the arrival of ships bringing wine to the British factory in Istanbul.

The final sort of gifts that might be considered as *pīşkeş* were those presented on a particular official's appointment to a new office, accounting for around 17% of total gifts given. Until 1774, the standard practice was to present gifts to the grand vizier and *kaymakam* on their appointments, as well as less regularly on the appointment of a new *reisülküttab*, *çavuşbaşı*, *bostancıbaşı*,

Table 6: *Kaftans presented on the grand vizier's appointment, 1693–1768*

| **Grand vizier** | **Cloth kaftans** | **Satin kaftans** | **Tabby kaftans** | **Velvet kaftans** | **Brocade kaftans** | **Fabric pieces** | **Total gifts** |
|---|---|---|---|---|---|---|---|
| Mustafa Paşa (1693) | 16 | 7 | 9 | 6 | 8 | - | 46 |
| Ali Paşa (1695) | 15 | 10 | 4 | 2 | 10 | 2 | 43 |
| Mehmed Paşa (1695) | 16 | 12 | 7 | - | 14 | - | 49 |
| Numan Paşa (1710) | 20 | 12 | 1 | - | 15 | 3 | 51 |
| Mehmed Paşa (1710) | 18 | 12 | 1 | - | 15 | 3 | 49 |
| Yusuf Paşa (1711) | 17 | 8 | 1 | - | 7 | 2 | 35 |
| Süleyman Paşa (1712) | 18 | 12 | 1 | - | 16 | 3 | 50 |
| Ali Paşa (1713) | 18 | 12 | 1 | - | 16 | 3 | 50 |
| Halil Paşa (1716) | 18 | 12 | 1 | - | 19 | 3 | 49 |
| Mehmed Paşa (1730) | 17 | 11 | 1 | - | 19 | 2 | 46 |
| İbrahim Paşa (1731) | 19 | 8 | - | - | 15 | 3 | 49 |
| Osman Paşa (1731) | 18 | 12 | 1 | - | 17 | 3 | 49 |
| Ali Paşa (1732) | 19 | 13 | 1 | - | 17 | 3 | 53 |
| İsmail Paşa (1735) | 19 | 13 | 1 | - | 10 | 3 | 53 |
| Mehmed Paşa (1738) | 18 | 11 | - | - | 10 | 4 | 43 |
| Ahmed Paşa (1740) | 17 | 12 | - | - | 10 | 3 | 42 |
| Ali Paşa (1742) | 17 | 12 | - | - | 10 | 3 | 42 |
| Hassan Paşa (1743) | 17 | 12 | - | - | 10 | 3 | 42 |
| Mahir Paşa (1768) | 21 | 14 | - | - | 10 | - | 45 |
| Mehmed Paşa (1768) | 21 | 14 | - | - | 10 | - | 45 |

*Beyoğlu voyvodası*, *Galata voyvodası*, and a number of other customs and administrative officials. The most formalised and regularised of these were the gifts given to the very highest officials, the grand vizier and *kaymakam*. Of the fifty grand viziers appointed between 1693 and 1768, the final recorded example of this practice, records have survived for twenty such occasions. The picture painted is again one of regularity, with essentially the same officials as on the ambassador's arrival being given the same amount and quality of goods. Table 6 illustrates the number of the different types of textile gifts presented on the grand vizier's appointment between 1693 and 1768 clearly indicating that gifts given were largely regular, although with a clear change in both quality and quantity from 1738, a pattern to which I shall return.

Other examples of officials who received gifts on their appointments were the *kaymakam*, with fourteen examples (thirteen between 1693 and 1716 and one in 1774), the gifts given on those occasions being almost identical in quality and quantity to those given on the grand vizier's appointment. New *bostancıbaşı*s received gifts regularly until 1766 of between six and ten high-quality kaftans, and after 1768 just one cloth and one satin kaftan (occasionally supplemented by 50 *guruş* in cash), that practice continuing until the end of 1798. A number of other officials – the *çavuşbaşı*, *kahya*, and *Galata voyvodası* – only received gifts, generally of two kaftans, until the 1710s, whilst the *gümrük emini* received his two kaftans until 1730. A final example of this sort of regular *pīşkeş* was that paid to the *kapudan-ı derya*, also known as the *kapudan paşa*, the chief admiral of the Ottoman navy, on his departure with the fleet either in wartime or on his more regular voyages to collect taxes from the Ottoman islands or to engage in anti-piracy patrols. He would receive eight or so rich kaftans, and members of his court, such as his *tercüman* (translator), his *kahya* (chief secretary), and the *tersane emini* (intendant of the dockyards) would also receive one or two kaftans. This practice continued until the war with Russia between 1768 and 1774, when the *kapudan paşa* Hüsameddin Paşa sailed off with the fleet to meet their doom at the Battle of Çeşme in 1770.

The pattern that emerges on occasions of gift-giving for *ḫilʿat* and especially *pīşkeş* is one of small but noticeable cuts in expenditure at the end of the 1730s, and huge cut-backs from the mid-1770s. This is of course only reflective of the data in the embassy accounts; the private expense accounts of the later ambassadors show that, although the amounts of official gifts given at the Company's expense decreased, expenditure on *hibe*, informal social gifts, continued to some degree, now on the ambassador's account to reclaim from the British government. The decrease in the *pīşkeş* gifts that represented a kind of tribute to the officials of the Ottoman state says, perhaps, as much about changes in the structure of the Ottoman state as it does about changes in the balance of British–Ottoman relations. The data, however, shows that something clearly changed in terms of gift-giving patterns from the 1730s and again in the 1770s. Just how far the less informal gift-giving social gifts might be representative of broader diplomatic trends is the subject of the next section of this analysis, which will examine the trends in consumption of *hibe* gifts accounting for 27% of recorded embassy expenditure.

## Trends in expense and consumption

When thinking about the sorts of gifts given by British ambassadors to Ottoman officials, we need to consider the context or materiality of the objects, but also their financial and logistical background. To give one example from the Ottoman side of things, as part of the preparations for Yusuf Agah Efendi's dispatch to London it was decided to gift George III some horses, much prized in Britain at that time. Not only would the horses themselves be expensive but, as Yusuf Agah petitioned, would require a significant amount of accompanying material and effort:

> As the imperial presents [*hedāyā-yı hümāyūn*] are to be taken by sea to Britain, it is submitted that two hundred bushels of barley and seventy-five *kintar*s of straw, being approximately enough provisions for four months' journey for the five Egyptian and Turkmen horses [*beş res-i Mısrī ve Türkmen atlarıñ*], be purchased through the means of the superintendent of grain, along with five each of horse-cloths, saddle-cloths, saddle-girths, and bridles, ten sets of ligatures and tethers, and a sufficient quantity of grooming equipment.[71]

The total cost of the supplies, not including that of the horses themselves, was calculated to be 16,125 *akçe*s (just over 134 *guruş*), a substantial sum in itself. Thus, with every gift, along with the issue of suitability, came the question of cost and logistics.[72] In order to better understand this in practice, this section will provide a detailed quantitative and qualitative analysis of the gifts given by the British to Ottoman officials. The surviving accounts provide information on the provenance, quality, quantity, and cost of the Company gifts, as well as their recipients and the occasions on which they were presented. This is particularly important, as it shows all sorts of gifts being given, the records of which are not preserved anywhere else. As such, the accounts ledgers show that social gifts remained an important part of the framework of diplomatic practice throughout the eighteenth century as an important means of ensuring the cooperation of Ottoman officials with commercial and political matters at all levels.

Textiles were the most diplomatically and commercially significant gifts presented by the British. Of the 10,545 individual gifts listed in the 8,354 entries in the surviving embassy accounts by my last count, 7,429 (70.5%) are kaftans and 1,084 (10.3%) are lengths of fabric, meaning that textile goods accounted for 80.8% of goods given, which in terms of costs equated to 64.6% of total expenditure on gifts going on textile goods. The most important of these were the kaftans (often recorded as 'vests'), generally given on occasions of *ḫilʿat* and *pīşkeş* but for numerous other purposes as well.[73] The majority

71 BOA/C.HR/176/8785, 26 Safer 1208 [2 October 1793].

72 For the discussion of another such example, see: Michael Talbot, 'Feeding an elephant in eighteenth-century Istanbul', *Tozsuz Evrak* (September 2013), docblog.ottomanhistorypodcast.com

73 Some beautifully illustrated examples can be found in a court costume book annotated in English and Ottoman Turkish, *The Grand Signor's Court* (c. 1620), BM, ME.SL 5258.

of the kaftans given – 3,650 recorded, or 49% of the total – were made from cloth, meaning wool cloth of the sort that formed the mainstay of British trade with the Ottoman Empire until the end of the eighteenth century. The entries of the late 1690s and early 1700s noted that the cloth came from Worcester and Salisbury, both major centres of English cloth production. Several of the entries revealed that the cloth was often dyed red or scarlet, a colour highly symbolic in the intermittently enforced Ottoman sumptuary laws, being the preserve of Muslim elites.[74] The question of production is a curious one, as there is no mention in either the British or the Ottoman sources about how these gift kaftans were actually made. It seems reasonable to assume that the fabric would have been given to the court tailors in Istanbul who would have fashioned them into kaftans.[75] However the garments were produced, they were made largely from British cloth, and so presenting large amounts of British manufactures to the most important members of the Ottoman state should be viewed in many ways as encouraging consumption of British goods. Over the period, the sultans received some 140 cloth kaftans, and the grand viziers 276, although many of these were recorded as being simply sent straight to the imperial treasury, perhaps to be re-gifted at a later stage. However, the range of officials who received cloth kaftans and lengths is good evidence that as well as honouring the recipient within the conventions of Ottoman gift-giving, the British also aimed to promote their commercial standing through their gifts.

The remaining 3,779 kaftans represented the other side of British commercial interest, silk. At the cheaper end were 'tabby' (often called 'broad' tabby) kaftans, a simple weave given in relatively small numbers (342), and often noted as being from 'Morilla', as the fabric had been manufactured in the major textile centre of Morella in Valencia. More common at the lower end of the scale, costing about the same as cloth kaftans, were those made from satin, sometimes noted using the Italian term '*raso*'. As noted in the previous discussion, the most common form of gift presentation was a pair of kaftans, one of cloth and the other of satin, and this is reflected in the large number (1,856) of satin kaftans being presented. The majority of the satin was manufactured in Florence or in the Florentine style (1,025 specifically noted as Florentine), with a number in the earlier period recorded as coming from or being in the style of Lucca. Italian silk production was very important in the

[74] See: Charlotte Jirousek, 'The transition to mass fashion system dress in the Ottoman Empire' in Donald Quataert (ed.), *Consumption Studies and the History of the Ottoman Empire, 1550–1922: An Introduction* (Albany NY, 2000), 201–42; Madeline C. Zilfi, 'Goods in the mahalle: Distributional encounters in eighteenth-century Istanbul' in Quataert (ed.), *Consumption Studies*, 289–312; Shirine Hamadeh, 'Public spaces and the garden culture of Istanbul in the eighteenth century' in Aksan & Goffman (eds), *Early Modern Ottomans*, 277–312, especially 300–6.

[75] I am very grateful for the insights Professor Hülya Tezcan gave me on court textile production when we met in Istanbul in May 2011. Hülya Tezcan, 'The imperial robe collection at Topkapı Palace Museum' in Patricia L. Baker, Hülya Tezcan & Jennifer Wearden (eds), *Silks for the Sultans: Ottoman Imperial Garments from Topkapı Palace* (Istanbul, 2007), 10–30. See also: Jennifer Wearden, 'The technical skill of Ottoman craftsmen' in Baker, Tezcan, & Wearden (eds), *Silks for the Sultans*, 45–56; Hülya Tezcan, *19.yy Sonuna Ait Bir Terzi Defteri: A Late 19th Century Tailor's Order-Book* (Istanbul, 1992).

British Mediterranean trade, and, as noted earlier, from the 1720s outstripped the amount of silk being purchased by the British in the Ottoman Empire.

At the higher end of the kaftan market were the finer weaves of silk and brocade originating in Italy or the Ottoman Empire itself, with four main types of such luxury textiles noted in the embassy accounts. The first was a floral Venetian fabric called 'damaschetto con oro', a rich damask with gold thread used mainly in the period up to 1720, and totalling 286 kaftans. The second was 'Hattai con oro', a weave of silk and gold, often with floral decorations, with 163 kaftans given between the 1710s and 1740s. The third was 'Samis', a silk-gold weave originating in Iran that had, via Byzantium, been immensely popular in medieval Europe as 'samite'. Manufactured in Italy, fifty-six kaftans of that fabric were presented in the late seventeenth century. Finally, there was 'Ajem brocade', the richest of the silk-gold weaves, made from Iranian silk, with 849 kaftans given. These European, Ottoman, and Iranian fabrics were indicative of market relations of luxury textiles in this period; raw silk from Iran purchased via the Ottoman Empire, sent to the manufacturing centres of Tuscany or northern Syria, and returned to the markets of the Ottoman realms to be purchased by Northern European merchants and Ottoman elites.

The prices of these garments remained relatively stable throughout the eighteenth century, as shown in table 7. Converting the price from the *guruş* to grams of silver using Pamuk's figures, one can clearly see the impact of debasement on price inflation, and, more importantly, on the stability of prices for luxury textiles in this period. The one exception is the 'ajem brocade', which saw a sharp rise in the cost of the fabric due to the disruption of the trade routes to Iran in the 1720s and 1730s. The cloth prices overall fluctuated more than the satin and tabby, probably due to the changing demands for British woollen goods at various points throughout the century compared to a fairly constant demand for Italian silk goods. As a comparison, among the *ḫilʿat*s distributed to Charles Arbuthnot's retinue on his arrival in 1805 were forty camlet garments (*şālī kerāke*) that cost the Ottoman treasury 60 *guruş* each, compared to 61.2 *guruş* paid by the British for cloth kaftans.[76] The two *ḫilʿat*s made with the finest sable-back fur (*āʿalā ṣırt-ı samūr kürkūñ*) given to Arbuthnot on that occasion cost 6,000 *guruş* each.

With their central role in Ottoman gift-giving practices, and with their materials so central to British commercial interests in the Ottoman Empire for most of the century, it is unsurprising that kaftans dominated British gift-giving at the Ottoman court. The great decrease in Levant Company expenditure on gifts after 1774 is directly linked to a decline in the giving of kaftans. Until that point, the importance of these gifts was almost universally recognised and accepted among the British in Istanbul. In February 1747, not long after his arrival in the Ottoman Empire, James Porter noted that the Istanbul factory had permitted an extra 3,000 *guruş* for gifts, '[a]s the presents

[76] BOA/C.HR/185/9212, 27 Cemaziülahir 1220 [21 September 1805]. See also BOA/C.HR/23/1142, 10 Cemaziülahir 1214 [8 November 1799], from the Earl of Elgin's arrival, that gives a figure of 5,300 *guruş* for a similar garment.

Table 7: *Price of kaftans in* guruş *and silver grams, 1693–1803*

| **Year** | **Cost in *guruş*** | | | | **Cost in silver grams** | | | |
|---|---|---|---|---|---|---|---|---|
| | **Cloth kaftan** | **Satin kaftan** | **Tabby kaftan** | **Brocade kaftan** | **Cloth kaftan** | **Satin kaftan** | **Tabby kaftan** | **Brocade kaftan** |
| 1693 | 17.5 | 20 | 10 | 50 | 273 | 312 | 156 | 780 |
| 1703 | 25 | 20 | 12 | 50 | 395 | 316 | 189 | 790 |
| 1713 | 25 | 20 | 12 | 50 | 385 | 308 | 185 | 770 |
| 1723 | 25 | 22.5 | 13.5 | 55 | 395 | 356 | 213 | 869 |
| 1733 | 25 | 25 | 13.5 | 60 | 373 | 373 | 201 | 894 |
| 1743 | 25 | 22.5 | 13.5 | 70 | 363 | 326 | 196 | 1015 |
| 1753 | - | - | - | - | - | - | - | - |
| 1763 | - | - | - | - | - | - | - | - |
| 1773 | 30 | 30 | 19.5 | 75 | 345 | 354 | 224 | 863 |
| 1783 | 42.5 | 30 | 19.5 | 80 | 425 | 350 | 195 | 872 |
| 1793 | 42.5 | 35 | 22 | 120 | 293 | 242 | 152 | 708 |
| 1803 | 61.3 | 40 | 27 | 120 | 361 | 236 | 159 | 708 |

of the Levant Company are accustomed to give to the Grand Signor and great officers of the Porte are very trifling and make no figure, and as the French and even the Neapolitans are and have been liberal to profusion'.[77] However, during his ambassadorship began the rumblings of dissent, with suggestions of giving gifts to the grand vizier on his daughter's wedding dismissed, with Porter complaining about 'how much against our dignity such voluntary and unprecedented impositions of tribute were'.[78] In 1755 he claimed that he had managed to avoid an audience with the newly enthroned Osman III (r. 1754–7), at which he would have been required to present and receive royal letters, claiming that this would have been 'onerous to the nation, and of no other use but an empty honour to the ambassador'.[79] Given the importance of letters in the ceremonial of friendly diplomacy at the Ottoman court, it is unclear how Porter, who seems to have enjoyed reporting himself in such contrary stances, might have got out of such a crucial ceremony.

The real change in attitude, however, came during the time of John Murray, who wrote proudly back to London in 1767 that, during his first ten months as ambassador, he had not 'given an asper [*akçe*] of the company's money more than the usual presents, and that there has not been a single article of the Capitulations infringed'.[80] Perhaps wary of implications of thriftiness at a time that Britain was attempting to influence Ottoman politics on the outbreak of war with Russia, the secretary of state reminded Murray that 'presents are so necessary in carrying on business in the East', and granted him an allowance of between 8,000 *guruş* and 10,000 *guruş* 'in support of the dignity of your character'.[81] Yet the change in policy appears to have come from the Ottoman government itself. On his first audience with the grand vizier Mehmed Paşa in 1775, the vizier did not accept the gifts presented as usual *pīşkeş*. Such actions were not without precedent; in a time of great instability at the top of the Ottoman government in the 1710s, both Numan Paşa (1710) and Mehmed Paşa (1710–11) returned their gifts on their appointment, although just why they did so is not recorded. In the 1775 case, the recent exemption of Russia and the Habsburgs from such *pīşkeş* had set a precedent. Murray was thrilled: 'If the [ambassadors] succeed to abolish this shameful custom, which we have resolved to try, and which I have taken many opportunities to disapprove of as beneath the dignity of the Porte to accept it, it will put all the courts upon the same footing with those of Vienna and Petersburg.'[82] Denouncing appointment and *Ramazan Bayramı* gifts as 'tribute', the British, French, Dutch, Venetian, Swedish, Prussian, and Neapolitan ministers all agreed to stop giving most of the established gifts. Grand viziers, *kaymakam*s, and all the other officials who had received *pīşkeş* on their appointments no longer did so, and the annual

77 TNA/SP97/33 James Porter to the Duke of Newcastle, 21 February 1747.

78 TNA/SP97/34 James Porter to the Duke of Bedford, 2 March 1750.

79 TNA/SP97/38 James Porter to the Earl of Holdernesse, 16 August 1755 (Secret). He avoided this again some years later: TNA/SP97/40 James Porter to William Pitt, 4 January 1758.

80 TNA/SP97/43 John Murray to the Earl of Shelburne, 15 April 1767.

81 TNA/SP97/44 Viscount Weymouth to John Murray, 1 November 1768; 23 November 1768.

82 TNA/SP97/50 John Murray to the Earl of Rochford, 17 October 1774.

*pīşkeş* at *Ramazan Bayramı* saw the number of kaftans given decrease from fifty-four in 1773 to ten in 1774, and those only of cloth. The impact on the embassy's finances was immediate, with average annual expenditure on gifts after 1774 at 35% of its previous level.

The attitude towards the more informal *hibe* gifts was different, however. Sir Everard Fawkener described them as:

> Little presents and gratifications which here make an essential part of all intercourse and are expected as tokens of respect, where they are not sought after for the value, but which is seldom the case, and where an acquaintance is once made, there is a constant train of little wants.[83]

This observation really gets at the heart of the most common form of Ottoman gift-exchange. Certainly, the major occasions were essentially establishing formal relationships with high Ottoman officials, and in expressing the Ottoman world-view. However, on a daily basis, *hibe* gifts were absolutely crucial in forming working relationships and even friendships between the ambassador and members of the Ottoman government. Such gifts continued even when the major occasions had been abolished and the expenses of the embassy gradually shifted more to the British government. As a set of objects, they also provide a crucial insight into luxury consumption among Ottoman elites, who often suggested appropriate gifts.

Some of the more popular were those to do with mechanics and science, most importantly clocks and watches.[84] According to the surviving Levant Company accounts, a total of 457 timepieces, consisting of 434 watches and 23 table clocks, were presented between 1693 and 1803, and doubtless a much larger number were given on the ambassadors' expense accounts. Even as an indication, this was a remarkable number, and timepieces accounted for 12.6% of expenditure on gifts. The Ottomans had their own tradition of horology and, as Kemal Özdemir has demonstrated, large mosques often contained timekeeping rooms or even separate buildings called *muvakkithane*s, and these were crucial in calculating prayer times and festivals. As a result, the Ottomans had a whole range of hourglasses, sundials, and even mechanical devices to help in such calculations, in addition to other aids such as the *kıblenuma*, a portable compass that gave the direction of the *kıble*, the direction towards which Muslims pray.[85] There was little chance in the eighteenth century of European watches supplanting the older methods of time-measurement in the *muvakkithane*s, because there simply was not the need, although the growing use of European timepieces in the Ottoman context was certainly noted in

83 TNA/SP97/40 Sir Everard Fawkener to the Duke of Newcastle, 15 March 1738/9 (Separate).

84 For further detail on this sort of gift, see: Michael Talbot, 'Gifts of time: Watches and clocks in Ottoman–British diplomacy, 1693–1803', *Jahrbuch für Europäische Geschichte* 17 (2016), 55–79.

85 D.A. King, 'Taḳīal-Dīn b. Muḥammad b. Maʿrūf' in *Encyclopaedia of Islam 2*, vol. X, 132–3; O. Kurz, *European Clocks and Watches in the Near East* (Leiden, 1975), 1–9; Kemal Özdemir, *Ottoman Clocks and Watches* (Istanbul, 1993), 29–36, 47–64.

contemporary literature.[86] The establishment of Swiss and French watchmakers and vendors from the end of the fifteenth century, therefore, did not bring something entirely new to Ottoman society and culture, but their technology and designs made European timepieces prized items among Ottoman elites.

By the end of the seventeenth century, the British dominated the Ottoman mechanical watch and clock market. In order to maintain this position, they needed to market their goods in a suitable manner. Watch- and clockmakers such as Markwick & Markham designed their pieces specifically for Ottoman customers, employing styles and materials they imagined were to Ottoman tastes, and often using Arabic numerals (as in ١, ٢, ٣, rather than 1, 2, 3 or I, II, III).[87] According to the British customs figures, an average of £2,000-worth of watches was exported to the Ottoman Empire each year in the eighteenth century, increasing sixfold over its course. Overall, the large number of watches given can be seen as aiming to encourage consumption of British goods, and that this tactic was successful judging by the trade statistics. Many were distributed as part of official ceremonies, especially as *pīşkeş* on the renewal of the customs tariffs, but a significant number were given as *hibe*, either at the ambassador's command (118) or at the request of the officials themselves (65). It appears that these watches and clocks were renewed, as the embassy accounts also include bills paid to British watchmakers to repair those broken by their Ottoman owners.

As well as timekeeping mechanisms, optical technology such as British-manufactured perspective glasses and telescopes proved popular as a gift in the earlier eighteenth century. Although such goods were not commercially significant, for most of this period they were an important part of diplomatic gift-giving. In the Company accounts, 177 different perspective glasses and telescopes were presented to high Ottoman officials, including the sultan, grand vizier, and *kapudan paşa*. The perspective glasses tended to be encased in tortoiseshell, often studded with gold or silver, depending on the quality of person receiving the gift. For instance, in 1712, Ahmed III received three perspective glasses and one telescope, the telescope 'japanned' (lacquered) and tipped with ivory and silver, and two of the perspective glasses of tortoiseshell studded with gold and silver, and the third gold enamelled and set with rubies and emeralds, with a total value of 495 *guruş*, or 6% of the total gift expenditure for that year. Other high officials received glasses of tortoiseshell studded with gold or silver. Several went to favourites of the high officials to gain access to their patrons, to procure the friendship of a specific individual, or to thank an official for their assistance in official business. These were items with significant cultural and material capital, and in the 1720s the accounts note that the Levant Company began facilitating the transport of these optical instruments.

86 Avner Wishnitzer, *Reading Clocks Alla Turca: Time and Society in the Late Ottoman Empire* (Chicago, 2015), especially chapters 1 and 2.

87 For some examples of this sort of timepiece, see: MOL, PC/C1478, Gold watch, London, c. 1780; VAM, MC/365-B-1897, Enamel and gilt watch, London, Markwick & Markham, 1750–75.

Perhaps of more general use to Ottoman eyes were British-manufactured spectacles, with some 138 pairs recorded as being given between 1707 and 1737. The spectacles were usually unadorned, although some had silver rims, so the material value was in their cases, which were often made of tortoise-shell or mother-of-pearl, with finer pieces studded with silver. As with the perspective glasses, they were given generally by the ambassador's order, most likely after a hint from the relevant official. A significant number of spectacles were specifically requested by high-ranking officials, including the *reisülküttab, çavuşbaşı*, and *defterdar* (chief finance minister), as well as a significant number of religious figures, such as the *şeyhülislam* (the chief religious scholar of the state).[88] Whether this was a fashion craze, or whether these spectacles were actually used, is unclear, although the research of Vincent Ilardi into fifteenth-century Florentine trade in the Levant and Toby Huff's fascinating study of intellectual curiosity demonstrate that there had been a long-standing consumption of spectacles (and perspective glasses) in the Ottoman realms, and so this may be an example of the British trying to crack into an existing market by promoting elite consumption of their goods.[89]

Some technological gifts were far rarer. A very small number of scientific instruments were presented to the highest Ottoman officials in the 1730s and 1740s, such as a silver-mounted barometer to the chief translator in 1732, and mathematical instruments to the *mulla* of Galata in 1733, the grand vizier's *kahya* in 1734, and the grand vizier, Nişancı Ahmed Paşa, in 1741 (the last two made out of gold), all requested by the officials themselves. A rather unusual piece of apparatus was requested of Sir Everard Fawkener in 1741. Sultan Mahmud I, after eleven years on the throne, had yet to sire an heir, something of great concern to the Ottoman government. Among a number of surgical instruments requested by a direct communication from the palace, was a microscope:

> I have been told seriously it is designed for a very extraordinary use, which is to examine the Sultan's seed. It would be happy if defects which can be remedied away may be discovered, but it is to be feared the faculty will hardly succeed where youth and beauty, and even variety have failed.[90]

As the sultan later died without producing an heir, it would seem that the investigation came to nothing, but this episode at the very least shows that some of the gifts had practical uses. Another example is a number of maps and atlases presented to high-ranking officials in the earlier part of the eighteenth century. They may have been for curiosity, but a map of Iran given to grand vizier İbrahim Paşa in 1724 undoubtedly was requested because of the war with Iran,

88 A potential example can be seen in VAM, FWC/W.5-1970, Tortoiseshell spectacles and mother-of-pearl case, England, c. 1685–8.

89 Vincent Ilardi, *Renaissance Vision from Spectacles to Telescopes* (Philadelphia, 2007), 119–23; Toby E. Huff, *Intellectual Curiosity and the Scientific Revolution: A Global Perspective* (Cambridge, 2010), 120–56, 206.

90 TNA/SP97/31 Sir Everard Fawkener to the Duke of Newcastle, 26 December 1741.

and a map held in the Ottoman archives in Istanbul would appear to be a copy made from a European map, very possibly from that very gift.[91] All of these gifts had a variety of purposes, and were requested or given for a variety of reasons. Beyond the trends established by the overarching data, the individual case studies reveal far more nuance and insight into gift-giving practices on a daily level. Watches, perspective glasses, telescopes, and spectacles are all excellent examples of social gifts given by the British embassy to a variety of Ottoman officials in order to cement their friendship, but also to promote British technology and British manufacturing. Yet they must also have been important objects of social capital, as well as of practical use.

The utility of other kinds of gift is far more evident. Numerous barrels of English (often glazed) gunpowder presented to military officials such as the *topcubaşı* (chief of the gunners) and the *çorbacı* (lit. soup server, a colonel of the janissaries) of Galata. It seems that these were used for hunting rather than military purposes. Similarly a number of firearms were given, often produced specifically for the 'Oriental' market, generally pistols (trimmed with silver for the higher officials), but also hunting guns ('fowling pieces') given to the sultan, grand vizier, and other high-ranking members of state.[92] Hunting was a favourite pastime of the Ottoman elite, and it is likely that a number of guns, pistols, and barrels of gunpowder requested by officials such as the *bostancıbaşı* were presented again as gifts for the sultan's use. The gifting of guns and gunpowder is also interesting from a commercial point of view, so that although the British were prohibited in their Capitulations from exporting gunpowder and weapons, traffic the other way was perfectly acceptable.

Textiles and technologies of various forms provided the majority of British *hibe* gifts to Ottoman officials, from official kaftans to watches to guns. Such gifts also provide insights into different patterns of consumption at the Ottoman court, with waves of fashion favouring certain forms of watch or items like spectacles. One final sort of *hibe* gift that gives a sense of consumption trends on a very individual level were the various consumable items, specifically food, drink, medicine, and perfumes. As will be seen in the next chapter, food was an important feature of Ottoman court ceremonial. It was customary, for instance, for the grand vizier to send fruit and flowers to a new ambassador on his arrival. Consumption of food and other items, from perfumes to flowers, was an important sign of the wealth of the Ottoman court. Indeed, flowers were to become synonymous with the period of Ahmed III's rule under the vizierate of İbrahim Paşa (1718–30), otherwise known as the *Lale Devri*, the Tulip Era.[93] This was painted as an era of luxury, of feasting, of

[91] BOA/HRT.h/103a, Zilkade 1142 [1730]. The original would most likely be Guillaume Delisle's *Carte de Perse dressée puor l'usage du Roy* (1724), a copy of which is in the British Library: Guillame Delisle, *Carte de Perse* (Amsterdam, c. 1730).

[92] For an example of a pistol, see: MOL, PC/A15624, Pistol for the Ottoman/Indian market inlaid with silver and ivory, William Parker & Joseph Bunney, London, c. 1808.

[93] The original term was coined (along with 'Tulip-mania', '*lāle merāḳı*') by an Ottoman historian: Ahmed Refik [Altınay], *Lāle Devri* (Istanbul, 1331 [1915]). Ariel Salzmann, 'The age of tulips: Confluence and consumer culture (1550–1730)' in Donald Quataert (ed.), *Consumption*, 83–106;

beautiful gardens, and of extravagant festivals, receiving its name for the huge sums Ottoman elites were prepared to pay for certain kinds of tulips. Even outside the confines of that historiographical era, however, we see evidence of the Ottoman love of flowers in the many hundreds of hyacinth, tulip, and daffodil roots gifted by the British, particularly in the later 1730s. In the same period, canary birds along with British-manufactured cages were given to high officials, doubtless to ornament their gardens.[94] In diplomatic gifts, therefore, we can find evidence for trends in Ottoman consumption.

Gifts of food were commonly given until the beginning of the 1740s, sometimes from the ambassador's household stores. Some forms became regularised, such as the annual gift of around two *okka*s each of cloves, cinnamon, and nutmeg to the sultan's kitchen via the *bostancıbaşı* until 1741, accompanied, for some unknown reason, by several sorts of paints for the sultan's use. Just as the Ottoman court would send gifts of fruit on the ambassador's arrival, if the sultan visited the palaces in Beyoğlu or Galata, or if the ambassador encountered him in the countryside during the hot summer months, it was customary for the ambassador to send him a gift of sweetmeats. Sweet things such as chocolate, sugar loaves, and Venetian treacle were among the most popular goods requested by high Ottoman officials, as well as more luxurious items like green tea or Indian tea. The ambassador was acting as more than a luxury grocer, but, rather like in the case of the textile and technological gifts, was catering to the tastes and interests of Ottoman officials in order to better advance the interests of his merchants. Giving sweets and chocolates could secure a tenuous friendship, and it is again at a more individual level that we can see how this happens.

For example, there seems to have been a small tradition between around 1703 and 1715 that the ambassador present the *kapudan paşa* with one or more large Cheshire cheeses, standard issue on Royal Navy ships, often accompanied by strong fish such as anchovies, red herring, or stockfish, and occasionally olives or pickles; between 1704 and 1706, this gift of cheese was also accompanied by 'strong beer'.[95] Indeed, alcohol appears regularly in different forms among the gifts given to Ottoman elites well into the 1730s. There was the occasional bottle of wine, such the bottle of 'Old Hock' given to the chief translator – a non-Muslim – in 1710. However, most common were spirits and liqueurs, and it is likely that these were (literally, not figuratively)

Mustafa Armağan (ed.), *İstanbul armağanı: Lâle Devri* (Istanbul, 2000); B. Deniz Çalış, 'Gardens at the Kağıthane commons during the Tulip Period (1718–1730)' in Michael Conan (ed.), *Middle East Garden Traditions: Unity and Diversity* (Washington DC, 2007), 239–68. For a historiographical critique of the concept of the Tulip Era, see: Can Erimtan, *Ottomans Looking West? The Origins of the Tulip Age and its Development in Modern Turkey* (London & New York, 2008).

94 In a later period, François Pouqueville noted that singing canaries adorned the gardens of Ottoman officials: F.C.H.L. Pouqueville, *Travels through the Morea, Albania, and several other parts of the Ottoman Empire, to Constantinople, during the years 1798, 1799, 1800, and 1801*, trans. anonymous (London, 1806), 162.

95 Henry Phelps Brown & Sheila V. Hopkins, *A Perspective of Wages and Prices* (Cambridge, 1981), 26.

medicinal, as the most usual type, a liqueur of the sundew flower distilled on Corfu called 'rossolis', was supposedly a general curative and aphrodisiac.[96] Another such tonic, 'barbadoes water', an expensive and strong cordial believed to protect against plague, was given to the grand vizier İbrahim Paşa in 1723.[97] Other medicinal tonics were distillations such as 'spirit of amber' for rheumatism, 'oil of amber', an anti-hysteric and aphrodisiac, 'cinnamon water' and 'cinnamon oil' for digestive problems, and the wonderful 'theriac', a cure-all potion concocted from almost seventy ingredients.[98] These were given to only the highest members of the Ottoman state, especially the sultan, grand vizier, and other senior members of the court.[99] One rather unusual item, given only to the sultan and the grand vizier for the ambassador's arrival audience from 1766, was a bezoar stone. Hugely expensive and presented in an ornamental case, it was a cure-all medicine, supposedly with particular efficacy against poisons (the word itself may come from the Persian *pāzahr*, 'antidote'), made from a mass of indigestible matter found in the digestive system of the bezoar ibex.[100] Finally, a number of perfumes and essences were given at the request of various Ottoman officials, along with silver boxes to hold fragrant plants and woods such as aloes, agarwood, and sweetwood. The British also gave raw ambergris, 'spirit of ambergris', 'Hungary water', and various Italian essences.[101] These were popular until the end of the 1730s, and were given to only the highest officials. The embassy accounts noted that a box of essences was presented to the mother of the *reisülküttab* in 1715, and four boxes of Italian perfumes were sent to the 'sultana' of the grand vizier in 1723; these two gifts, along with six cubits of cloth to the sultan's mother (*valide sultan*) in 1713, constitute the only recorded gifts presented to Ottoman women. All of these foodstuffs indicate a more personal relationship with these different Ottoman officials. The food, drink, medicine, and perfumes given by the British embassy are in some ways the archetypal *hibe* gifts, small but

96 Thomas Short, *Medicina Britannica: or, a Treatise on such Physical Plants, as are Generally to be found in the Fields or Gardens in Great-Britain, Containing a particular Account of their Nature, Virtues, and Uses* (London, 1746), 243; Xavier Scrofani, *Voyage en Grèce, de Xavier Scrofani, Sicilien, Fait en 1794 et 1795*, trans. J.F.C. Blanvillain, 3 vols (Paris & Strasbourg, Year IX [1801]), vol. III, 14; Ambrose Cooper, *The Complete Distiller* (London, 1757), 215–17. On the permissiveness of alcohol in Ottoman medicine, see: Miri Shefer-Mossensohn, *Ottoman Medicine: Healing and Medical Institutions, 1500–1700* (Albany NY, 2009), 89–92.

97 Cooper, *Complete Distiller*, 214–15; Charles Carter, *The Compleat City and Country Cook: or, Accomplish'd Housewife* (London, 1732), 193–4.

98 See: VAM, CC/C.187-2003, Ceramic Theriac container, Delft, 1725–75.

99 Cooper, *Complete Distiller*, 134–5; *Encyclopædia Perthensis: or, Universal Dictionary of the Arts, Sciences, Literature etc*, 2 vols (Edinburgh, 1816), vol. I, 556; Moyse Charas, *Theriaque d'Andromacus* (Paris, 1685).

100 Thomas Pope Blount, *A Natural History* (London, 1693), 30–7; Peter Borschberg, 'The Euro-Asian trade in bezoar stones (approx. 1500 to 1700)' in Michael North (ed.), *Artistic and Cultural Exchanges between Europe and Asia, 1400–900* (Farnham, 2010), 29–44. For an example of a container, see: BM, PEC/HG.804, Silver bezoar container, London, late 17th century to 18th century.

101 Cooper, *Complete Distiller*, 153–4; Robert James, *Pharmacopœia Universalis* (London, 1747), 646; Carter, *The Compleat City and Country Cook*, 241.

important signs of friendship that worked in conjunction with other kinds of gift to build a working relationship within the Ottoman diplomatic framework.

## Conclusion

All of these gifts described above, from tea to bezoars to kaftans, cost money, and in their sum they were a great burden to the Levant Company. It was a burden, however, that was both expected and necessary. As I am particularly interested in the relationship between diplomatic finance and diplomatic practice, it seems clear that overall changes in expenditure on British diplomatic gifts, especially *hibe* gifts, can be directly related to the financial difficulties faced by the Company in the eighteenth century. There is a clear correlation between the decreasing volume of British–Ottoman trade, the concurrent decrease in income available to the Levant Company, and an evident decrease of Company expenditure on diplomatic gifts, the bill for which, as has been noted, was increasingly paid for by the Crown from the middle of the century. There were a variety of factors that can explain why the different sorts of *hibe* gifts were given, from commercial opportunism to personal taste. However, the overall decrease in expenditure on *hibe* and other gifts across the century must be largely linked to the financial fortunes of the Company. Because gifts were such a crucial part of the diplomatic framework, as the Company began to suffer the Crown eventually began to pick up the tab, providing the ambassador with an allowance to ensure that gifts could be purchased. Indeed, although the embassy accounts show a marked decrease in the amount of *hibe* gifts given after 1740 as a result of the poor financial state of the Company, this does not mean that the practice died out. Instead, the ambassadors continued to give such gifts to form friendships and honour Ottoman officials on their personal accounts to be recompensed (or not) by the British government. This explains, for instance, the chronic debt Sir Everard Fawkener found himself in on his departure from Istanbul, and why the British government introduced a set allowance during the time of James Porter. Although many of the personal accounts and bills of the ambassadors have not survived, those that have show that much the same sort of gifts were given later on in the century. For example, Sir Robert Ainslie's draft on the British Treasury covering the period from May 1789 until May 1790, includes English pistols sent to the grand vizier, an ornamented gun to Selim III along with glazed gunpowder, perspective glasses to the grand vizier's officials, a gold watch and sugar to the *reisül-küttab*, embroidered velvet to 'a friend' in the palace, and a gold snuff box to the chief translator.[102]

Whilst the ambassadors in the later part of the eighteenth century were able to cut back on the more formal and problematic forms of gift-giving that constituted *pīşkeş*, the ambassadors continued to give gifts as *hibe* to form social bonds and develop alliances with Ottoman officials. Although Company

[102] TNA/FO78/11 Sir Robert Ainslie to the Duke of Leeds, 22 June 1790.

expenditure on those less formal occasions decreased as their financial state deteriorated, the allowances provided by the British government permitted a continuance of this necessary practice. In all, the gifts given as *hibe* were varied, and provide an interesting view of the relationship between British commercial interests, Ottoman elite consumption, and diplomacy, and show how far the British conformed to Ottoman conventions of gift-exchange. Far from the arbitrary or corrupt nature assigned to them by many in Britain at the time, the Ottomans had clear conventions of gift-giving and the British understood and, through necessity, actively engaged in them.

When the Ottomans dispatched a resident ambassador to London, they sent him with a variety of rich gifts, and there were numerous discussions involving Sultan Selim III himself about what would be appropriate.[103] Above all, the Ottomans were concerned that they should provide gifts appropriate to the occasion, and the degree of discussion was crucial given that precedents would be set with those first embassies. For the British, the precedents had long been set in Istanbul. Although many of the ambassadors viewed Ottoman officials as greedy and corrupt for accepting those gifts, fundamentally they understood that they had to conform to those conventions if they were ever to successfully represent British interests. Gift-giving was therefore a central mechanism in the day-to-day interaction of British diplomats and members of the Ottoman state, and, as will be seen, formed one part of a wider set of practices of ceremony and etiquette that the British were obliged to follow. Quite simply, the framework of diplomatic relations relied on the giving of gifts as an essential and fundamental part of diplomatic practice, without which no commercial or political business could progress. This reflects the narratives put forward in the British Capitulations, of the giving of gifts preceding the granting of privileges.

Beyond questions of appropriateness and obligation, there is the issue of finance and commerce. Abraham Stanyan's advice to the Swedes in 1729 on how to prepare an embassy to the Ottoman court gives an indication of British attitudes:

> It is so ancient and general a custom of foreign ministers to bring presents with them for the Grand Signor and grand vizier at least, that it would be looked upon as a sort of slight, if not an affront to come without any, and would be prejudicial to the minister himself both in his treatment and his allowance for his entertainment. But they need not be very costly; vests of cloth of the most fanciful colours, gay silks with gold flowers more showy than costly or rich in brocade, a few of the smallest gold repeating watches, fine spying glasses, and large looking-glasses are the toys that will be the most acceptable to the present court here.[104]

[103] BOA/HAT/145/6076, 29 Zilhicce 1204 [9 September 1790]. A detailed list of items presented to the king, queen, and ministers of state in 1793 with costings can be found at: BOA/HAT/950/40832B, 19 Rebiülahir 1208 [23 November 1793].

[104] TNA/SP97/25 Abraham Stanyan to the Duke of Newcastle, 19 April 1729.

However, as the financial analysis above revealed, British gift-giving in Istanbul was far from cheap, consuming around 10% of the Company's expenditure. Moreover, the items that Stanyan dismissed as mere toys held important social and material capital at the Ottoman court. But it is in the overwhelming dominance of textiles in gift-exchange between the British and Ottomans that we see a more complex relationship, beyond 'fanciful colours [and] gay silks'. For the British, it was a chance to market woollen manufactures, their most important export, which is why they were presented in such large numbers to the Ottoman court in the form of cloth kaftans. The commercial link can be said to apply to other British manufactures presented, especially timepieces. Thus, the interdependent link between diplomatic practice and finance can be clearly seen through gifts, which also demonstrate the importance of abiding by social conventions, and the ability to adapt those conventions to potential commercial benefit. From the Ottoman perspective, the gifts they gave and received were part of their socio-economic system. Ottoman officials receiving diplomatic gifts gained an important addition to their economic and social capital, where gifts could be passed on as new gifts or stored as savings. Moreover, the symbolism of clothing and being clothed meant that the giving and receiving of garments and fabrics was not simply important from an economic perspective, but from the point of prestige as well. When the Ottoman sultan and his officials received kaftans from the British ambassador on behalf of his nation, it was a symbol of the ambassador's respect for the Ottoman state, and when the ambassador received robes in return from the sultan and grand vizier, he was implicitly accepting their benevolence and authority.

Gift-giving was not something static. Although certain occasions tended to have the same quantity and quality of gifts given throughout the period under examination, the items that caught the interest of Ottoman officials changed as fashions and tastes changed, and varied from individual to individual. Most importantly, gift-giving provides a clear and compelling bridge between the demands of British–Ottoman commercial relations, and the ceremonial imperatives within which diplomacy was practised. Certainly, it was useful for the British to promote their merchandise via the gifts they presented to the Ottoman court, but, as Stanyan noted, not to give gifts would have been inconceivable. There were changes over time, as with ending of *pīşkeş* gifts, but the British were unable to argue for an end to gift-giving practices in general in this period. Much as gift-giving may have been resented, it formed the financial and symbolic basis of the theatre of ceremonial, without which show the basic business of diplomacy could not have been performed.

# 5

# Diplomacy as performance

## Ceremonies and spectacle

The arrival of the Ottoman ambassador Yusuf Agah Efendi to London in early 1795 was marked by a number of official ceremonies.[1] After being treated to speeches and 'a cold collation' at his residence, the ambassador processed to St James's Palace with his small retinue in a convoy of a dozen coaches accompanied by footmen and attendants, with a group of soldiers at the front clearing the way. They were received at the palace by a parade of soldiers, and the ambassador was escorted inside towards the main audience hall. Arriving at the door, he was flanked by the Lord Chamberlain on his right, and the Earl of Jersey on his left, and on entering the hall he made 'three profound reverences', which were acknowledged by the king. This moment was imagined in Mather Brown's painting, which aimed to provide a new image of the Ottoman place in the diplomatic world at the end of the eighteenth century, with the Ottoman ambassador bowing low in humility before a British monarch.[2] After this, Yusuf Agah gave a speech that was translated by his own *tercüman*, and delivered his credentials to Lord Grenville, kissing it before handing it over. The king replied, and the ambassador withdrew, again making three reverences.

The use of such ceremonial in diplomatic practice provided a means of regulating relations performing rhetorical notions of geopolitics. The ceremonies that accompanied formal meetings between the British ambassadors and the sultan, grand vizier, and other officials were part of a carefully choreographed performance of the Ottoman world-view, albeit one sufficiently flexible that it changed over time. As with Ottoman conventions of gift-giving, the British did not always have a particularly positive view of those practices.

1 TNA/FO78/14 Edward Smith to Lord Grenville, 21 December 1793; TNA/FO78/15 Untitled and undated memorandum (probably January 1794); LMA/SC/PZ/WE/02/0356 Reception at the St. Jamess Palace, *The Morning Post*, 10 January 1794; LMA/SC/PZ/WE/02/0760 Arrival of the Turkish Ambassador, with text cuttings; *TLG* no.13611, 7 January 1794, 23.

2 *His Majesty and the Officers of State Receiving the Turkish Ambassador and Suite*. Coloured engraving by Daniel Orme after a painting by Mather Brown, 1797. GAC, 16159.

However, as with gift-giving, it was necessary for the British to comply in order to ensure good relations with the Ottoman state. The idea of the actual display of friendship – *iẓhār-ı muṣāfāt ve iḫlāṣ ve işʿār-ı meveddet* (displays of amity and sincere friendship, and signs of amicability), to quote the British Capitulations – gave ceremonial a key role in physically articulating this important concept within the diplomatic framework.[3] Moreover, public ceremonies were a means to maintain Britain's prestige in relation to the other resident European embassies. In order to conceptualise Ottoman diplomatic court ceremony on particular occasions and on a daily basis, as well as British and other European traditions in Istanbul, this chapter will examine the main themes through the first audience of the ambassador with the grand vizier and the sultan.[4] First to be examined will be broader ideas of performative diplomacy, along with notions of space and spectacle through processions. This will be followed by a discussion on how the audience with the grand vizier was indicative of daily rituals, compared with that of the sultan that was intended to show the power, wealth, and hospitality of the Ottoman state. Finally, I consider the importance of representation, through British depictions of the audience with the sultan, and rivalry among the European diplomats in Istanbul.

Diplomacy has at its heart various sorts of rituals that, whilst perhaps appearing frivolous, petty, or archaic, contain various layers of meaning that form a crucial part of diplomatic language.[5] One very concise and convincing explanation of the importance of ritual in social contexts has been provided by the anthropologist Ioan Lewis, who argues that 'ritual demarcates, emphasizes, affirms, solemnizes and also smoothes over critical changes in social relationships. It is an all-purpose solvent, an inexhaustibly resourceful regulatory agent'.[6] Similarly, Jeffrey K. Walker contends that, because ritual and prestige were inseparable in diplomatic practice, 'even a seemingly meaningless change in protocol might lead to a nasty diplomatic imbroglio', and, using Lewis's framework, emphasised that ambassadors were not simply messengers of treaties or protectors of commerce:

> Because the importance of diplomatic intercourse cannot be quantified merely in numbers of trade contracts signed or amount of foreign aid received, states will continue to engage in the ritual of representative character diplomacy to allow some tangible, albeit ritualistic mechanism for directly manifesting

[3] TNA/SP108/540.

[4] I have gone into further detail on the importance of ceremonial, particularly in the context of access to the sultan: Michael Talbot, 'Accessing the Shadow of God: Spatial and performative ceremonial at the Ottoman court' in Dries Raeymaekeres & Sebastiaan Derks (eds), *The Key to Power? The Culture of Access in Princely Courts, 1400–1750* (Leiden, 2016), 101–23.

[5] Richard Sennett, *Together: The Rituals, Pleasures and Politics of Co-operation* (New Haven, 2012), 240–2; William Roosen, 'Early modern diplomatic ceremonial: A systems approach', *The Journal of Modern History* 52:3 (1980), 452–76.

[6] Ioan M. Lewis, *Social and Cultural Anthropology in Perspective*, 3rd edn (New Brunswick NJ, 2003), 136.

honour, disdain, or anger toward a nominally coequal sovereign in an intrinsically personal and human way.[7]

What, though, if the notions of equality present in modern diplomatic structures were absent? For the majority of the period under examination here, the Ottoman state certainly did not view Britain as an equal. These diplomatic rituals, as with any rituals, were only given meaning by those participating in and viewing them. Using Pierre Bourdieu's assertion that ritual practice is a means to enable encounters between opposites primarily via polysemy, I have been very much persuaded by Sarah Beckworth's analysis of ritual in fifteenth-century York, which argued that 'ritual does not so much assert a set of monolithic beliefs as construct a series of tensions'.[8] The question of tension in the Ottoman case is an interesting one. Ottoman ceremonial – procession, displays of power, feasting, and audience – all contained some elements of tension, tension of space, of passivity, and of reception. Yet polysemy seems to have permitted participation in these rituals largely without an overt expression or manifestation of those tensions; that is, multiple layers of meaning and interpretation enabled equal participation in potentially unequal settings.

Indeed, in thinking about the nature of diplomatic ceremonial, it is entirely counterproductive to attempt to separate form and meaning; and the significance of such events, be they rare or daily, in helping the ambassadors to understand Ottoman culture, and then using that knowledge to their own advantage, cannot be overstated.[9] Moreover, the particular context of the Ottoman court, in common with other Asian empires, saw the European ambassadors forced to deal with tensions between different kinds of court ritual and notions of submission and homage, and the blurred distinction between 'ritual' and 'reality'.[10] It is here that the centrality of 'performative ceremony' to diplomatic practice proves to have fascinating implications for understanding the enactment of rhetorical relations and the methods by which encounters between Ottoman elites and European diplomats were mediated

7 Jeffrey K. Walker, 'Fiction versus function: The persistence of "representative character" theory in the law of diplomatic immunity' in Harvey J. Langholtz & Chris E. Stout (eds), *The Psychology of Diplomacy* (Westport CT, 2004), 243–68 at 259–61. See also: Harvey J. Langholtz, 'The psychology of diplomacy' in Langholtz & Stout, *The Psychology of Diplomacy*, 1–18; Chris E. Stout, 'A psychologist in the diplomat's court: A primer' in Langholtz & Stout (eds), *The Psychology of Diplomacy*, 19–28.

8 Pierre Bourdieu, *Outline of a Theory of Practice*, trans. Richard Nice (Cambridge, 1977), 120; Sarah Beckwith, 'Ritual, theater, and social space in the York Corpus Christi Cycle' in Barbara A. Hanawalt & David Wallace (eds), *Bodies and Disciplines: Intersections of Literature and History in Fifteenth-Century England* (Minneapolis, 1996), 63–86 at 67–8.

9 See: Richard C. Trexler, *Public Life in Renaissance Florence* (Ithaca NY, 1991), 279–331; William N. Fenton, 'Structure, continuity, and change in the process of Iroquois treaty making' in Francis Jennings (ed.), *The History and Culture of Iroquois Diplomacy: An Interdisciplinary Guide to the Treaties of the Six Nations and Their League* (Syracuse NY, 1985), 3–37 at 18–21.

10 Hevia, *Cherishing Men from Afar*, 1–25, 74–9. See also D.R. Howland, *Borders of Chinese Civilization: Geography and History at Empire's End* (Durham NC, 1996), 15–18; L.J. Newby, *The Empire and the Khanate: A Political History of Qing Relations with Khoqand c.1760–1860* (Leiden, 2005), 1–20.

and controlled, something which has received increasing attention in the Ottoman context, particularly within a spatial framework.[11] By considering these various issues – form, meaning, submission, performance – within this particular context, I have charted changes in the ceremonial experienced by the British ambassadors at the Ottoman court across the period under examination, and what follows is a composite narrative of the ceremonies undertaken by British ambassadors on their arrival in the Ottoman Empire based on their own accounts. In that regard, Winchilsea, Harvey, Trumbull, Hussey, Sutton, Kinnoull, Murray, and Ainslie all left detailed narratives, the others giving the events a far briefer mention.[12] Additionally, I have consulted Ottoman

[11] Benjamin H. Irvin, *Clothed in the Robes of Sovereignty: The Continental Congress and the People Out of Doors* (Oxford, 2011) 168–80. For some studies dealing with this sort of ceremonial, see: Gülru Necipoğlu, 'Framing the gaze in Ottoman, Safavid, and Mughal palaces', *Ars Orientalis* 23 (1993), 303–42. See also: Ebru Boyar & Kate Fleet, *A Social History of Ottoman Istanbul* (Cambridge, 2010), 28–71; Nurhan Atasoy, 'Processions and protocol in Ottoman Istanbul' in Karin Ådahl (ed.), *The Sultan's Procession: The Swedish Embassy to Sultan Mehmed IV in 1657–1658 and the Rålamb Paintings* (Istanbul, 2006), 74–113. An interesting point of comparison is Robert M. Croskey, 'The diplomatic forms of Ivan III's relationship with the Crimean khan', *Slavic Review* 43:2 (1984), 257–69. Beyond the Ottoman context, Canepa and Dillon's work have been particularly helpful: Canepa, *Two Eyes of the Earth*, 130–44; Janette Dillon, *The Language of Space in Court Performance 1400–1625* (Cambridge, 2010), 76–102.

[12] Unless otherwise noted, my analysis is based on the following accounts: TNA/SP97/17 A narrative of ye succesese of my Voyage from Smirna to Constantinople, my arrivall there, ye manner of my entry to Pera, and my audience with ye Grand Vizier and Grand Seignour, March 1661; TNA/SP97/19 Sir Daniel Harvey to the Earl of Arlington, 31 January 1669/70; George Abbott, *Under the Turk in Constantinople: A Record of Sir John Finch's Embassy, 1674–1681* (London, 1920), 86–104, 136–46; BL, Stowe 219 Baron Chandos to William Raye, 8 August 1681; BL, Stowe 219 Baron Chandos to the Levant Company, 23 September 1681; BL, Add. 72554 The Newes sent my Lord President, 15 September 1687; BL, Add. 72544 An Acct. of his Excy's Aud:ce of ye G. Sigr., August 1688; TNA/SP97/20 Sir William Hussey to the Earl of Nottingham, 3/13 June 1691; TNA/SP97/20 Narrative of Sir Wm. Husseys going to audience to Vesir Passa govr. to the present Vizir, & Chimacham of Cons:ple, 29 June 1691; SOAS/SC:PP/15/65 Sir Wiliam Harbord to the Earl of Nottingham, 9/19 March 1691/2; TNA/SP97/20 Baron Paget to the Earl of Nottingham, 13/23 October 1693; TNA/SP97/21 A Relation of the Publick Audience which Sir Robert Sutton Ambassad:r from his Majesty of Great Brittaine to the Ottoman Porte had of the Grand Vizir the 3d of March O.S. 1701/2 at Adrianople; TNA/SP97/21 A Relation of the Publick Audience which Sir Rob:t Sutton Amabssad:r from his Maj:ty of Great Brittaine to ye Ottoman Porte had of ye Grand Sig:r, 10 March 1701/2; TNA/SP97/24(1) Edward Wortley-Montagu to Joseph Addison, 10 April 1717; TNA/SP97/24(2) Abraham Stanyan to James Craggs, 29 April 1718; TNA/SP97/26 Account of His Excellency the Earl of Kinnouls Visits to the Grand Vizir and Grand Signior, May 1730; TNA/SP97/28 Sir Everard Fawkener to the Duke of Newcastle, 12 April 1736; TNA/SP97/28 Sir Everard Fawkener to the Duke of Newcastle, 27 April 1736; TNA/SP97/33 James Porter to the Duke of Newcastle, 21 February 1746/7; TNA/SP97/33 James Porter to the Duke of Newcastle, 18 March 1746; TNA/SP97/41 Henry Grenville to the Earl of Egremont, 2 April 1762; TNA/SP97/41 Henry Grenville to the Earl of Egremont, 31 May 1762; TNA/SP97/43 John Murray to Henry Seymour Conway, 30 June 1766; TNA/SP97/52 Sir Robert Ainslie to Viscount Weymouth, 3 December 1776; TNA/FO78/15 Robert Liston to Lord Grenville, 10 October 1794; TNA/FO78/15 Robert Liston to Lord Grenville, 25 October 1794; TNA/FO78/24 Earl of Elgin to Lord Grenville, 25 November 1799; TNA/FO78/24 Earl of Elgin to Lord Grenville, 28 December 1799; TNA/FO78/40 William Drummond to Lord Hawkesbury, 23 June 1803; TNA/FO78/46 Charles Arbuthnot to Lord Mulgrave, 10 September 1805.

documents that give an insight into their view of the occasions discussed, including some archival notes on expenditure and narratives. Of particular interest has been Hakan Karateke's edition of an Ottoman protocol register (*teşrifat defteri*), but one very interesting text has been the early nineteenth-century Ottoman historian Esad Efendi's collection of ceremonial examples in the *Teşrīfāt-ı ḳadīme* (*Ancient ceremonial*, published 1287/1870).[13]

The first crucial spatial element of interaction between the ambassadors and the Ottoman state was one of separation. The resident ambassadors were physically separated from the centre of the Ottoman state by the Golden Horn. As had been the practice since Byzantine times, when the Genoese had first established a colony opposite the walled city of Constantinople, the area of Galata, the small peninsula on the extreme eastern point of the north side of the estuary, had been home to foreign merchants and ambassadors. The Ottomans retained this situation following the conquest, and in time the area, which became known as *Frengistan*, 'abode of the Franks', expanded northwards outside the walls of Galata. That neighbourhood became known as Beyoğlu, supposedly a Turkification of Italian *bailo* (the title of the Venetian ambassador), although the Europeans, as they were wont to do, continued to refer to the area by its Byzantine name of Pera. The British ambassador's residence was situated in the Tepebaşı district of Beyoğlu, in the area where the current British consulate is situated just to the west of what was known as the 'Main Street of Pera', which correlates to today's İstiklâl Caddesi, leading from the walled city of Galata in the south to the Galata Palace in the north. The British Palace, as it was known, was a rather problematic building, as we shall see shortly. It was set slightly away from the other embassies, with the French, Venetian, Dutch, and Swedish buildings situated on the Main Street or slightly off it.[14] The majority of business between the British ambassador and the Ottoman state required regular crossings of the Golden Horn. This meant extra expenditure for the embassy in the hiring of boats whenever their translators took messages and declarations to the *reisülküttab* or grand vizier. It also meant that official business could be delayed in bad weather, with the messenger having to take a longer route to cross at a narrower point or waiting for the weather to clear up. All meetings between the ambassador and the high Ottoman officials, for whatever daily business might be needed to be dealt with, and for all ceremonial matters, required this journey across the water and the expense, time, and effort that it entailed. The spatial separation was in a way coincidental, but the development of Galata/Beyoğlu as *Frengistan* created a symbolic distance that was absorbed into the performance of daily and official diplomatic encounters.

[13] Hakan T. Karateke (ed.), *An Ottoman Protocol Register Containing Ceremonies from 1736 to 1808: BEO Sadaret Defterleri 350 in the Prime Ministry Ottoman State Archives, Istanbul* (Istanbul & London, 2007); Esad Efendi, *Teşrīfāt-ı ḳadīme* (Istanbul, 1287 [1870]). I originally encountered Esad Efendi's volume via a modern Turkish translation: Esad Efendi, *Osmanlılarda Töre ve Törenler (Teşrifât-ı Kadîme)*, trans. Yavuz Ercan (Istanbul, 1979).

[14] F. Kauffer & I.B. Lechevalier, *Plan de Constantinople/Plan von Constantinopel* (Weimar, 1807). I am grateful to Shifra Braier for pointing me in the direction of this particular source.

For an audience with the sultan, as with all other business in Istanbul proper, the ambassador therefore had to cross the water, and the journey down to the docks became a good opportunity to show off his person and his retinue. First, he processed from his residence to the nearest ferry port at Tophane, a distance of around two miles. This part of the ceremony usually began at around 9 or 10am for the audience with the grand vizier, and before sunrise for that with the sultan. The procession made its way on foot through the streets of Beyoğlu, led by flaming links ('flambeaus') in the darkness before dawn in the case of their visit to the sultan.[15] On reaching the port, they were met by a number of small boats provided by the Ottoman state to take them on the half-a-mile-or-so journey across the Golden Horn. The audience was on occasion delayed by bad weather making the water too choppy to pass, such as in the case of Sir Everard Fawkener's first attempt in late March 1736, and the Earl of Elgin's in November 1799, which Lady Elgin recorded with disappointment as the dinner and ball she had planned had to be postponed, resulting in a great quantity of wasted food.[16]

If there were any European armed vessels at anchor as the ambassador and his party crossed the water, they would give a gun salute as they passed by. The practice of giving salutes with cannon fire originated in the seventeenth century, and the Ottomans embraced it enthusiastically.[17] Thomas Coke claimed that Trumbull was the first British ambassador to receive such an honour, being saluted by British, French, and Dutch ships as he crossed for his audience, although the practice was certainly around by the time of the Earl of Winchilsea. Hussey, Kinnoull, Ainslie, and Elgin all specifically reported being saluted by ships, usually receiving a royal salute of twenty-one guns as the representative of the British monarch. Ottoman practices recorded by the British include firing salutes for the sultan on his way to coronation at Eyüp, on the setting out, return, or appointment of a *kapudan paşa* (when the whole fleet would salute), on news of a military victory, and on the birth of a prince or princess.[18] Imperial pregnancies were, in fact, also a period during which the firing of cannon was prohibited, along with the holy month of Ramadan. There are numerous examples of violations of such orders, and the disputes they caused, such as a British ship firing at night-time in Ramadan in 1732, which caused the Earl of Kinnoull to be summoned to the grand vizier for an official complaint, and two

15 TNA/SP97/26 An Account of His Excellency the Earl of Kinnouls Visits to the Grand Vizir and Grand Signior, May 1730.

16 TNA/SP97/28 Sir Everard Fawkener to the Duke of Newcastle, 27 March 1736; Mary Nisbet, Countess of Elgin, *The Letters of Mary Nisbet of Dirleton, Countess of Elgin*, ed. Hamilton Grant Nisbet (New York, 1928), 48–9.

17 Boyar & Fleet, *Ottoman Istanbul*, 48.

18 TNA/FO78/10 Sir Robert Ainslie to the Marquess of Carmarthen, 15 April 1790; TNA/SP97/31 Sir Everard Fawkener to the Duke of Newcastle, 14 January 1739/40; BL, Stowe 219 Baron Chandos to William Raye, 24 December 1681; TNA/SP97/26 Earl of Kinnoull to the Duke of Newcastle, 27 September 1730; TNA/SP97/50 John Murray to the Earl of Rochford, 17 November 1774; TNA/SP97/53 Sir Robert Ainslie to Viscount Weymouth, 17 May 1777; TNA/SP97/26 Earl of Kinnoull to the Duke of Newcastle, 24 March 1731/2; TNA/SP97/55 Sir Robert Ainslie to Viscount Weymouth, 17 March 1779.

British merchants to be taken prisoner until guarantee was made that the captain would be punished.[19] That incident supposedly caused a general prohibition on cannon fire by European ships, which was only lifted in 1736.[20]

Having crossed safely, they embarked on the southern side of the Golden Horn at Bahçe Kapısı, now on the spot of the sprawling ferry docks at modern Eminönü. There, the group was met by the *çavuşbaşı*, and the ambassador would rest in a kiosk and receive refreshments, specifically the trinity of Ottoman diplomatic hospitality of coffee, sherbet, and sweetmeats. After having rested and eaten, the ceremonial really got underway, including on each occasion the same basic groups of people accompanying the ambassador in a formal procession. At the front of the group would be the *çavuş*es, the ushers of the palace, whose commander would greet the ambassador on his arrival at Bahçe Kapısı, bringing with him a large number of horses from the grand vizier's or sultan's stables in order to provide mounts for the ambassador and his retinue. This part of the ceremony was usually uneventful, aside from a period when the *çavuşbaşı* attempted to secure a position at the ambassador's right hand, the position of honour. Noted specifically by Sutton, who placed his secretary there to avoid any disruption, Kinnoull proudly reported it a sign of favour that it was not attempted on his procession. Although Porter complained of the practice in his memoirs, the issue seems to have become less important by John Murray's audience in 1766, when the *çavuşbaşı* rode beside him with no procedural problems.[21] In general, the *çavuş*es took the lead, followed by a detachment of janissaries, some belonging to the Ottoman government, others who were employed by the embassy, who provided security for the procession.

Following close behind those Ottomans came the British part of the contingent. Although Winchilsea wrote that he had 'English trumpets' heralding his approach, such a practice was not reported at later processions. The ambassador was accompanied by four main groups: the translators; footmen and grooms; his gentlemen; and the British merchants. The translators, often accompanied by the apprentice translators known as the *giovani di lingua*, would play an important part in the audiences, and were among the most valued members of the ambassador's household, or 'family'. The footmen and grooms came in various guises. The footmen tended to be liveried, and, reflecting the ambassador's dual obligations to Crown and Company, half of them tended to be dressed in the Levant Company's livery, and the other half in that of the British monarch. Although there are no surviving depictions of the Company's livery, it was described in the ambassadorial narratives as being in the 'Turkish' or 'Greek' style, which Kinnoull and Murray noted as being white in colour.[22] The royal livery was scarlet cloth lined with satin, and a note in the embassy

19 TNA/SP97/26 Earl of Kinnoull to the Duke of Newcastle, 24 March 1732.

20 TNA/SP97/28 Sir Everard Fawkener to the Duke of Newcastle, 1 March 1736.

21 Porter, *Observations*, vol. II, 35.

22 The fashion of having 'Turkish'-style servants' attire has been analysed in a fascinating article on European court festivities in this period: Edmund A. Bowles, 'The impact of Turkish military bands on European court festivals in the 17th and 18th centuries', *Early Music* 34:4 (2006), 533–60.

accounts from May 1710 gave the price for twelve new liveries made from fifty-four pikes of scarlet cloth with satin facings that, along with buttons and the tailor's fee, came to 261 *guruş*. At 21.75 *guruş* per livery, their cost was similar to the price of a cloth kaftan at 25 *guruş*, adding to the already large cost of such occasions. After the footmen came the grooms, some of whom were noted as 'gentlemen of the horse', riding in front of others leading liveried horses from the ambassador's stable. Following them rode the ambassador himself, surrounded by footmen and accompanied by the embassy secretary, who would be holding the monarch's letter to the sultan or grand vizier in a brocade or velvet sabertache. Then came the gentlemen, numbering anywhere between ten and twenty men, and who would accompany the ambassador into the audience itself and would receive *ḫilʿat*s. Decked in their finery, they formed a sort of honour guard. Finally, in a numerous gaggle, came the British 'nation', all the merchants and their servants who were inclined to attend. Additionally, if the ship that had brought the ambassador to Istanbul was still docked in the port, the captain and crew might also accompany the procession at the rear. In the case of Winchilsea, Elgin, and others, their wives accompanied them in carriages at the very back of the procession. With ushers, guards, footmen, household, and merchants, the whole troupe consisted of well over one hundred individuals, and dozens of horses provided by the Ottoman imperial stables in a show of wealth and generosity on the part of the Ottoman state.

The procession of the British ambassador to his audiences had elements of tension within the spatial aspect of his progress, but it was made palatable through polysemic interpretation. Every ritual contains an element of tension, primarily through the possibility of non-participation. Rituals and other sorts of social performances, therefore, have to contain elements to encourage participation. As such, the procession of the ambassador contained a number of layers. For the British ambassador and merchants, it was a public display of their status and wealth, a showcase of the dignity of the ambassador and of the British presence in Istanbul. For the Ottoman state, however, it was a demonstration to the populace of its capital of a foreign nation paying submission to the sultan, with a symbolic journey from 'European' *Frengistan* to 'Ottoman' Istanbul. The fact that the British processed not up some grand imperial avenue, but through streets filled with markets, mosques, and the homes of the ordinary residents of the city gives us a good sense of the intended audience, yet the nature of the procession allowed the British to believe that they were the ones displaying British might and wealth to the people of the Ottoman capital. From the Ottoman perspective, it was not a question of the British impressing the locals, but rather the procession was to show the inhabitants of Istanbul that those foreigners in all their finery were obliged to make the effort to show their deference to the sultan. One of the claims made in that monarch's titles spoke of ambassadors coming 'to our Threshold of Felicity, which is the refuge of asylum of the sultans of the earth, the place of retreat of the sovereigns of the globe'.[23] The ritual of the

[23] BOA/TS.MA.d/7018/002 fol. 7.

British ambassador processing his audience was therefore a performance of that concept of kingship, yet, because of the potential to read other meanings into the procession, the British were willing participants whilst being obliged to participate. This was only one element of performative diplomacy, and the procession was only the beginning of the audience process. On arriving at the palace, a whole different set of performances and displays designed to show off the power, wealth, and generosity of the Ottoman state required the ambassador's participation.

## Displays of hospitality and power

Having made the journey from *Frengistan* to the heart of imperial Istanbul, the ambassador would go to audience either with the grand vizier or with the sultan. The grand vizier's audience rituals were more indicative of daily practices of meetings between Ottoman and embassy officials. The audience with the sultan, however, involved a gradual procession of the ambassador from the public spaces of the imperial palace to the private space of the monarch, and each progression required participating, passively or actively, in Ottoman diplomatic performance. As with the procession, these rituals could be interpreted differently by the participating parties, allowing equal participation in otherwise unequal conditions. Above all, this performance blurred the lines between ritual and reality, with the ambassador acting in the stead of his monarch to receive the friendship of the sultan anew through this very public display of *dostluḳ*, friendship.

In order to notify the ambassador of his audience dates, it was customary for the grand vizier or *reisülküttab* to send a messenger with flowers and fruit – perhaps symbolic of the beauty and bounty of the Ottoman state – to the embassy with an oral message.[24] The audience with the grand vizier was, compared with that with the sultan, much more informal, and, being before the audience at the imperial palace, more of an introduction to daily Ottoman diplomatic practices. Arriving at the Bab-ı Ali, where the grand vizier held court, the incoming ambassador, often accompanied by the outgoing ambassador, was led to an audience room in which two velvet stools were set up a short distance from a raised and cushioned platform that the British referred to as the 'sofa'.[25] By this gesture, Ottoman ceremonial made provision for the European manner of sitting. It was customary for the grand vizier to keep the ambassador waiting for a short while, and it was seen as a particular point of honour and respect if he entered the room almost at the same time as the ambassador. The ambassador and grand vizier exchanged salutes by bowing heads, and the *selam ağası* would offer prayers for the welfare of the sultan and grand vizier. This part of the ceremony was described by the traveller

[24] For a disucssion of the role of fruit and flowers in Ottoman iconography, see: Deniz Çalışır, 'Osmanlı görsel kültüründe meyve teması: Geleneksel natürmort resimleri bağlamında bir değerlendirme', *Turkish Studies* 3:5 (2008), 65–86.

[25] For an illustration, see: GAC, 3317 *Audience of a European Ambassador with Grand Vizier* by Antonio Guardi & Studio, c. 1740.

Charles MacFarlane, supposedly witnessing the audience of a new Dutch ambassador in 1828:

> A string of attendants ranged on one side of the room set up a chorus of salutations that began with *Selam-alekim, ve alekim Selam*, and ended with the shout of Hu! Hu! – the whole loud, wild, yet monotonous, and of such a length, that I thought the choristers were going on to 'the crack of doom.' It will be understood, that these were the Asiatic greetings of peace and good will, but they sounded to my ear much more like an Indian war-whoop.[26]

This rather disparaging account of this part of the ceremony is a perfect example, as will be discussed shortly, of how the ceremony became distorted back in Britain via negative accounts, a rejection of polysemy, and a highlighting of the tensions inherent in these audiences. Nonetheless, the participants having responded to the *selam ağası* arranged themselves into certain positions, and a royal letter would be handed to the grand vizier. The incoming ambassador would then make a brief formal speech, in which he would ask that the vizier ensure that the Capitulations would be fully observed, and that British subjects would be entirely protected, giving assurances of Britain's friendship. The vizier would then reply, assuring the ambassador that, so long as the British maintained the Capitulations on their side, the Ottoman government would abide by them as well. This was an almost verbatim performance of the narrative of the Capitulations by the ambassador and the vizier:

> As long as this pact, covenant, and pledge is faithfully and purely observed by the aforementioned queen on a fixed foundation enduring the passage of time, from our part we will also hold these provisions of covenant and safety, and regulations of peace, harmony, and old friendship with full-force and with esteem.[27]

The rhetoric of friendship and its maintenance was thus cemented via this part of the ceremonial, also acknowledging the political significance of the grand vizier.

Official speeches completed, the ambassador and grand vizier would enjoy a private entertainment.[28] The social lubricants of coffee, sherbet, sweetmeats (often reported as rose-flavoured, or rose conserve), and perfumes would be brought in. These were the absolute bread and butter, as it were, of interactions between the Ottomans and the British, and indeed within Ottoman elite society in general, with coffee and sherbet being a minimum provision in all meetings.[29] The practice of coffee drinking had been introduced to Britain in

[26] Charles MacFarlane, *Constantinople in 1828: A Residence of Sixteen Months in the Turkish Capital and Provinces* (London, 1829), 328.

[27] TNA/SP108/540.

[28] VAM, PDPC/D.124-1895 *A British Official [probably the Ambassador Stratford Canning] dining with the Kaymakam of Istanbul*, painting by an anonymous Greek artist, c. 1809.

[29] Suraiya Faroqhi, *Subjects of the Sultan: Culture and Daily Life in the Ottoman Empire* (London

the mid-seventeenth century, and by the eighteenth century was a firm part of urban elite culture.[30] In modern Turkey, there is a saying that one cup of coffee is remembered for forty years, and doubtless the emphasis on the sharing of coffee in particular as a social bond existed in the Ottoman context as well.[31] These refreshments were not simply symbols of hospitality and togetherness, but, as Eyal Ginio argued, were signs of wealth, with sweets and drinks like coffee and sherbet indicating high social status.[32] Meeting rituals involving coffee, sweetmeats, and other refreshments were such an important part of practice that the British embassy had a special budget set aside for those items for when Ottoman officials and others came to the embassy on business or on social calls. The embassy accounts show a regular expenditure on coffee, sherbet, sweetmeats, and conserves, as well as perfumes, liquors, tobacco, pipes, and wine, forming as much as between 0.5% and 2% of total embassy expenditure in the period 1710–35. A set limit of 100 *guruş* per annum was implemented from 1738, rising to 185 *guruş* by the 1760s. No business meetings, therefore, would be conducted without those foodstuffs, which would be consumed by the participants as equals. The consumption of coffee and sweetmeats in the specific setting of diplomatic meetings is one clear example of the British conforming to, and even embracing, Ottoman social practices.

All audiences and conferences between the British ambassador and Ottoman officials would be accompanied by these social lubricants, and in the audience with the grand vizier this was an occasion for the exchange of pleasantries. It is, of course, difficult to know what was actually said, but from the ambassadors' accounts, conversations focused on the ambassador's journey, health, and family. As with all such exchanges, this was mediated through translators, be they those of the Ottoman court or those of the embassy. The lingua franca until the beginning of the nineteenth century was Italian, a language with which only a few of the ambassadors were conversant, and so documents and oral relations might have to go through both Italian and French or Latin before ending up in English or Ottoman Turkish. The importance of those translators cannot be overstated, and without them diplomatic interactions at all levels were all but impossible. The dynasties of translators who served the British embassy deserve further study, not just as diplomatic translators, but as businessmen and cultural nodes as well.[33]

& New York, 1995), 220; Ralph S. Hattox, *Coffee and Coffeehouses: The Origins of a Social Beverage in the Medieval Near East* (Seattle, 1985).

30 For an interesting study on this subject, see: Brian Cowan, *The Social Life of Coffee: The Emergence of the British Coffeehouse* (New Haven & London, 2005).

31 'Bir fincan kahvenin kırk yıl hatırı vardır.'

32 Eyal Ginio, 'Aspects of Muslim culture in the Ottoman Balkans: A view from eighteenth-century Salonica' in Dimitris Tziovas (ed.), *Greece and the Balkans: Identities, Perceptions, and Cultural Encounters since the Enlightenment* (Aldershot & Burlington VT, 2003), 114–26 at 120. See also: Ussama Makdisi, *The Culture of Sectarianism: Community, History, and Violence in Nineteenth-Century Ottoman Lebanon* (Berkeley & Los Angeles, 2000), 28.

33 For an important study on the nineteenth-century translators, see: Berridge, *British Diplomacy*, 49–75; G.R. Berridge, 'Dragomans and oriental secretaries in the British embassy in Istanbul'

Baron Paget, perhaps unfairly, described his translators in 1693 as 'the dullest souls I ever met with', but they had a difficult role to fulfil.[34] The British embassy was served by a number of Levantine (Catholic and Italian-speaking) Ottoman families, from the Timonis in the late seventeenth century to the Pisanis at the end of the eighteenth, with other figures such as Antonio Perone under Paget, Lucca Chirico under Stanyan, Andronico Geracchi under Kinnoull, Antonio Crutta under John Murray, and Antonio Danè under Ainslie. In 1749, after a solicitation by the long-serving Antonio Pisani, the chief translator of the embassy was granted the title of 'His Majesty's Interpreter of the Oriental Languages' in order to put him on a par with those of the other embassies.[35] Aside from the Earl of Kinnoull's ill-founded suspicions that Chirico was a French spy, relations between the translators and ambassadors were generally cordial, quite simply because such a relationship relied entirely on the trust of the ambassador that the messages relayed to and from the Ottoman court were accurately conveyed and translated. Comparisons between official *taḳrīr*s (declarations) in English, Italian, and Ottoman Turkish show that the ambassadors were generally in good hands, and there were very few complaints by the ambassadors about their translators. The embassy would employ at least three senior 'dragomans' (the English corruption of *tercüman*), with a number of *giovani di lingua* being trained and schooled in the embassy. This is why one finds dynasties of translators such as the Pisanis, as it was common for father or uncle to teach sons or nephews, and certainly in the British case from the 1760s dragomans such as Stefano and Bartolommeo Pisani became skilled not just in Ottoman Turkish and Italian, but in French and English as well. This is not to mention the powerful official Ottoman court translators, such as the Mavrokordátos family in the late seventeenth and early eighteenth centuries. Thus, the small talk between the ambassador and the grand vizier over coffee and sweets represented conventions of Ottoman hospitality, but, as with all official business, required the mediation of individual translators and so relied on their talents to translate both linguistically and culturally.

Coffee drunk, confections devoured, and compliments exchanged and translated, the ambassadors and their gentlemen would receive their various kaftans from the vizier, and occasionally the ambassador might receive silk handkerchiefs as well as a more personal token of friendship. Following this ceremony, the ambassador and his retinue would leave, and return to the embassy in the same order of procession as they arrived. Although the form of the ceremony barely changed in the century-and-a-half between Winchilsea's

in Yurdusev (ed.), *Ottoman Diplomacy: Conventional or Unconventional?*, 151–66. See also: Alexander H. de Groot, 'Dragomans' careers: The change of status in some families connected with the British and Dutch embassies at Istanbul, 1785–1829' in Alastair Hamilton, Alexander H. de Groot & Maurits H. van den Boogert, *Friends and Rivals in the East: Studies in Anglo-Dutch Relations in the Levant from the Seventeenth to the Early Nineteenth Century* (Leiden, 2000), 223–46.

34 SOAS/SC.PP/1/6 Baron Paget to William Blathwayt, 28 May/7 June 1693.

35 TNA/SP97/34 James Porter to the Duke of Bedford, 25 August 1749; TNA/SP97/34 Duke of Bedford to James Porter, 12 October 1749.

arrival in 1661 and Arbuthnot's in 1805, there was certainly a change in the tone of the ceremony as time went on. In the earlier period, British accounts noted a definite tone of haughtiness at these audiences. Having been introduced as a great noble, Winchilsea aimed to demonstrate Charles II's high opinion of the Ottoman Empire by pointing out that he had been the first diplomat to be dispatched by the king, sent even before those to Christian monarchs. Winchilsea reported the reply of the Köprülü Mehmed Paşa, using Ottoman universalist rhetoric, that this 'was but reason, since the Grand Seignior was an emperor, and they but kings, and he the greatest and most sovereign potent one of the whole world'.[36] From the time of Kinnoull's audience in 1730, this sort of language was no longer reported, and the adjective 'civil' was the one most employed to describe the ambassadors' reception by the grand vizier. The earlier distance that had existed in the late seventeenth century, under the powerful Köprülü viziers in particular, had to a large extent ended. Whilst the format remained the same, the experience of the earlier ambassadors such as Winchilsea, Finch, and Chandos was very different to the friendly and increasingly deferential receptions accorded to later ambassadors like Ainslie, Elgin, and Arbuthnot. This provides further clues to the changing political balance, but also shows that these audiences remained an important feature of the performance of relations nonetheless.

The audience with the grand vizier was important in introducing the ambassador to the real power in the Ottoman state, yet it was also an introduction to the basic rituals of business, specifically meetings mediated by translators, and accompanied by the social lubricants of caffeine and sugar. The audience with the sultan, however, was far more symbolic in representing the meeting of two states. The ambassador was the representative of the British monarch, and the sultan was the personification of the might of the Ottoman Empire. Thus, the way in which the British ambassador was received by the Ottoman monarch was the physical representation of British–Ottoman relations. The ceremony itself incorporated a wide range of traditions and customs, and, unlike the audience with the grand vizier, did noticeably change over the period under examination, specifically at its very end in the reign of Selim III. It also contained problems of participation, in that certain elements were interpreted as enforcing the submission of the British ambassador. As with the procession to the palace, the rituals associated with the audience with the sultan were public enactments of Ottoman universalist monarchy, but at the same time were not so full of tension as to negate polysemy and preclude voluntary participation.

In his survey of traditional Ottoman court ceremonial, Esad Efendi gave the basic mechanics of an ambassador's meeting with the sultan in the seventeenth and eighteenth centuries:

> For ambassadors coming with letters from Muslim rulers and from the Christian states, if [the letter] shall be presented at the imperial council, on

[36] TNA/SP97/17 A narrative of ye sucksese of my Voyage from Smirna to Constantinople.

> the day council is held the ambassador enters the imperial presence in the petition-hall and, completing his declaration, the letter is taken from the ambassador's hands to the standard-bearer. Then it is delivered to the row of viziers and is passed by hand along that line to His Highness the grand vizier. At the same time on the imperial throne, situated on the sofa, His Majesty our majestic and noble lord may command an imperial speech [to be given]. If not, he commands a sign [to be made], and His Highness the grand vizier and the court translator intervene and give the ambassador an explanation, after which the ambassador is sent away.[37]

Yet this does little to provide a sense of the spatial and symbolic protocols that preceded the main moment of the encounter between sultan and ambassador. The date for the audience with the sultan was generally determined by days on which the janissaries received their pay from the Ottoman government, and this particular occasion was chosen, according to the Earl of Winchilsea, as 'the Ottoman court appears then in its greatest splendour, which they were desirous I should see and admire, and report their greatness to my master with the best advantage'.[38] This was therefore a carefully choreographed piece of performative diplomacy, with the date of performance specifically selected to best convey the message of Ottoman power and superiority. The ceremonial of the audience with the sultan was complex, and can be divided into three sections, each fulfilling a different role.[39] The first section aimed to display the military power, material wealth, and justice of the Ottoman state, and the second part demonstrated Ottoman hospitality. The final part of the ceremonial, the audience with the sultan itself, the most potentially problematic part from the perspective of voluntary participation, will be discussed in more detail below.

The first part of this ceremonial was intended to awe the ambassador with the might and wealth of the Ottoman state. Arriving at the outer gate of Topkapı Palace, known as the Bab-ı Hümayun, 'the imperial gate', the ambassador and his retinue dismounted. Moving into the palace's Second Court through the imposing Babü's-selam or 'gate of greeting', the ambassador would be greeted by the sight of thousands of janissaries on parade, standing utterly still in complete silence; Winchilsea estimated 5,000, Trumbull 6,000, Sutton 3,000, Kinnoull 4,000. As noted above, the audience with the sultan was almost always scheduled to coincide with the day on which the janissaries received their quarterly pay. An important part of that process involved large dishes of pilaf rice being placed on the ground in the Second Court, and, on a signal being given, the thousands of assembled troops would scramble across the courtyard to devour it. Food formed a central part of janissary

[37] Esad Efendi, *Teşrīfāt-ı ḳadīme*, 79–80.

[38] TNA/SP97/17 Earl of Winchilsea to Sir Edward Nicholas, 4 March 1661.

[39] Images of these three stages of the ceremonial can be found in the paintings of Antonio Guardi and Studio in c. 1740: GAC, 3319 *European Ambassador in the Second Court of Topkapi Palace*; GAC, 3318 *Dinner Given by Grand Vizir to European Ambassador*; GAC, 3316 *Audience of a European Ambassador with the Sultan.*

identity. Indeed, the janissaries were organised according to food: as a unit they were referred to as an *ocaḳ* (hearth); their battalions were headed by a *çorbacı* (soup-maker); and they signalled their displeasure by turning over and beating their *kazgan*s (cauldrons). The feeding of the janissaries showed the renewal of the bond between the corps and the sultan, and they demonstrated their pleasure by rushing across the court to greedily devour the rice, which must have been quite a sight. The ambassadors were therefore treated to two spectacles with separate but clear messages. The strength and discipline of the military contingent emphasised the military might of the Ottoman Empire, and was a nod to the consequences of having unfriendly relations with the Sublime State. At the same time, the feeding of the janissaries demonstrated their loyalty to the sultan, but also hinted at the wealth and bounty of the state in providing such a large body of men with such a great quantity of food.

The next show of imperial power came when the ambassador would be led across the court to the Divan-ı Hümayun, the imperial council hall. There, he would be presented to the grand vizier, who was assembled in full council with the other important ministers of state. As in his formal audience with the grand vizier, a velvet stool was provided for the ambassador and, with the sultan observing proceedings through a grate in the wall, the imperial council would dispense various functions of state. For instance, Winchilsea, Harbord, and Murray reported that the coins for the janissaries' pay would be inspected for quality and quantity, whilst Trumbull, Sutton, and Ainslie wrote that petitions were presented, heard, and judged. Another example of a performative display, this provided a new level to the ideas conveyed through the parade of the janissaries in showing that the Ottoman state operated under an ordered set of laws. Together, these two initial pieces of imperial theatre, the display of the Ottoman military and of the justice of the Ottoman state in action, were clearly designed to impress the ambassadors with the Empire's might on the one hand, and its ordered state on the other. Together, these two functions of state provided a powerful moral to foreign ambassadors: if peace were maintained, the ambassador and his nation might expect the due process of Ottoman justice for their merchants; if not, the army was well paid, well fed, and ready to fight for an organised and efficient state. However, in terms of polysemy, it could easily be seen as a display performed to honour the ambassador, rather than to threaten or awe him, with the parade a sign of respect as in the European context, and his inclusion in an imperial council meeting akin to the more regular sort of court presence ambassadors undertook in Europe.

After this display of statecraft, the second section of the audience ceremony would begin, which involved a demonstration of Ottoman hospitality via the provision of a feast. Feasting formed a central part in diplomatic ceremonial, and hospitality, with its numerous conventions, continue to form a great part of culture in the lands of the former Ottoman state, particularly in modern Turkey where the concept of *misafirperverlik* is still an important tenet in many social contexts. A combination of the Arabic *musāfir*, 'guest/traveller', the Persian '*perver*', 'care/cherish', and the Turkish suffix '*-lik*' denoting an abstract noun, *misafirperverlik* is one of those wonderfully mixed words that in its sum denotes a key notion of hospitality.[40] The feast provided by the grand vizier was not the institutionalised form of hospitality practised in hotels and hostels; rather, the hospitality offered on this occasion was more akin to domestic hospitality, as with the provision of coffee and confections described above, only in this case more in the context of explicit diplomatic performance.[41] Eating and drinking were a crucial part of diplomatic interaction, yet unlike the more informal practice of consuming coffee and sweetmeats at the audience with the grand vizier, the occasion of an audience with the sultan involved the rather different matter of a state banquet.

Britain, of course, had its own traditions of formal state dining. From the sixteenth-century banqueting hall in Hampton Court to the grand dining room in the Brighton Pavilion at the beginning of the nineteenth century, formal eating rooms were central features of British palaces. Perhaps the most notable example of state dining, however, was the famous *grand couvert*, the public performance of eating by the French king and queen in front of the court at Versailles, with the monarch being served dozens of expensive and rich dishes of different sorts in quick succession, and with a display of food on the table as representative of the bounty of France and its commerce in what Peter Brown has called a 'medieval service'.[42] One of the foremost cookbooks of the day, François Massialot's *Le cuisinier roïal et bourgeois* (*The royal and bourgeois cook*, 1705), opened its third revision in 1734 with the proud declaration that 'the pleasure of the table belongs to all ages, sexes, and nations, and there is no-one who does not desire to be served in the French style'.[43] One great example of this from the British case can be found in Francis Sandford's wonderful illustrated book of James II's coronation in 1685,

[40] For an example of such a construction: Bayram Nazır, *Ottoman Hospitality and Its Impact on Europe* (Istanbul, 2008), especially 3–4.

[41] For some discussions on defining hospitality, see: Olivia Remie Constable, *Housing the Stranger in the Mediterranean World: Lodging, Trade, and Travel in Late Antiquity and the Middle Ages* (Cambridge, 2003). See 1–11 for her succint and convincing theoretical framework. For another discussion, see: Amy Singer, 'The "Michelin Guide" to public kitchens in the Ottoman Empire' in Amy Singer (ed.), *Starting with Food: Culinary Approaches to Ottoman History* (Princeton NJ, 2011), 69–92; Conrad Lashley, 'Towards a theoretical understanding' in Conrad Lashley & Alison Morrison (eds), *In Search of Hospitality: Theoretical Perspectives and Debates* (Oxford, 2000), 1–17; Elizabeth Telfer, 'The philosophy of hospitableness' in Lashley & Morrison (eds), *In Search of Hospitality*, 38–55; Kevin O'Gorman, L.R. McLellan, & Tom Baum, 'Tourism in Iran: Central control and indigeneity' in Richard Butler & Tom Hinch (eds), *Tourism and Indigenous Peoples: Issues and Implications* (Oxford, 2007), 251–64.

[42] Peter Brown, 'Dining by design' in Harlan Walker (ed.), *The Meal: Proceedings of the Oxford Symposium on Food and Cookery, 2001* (Totnes, 2002), 58–66 at 63. See also: Jeroen Duindam, *Vienna and Versailles: The Courts of Europe's Dynastic Rivals, 1550–1780* (Cambridge, 2003), 166–80; Anne Lair, 'The ceremony of dining at Napoleon III's court between 1852 and 1870' in Daniëlle de Vooght (ed.), *Royal Taste: Food, Power and Status at the European Courts after 1789* (Farnham, 2011), 143–70 at 145–7.

[43] François Massialot, *Le nouveau cuisinier royal et bourgeois*, 3 vols (Amsterdam, 1734), vol. I, 1. See also: Sean Takats, *The Expert Cook in Enlightenment France* (Baltimore, 2011), 98–119; Maurice Bensoussan, *Les particules alimentaires: naissance de la gastronomie au XVIe siècle* (Paris, 2003).

which gave the detailed setting of each of the tables along with the placing of the 145 different dishes served.[44] Eating habits, however, changed greatly during the eighteenth century, with the introduction of new implements such as forks, and new conventions of dining etiquette. Finally, at the beginning of the nineteenth century, the old French style was slowly being challenged by *service à la russe*, which saw dishes served individually in set courses in a way that modern diners would recognise.[45]

The Ottoman state had its own version akin to *service à la français* in the formal feasts it provided for its own officials and for visiting ambassadors. This dining experience differed from the performative display of the military parade and viewing of the imperial council as it required the active participation of the ambassador and his retinue. With the business of state over in the *divan*, a number of low tables (between three and five) known as *sofra*s were brought into the council chamber, which was the usual practice in such meetings when dinner served at noon would provide a formal break in the long deliberations of the ministers.[46] There were set seating patterns at diplomatic feasts, with the ambassador and grand vizier sat together at one table attended by their chief translators, some mixed tables of British gentlemen and Ottoman officials (including high officials such as the *defterdar* and *nişancı*), and one separate table for the *kazasker*s of Rumelia and Anatolia, two top Ottoman religious judges who were separated from the non-Muslims. The rest of the retinue had tables laid for them in the gallery outside the hall. With the company seated, dinner would be served, with communal bowls and an almost constant flow of food brought to the table. The one thing that does seem to have consistently attracted comment from British participants was the lack of knives, or any sort of cutlery except for spoons, which Murray described as made from horn. Soups and liquid dishes were eaten with the spoons, whilst the more solid courses would be eaten with the right hand. Winchilsea quipped that 'we had no knives laid for us to cut, for supposing the sharpness of our stomachs would make amends for the want of knives'.[47] A similar criticism came in Isaac Bickerstaff's 1775 comedy *The Sultan or, a Peep into the Seraglio*, in which the spirited British slave girl Roxelana, discovering that there were no knives provided, cried in horror, 'what, do they mean to make me sit squat like a baboon, and tear my meat with my fingers?'[48] Many of the accounts also noted the speed at which the dishes were brought to the table and then removed, so that the diner would only have opportunity to have a short taste of the food before it was whisked away in yet another display of the sultan's wealth.

Winchilsea reported being served twenty courses, Sutton one hundred individual dishes, and the others all concurred that a great many plates of

44 Francis Sandford, *The History of the Coronation of the Most High, Most Mighty, and Most Excellent Monarch, James II* (London, 1687), 110–11.

45 Edward Muir, *Ritual in Early Modern Europe* (Cambridge, 1997), 134–40.

46 Mehrdad Kia, *Daily Life in the Ottoman Empire* (Santa Barbara CA, 2011), 59–61.

47 TNA/SP97/17 A narrative of ye suckses of my Voyage from Smirna to Constantinople.

48 Isaac Bickerstaff, *The Sultan or, a Peep into the Seraglio* (Cork, 1781), 22.

food had been presented. A commonly cited source is that of Paul Rycaut, but the most detailed account can be found in the diary of the embassy chaplain under Harvey and Finch, John Covel, who attended Finch's arrival audience in 1674.[49] Although he confessed that he could not remember exactly every single dish, the menu he provided is striking enough:

> Six roast chickens brought piled one upon another, without sauce;
> A dish of roast pigeons;
> *Kibóbs* [*kebap*s], bits of flesh, the first roasted, the last boiled; this was ready mammocked, and cut to our hands;
> Several sorts of *dolmáh* [*dolma*], which is minced meat stuffed into pieces of gourds, or gobbeted in vine leaves or the like, and so boiled;
> Several *Cherbaws* [*çorba*s], pottages made of rice, wheat, etc., some sweet, some savoury;
> *Pelo* [*pilav*], rice boiled with pieces of a hen;
> Rice jellied, a perfect fool in a platter;
> Slip-slop of dates and pine kernells;
> A great baked pie in a platter, with puff pastry above and minced beaten meat, well-seasoned underneath;
> A puff pastry pudding in a platter, plain;
> Another, sweetened with honey.

Halfway through this feast, the guests were served with lemon sherbet, which Covel described as being 'brought in a *fingeon* [*fincan*], of Polish glass, gilt on the verge at the top'. This account correlates with lists of provisions from the imperial kitchens on such occasions, and with two very important analyses of formal state dining at the Ottoman court: Joanita Vroom's analysis of the Dutch ambassador Cornelis Calkoen's arrival audience in 1727; and Hedda Reindl-Kiel's discussion of official meals in the seventeenth-century Ottoman court.[50]

This manner of feasting was still practised at the beginning of the nineteenth century. As Özge Samancı has demonstrated, it was only with the move away

49 Rycaut, *History*, 150–3; John Covel, 'Extracts from the diaries of Dr. John Covel, 1670–1679' in Bent (ed.), *Early Voyages*, 99–288 at 260–4.

50 The first relates to Sutton's audience and the second to Elgin's: BOA/D.BŞM.MTE.d/10792, 29 Şaban 1113 [28 January 1702]; BOA/C.HR/14/654, 9 Receb 1214 [7 December 1799]; Joanita Vroom, '"Mr. Turkey goes to Turkey," or: how an eighteenth-century Dutch diplomat lunched at Topkapı Palace' in Amy Singer (ed.), *Starting with Food*, 139–76; Hedda Reindl-Kiel, 'The chickens of paradise: Official meals in the mid-seventeenth century Ottoman palace' in Suraiya Faroqhi & Cristoph K. Neumann (eds), *The Illuminated Table, the Prosperous House: Food and Shelter in Ottoman Material Culture* (Würzburg, 2003), 59–88. Other useful works on the organisation of the palace kitchens, and on the historiography of food in Ottoman studies, include: Suraiya Faroqhi, 'Introduction' in Faroqhi & Neumann (eds), *The Illuminated Table*, 9–34; İsmail Hakkı Uzunçarşılı, *Osmanlı Devletinin Saray Teşkilâtı* (Ankara, 1945), 379–92, 460; Metin Saip Sürücüoğlu, 'Osmanlı İmparatorluğu'nda Mutfak teşkilatı protokol tören ve şenlik yemekleri' in Kamil Toygar (ed.), *Türk Mutfak Kültürü Üzerine Araştırmalar* (Ankara, 1999), 49–81.

from Topkapı Palace under Mahmud II (r. 1808–39) that the mode of eating and the general setting of formal dining really began to adopt more of the European style.[51] The message of the feast given in the presence of the ambassador was clear. If the passive participation in the earlier displays had been intended to show the might and wealth of the Ottoman state, then active participation in the feast was to demonstrate that the Ottoman state was generous and hospitable to visitors and guests, as well as to further that sense of power. It is interesting, however, to note that whilst the setting of the feast in the *divan* hall, along with the quantity of food provided, was designed to impress the ambassadors, the fact that Ottomans and Britons were sitting together at the same tables, eating the same food, and sharing from the same bowls, represented a degree of equality under the sultan.[52] From another viewpoint, as with the performative displays, the ambassadors could interpret the feast as the Ottoman state honouring them and their master through providing such a vast and costly meal.

The first two rituals at the palace were full of meaning for British and Ottoman participants, specifically through demonstrations of power, and offerings of hospitality. In regular diplomatic practice, of the kind introduced at the audience with the grand vizier, coffee and sweetmeats provided a ritual element to meetings that, along with the necessary mediation of translators, gave an element of familiarity to such encounters. The ceremonial at the audience with the sultan, however, as with the procession, formed part of a more symbolic enactment of relations between Britain and the Ottoman Empire, something I have attempted to visualise in figure 7, where each stage of the ceremonial saw the ambassador required to undergo certain preconditions in order to move towards the presence of the sultan.

Not only did the ambassador have to process across the Golden Horn in a symbolic journey from *Frengistan*, but on arrival at the imperial palace was obliged to witness displays of Ottoman military power, material wealth, and ordered justice. This was then followed by participation in a formal state feast that demonstrated the generosity and hospitality of the Ottomans towards foreign guests. As with the procession, these elements of performative diplomacy could be interpreted in a number of ways. For the ambassador, the displays could be seen to be honouring his visit, with the effort and expense entailed showing Ottoman respect for him and his nation, especially considering that at the feast Ottomans and Britons sat and ate largely as equals. Simultaneously from the perspective of the Ottoman state, the displays demonstrated the might, wealth, and justice of their state, demonstrating the consequences of friendly and unfriendly relations, and the feast showed that

[51] Özge Samancı, 'Pilaf and bouchées: The modernization of official banquets at the Ottoman palace in the nineteenth century' in de Vooght (ed.), *Royal Taste*, 111–42. An interesting point of comparison is with similar processes in Meiji Japan in the mid-nineteenth century: M. William Steele, *Alternative Narratives in Modern Japanese History* (London, 2003), 110–32.

[52] Azam Torab, *Performing Islam: Gender and Ritual in Iran* (Leiden, 2007), 83, 115; Martin Jones, *Feast: Why Humans Share Food* (Oxford, 2007); Sidney W. Mintz & Christine M. Du Bois, 'The anthropology of food and eating', *Annual Review of Anthropology* 31 (2002), 99–119.

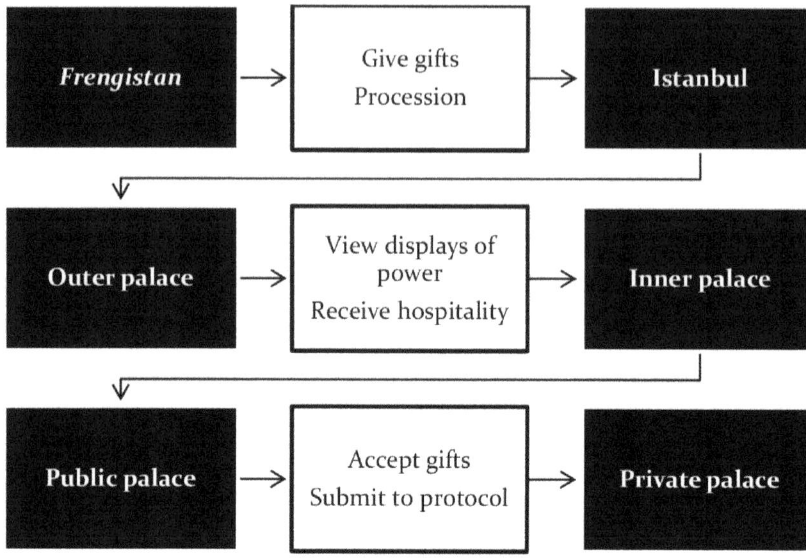


Figure 7: Levels and conditions of access in the audience with the sultan

all the participants were equally dependent on the sultan for their sustenance. These multiple layers of meaning ensured participation in these rituals of diplomacy, yet until this point in the ceremonial there was sufficient subtlety to permit polysemy. However, the final part of this ceremonial, the audience with the sultan, is a clear example of the importance of multiple meanings and interpretation in diplomatic rituals.

## Ritual and representations

Dinner eaten, the ambassador and his gentlemen moved from the *divan* hall across the spacious Second Court, with the massive chimneys of the kitchens forming an imposing sort of colonnade, and another reminder of the sultan's wealth. They then reached the beautiful and imposing Babü's-saadet, the 'gate of felicity', signifying the entrance to the Enderun, the inner and private part of the palace. There, the ambassador and a number of specially selected gentlemen would be vested with their *ḫilʿat*s. Spatially, the ceremony began to take on an air of privacy and confinement, in contrast to the wide-open spaces of the first courts of the palace. The Babü's-saadet was wide and tall, but its passage was low and narrow, acting as a funnel. Through the gate was the covered kiosk of the Arz Odası, the petition-hall where the sultan received high officials and ambassadors. The side of that kiosk facing the Babü's-saadet was fronted by an arcade of marble columns with a low ceiling linking it to the gate, and two doors either side of a large grated window. In front of that window the ambassador's gifts were displayed, having been ferried to the palace prior to the audience. The view of the more private parts of the palace was obscured by the audience chamber itself, focusing attention on the door through which the sultan sat and the window before which the gifts were displayed.[53] The display of the costly gifts the British had provided, along with the experiences of the procession, the parade and feeding of the soldiers, the dispensing of justice, the feast, and the robing, and the spatial layout of the palace all combined, from the Ottoman perspective, to demonstrate the sultan's authority and the ambassador's role as a pseudo-subject.

On reaching the entrance to the petition-hall, the ambassador and his retinue were approached by number of *kapıcı*s or *çavuş*es. Two of those officials would restrain each of the foreigners by holding their arms, and, on entering the audience hall, would push behind their necks to make them bow low before the sultan. This was potentially a very humiliating event, especially considering European attitudes towards the inviolability of the person of the ambassador, and it thus required a process to make it palatable. The most common European explanation for this particular custom can be found in the sixteenth-century memoirs of the Habsburg ambassador Ogier Ghiselin de Busbecq, and in Rycaut's history.[54] The story went that, during an audience, a Serbian nobleman had concealed a knife under his cloak and murdered Murad I (r. 1362–89), and consequently weapons were banned from the audience chamber and visitors were to be restrained as a security measure.[55] However, Esad Efendi's description of the ceremonial for the grand vizier and şeyhülislam attending the sultan before viewing the Prophet's Mantle (*ziyāret-i ḥırka-ı şerīf*) demonstrates that such physical restraining was a common practice:

> The right arm of His Highness the grand vizier was taken by the sword-bearer, and his left arm by the chief of the imperial doormen; and His Highness the şeyhülislam was taken under his arms [*ḳoltuḳlarına girüb*] by two individual imperial doormen.[56]

Therefore, this practice was not imposed on European diplomats simply to humiliate them, but was a ritual participated in by the highest Ottoman officials. Nor were such practices limited to the Ottomans, as demonstrated in a narrative of an embassy from the Duke of Holstein to Shah Safi of Iran in 1637, in which Safavid officials 'took them under the arms, one after the other, and brought them to the king'.[57] The author of that account was sympa-

53 Necipoğlu, 'Framing the gaze', 305.

54 Rycaut, *History*, 154; Ogier Ghiselin de Busbecq, *The Turkish Letters of Ogier Ghiselin de Busbecq, Imperial Ambassador at Constantinople, 1554–1562*, trans. Edward Seymour Forster (Oxford, 1927), 58–9.

55 For some interesting discussions on the subsequent literary and nationalistic representations of this event, see: Branimir Anzulovic, *Heavenly Serbia: From Myth to Genocide* (New York, 1999), 13–17; Tatyana Popović, *Prince Marko: The Hero of South Slavic Epics* (Syracuse NY, 1988), 21–37.

56 Esad Efendi, *Teşrīfāt-ı ḳadīme*, 15.

57 Adam Olearius, *The Voyages and Travels of the Ambassadors from the Duke of Holstein, to the Great Duke of Muscovy, and the King of Persia*, trans. John Davies (London, 1662), 272.

thetic to the rationale behind this custom, saying that it 'is very necessary, and must now be looked on as a particular honour done the ambassadors, though it be said, and that very probably, that with the same labour, they secure the prince's life'.[58] In the Ottoman case, there was certainly sense in demanding that the ambassadors should be disarmed and restrained, as there were no armed soldiers in the audience chamber. Refusing to be restrained could have been interpreted as a threat to the sultan's life, and armed men were denied access to the Enderun. For instance, when an early eighteenth-century French ambassador refused to remove his sword, he was denied his audience, his gifts were returned, and his *ḫilʿat*s taken back.[59] Despite the potential humiliation of being manhandled before a foreign monarch, it was possible to give the ritual of greeting the sultan an alternative meaning by highlighting the explanation that this was a matter of security not humiliation, and that it was in fact honourable as it was a ritual reserved for ambassadors and high Ottoman officials. This is not to say that there was no attempt at all to instil some humility in foreign ambassadors through such a ritual; yet there was clearly something more to this practice than simple humiliation.

The tone of this part of the ceremony changed greatly towards the end of the eighteenth century. For instance, there was a long-established custom that the sultan never spoke to the ambassador, nor looked directly at him, instead staring off at an angle in a stance of superiority. This began to change from the 1760s, at least according to the accounts of the British ambassadors. Murray recorded that the sultan's expression in his audience in 1765, far from being aloof, was rather friendly, and Ainslie was surprised when Abdülhamid I turned halfway to look at him for the whole audience. Robert Liston commented on the removal of the 'sullen and contemptuous dignity' that sultans had previously employed, and was given a 'gracious and attentive' reception by Selim III. Of course, how far these were genuinely reflective of the audience or attempts by the ambassadors to impress their superiors in London is unclear. Nonetheless, as Selim's reign progressed, audience customs evidently begin to change. Drummond reported that '[t]he emperor spoke to me several times, which I believe never happened before at a first audience', asking after George III's health and praising Britain's friendship with the Sublime State. Drummond even reported that, following his audience of leave later in 1803, he was given a tour of some of the interior and private parts of the palace at the sultan's invitation.[60] A change in ceremonial can also be discerned through a new sort of honour to go along with the *ḫilʿat*, the European-style Order of the Crescent (*hilāl nişānı*).[61] Both Drummond and Arbuthnot received the first-class version of this award in 1803 and 1805 respectively.[62] The friendly reception, conver-

[58] Ibid.

[59] SOAS/SC.PP/3/20 Baron Paget to Lord Jersey, 10 January 1700/1.

[60] TNA/FO78/40 William Drummond to Lord Hawkesbury, 13 November 1803.

[61] An example can be found at NMM, REL0121 Embroidered star of a Knight of the Ottoman Order of the Crescent, 1799–1805.

[62] TNA/FO78/40 William Drummond to Lord Hawkesbury, 24 June 1803; TNA/FO78/46 Charles Arbuthnot to Lord Mulgrave, 10 September 1805. Then, as now, the British monarch had to

sation, and chivalric order received by those last two ambassadors would have been entirely alien to their predecessors even fifty years earlier.

Despite these later changes, the ceremonial surrounding a British ambassador's audience with the Ottoman sultan was fairly consistent throughout the eighteenth century. As such, narratives of these events became fairly standardised, and an embassy chaplain in the late eighteenth century noted in his travel memoirs that 'scarcely an author on the Levant, from the earliest accounts, has omitted to describe the ceremonies of the audience of the sultan or vizier'.[63] However, there are subtle differences in some of these accounts that reveal British attitudes towards the audience. In several literary accounts, the encounter with the sultan was presented as being typical of the haughty manners of the 'East', including in the fictional correspondence of the *Turkish Spy*, and particularly in Charles MacFarlane's account of life in Istanbul, which spoke of 'all the punctilios of oriental respect'.[64] MacFarlane's words implied something hollow but excessively precise, and the idea of 'oriental respect' was presented as a contradiction in terms. One similarly critical account was by a Scottish merchant, Thomas MacGill, who travelled extensively in the Ottoman realms, giving a dramatic account of Charles Arbuthnot's 'farce' of an audience with Selim III in 1805. In his description of the conveyance of the ambassador through the Babü's-saadet to meet the sultan, the *kapıcı*s who held the ambassador and his retinue by their arms were transformed into beasts:

> This guard was composed of the ugliest monsters that ever wore the human form; their features were horrible with the flesh depending from them; their faces were of the most deadly hue. Each infidel was now adorned with two eunuchs, who laid a paw on each shoulder, to signify when he was to bend before the King of Kings, and also to prevent outrage in his presence.[65]

MacGill's account is a good example of a response to a ritual practice in which the tensions were so strong due to the perceived injustice of inequality between the participants that they elicited an extremely negative reaction from

grant permission to wear foreign orders. For Drummond's permission: BOA/HAT/245/13789, 30 Rebiülevvel 1218 [1803].

63 James Dallaway, *Constantinople Ancient and Modern, with Excursions to the Shores and Islands of the Archipelago and to the Troad* (London, 1797), 26.

64 *Letters Writ by a Turkish Spy, Who liv'd five and forty Years undiscover'd at Paris*, 8 vols (London, 1734), vol. VI, 3–4; MacFarlane, *Constantinople in 1828*, 91. See also: Roger North, *The Life of the Honourable Sir Dudley North, Knt., Commissioner of the Customs, and afterwards of the Treasury to his Majesty King Charles the Second* (London, 1744), 76; Johann Christian von Struve, *Travels in the Crimea: A History of the Embassy from Petersburg to Constantinople, in 1793* (London, 1802), 173, 219. For a comparison with Byzantine etiquette see: Averil Cameron, 'The construction of court ritual: The Byzantine Book of Ceremonies' in David Cannadine & Simon Price (eds), *Rituals of Royalty: Power and Ceremonial in Traditional Societies* (Cambridge, 1987), 106–37.

65 Thomas MacGill, *Travels in Turkey, Italy, and Russia, During the Years 1803, 1804, 1805, and 1806*, 2 vols (London & Edinburgh, 1808), vol. II, 9–10.

the observer. For MacGill, it was intolerable to see the representative of the British monarch manhandled before this foreign ruler.

A similar case from the perspective of a participant came from the pen of the former ambassador James Porter. Porter viewed the whole ceremony as an insult, saying that '[p]ersonal vanity, or national pride, has not permitted Christian writers to set this ceremonial in its true light; nay, some ambassadors have been for softening and palliating the worst of its indecorum'.[66] He may well have been referring to the tone set in publications such as *The London Gazette*, and more likely to popular magazines such as *The Weekly Amusement* and *The Historical Register*, the latter having described the Earl of Kinnoull's audience as an example of 'Turkish civility and magnificence'.[67] Porter's criticisms were echoed by later writers, such as Richard Robert Madden who claimed that 'nothing can equal the absurdity of that ceremony except its humiliation'.[68] These rejections demonstrate that tensions within this diplomatic ritual were certainly present. However, it is important to note that, despite his later printed objections, Porter still participated in the audience ceremonial at the time without fuss. As with gift-giving, ambassadors might have grumbled and objected in private, but the importance of participating in performative diplomacy for the benefit of their general duties made it almost impossible to avoid. Without undergoing the audience with the sultan, no formal business could proceed, and thus as a key part of the diplomatic framework in terms of conforming to Ottoman practices, the ambassador simply had to grin and bear it.

Moreover, despite the views of Porter and others, there were enough neutral or positive representations of the audience ceremonies to suggest that even this ceremony was given either an alternative interpretation or simply ignored as mere form. Such narratives could have been due to embarrassment over the formal manhandling of a British ambassador, or, perhaps more likely, because it was not widely seen as problematic. For instance, MacGill's work was heavily criticised by *The Critical Review* – with one of his more colourful passages described as having 'all the properties of the most drastic vomit' – for suggesting that the Earl of Elgin had publicly declared his frustration at the length of the ceremony.[69] 'We were convinced,' wrote the reviewer, 'that this statement was erroneous; and we were at least certain that neither Lord Elgin nor any other British ambassador would offer such a deliberate insult to the usages, however trivial or tedious, of a foreign court.'[70] That is an important

[66] Porter, *Observations*, vol. II, 41–2.

[67] *The Weekly Amusement: or, the Universal Magazine*, 3 vols (London, 1735), vol. III, 26 July 1735, 971–93 at 971–81; *The Historical Register, containing an Impartial Relation of all Transactions, Foreign and Domestick*, vol. XV, no. 60 (London, 1730), 237–310 at 263–7.

[68] R.R. Madden, *Travels in Turkey, Egypt, Nubia, and Palestine, in 1824, 1825, 1826, and 1827*, 2 vols (London, 1829), vol. I, 106.

[69] MacGill, *Travels*, vol. II, 8.

[70] 'Art. X: Travels in Turkey, Italy, and Russia, during the Years 1803, 1804, 1805, and 1806, with an Account of some of the Greek Islands. By Thomas Macgill', *The Critical Review: or, Annals of Literature*, 3rd series, 24 vols (London, 1808), vol. XV, 76–88 at 85–6.

statement, in that no matter how far the British ambassador disagreed with the method or tone of the audience, so long as British interests were not being harmed, it would have been completely against the practice of diplomacy to be openly critical of those customs. Thus, within the generally unwritten demand to conform to the practices of other courts was the acceptance of such rituals. One revealing account comes from the personal letters of the Countess of Elgin. Lady Elgin claimed to have been actually present in the audiences themselves, disguised as a young nobleman. She said that 'nothing could exceed the civility I received from everybody' at the audience with the *kaymakam*; indeed, she said that 'I never knew what politeness was until I met with Turks.'[71] She noted the splendour of the enthroned sultan, and, in common with her husband's narrative, commented on his particularly friendly demeanour. Her account of the *kapıcı*s stands in complete contrast to MacGill's: 'We had each two men in superb gold embroidered dresses, who put a hand on each shoulder, and in this form we entered the room where the [sultan] was sitting on his throne.'[72] Lady Elgin had clearly managed to interpret this part of Ottoman ceremonial in a positive manner.

Writers such as Porter were perhaps so critical of the audience ceremony because they thought it damaged their own, and therefore Britain's, honour. Although there may have been some general prejudice against the practices of the Ottoman court, the fear of damaging Britain's image was more linked to the perceptions of other European powers. As all European ambassadors underwent this ceremony, there was nothing to be embarrassed about in that sense. However, the British were just as concerned – if not more concerned on occasion – about the image they conveyed to other European nations in Istanbul. Just as Ottoman ceremonies were designed to convey the Ottoman world-view, European diplomatic rituals were manifestations of the complexities of inter-European rivalries. The most common practices were royal celebrations and formal visits, designed to project the power of their ruler on the one hand, and to emphasise the hierarchy among European states on the other. For the British, the problems of finance once again came to the fore, with great expenditure required on participating in European ceremonial, as well as maintaining an embassy building that was necessary as a space for entertainment and business.

A number of occasions required specific performative reactions. Royal deaths necessitated a public demonstration of loyalty through the wearing of mourning dress by the ambassador and his household, which, as Chandos, Sutton, and Stanyan noted, the ambassador often had to pay for from his own pocket.[73] Royal births and birthdays required national celebration, so that on William III's birthday in 1700, Paget reported that all the British ships in port

71 Her two accounts of the audience with the grand vizier and with the sultan can be found in: Nisbet, *Letters*, 47–57.

72 Ibid., 56.

73 TNA/SP97/20 Baron Chandos to the Earl of Sunderland, June 1685; TNA/SP97/21 Sir Robert Sutton to the Earl of Nottingham, 7 March 1702/3; TNA/SP97/25 Abraham Stanyan to the Duke of Newcastle, 6 October 1727; TNA/SP97/41 James Porter to William Pitt, 17 December 1760.

fired salutes, and the merchants celebrated with music, 'cheerful recreations' and many toasts to the king's health.[74] One of the grandest of the recorded celebrations held by the British embassy was on the birth of James II's son in 1688, when the embassy was decorated with illuminations and an ornate triumphal arch adorned with imagery glorifying the dynasty in a garden lined with coloured lamps, whilst a great feast was held accompanied by 'Turkish' music and even a 'Turkish comedy' for all the European diplomats and merchants.[75] European ambassadors were also expected to participate in the celebrations of the birth of Ottoman royal children, notably in the grand entertainments during the reign of Ahmed III. Entries in the embassy accounts note expenditure on 'the public celebration' for the births of princes in 1705, 1706, 1707, and 1709. A total of 897.5 *guruş*, a significant sum, was spent on lamps, oil, wax, and tallow candles for illuminations, garlands, fabrics, and tinsels to make an arcade at the embassy gate, plus carpenters, joiners, and painters to construct it, watchmen, plus coffee, rossolis, and other refreshments, along with waiters to serve them.

The embassy building played host to a variety of diplomatic ceremonies, whether for celebration of royal birthdays or the births of imperial princes. Yet, the building itself was a source of major embarrassment, particularly when compared to the other European embassies in Istanbul. This provides a clear example of how finance, or the lack of it, affected diplomatic practice. As noted above, the building was situated slightly away from the other European embassies and was rented, unlike the purpose-built grand buildings of the French, Venetians, and Dutch, of which only the Venetian embassy still survives (built in 1781, today the Italian consulate).[76] The British ambassadors themselves paid the rent, and, after a fire in 1725, Stanyan earnestly hoped that he would not have to fund the rebuilding as well.[77] A year later, with Crown and Company reluctant to contribute, the matter was still unresolved, his household living in one half of the Dutch embassy. The Company finally allotted 6,000 *guruş* to the rebuilding, although Stanyan had already laid out 9,000 *guruş*.[78]

By the time of Sir Robert Ainslie's arrival in 1776, the new ambassador reported that 'there was not a single room which was either wind or water tight', and he attempted numerous repairs.[79] Robert Liston found the building in such a poor state that he convened an emergency assembly of the Istanbul factory, which resolved that the Company should purchase the land rather than continue to rent it, and pay for a new embassy to be constructed out of brick, rather that repairing the existing wood and clay structure.[80] A report by

74 SOAS/SC.PP/3/20 Baron Paget to Robert Yard, 10 January 1700/1.

75 BL, Add. 72554, Copie of ye Relation of ye Allegrezza sent to my L.P. upon ye birth of ye P. of Wales, 18 October 1688.

76 See: Tuna Köprülü, *İstanbul'daki Yabancı Saraylar* (Istanbul, 2005).

77 TNA/SP97/25 Abraham Stanyan to the Duke of Newcastle, 25 October 1725.

78 TNA/SP97/25 Abraham Stanyan to the Duke of Newcastle, 24 January 1726/7.

79 TNA/SP97/53 Sir Robert Ainslie to Viscount Weymouth, 17 June 1777.

80 TNA/FO78/15 Extract of the Minutes of the Assembly of the British Factory held at the Palace in Pera of Constantinople, 30 June 1794.

an Ottoman master builder noted that repairs to the existing structure would last fifteen years and cost 25,000 *guruş*, whilst a new build, which he advised, would cost 60,000 *guruş*.[81] No action was taken, and further correspondence reveals more about the nature of the embassy building. The Timoni family, who had served as embassy translators for many generations, held the land as a freehold under Ottoman law, and demanded increased rent of 3,000 *guruş* per annum for a five-year lease, whilst the property itself could be bought for around 55,000 *guruş*.[82] Liston therefore told the Company that the sum of £15,000 would be necessary 'to purchase the ground and to rebuild the palace in a handsome manner'.[83] The Company's representatives met with the secretary of state and the former ambassador Ainslie, pleading that it was impossible for the Company finance to fund either repair or construction.[84] It was something of a stroke of fortune, then, that the embassy burned down in 1799. The chargé d'affaires, John Spencer-Smith, moved into the French embassy that had been vacated following Napoleon's invasion of Egypt, and remained there until 1801, when Selim III gifted the land in Tepebaşı for a new embassy to thank Britain for its support against the French in Egypt.[85] Elgin began construction of the new palace, which was finally completed in 1805, modelled on his beautiful (and similarly situated) manor at Limekilns in Fife.[86] This was a grand building, with the first floor alone containing four 'luxury' rooms, a ceremonial room, a great hall, a dining room, a bedroom, a grand staircase, a large antechamber, a library, and an office.[87] It provided a much-needed boost to British prestige. However, the fact remains that the British ambassadors had spent the previous century in accommodation that was well below the standard of the other European embassies, and, in a position that required the provision of constant entertainment, that must have been highly embarrassing.

Despite the shoddy state of the building itself, the embassy hosted the rituals of the European ambassadors, whose lives were governed by rounds of visits and dinners given and returned in particular orders and manners and, unlike those between the British and the Ottomans, these were incredibly subject to dispute. Several examples of faux pas and breaches of protocol can be found in the correspondence: the Dutch minister visiting the French ambassador before Chandos; Stanyan avoiding sending servants to greet the new

81 TNA/FO78/15 Copy of the Greek Master Builder's Report, 30 June 1794.

82 TNA/FO78/16 Robert Liston to Lord Grenville, 10 February 1795.

83 TNA/FO78/16 Robert Liston to the Levant Company, 10 December 1794.

84 TNA/FO78/16 Robert Liston to the Levant Company, 10 December 1794; TNA/FO78/16 S. Brianquet to Lord Grenville, 30 January 1795.

85 TNA/MPK1/46/2 Plan de l'ancien Palais de France situé à Péra lez Constantinople approprié par la Porte Ottomane à l'usage de L'Ambassade de la Grande Bretagne, Dédié à Son Excellence Monsieur Spencer Smith Ministre Plénipotentiaire de Sa Majesté Britannique par son tres humble et obéissant serviteur Kauffer Ingénieur au service de la Porte Ottomane; Nisbet, *Letters*, 150.

86 Nisbet, *Letters*, 157–64.

87 BM, GRA/AN1169826001 *Premier Etage du Palais: English Embassy at Constantinople.* Ink drawing by Charles Robert Cockerell, 1810.

Habsburg internuncio to avoid an argument over precedence with the French; and Fawkener's dispute with the Russian minister over who should visit the French ambassador first.[88] By the middle of the eighteenth century, conventions became more settled, linked to the order of precedence the Ottomans had gradually established for audiences. For instance, on John Murray's arrival in 1766, he first notified the senior mercantile nations, that is, those with the longest relations with the Ottomans, the French, Venetian, and Dutch ambassadors (in Ottoman ceremonies, Britain came after France), with visits made and returned. The following day, Murray notified the second division of diplomats, the Habsburg internuncio, the Swedish, Danish, and Prussian envoys, and the Russian resident, who visited him the same day and whom he visited the day after. In order to avoid questions of precedence, the Neapolitan envoy, and later also the Spanish envoy, gave and received all of their visits, and took their audiences, eleven days after the rest. As the Ottoman audience ceremonies were partly an enactment of Ottoman universalist monarchy, so these visits could be said to be a performance of fractious and discordant European geopolitics.

For much of the eighteenth century, the Company paid for the expenses of these visits, with the surviving embassy accounts showing significant expenditure on visits between 1700 and 1736, notably for the liverymen who accompanied and attended him on all visits. Liverymen received 2 *guruş* per day, a good wage indeed, ten times that of Ottoman unskilled workers, with ten men taken for regular visits and over twenty for special occasions, thus costing 20–40 *guruş* per visit, plus any clothes they might need. If one considers that in that period the accounts record seventy-eight visits given and seventy-nine received, one can see why the Company was reluctant to pay. When the Company would not or could not pay, the ambassador simply had to lay out the expenses himself, so important were these visits to inter-European interaction in Istanbul. As with Ottoman ceremonial, it was inconceivable that the British ambassador should not participate. Nonetheless, not many British ambassadors seem to have enjoyed these practices and the disputes they almost inevitably ignited. On one disagreement between some of the ambassadors over the order of precedence for their wives in 1784, Sir Robert Ainslie wrote to London that '[f]or my part, I shall only laugh in my sleeve, and endeavour to be civil to all parties'.[89] The point of these disputes, however petty, was to ensure that due honour and respect were given to the ambassador as a representative of his state. For such reasons, a Danish envoy complained to the grand vizier because the Ottomans did not include all the titles of his king, and a Russian envoy-extraordinary was refused the right hand of ambassadors on visits because they outranked him.[90] The notion of offence was the main concern, and although

[88] TNA/SP97/20 Baron Chandos to the Earl of Sunderland, 12 May 1686; TNA/SP97/24(3) Abraham Stanyan to James Craggs, 6 May 1720; TNA/SP97/31 Sir Everard Fawkener to the Duke of Newcastle, 23 March 1740/1 (Separate and Private).

[89] TNA/FO78/05 Sir Robert Ainslie to the Marquess of Carmarthen, 9 August 1784.

[90] TNA/SP97/48 John Murray to the Earl of Rochford, 3 April 1772; TNA/SP97/26 Earl of Kinnoull to the Duke of Newcastle, 19 November 1731.

writers like Porter and MacGill highlighted supposed Ottoman offences, the British ambassador spent far more time and energy in disputes over etiquette with the other ambassadors.

Honour and image were central to the practice and reception of diplomatic ritual and ceremonial in eighteenth-century Istanbul, both between the British and the Ottomans and between the British and other Europeans. Indeed, the latter were usually more problematic than the former. One of the reasons, perhaps, that the audience with the sultan was only occasionally mocked or criticised was because, manhandling of the diplomat aside, there was not much objectionable content. The military and governmental displays, the feast, and even the audience itself, whilst certainly a clear demonstration of Ottoman state ideology to a foreign ambassador, could also be absorbed by the ambassador as honouring him and his country. Whilst the daily interactions with other European diplomats were highly ritualised, complex, and expensive, those with Ottoman officials were largely hassle-free and much cheaper. Indeed, it could be argued that the British were more preoccupied and concerned with maintaining their position within European ceremonial than they were with the rituals of Ottoman performative diplomacy, evidenced by the constant disagreements over diplomatic protocol, the great expenditure on entertainments and daily rituals, and the embarrassment at the condition of the embassy building. Maintaining a good image, however, was important, as the ambassador was, after all, the representative of the British government in Istanbul. As well as taking part in the complexities of European protocol, in order to maintain his honour and position, it is clear that the ambassador was obliged to participate in Ottoman diplomatic ceremonial. The audience with the sultan is a case in point. Some writers represented it as degrading, others as honourable, but, regardless, all the ambassadors participated in that ritual, ultimately because they were able to interpret it in a manner that permitted their participation, and because they appreciated the necessity in conforming to Ottoman practices to further the interests of their government, and especially of their trading subjects.

## Conclusion

When Yusuf Agah underwent his audience with the king in London, all of the rituals he would have been familiar with from Istanbul were present, if in a rather different form, including processions, formal dining, military displays, and a highly ritualised encounter with the sovereign. In Istanbul, too, daily diplomatic life was dominated by ceremonial and rituals. From the grand balls and feasts on special occasions, to the rounds of visits and coffee drinking that accompanied ordinary business, diplomacy was formed of a whole variety of practices that were performative. As with conventions of gift-giving, participation in the festivals, court ceremonies, and rituals of daily etiquette in Istanbul was an unavoidable and essential part of diplomacy. What made the performative aspect of diplomatic practice generally palatable to the British was the ability to interpret those practices in a number of different ways. The procession, the viewing of Ottoman might, wealth, and justice, the feasting, and the audience ceremonies were all polysemic, so that whilst they were designed by the Ottomans to present a performance of universalist monarchy to the ambassador of a lesser state, for the British, the effort and expense made by the Ottoman government on those major formal occasions could be seen as honouring Britain. The representations of the ceremonial around the audience with the sultan demonstrate the ability of participants and observers to interpret the same ritual in ways that suited their interests and world-view.

One interesting issue is how far the grand and formal audiences on the arrival of a British ambassador were reflective of wider daily diplomatic rituals. In terms of ceremonial space in the practice of daily diplomacy, where the ambassador relied on the translators to convey messages, decrees, and petitions between Istanbul proper and Galata, there was an enforced separation provided as much by linguistic differences as by the waters of the Golden Horn. However, in terms of performance, daily business contacts between the ambassadors and officials of the Ottoman state were governed by conventions designed to facilitate interaction and communication, from serving coffee and sweetmeats at meetings at the houses and palaces of Ottoman officials and at the British embassy, where ministers would speak freely to each other through their translators, to the grand ceremonies like the formal audience with the sultan designed to present its specific message of power, wealth, and hospitality. Grand gestures like the forced bowing before the sultan worked hand in hand with small activities like taking coffee to facilitate business and define relationships, and were thus a crucial component of the diplomatic framework. Such ceremonial with the Ottomans worked in conjunction with the diplomatic practices among European ambassadors, with constant rounds of visits, return visits, banquets, and balls, not infrequently complicated by disputes over precedence and other details that were seen to have reflected upon the honour of the ambassador and his state within European geopolitics. For interactions with both Ottomans and Europeans, the British were once again let down by the financial situation of the embassy. Just as they often struggled to give gifts at the same level as their rivals and allies, it was also the case that the embassy building, the size and quality of the ambassador's retinue, and the budgets for entertainment often fell short of expectation. This would have had a great impact on the perceptions of the British mission in Istanbul, and at the turn of the nineteenth century the British showed an awareness of this problem with the rebuilding of the embassy in a style that would impress visitors and provide ample space for diplomatic entertainments.

This also, perhaps, reflects a new sense of Britain in the Ottoman Empire and in the world, with the embassy completed just a few short years before the ambassador and nation would flee Istanbul under the shadow of war. As with gift-giving practices, some Ottoman court rituals, notably those involving the sultan, changed towards the end of the eighteenth century, in part due to reforms within the Ottoman state, but also as a result of changing political realities. However, as with social gifts, the most basic interactions of coffee drinking, visits, and celebrations remained largely the same, as did the arguments over precedence among the Europeans. Many of the details and disputes may seem petty and trivial, but the performance of diplomatic relations was absolutely crucial in establishing a set of boundaries and conventions. In the case of the formal audience ceremonials and ambassadorial visits, the ambassador was a personification of his state, and that required him to participate in diplomatic performances, passively and actively depending on the ritual, as to fail to do so in an appropriate manner would have been detrimental to his ability to represent his state's interests. Without the social lubricants of gift-exchange and performative ritual, which required finance that the British were often lacking, there would be no chance of the British ever representing their interests to the Ottoman government, or of resolving disputes. It is to the resolution of those disputes, the primary purpose of the ambassador's residence, to which we now turn.

# 6

# Negotiating disputes

## Freedoms, debts, and violence: Consular functions and diplomatic notes

In the late summer of 1764, a violent brawl erupted at a tavern in London, caused initially by a disagreement between two seamen. The pub was gutted, with all the furniture smashed and all the food and drink ransacked; the owner lost everything. The landlord of that particular establishment happened to be an Ottoman subject from Athens, who is recorded in the petitionary records as Thomas Berzuoni. This Berzuoni was a merchant who went to London to trade but, due to a great decrease in commerce during the Seven Years' War, had instead invested his money into renting a pub to earn some cash whilst waiting for business to pick up again.[1] Just before his six-month's lease was over, and just before he was to sail for Istanbul to return home, this violent event ruined his investment and left him with nothing. He tried to gain some sort of redress from British courts and judicial and political authorities, but to no avail. Destitute and desperate, his wife wrote to Henry Grenville, the ambassador in Istanbul, to see if he could put some pressure on the authorities in London to help Berzuoni.[2] Few of these sorts of cases are recorded, but when they are, it is evident that the lack of Ottoman diplomatic or consular representation in Britain made it very difficult for Ottoman subjects involved in any kind of dispute to find justice, and usually resulted in pressure being applied on their behalf via the ambassador in Istanbul. A key duty of the British ambassador was to represent the interests of merchants with the Ottoman government, particularly commercial disputes and other sorts of litigation. Poor Berzuoni, however, was thirty years too early for an Ottoman ambassador in London to be able to provide him with similar assistance.

The majority of the British ambassador's time was spent intervening in commercial disputes between British and Ottoman subjects. The major

1 Perhaps this Berzuoni was a manifestation of the so-called 'Eastern invasion', the prominence of Greeks in Ottoman commercial shipping in the eighteenth century: Harlaftis, 'The "Eastern invasion"'.

2 TNA/SP97/42 Henry Grenville to the Earl of Halifax, 10 September 1764. Berzuoni's wife's petition in Italian and English is enclosed with this letter.

diplomatic disputes that occurred centred on daily commercial disputes on the one hand and the resolving compensation claims of Ottoman subjects wronged by British privateers on the other. As we shall see, the implementation of British foreign policy, the high diplomacy of traditional historiography, played only a minor role, except when, as the eighteenth century wore on, that foreign policy resulted in violence against Ottoman shipping. For the most part, many of the ambassador's interactions with the Ottoman state constituted what are now termed as 'consular functions',[3] When a parliamentary committee in 1835 asked James Henderson, the former consul-general at Bogota, how he defined consular duties, he answered, 'I consider the duties of a consul to be to protect interests of British commerce, and the interests of His Majesty's subjects abroad, in every shape in which they may stand justly in need of his protection and support.'[4] The report pointed to the overriding importance of commercial matters, and the difficulty in separating diplomatic and commercial functions. Indeed, from the Ottoman perspective, trade and diplomatic relations were intimately linked. The initial description in the Capitulations of the people covered by that agreement were 'the British nation and merchants, and merchant nations coming under the British flag' (*İngiltere ṭāʾifesi ve tüccārı ve İngiltere bayrağı ile yürüyen tüccār ṭāʾifesi*), showing merchants and trade to be at the heart of relations.

Although ranked higher than the consuls who served Company's interests in the provincial factories, the ambassador in Istanbul often found himself acting as a consular official for the merchants resident in Istanbul, and occasionally for those in the provinces as well. Above all, the difference between him and other consuls was that he dealt directly with the central authorities.[5] The often-rambling narratives and gossip of high political matters that dominated the diplomatic correspondence with London did not accurately reflect his workload. The surviving material in the Ottoman archives clearly demonstrates what sort of matters shaped daily interactions, revealing two main areas in which the ambassadors tended to intervene on behalf of British subjects. The first was to ensure the freedoms of person and movement guaranteed in the Capitulations, and the second to pressure the Ottoman government in cases of contentious commercial disputes, generally cases that could not be resolved at a local and consular level.

The most common diplomatic tool was the *taḳrīr*, which can be translated as 'declaration', 'memorandum', or 'note'; in the context of diplomacy it was usually either a report or a diplomatic note.[6] There are a large number of these documents in the Ottoman and British archives, and they are a fascinating and

3 Ernest Satow, *Satow's Diplomatic Practice*, 6th edn, ed. Ivor Roberts (Oxford, 2009), 78–9.

4 Parliament of the United Kingdom, 'Report from the Select Committee on Consular Establishments' in *Reports from Committees: Sixteen Volumes. (2) Army (Colonies); Consuls; Militia; General Darling* (London, 1835), vol. VI, 9.

5 Satow, *Diplomatic Practice*, 79.

6 Michael Talbot, 'Petitions of the supplicant ambassador: British commercial representations to the Ottoman state in the eighteenth century', *Osmanlı Araştırmaları / Journal of Ottoman Studies* 46 (2015), 163–91.

underused corpus of material that reveals much about diplomatic practice. *Taḳrīr*s were the most important means of communication between the embassy and the Ottoman government.[7] As well as being declarations, *taḳrīr*s often resembled legal petitions, full of formulaic language that helped to signify social and political distinctions and relationships.[8] However, whereas petitioning was acceptable in the relationship between state and subject, this might have been viewed as humiliating in a diplomatic context if framed in the same terms.[9] As Anton Minkov demonstrated in his examination of petitions (*ʿarżuḥāl*) in the Ottoman Balkans, petitions received 'from all strata of society' tended to conform to particular conventions of formulation and language.[10] British *taḳrīr*s, when translated into Ottoman Turkish, employed some of the language and form of Ottoman petitions, but at the same time functioned as diplomatic notes. As such documents aimed to present complaints or requests within the framework of the Capitulations or Ottoman law, they tended to assume a more legal and petitionary language, just as modern diplomatic notes have their own linguistic conventions based on international law.[11]

*Taḳrīr*s, therefore, were flexible documents, a combination of declaration and petition, and skilful pieces of writing by the translators who had to convey the sense of the original English or Italian memorial within the conventions and language of Ottoman petitionary writing.[12] Each *taḳrīr* contained three

[7] Kristina Spohr Readman, 'Memoranda' in Miriam Dobson & Benjamin Zieman (eds), *Reading Primary Sources: The Interpretation of Texts from 19th and 20th Century History* (Abingdon & New York, 2009), 123–40 at 123; P.M. Holt, *Early Mamluk Diplomacy, 1260–1290: Treaties of Baybars and Qalāwūn with Christian Rulers* (Leiden, 1995), 6–11; Karsten Plöger, *England and the Avignon Popes: The Practice of Diplomacy in Late Medieval Europe* (London, 2005), 11–12, 179.

[8] See: Ronald C. Jennings, 'Kadi, court, and legal procedure in 17th C. Ottoman Kayseri', *Studia Islamica* 48 (1978), 133–72; Michael Ursinus, *Grievance Administration (Şikayet) in an Ottoman Province: The Kaymakam of Rumelia's 'Record Book of Complaints' of 1781–1783* (Abingdon & New York, 2005); Süleyman Demirci, 'Complaints about avâriz assessment and payment in the avâriz-tax system: An aspect of the relationship between centre and periphery. A case study of Kayseri, 1618–1700', *Journal of the Economic and Social History of the Orient* 46:4 (2003), 437–74; Boğaç A. Ergene, *Local Court, Provincial Society and Justice in the Ottoman Empire: Legal Practice and Dispute Resolution in Çankırı and Kastamonu (1652–1744)* (Leiden, 2003), especially 125–41. For an interesting comparative study: Geoffrey Koziol, *Begging Pardon and Favour: Ritual and Political Order in Early Medieval France* (Ithaca NY, 1992), 25–58.

[9] This point has been discussed in respect of a very interesting case between the British and Shawnees in mid-eighteenth-century Carolina. See: Ian K. Steele, 'The Shawnees and the English: Captives and war, 1753–1763' in Daniel P. Barr (ed.), *The Boundaries between Us: Natives and Newcomers along the Frontiers of the Old Northwest Territory, 1750–1850* (Kent OH, 2006), 1–24, especially 1–5.

[10] Anton Minkov, *Conversion to Islam in the Balkans: Kisve Bahası Petitions and Ottoman Social Life, 1670–1730* (Leiden, 2004), 111–13. For a comparison, see Pierre Chaplais's analysis of the structure of English diplomatic documents in the medieval period: Pierre Chaplais, *English Diplomatic Practice in the Middle Ages* (Cambridge, 2003), 102–23.

[11] Dietrich Kappeler, 'Texts in diplomacy' in Jovan Kurbalija & Hannah Slavik (eds), *Language and Diplomacy* (Msida, 2001), 201–6 at 202; Bolewski, *Diplomacy and International Law*, 15–16.

[12] An interesting discussion of the role of translators in such legal cases can be found in Kemal Çiçek, 'Interpreters of the court in the Ottoman Empire as seen from the Sharia court records of Cyprus', *Islamic Law and Society* 9:1 (2002), 1–15.

main elements, the first being the greeting line. Some were headed with the title 'the translated declaration of your supplicant, the British ambassador' (*İngiltere elçisi dāʿīleriniñ taḳrīr tercümesidir*), which indicates that the original was delivered in Italian and translated by the translators of the Sublime Porte. Those written in Ottoman Turkish by the translators working for the British embassy conveyed formal greetings, specifically with the phrase '*devletlü saʿādetlü sulṭānım ḥażretleri sağ olsun*' (your highness, my great and felicitous sultan, health unto you). The second feature of the *taḳrīr*s was the ambassador's mark. This took two forms, the first being the ambassador's seal, often with his coat of arms. It would appear that on occasion the ambassador would even have an Ottoman-language seal made for use on these documents, as Charles Arbuthnot did.[13] Seals were relatively common, but far more usual was for a simple cypher to be placed at the bottom of the document. The cypher bore the phrase '*ed-dāʿī elçi-i İngiltere*' (the supplicant, the ambassador of Britain). *Dāʿī* is a tricky word to translate, but, having its root in an Arabic word for prayer, *duʿāʾ*, it would have been understood by the Ottomans in terms of supplication, as in humble petitioning, being a standard part of the language of Ottoman petitions.[14] The British ambassadors certainly did not employ such a term in their own documents and probably were unaware of the connotations of the term, mainly because they could not read Ottoman Turkish and the Italian texts contained a different sense. On the rare occasion that translators did give the Ottoman sense in the Italian text, there was trouble. One example of this comes from 1694, when Baron Paget was examining a petition drawn up by the translators of the consul in Izmir. He took particular exception to a passage containing the phrase '*alli poveri pietosissimo*' (to the most pitiful paupers) in reference to British consular officials, which, in his opinion, 'sounds as if the petitioner were rather to beg an alms than requiring justice according to our Capitulations'.[15] On the whole, however, there were few recorded issues regarding the language used in the Ottoman-, Italian-, and English-language versions of *taḳrīr*s. The embassy translators had to fit the English, Italian, or French originals into the linguistic conventions of the Ottoman state, which insisted that all requests to the Ottoman government be framed in the language of a supplicant petitioner.

The final element of the *taḳrīr* was the text itself, which, although differing from document to document depending on the matter at hand, contained certain stock phrases that place these documents within the wider corpus of legal documentation in the Ottoman state. Above all, these documents show the ways in which the British ambassadors, as diplomats exercising consular functions, brought commercial issues to the attention of the Ottoman government. The following examples of *taḳrīr*s, taken as an indicative sample

[13] See: BOA/C.HR/19/930, 21 Ramazan 1220 [13 December 1805]. The seal reads, 'Çarlis Arbutnot'.

[14] An example of Ottoman subjects using the same term can be found in Ursinus, *Grievance Administration*, 95.

[15] SOAS/SC.PP/2/10 Baron Paget to William Raye, 2 April 1694.

of the wider body of documents in the British *düvel-i ecnebiye defteri* (foreign states register) in the Ottoman archives, give a very strong indication of the common daily issues that required the ambassador's attention. These also put paid to the idea that there are few records concerning British merchants and British commerce in the Ottoman archives.

The first set of *taḳrīr*s indicates the attempts of the ambassadors to protect the freedoms granted to British subjects under the Capitulations, the most common of which concerned the freedom of movement of British ships. This example from 1185/1771 is just one of many from the later eighteenth century:

> Our captain John James, one of the British captains, has been bringing and taking goods by sea with his ship. Having paid all of the customs duties and taken a receipt [*tezkere*] for them in accordance with the imperial Capitulations, he is now seeking to make his return. After inspection according to custom [*muʿtād üzere*] at the Bosphorus Castles has been performed, he should not be [searched] even one additional time. A noble command is petitioned and requested for a permission to sail as is customary so that he should not be obstructed in his passage and journey.[16]

This demonstrates the legal significance of a particular custom (*muʿtād*) outside the articles of the Capitulations. Moreover, the emphasis here that the captain possessed a *tezkere* for his customs payments implies that there were attempts to exact duties contrary to the Capitulations during these customary searches. At the most basic level, therefore, this was an assertion of the first article of the Capitulations, which protected the freedom of British ships to travel to and from Ottoman ports, and of the numerous articles forbidding exaction of undue custom, and demonstrate the ambassador's regular role in ensuring their implementation.[17]

Although such petitions were the norm, the ambassador's diplomatic skills were often tested by ever-present commercial disputes, and the following three examples provide case studies on the sorts of disputes taking place, and the ambassador's role in settling them. The first took place in Istanbul, and the other three relate to the provincial cities of Aleppo, Latakia, and Baghdad. In Istanbul in 1203/1789, the merchant James Barbaud was engaged in the contract for supplying the Ottoman government with naval stores, an increasingly important part of British–Ottoman trade in the later eighteenth century.[18] Unfortunately for Messrs Barbaud & Co., the Ottoman government had not been forthcoming with payment. The *taḳrīr* noted that Barbaud had supplied two units of new ship cables and one unit of anchors on the basis of immediate

[16] BOA/A.DVN.DVE(3)/81/92, 2 Cemaziülahir 1185 [11 September 1771]. See also, for instance: BOA/A.DVN.DVE(3)/81/72, 5 Cemaziülahir 1183 [5 October 1769]; BOA/A.DVN. DVE(3)/83/54, 4 Cemaziülahir 1203 [1 March 1789].

[17] For instance: Articles XXXI/24, LI/40, LVI/41, LX/46, LXI/47. On ship's permissions more generally, see: İdris Bostan, 'İzn-i Sefine Defterleri ve Karadeniz'de Rusya İle Ticaret Yapan Devlet-i Aliye Tüccarları, 1780–1846', *Türklük Araştırmaları Dergisi* 6 (1990), 21–35.

[18] BOA/A.DVN.DVE(3)/83/58, 2 Şaban 1203 [28 April 1789].

payment (*bahāsı muʿacelā*). The total owed was 5,205 *guruş*, roughly the equivalent of £460 (perhaps £50,000 today), so there was some urgency in terms of Barbaud & Co.'s cash flow. On the *taḳrīr*, the comments by Ottoman officials discussing the case concluded that there should be an official enquiry (*istiʿlām*) made by the *kapudan paşa*. As later correspondence from the main supplier in London, Edmund Hill, indicates that he was owed the huge sum of 175,064 *guruş* for iron shot and 3,593 barrels of gunpowder, clearly ambassadorial intervention could not always persuade the Ottoman government to pay up on time.[19]

The second example, involving the British factory in Aleppo and the governor of Baghdad, demonstrates the problem of insufficient documentation. Seeking to expand their trade to Baghdad and Basra, the British merchants of Aleppo sent an Armenian agent to sell some merchandise in Baghdad in late 1749. However, the British merchants neglected to provide him with the correct certificates and receipts to legally prove ownership of the goods.[20] The Ottoman governor, needing to pay the troops of the garrison, seized the British goods, which had been stored for safekeeping in the Baghdad customhouse, promising the agent that he would be compensated. However, in a second error, the Armenian took no receipts for the goods or the promise, and as a result the only proof of the provenance and value of the merchandise came from a letter by the agent, and a declaration of the qadi of Aleppo. The total debt came to the enormous sum of 91,331 *guruş*, the major creditor being the *tercüman* of the British factory in Aleppo who lost 60,000 *guruş* in this seizure. After several attempts to gain compensation, James Porter sent a rather forceful *taḳrīr* insisting on refunds for any damage and loss incurred (*żarar ve ziyānıñ tażmīni*), and complaining that resolution of the case had been impeded and delayed (*ʿavḳ ve tāḫīrine*).[21] After almost a year of petitions and declarations, the Ottoman government agreed to pay damages to the British merchants in instalments of 5,000 *guruş* until the debt was repaid.[22] Porter wrote to the Duke of Newcastle that the issue 'has been attended with a series of extreme disagreeable incidents to me, in great part owing to the mismanagement of those concerned, and by the irregularity, precipitancy and rapaciousness of this government'.[23] Despite his disdain for Ottoman justice, even Porter had to admit that the dispute was exacerbated due to the lack of proper documentation on the part of the British merchants, hindering their ability to prove ownership and the value of the goods involved.

19 TNA/FO78/12A Edmund Hill to Lord Grenville, 4 August 1791; TNA/FO78/12A Messrs James Barbaud & Co. to Edmund Hill, 15 June 1791; TNA/FO78/12A Messrs James Barbaud & Co. to John Fish, undated (c. June 1791).

20 TNA/SP97/34 James Porter to the Duke of Bedford, 24 October 1749.

21 TNA/SP97/34 James Porter to the Duke of Bedford, 24 January 1749/50; 24 January 1749/50 (Private); TNA/SP97/34 James Porter to the Duke of Newcastle, 22 June 1750; BOA/A.DVN. DVE.(3)/81/13, 15 Receb 1163 [20 June 1750].

22 TNA/SP97/34 James Porter to the Duke of Newcastle, 23 July 1750.

23 Ibid.

Perhaps the most common cause of dispute was bankruptcy. For example, a *taḳrīr* received from the British consul in Latakia in 1181/1767 began by describing the bankruptcy of Monsieur Boumaster, to whose estate a certain Mustafa Bey owed 17,000 *guruş*.[24] The failure to collect that debt meant that no dividend could be paid to Boumaster's creditors, consisting primarily of European merchants, and the governor of Latakia, who consequently imprisoned Mustafa Bey. In turn, Mustafa Bey had accused the former British consul, Edward Purnell, of absconding with the sum in question, 'in the hope that the aforementioned pasha would free Mustafa Bey after collecting the assets for himself and for the aforementioned Frank merchants'.[25] Murray assured the secretary of state in London that this was untrue, and that Purnell was actually one of the largest creditors.[26] The secretary of state instructed Murray to encourage the Ottoman government to 'exert itself in obliging such of their subjects as are indebted to the estate of Mr Boumaster, to pay their debts'.[27] Therefore, Murray's *taḳrīr* spoke of Mustafa Bey's conduct as perfidy (*ġadr*), and demanded 'in accordance with the requirements of the noble [Islamic] law and the imperial Capitulations' (*şerʿ-i şerīf ve ʿahdnāme-i hümāyūn mūcebince*) that a collection for the debt be made.[28] Here, we see the petition making reference to multiple Ottoman legal systems – Islamic shari'a and the sultanic grants of the Capitulations – to strengthen their argument. This resulted in the matter being settled, with the sum secured from Mustafa Bey divided *pro rata* among Boumaster's creditors.[29] Here, again, we see the ambassador in Istanbul becoming involved in provincial disputes. As I have argued elsewhere, this was possible through a clever use of the Capitulations.[30] Article 16/XXIV specifically states that 'lawsuits with a value of more than four thousand *akçe*s [*dört biñ aḳçeden ziyāde olan daʿvāları*] are to be heard at the Threshold of Felicity, and may not be heard in any other place'. Due to inflation and the devaluation of Ottoman currency, 4,000 *akçe*s (33.33 *guruş*) was far less substantial a sum in the eighteenth century than when this article had been issued in the early seventeenth, and clearly not every single case worth that amount would be sent to Istanbul. Instead, the consuls only seem to have sent cases for the ambassador to take to the *divan* when they were unable to get a favourable or timely response from the local Ottoman authorities in the provinces. Therefore, as well as dealing with the debts, bankruptcies, and disputes involving the British merchants in Istanbul, the ambassador also brought difficult provincial cases to imperial attention.

Resolving commercial and legal disputes was a key part of the ambassador's role, the pivotal link in the framework of diplomatic practice between

24 BOA/A.DVN.DVE(3)/81/73, 1 Receb 1183 [31 October 1769]; TNA/SP97/43 John Murray to the Earl of Shelburne, 15 April 1767.

25 BOA/A.DVN.DVE(3)/81/73.

26 TNA/SP97/43 John Murray to the Earl of Shelburne, 15 April 1767.

27 TNA/SP97/43 Earl of Shelburne to John Murray, 5 June 1767.

28 BOA/A.DVN.DVE(3)/81/73.

29 TNA/SP97/43 John Murray to the Earl of Shelburne, 17 August 1767.

30 Talbot, 'Petitions of the supplicant ambassador', 178–9.

the preparatory work of conforming to Ottoman gift and ceremonial practices and ensuring the successful trade of the British merchants that funded the embassy. In a sense, these documents were the final result of a series of diplomatic practices, with much relying on the relationships developed through gift-giving and ceremonial. For instance, when Ainslie attempted to secure a payment owed to John Humphreys & Sons, he attended an audience with the *reisülküttab,* upon which occasion he reported that 'independent of the usual etiquette employed on similar occasions, [the *reisülküttab*] thought proper to give me an extraordinary mark of attention, by sending the dragoman of the Porte with an invitation for me to partake of a collation, provided on purpose'.[31] Gift-giving was also a crucial part of the process of persuasion, and the spying glasses, pistols, china, and watches presented to various Ottoman officials in Ainslie's accounts presented in the second half of 1787 alone cost the British government over 6,000 *guruş*.[32] Such practices enabled the ambassador to have his *taḳrīr*s properly considered, and those documents shed an important light onto the sort of cases that ambassadors dealt with on a daily basis.

However, from time to time the ambassador had to deal with other sorts of interaction between British and Ottoman subjects, particularly violent ones. Eighteenth-century ambassadors did not deal with violence against British subjects to anywhere near the same degree as their seventeenth-century counterparts due to the great decrease in cases of enslavement by the North African fleets. For Britons resident in Ottoman cities, violence specifically targeting Europeans was rare. Violence sometimes occurred during raucous celebrations, such as an attack on the British nation in Izmir celebrating the king's birthday in November 1696 that saw an embassy janissary and two servants wounded by musket fire.[33] On occasion, the British ambassador sought violent justice. When a young Ottoman spotted a British merchant duck hunting on the Golden Horn in 1779, he took offence for some reason and opened fire, wounding the merchant's Armenian servant; Ainslie sought retribution and the Ottoman government ordered the young man to be bastinadoed.[34] Violence between Europeans was far more likely, particularly during the many inter-European wars of the period. This was particularly notable in the French Revolutionary Wars of the 1790s, when Izmir was gripped by fighting between French and British sailors and merchants, leading Robert Liston to successfully request that the Ottoman government send warships to return order to the city.[35] As with Berzuoni's tavern, sailors were often at the centre of inter-European violence, as with a British sailor stabbed in a public house in 1772 in a drunken brawl among mariners of various nationalities.[36]

31 TNA/FO78/6 Sir Robert Ainslie to the Marquess of Carmarthen, 10 November 1785.

32 TNA/FO78/8 Sir Robert Ainslie to the Marquess of Carmarthen, 10 October 1787.

33 SOAS/SC.PP/5/27(iii) William Raye to Baron Paget, 12 November 1696.

34 TNA/SP97/55 Sir Robert Ainslie to Viscount Weymouth, 18 February 1779.

35 TNA/FO78/15 Robert Liston to Lord Grenville, 25 July 1794; TNA/FO78/15 Robert Liston to the Sublime Porte, undated [July 1794].

36 TNA/SP97/48 John Murray to the Earl of Rochford, 3 December 1772.

Far more telling for the story of British–Ottoman relations was the mob violence in major cities and ports occasionally sparked by Ottoman defeats. The British were particularly targeted following the destruction of the Ottoman fleet at Çeşme in 1770, with rioting in Izmir and Istanbul that saw a number of Ottoman Christians and Europeans killed. John Murray's secretary was attacked and barely escaped serious injury as two pistol bullets hit the walls of the embassy.[37] At the time of the violence against the British in Izmir, a forceful *taḳrīr* was issued concerning security of the factory there. The ambassador's declaration noted that the British had been suspected of aiding the Russians – which, as we shall see, was a well-founded suspicion – sparking a number of attacks that injured several Britons in Izmir:

> Recently, a sedition of order [*iḫtilāl-ı tanẓīm*] arose, and a sheer fabrication sown among the people [*maḥż kiẕb beynü'n-nās nesir olunan*] that the British were aiding the Russians in the present conflict [*İngilterelü Mosḳovlu'ya işbu muḥārebede imdād eyledi deyü*] ... this sort of lie and calumny is of evil consequence to the persons, property, and goods of the British consul and merchants resident in Izmir, [and so] let a special messenger be sent with a letter [of command].[38]

The *taḳrīr* further declared, echoing the language of the Capitulations, that Britain was a true and faithful friend (*ḫāliṣ ve ṣādiḳ dost*), noted widespread loss and damage (*żarar ve ziyān*), and that, in cases where Britons were in positions of danger and peril (*ḫaṭar ve tehilkede*), they should not be refused if they made an application for protection and security (*ḥimāyet ve emtiyet*).[39] The Ottoman commentary written around this *taḳrīr* indicates an acceptance of the petition, and that increased protection would be granted to British merchants. This unusual case demonstrates that *taḳrīr*s, when necessary, could be forceful in their language, and this particular example is far more akin to the sorts of documents used among European powers than the more usual commercial supplications employed at the Ottoman court.

However, it is also a good indication of a new feature within British–Ottoman relations. At a fundamental level, the ambassador needed to protect the freedom of movement and other privileges granted to the merchants. When problems did arise, primarily from disputes over bankruptcies or seizures of goods in Istanbul, he was responsible for resolving the situation with the Ottoman government, as he was for cases in the provinces when resolution attempts at the local level had failed. Finally, when British subjects were threatened with harm, the ambassador had to ensure the protection of their persons and property. The formal vehicle for bringing such issues to the attention of the Ottoman government were *taḳrīr*s, whose language and phrasing place them into part of a wider body of petitionary documents

37 TNA/SP97/46 John Murray to Viscount Weymouth, 3 December 1770.

38 BOA/C.HR/79/3907, 7 Rebiülahir 1184 [27 September 1770].

39 Ibid.

within the Ottoman bureaucratic and legal system. As with gift-exchange and ceremonial, there were some elements in the Ottoman-language versions of the ambassadors' declarations that were supplicatory in their tone, but these simply conformed to the conventions of such legal documents, and when necessary the language could be sufficiently forceful to ensure that the pressing nature of the ambassador's representation was conveyed. However, as the case of the violence in Izmir showed, the delicate balance of the diplomatic framework could be damaged when Ottoman and British interests collided on a geopolitical level, as in this case with Britain providing backing for Russia in a war against the Ottomans. *Taḳrīr*s are the documents of disputes, but largely of routine capitulatory disputes. The increasingly aggressive British attitude that developed over the eighteenth century in the Ottoman realms saw new sorts of dispute emerge regarding freedom of movement, not of British subjects but of Ottoman shipping.

## 'Ill-treated by friends': British privateers and Ottoman maritime territoriality

Between the late seventeenth century and the early nineteenth century, Britain fought France, and others, in six major conflicts: the Nine Years' War (1688–97); the War of the Spanish Succession (1701–14); the War of the Austrian Succession (1740–8); the Seven Years' War (1756–63); the American War of Independence (1775–83); and the French Revolutionary Wars (1793–1802). In each of those conflicts, British privateers were active in the Levant, and the repercussions of their actions reveal much about diplomatic practice. This sort of maritime violence also shows us something new in British–Ottoman relations. As a response to British privateering, the Ottomans instituted new maritime laws designed to keep out armed ships and to provide compensation for their merchants, particularly from the 1740s to the 1780s.[40] Privateering did huge damage to trade – the huge dips in British commerce in the early 1740s, the late 1750s, and the near collapse of commercial activity in the late 1770s were all due to these privateering wars. More than this, attacks on enemy shipping often meant attacks on Ottoman goods being freighted by that shipping, bringing the British and the Ottomans into a conflict that the Ottomans sought, in the interests of ancient friendship, to resolve peacefully.[41]

[40] I have gone into depth about this subject in other publications, notably in Michael Talbot, 'Ottoman seas and British privateers: Defining maritime territoriality in the eighteenth-century Levant' in Firges et al. (eds), *Well-Connected Domains*, 54–70, and in two forthcoming articles, entitled 'Separating the waters from the sea: The place of islands in Ottoman maritime territoriality in the eighteenth century', which will form a special edition on Ottoman insularity in *Princeton Papers*; and in 'Protecting the Mediterranean: Ottoman responses to maritime violence, 1718–1770' in *Journal of Early Modern History*. I have also discussed issues of privateering and Ottoman maritime legal practice in an episode of the *Ottoman History Podcast*, together with Sam Dolbee, Arianne Urus, and Güneş Işıksel, aired on 20 April 2015 (http://www.ottomanhistorypodcast.com).

[41] My research into this subject owes much to the following studies: Colin Heywood, 'The frontier in Ottoman history: Old ideas and new myths' in Daniel Power & Naomi Standen (eds), *Frontiers*

The Ottoman Mediterranean was a contested space in the eighteenth century, and the Europeans arrived with their own ideas of what maritime space meant.[42] Three major publications defined European attitudes towards maritime jurisdiction, the first being Hugo Grotius's *Mare Liberum* (*The Free Sea*, 1609).[43] Attacking Spanish and Portuguese claims over large swathes of ocean, Grotius argued that 'those things that cannot be occupied, or are never occupied, cannot be the property of anyone, for all property has arisen from occupation'.[44] Grotius's position was countered by the English jurist John Selden in *Mare Clausum* (*The Closed Sea*, 1636), which argued that it was possible to hold dominion over the sea (*dominio maris*) in order to secure maritime resources, ensuring that 'others are cut off or at least limited' in their access.[45] The third work, Dutch lawyer Cornelius van Bynkershoek's *De dominio maris dissertatio* (*Discussion on ownership of the sea*, 1703), proposed a compromise. He defined maritime territory as that which could be constantly defended: 'In general it must be said that the power of the land ends where the force of arms ends, for this is, as we have said, the means of protecting possession.'[46] This led to the development of the 'three-mile rule', based on the limit of the range of shore-based cannon, which principle is the foundation of modern concepts of maritime territoriality. This was an idea shared by the Ottomans, defined according to Ottoman official documentation,

*in Question: Eurasian Borderlands, 700–1700* (London, 1999), 228–50; Colin Heywood, 'Ottoman territoriality versus maritime usage: The Ottoman islands and English privateering in the wars with France, 1689–1714' in Nicolas Vatin & Gilles Veinstein (eds), *Insularités ottomanes* (Paris, 2004), 145–73; Colin Heywood, 'The Kapudan Pasha, the English ambassador and the Blackham frigate: An episode in Anglo-Ottoman maritime relations (1697)' in E. Zachariadou (ed.), *The Kapudan Pasha, his Office and his Domain: Halcyon Days in Crete IV: A Symposium Held in Rethymnon 7–9 January 2000* (Rethymnon, 2002), 409–38; Eyal Ginio, 'Piracy and redemption in the Aegean Sea during the first half of the eighteenth century', *Turcica* 33 (2001), 135–47; Maurits van den Boogert, 'Redress for Ottoman victims of European privateering: A case against the Dutch in the Divan-i Hümayun (1708–1715)', *Turcica* 33 (2001), 91–118; Robert D. Sack, *Human Territoriality: Its Theory and History* (Cambridge, 1986), 19–22. See also: İpek K. Yosmaoğlu, 'Constructing national identity in Ottoman Macedonia' in William Zartman (ed.), *Understanding Life in the Borderlands* (Athens GA, 2010), 160–88, especially 179–84.

42 Michael Talbot, 'Protecting the Mediterranean', forthcoming.

43 Peter Borschberg has written extensively on Grotius and notions of free trade in South-East Asia. For just two important pieces in a long bibliography, see: Peter Borschberg, *Hugo Grotius, the Portuguese, and Free Trade in the East Indies* (Singapore, 2011); Peter Borschberg, 'Grotius' theory of trans-oceanic trade regulation: Revisiting Mare Liberum (1609)', *Institute for International Law and Justice Working Paper* 14 (2005).

44 Hugo Grotius, *Mare Liberum sive de jure quod Batavis competit ad Indicana commercia dissertatio* (Leiden, 1609), 18.

45 John Selden, *Mare clausum sev de dominio maris libri duo* (London, 1636), 19–20. For a discussion of the Grotius–Selden disputes, see: James Muldoon, 'Is the sea open or closed? The Grotius–Selden debate renewed' in Kenneth Pennington & Melodie Harris Eichbauer (eds), *Law as Profession and Practice in Medieval Europe: Essays in Honor of James A. Brundage* (Farnham, 2011), 117–36.

46 Cornelius van Bynkershoek, 'De dominio maris dissertatio' in *De lege Rhodia de Jactu Liber Singularis et de Dominio Maris Dissertatio* (The Hague, 1703), 14.

either as a number of leagues (*birḳaç mīl*) or more specifically as three leagues (*üç mīl*) from the shore.[47] There was therefore a shared notion by the turn of the eighteenth century of limited maritory. The Europeans at the time simply seem not to have been interested in Ottoman traditions, with the early nineteenth-century Italian jurist Domenico Alberto Azuni asserting that, '[w]e know of no maritime legislation in the Ottoman Empire and in the Regencies established on the coast of Barbary subject to the sultan. It seems, moreover, that one finds there no other than those of the nations that trade there.'[48] This perception stemmed from a lack of codified Ottoman maritime law, which only occurred with the Commercial Code of 1850 and the Maritime Code of 1863.[49] Although Selden cited the Arabic texts of the Qur'an and a number of Arab geographers, there was thus a general sense that the Ottomans were outside or irrelevant to European debates on maritime sovereignty, something that seems to persist.[50]

There are two sources that indicate Ottoman attitudes towards maritime territoriality in practice. The first is in the Capitulations, with *müste᾽minīn*, those protected by treaty, entitled to free access of Ottoman ports. For instance, the British Capitulations granted that 'the British nation and merchants, and peoples and merchants coming by sea with the British flag, their various goods, and their ships and galleons, may come and go in security and peace to the Well-Protected Domains'.[51] The Capitulations also granted rights for 'enemy' (*ḥarbī*) nations to trade under friendly flags, with one article of the British Capitulations dating to the early seventeenth century specifying the merchants of Spain, Portugal, Ancona, Sicily, Florence, Catalonia, and Holland, none of which nations held friendly treaties with the Ottomans at that time.[52] Thus, the Ottoman Mediterranean was 'open', even to friendly merchants, and the freedom of movement was emphasised in the treaties. However, movement was restricted in the Black Sea for much of the eighteenth century to maintain the Ottoman commercial monopoly, and in the Red Sea past the port of Jeddah, to protect the commerce of Mecca and Medina and to prevent customs evasion. The second source comes from responses to violations of Ottoman waters during European assaults on each other's shipping during the numerous wars of the century. As Ottoman merchants increasingly used European

[47] BOA/C.HR/140/6968, end of Muharrem 1157 (middle of March 1744); BOA/C.HR/118/5877, middle of Safer 1193 (beginning of March 1779).

[48] Domenico Alberto Azuni, *Origine et progrès du droit et de la législation maritime, avec des observations sur le consulat de la mer* (Paris, 1810), 227.

[49] *Ḳānūnnāme-i ticāret* (Istanbul, 1281 [1865]); *Ḳānūnnāme-i hümāyūn-u ticāret-i baḥriye* (Istanbul, 1280 [1864]).

[50] Selden, *Mare clausum*, 16, 36, 41, 179, 227; G.J. Toomer, *Eastern Wisedome and Learning: The Study of Arabic in Seventeenth-Century England* (Oxford, 1996), 64–71. For a general and somewhat problematic overview, see: Hassan S. Khalileh, *Islamic Maritime Law: An Introduction* (Leiden, 1998). For an examination from an Islamic legal perspective, see: ʿAbd ar-Raḥmān ibn Aḥmad ibn Muḥammad ibn Fāyiʿ, *Aḥkām al-baḥr fī al-fiqh al-Islāmī* (Jeddah, 2000).

[51] BOA/A.(DVNSDVE.d)/35/1 fol. 2.

[52] Ibid., fols 9–11.

ships to freight their goods, especially those of the French, violence against French shipping by British privateers often meant violence against Ottoman shipping.[53] In 1696, following French and British ships making captures in and blocking up the port of Izmir, the *kapudan paşa*, Mezamorto Hüseyin, made an important declaration, supported by the qadi of Izmir, to the translators of the French, British, and Dutch consuls:

> [F]rom Andro [Andros] to Stanchoi [Kos] hither no acts of hostility should be committed; and that if any ship acted contrary thereto and took any other within those limits, [the Ottoman authorities] did engage to the party suffering that restitution should entirely be made him for all damages sustained by the captor.[54]

This extended the Ottoman maritime borders, and therefore legal jurisdiction, beyond the customary shoreline limit in order to protect shipping in the Aegean, meaning that any attack in that part of the Aegean would make the attacker liable to pay compensation. Paget opined that 'it is not possible to give limits to any seaport beyond canon shot without occasioning many undeterminable disputes', protesting to the Ottoman government that it was an 'innovation contrary to the laws of the ocean', and was concerned that it was a pretence for the Ottomans to exact 'avanias', a term used to describe unfounded claims against the Europeans, unfairly presupposing corruption and extortion in Ottoman claims and cases.[55]

Despite his fear of avanias, and public rejections of the new regulations, Paget respected the Ottoman ruling, and even attempted to ensure the compliance of British privateers. This was a good example of the circle of friendship in action, with Paget realising that it was necessary to maintain the peace in order to secure British interests. In 1697, one very active privateer, the *Blackham Galley*, took a French ship within the limits, and Paget was summoned to Edirne to receive an official protest from the Ottoman government. The ambassador could barely contain his rage at the captain: 'You have been told more than once at my house, what inconveniences the taking a prize within the limits might occasion … after that so near as Tenedos to take so inconsiderable a prize and bring so much trouble upon your owners and us is inexcusable.'[56] Therefore, although he protested against the regulations,

53 On this phenomenon, see: Panzac, *La caravane maritime*, passim.

54 SOAS/SC.PP/5/27(iii) William Raye to Baron Paget, 3 July 1696. On Mezamorto Hüseyin's maritime reforms, see: İdris Bostan, 'Mezamorta Hüseyin Paşa ve 1701 Tarihli Bahriye Kanunnamesi' in İdris Bostan & Salih Özbaran (eds), *Başlangıçtan* XVII. Yüzyılın Sonuna Kadar Türk Denizcilik Tarihi 1 (Istanbul, 2009), 281–91.

55 SOAS/SC.PP/3/17 Baron Paget to William Raye, 2 May 1697; SOAS/SC.PP/3/16 Baron Paget to Aléxandros Mavrokordátos, 19 February 1697/8; SOAS/SC.PP/2/13 Baron Paget to James Vernon, 14 December 1696. See: Wood, *Levant Company*, 124; Van den Boogert, *Capitulations*, 118–22, 155–7. See also: Merlijn Olnon, 'Towards classifying avanias: A study of two cases involving the English and Dutch nations in seventeenth-century Izmir' in Hamilton, de Groot, & van den Boogert (eds), *Friends and Rivals*, 159–86.

56 SOAS/SC.PP/3/16 Baron Paget to Captain Charles Newman, 5 June 1697.

Paget encouraged compliance in the interest of wider British commerce, as he realised that violations would be noted and prosecuted by the Ottoman state. Similarly, when the regulations were reissued in 1703, setting the limits from Samos, Ikaria, and Andros to Euboea, the secretary of state complained that the Ottomans were acting 'contrary to the law of nations and the known practice of war'.[57] However, Sir Robert Sutton requested special powers over privateers, concerned that their independence might 'bring avanias and pretences of reparation of affronts and injuries upon the Levant Company'.[58] As early as the turn of the eighteenth century, British foreign policy was bringing conflict between the British and the Ottomans, with the disregard for the welfare of friendly Ottoman merchants a policy greatly contrary to the displays of friendship the Ottomans desired.

These Ottoman maritime regulations were further developed during a crucial period in the 1740s. In the four years following the departure of Sir Everard Fawkener in 1742, the British embassy was left to the chargé d'affaires, Stanhope Aspinwall. In May 1744, Aspinwall received notice of the British declaration of war against France, and notified the *reisülküttab*, who expressed his concern that Ottoman trade would be disrupted.[59] Indeed, the Ottoman government had already received notifications of French anxiety, with one report speaking of the dangers of 'ships under the castles and in the ports of the Sublime State being seized and enslaved by pirates'.[60] The Ottoman government then issued a formal declaration to the European diplomats, noting the sultan's desire to maintain the freedom of navigation 'in the waters of his Well-Protected Domains, and in places under his jurisdiction' (*nell'acque dei suoi crestoditi Dominii, & in luochi della sua giurisdizione*).[61] The command ordered a dramatic extension of the maritime limits to a line between the Morea and the Gulf of Sirte:

> [I]n any of the islands that are under Ottoman rule, and in its waters towards the east of such a line, neither on the high seas nor on the coasts of Europe nor on those of Asia, there shall not be introduced any warships or privateers; and in the event that any of these come within the prescribed limits they are to be taken and confiscated ... And it will be the ambassador, resident, or agent at the Sublime Porte of that power whose ship was the first to attack and oppress the other ... who will be responsible for the losses incurred in goods or persons.[62]

This was a bold statement by the Ottoman authorities, essentially shutting off the entire Eastern Mediterranean to European armed ships in an effort to stop

57 TNA/SP97/21 Earl of Nottingham to Sir Robert Sutton, 23 January 1703/4.

58 TNA/SP97/21 Sir Robert Sutton to the Earl of Nottingham, 7/18 August 1702.

59 TLG no.8316, 3 April 1744, 8–9; TNA/SP97/32 Stanhope Aspinwall to the Duke of Newcastle, 12 May 1744.

60 BOA/C.HR 140/6968, end of Muharrem 1157 [mid-March 1744].

61 TNA/SP97/32 Affare da esser proposto, & amichevolmente notificato agli Ambasciatori, ai Residenti, & agli Agenti Franchi qui dimoranti, 17 May 1744.

62 Ibid.

the violence; however, Aspinwall objected that 'a line to be drawn across so large a sea is the most chimerical thing that was ever imagined'.[63] At least in the 1696 and 1703 regulations, the 150-mile line was based around islands; this new line extended for over 300 miles across the open sea. Despite British protests, based largely on the impossibility of proving the location of captures, the command was reissued to ensure compliance.[64] Indeed, in calling this border a '*ḥaṭṭ-ı mefrūż*', an imagined line, the Ottomans were making an important point: this was not a permanent border or territorial claim, but a temporary regulation.[65]

The 1744 declaration clearly laid responsibility for ensuring restitution or compensation on the European diplomats, and this had legal basis in the Capitulations, which mentioned pirates in general. Article XIX/12 placed responsibility on the Ottoman government for ensuring justice for victims of Ottoman piracy. It stated that if any group of pirates (*ḳorṣān ṭāʿifesi*) or mercenary ships roving at sea (*deryāda yürüyen levend fürḳatası*) pillaged and damaged (*ġāret ve ḫasāret*) British ships and goods, the Ottomans would seek and pursue (*saʿī ve iḳdām*) those corrupt people (*ehl-i fesād*), and seize back and return any ships, possessions, and merchandise without hindrance or delay (*bilā taʿallul*). The new regulations seemed to imply that just as Ottoman ministers were responsible for securing justice for British sufferers, so too were European ministers expected to secure compensation for Ottoman subjects, and therefore that the Capitulations should be considered as reciprocal in that regard. This was necessary at the juncture due to a completely different scale of violence. Whereas the privateers of the 1690s and 1700s had targeted shipping around Izmir, the 1740s saw focus shift to the entrance of the Aegean between Kythera, Crete, Karpathos, and Rhodes, and to the busy routes between Egypt, Cyprus, and the coast of Syria, where French ships freighting Ottoman goods played an important part in internal trade. In the summer of 1746, the privateer Fortunatus Wright of *The Fame* took a ship near Heraklion carrying a cargo of soap and oil to Alexandria belonging to several Ottoman subjects, stripping the merchants of their cash and clothes before dumping them back on Crete. In order to make their claim, Ottoman merchants had to provide evidence of the goods being their property. The merchants immediately went to the governor, qadi, and customs officer of Heraklion, who provided documents that fifteen of the group took to Istanbul to present to the Ottoman government and British embassy.[66] At an audience with the grand vizier, Aspinwall received strong protests, and was given three

63 TNA/SP97/32 Stanhope Aspinwall to the Duke of Newcastle, 12 May 1744.

64 BOA/C.HR/121/6030, Şabān 1157 [1744]; TNA/SP97/32 Commandamento diretto al Pascia di Canea, beginning of Şabān 1157 [1744].

65 BOA/C.HR/121/6030.

66 TNA/SP97/32 Traduzione della Lettera di Chriuperli Ahmed Pascia di Candia al Supremo Vizir, 19/29 August 1746; TNA/SP97/32 Traduzione dell'Arz o Sia rappresentazione del Cadi, o Sio Giudici di Candia, alla Fulgida Porta, 15 Cemaziülahir 1159 [4 July 1746]; TNA/SP97/32 Carico d'oglio, sappone, e d'altre mercanzie sopra la Nave Francese di Capitan Blanc nella Scala di Candi destinato per Alessandria, 15 Cemaziülahir 1159 [4 July 1746]; TNA/SP97/32 Nota

months to make restitution or satisfaction. Eventually, the merchants received full compensation of 20,435 *guruş* (around £250,000 in modern terms) from the Company's funds.[67]

As a further financial pressure, when a new ambassador, James Porter, finally arrived in 1747, the Istanbul factory voted to increase his audience gifts by 3,000 *guruş* in order to gain favour with the Ottoman government. The situation, however, got worse. HMS *Diamond* seized a large shipment of rice from Damietta destined for famine-stricken Cyprus, whilst *The Fame* stole 5,687 *guruş* from an Ottoman official en route to the Aegean islands to buy corn for Syrian Tripoli.[68] *The Fame* took four more ships carrying coffee and rice from Damietta to Izmir, Istanbul, and Payas; the merchants of Payas threatened to take British stock from nearby Iskenderun as compensation, whilst in Latakia, where merchants had a stake in the cargo, the governor warned the British consul that 'he could not be responsible for the consequences of the people's fury'.[69] Wright's final victim was a ship from Damietta to Cyprus carrying Egyptian rice, and pilgrims returning from Mecca. George Wakeman, the British consul at Larnaca, paid the 5,200 *guruş* ransom Wright demanded for the ship in order to free the pilgrims and avoid reprisals.[70] The seizure of much-needed provisions, and the abuse of Muslim pilgrims, caused outrage. The consul at Acre was forced to compensate irate merchants there, whilst in Cairo, the British factory feared violence from people 'exclaiming against the English for taking [Muslims'] effects'.[71]

In all this, Porter's hands were, in his opinion, tied, as 'by the Turkish laws if they appear with proofs the composition must be above half'.[72] As demonstrated in table 8, the majority of claims fell on the Company, which paid at least 80,000 *guruş* (around £1.6 million today) in compensation. This required the factories to take a number of loans repayable at the high rate of 10% interest, as well as to raise additional leviations on goods.[73] The actions of British privateers were severely damaging the financial balance of the diplomatic framework. One reason why the Company paid, rather than the British government whose privateers had caused all the trouble, was the issue

delle robbe appartenti alli Mercani, e passaggiere Turchi imbarciato nella Scala di Candi, 15 Cemaziülahir 1159 [4 July 1746]; TNA/SP97/32 Memorial, 19 August 1746.

67 TNA/SP97/32 Stanhope Aspinwall to the Duke of Newcastle, 20 August 1746; 17 December 1746.

68 TNA/SP97/33 James Porter to the Duke of Newcastle, 21 February 1746/7. See: James Grehan, *Everyday Life and Consumer Culture in Eighteenth-Century Damascus* (Seattle, 2007), 56–94, especially 81–2

69 TNA/SP97/33 Edward Purnell to James Porter, 24 March 1746/7; TNA/SP97/33 James Porter to the Duke of Newcastle, 23 June 1747.

70 TNA/SP97/33 George Wakemen to James Porter, 20 March 1746/7; TNA/SP97/33 George Wakeman to Henry Frissell (pseudonym of Fortunatus Wright), 25 March 1747; 26 March 1747, nos. 4 & 5; 27 March 1747; TNA/SP97/33 Henry Frissell to George Wakeman, 25 March 1747; 27 March 1747, nos. 7, 8, & 10.

71 TNA/SP97/33 Robert Barton to James Porter, 28 March 1747.

72 TNA/SP97/33 James Porter to the Duke of Newcastle, 30 January 1747/8.

73 TNA/SP97/33 James Porter to the Duke of Newcastle, 29 August 1747; 22 September 1747.

Table 8: *Privateer captures, claims, and compensation, 1744–7*

| Year | Privateer | Captured at/near | Cargo | Amount claimed (*guruş*) | Amount paid (*guruş*) |
|---|---|---|---|---|---|
| 1744 | The Ruby | Kythera | Rice, coffee | 19,714 | Settled by admiralty, full amount |
| 1744 | Unnamed | Crete | Unknown | Unknown | Restored |
| 1744 | The Ruby | Rhodes | Barilla | 21,000 | 21,000 |
| 1744 | The Ruby | Zakynthos | Cloth | Unknown | Unknown |
| 1745 | The Thames | Tripoli (Syria) | Unknown | Unknown | Restored |
| 1746 | The Fame | Crete | Oil, soap, raisins | 20,435 | 20,435 |
| 1746 | The Fame | Syrian coast | Money | 5,687 | 5,687 |
| 1746 | HMS Diamond | Cyprus | Rice | 396 *ardabs* (27 tonnes) | Restored |
| 1747 | The Fame | Syrian coast | Coffee | 16,412 | 16,412 |
| 1747 | The Fame | Syrian coast | Rice, coffee | 15,545 | 10,000 |
| 1747 | The Fame | Syrian coast | Rice, coffee | 4,677 | 1,599 |
| 1747 | The Fame | Larnaca | Rice | 5,200 | 5,200 |
| **Total** | | | | ***at least* 108,670** | ***at least* 80,333** |

of proof. Porter noted that whereas English law required 'an affirmative oath of the Turks of the property by the Alcoran [Qur'an], no Turk can take such an oath, they swear only to the negative, that such and such goods did not belong to such a person'.[74] It must be said that it is notable that British courts allowed Muslims their own forms of oath, with evidence that a British convert named Morgan and an Ottoman subject recorded as 'Hasbrahim Ben Aga Soderati' were sworn in using the Qur'an in the eighteenth century.[75] Yet, as Porter

74 TNA/SP97/33 James Porter to the Duke of Newcastle, 30 January 1747/8 (secret).

75 POB, t17650227-5, trial of John, Jeremiah, and Mary Ryan, 27 February 1765; POB, t17870523-91, trial of John M'Nally & Nicholas Ellicot, 23 May 1787.

noted, oaths in Islamic courts were usually sworn by those denying charges rather than claiming goods, who relied instead on legal proofs, and so in theory compensation could not be made under British law.[76] This also demonstrates that British courts were not willing to accept the written proofs of Ottoman merchants prepared by local judges, however voluminous, and whether or not they were registered with the British embassy or consulate.

One example of the burden of proof came in August 1744, when seventeen Ottoman merchants, mainly from Crete, lost their cargo of barilla, shipped from Tunis to Athens, to *The Ruby* off Kythera; some of the 'Moors' (i.e. North Africans) were taken to Malta for enslavement.[77] The privateer had also taken all of their documentation, and therefore two of the merchants, Osman and Ahmed, travelled to London for their case to be heard.[78] Aspinwall requested that 'this affair be treated somewhat in a public light, and not merely as a common lawsuit, for the Turks will not be able to make of the proofs which [English] law requires'.[79] After fifteen months, the secretary of state finally agreed to recommend the case to the Lords Commissioners for Prize Causes, who ruled that the prize had been unlawfully condemned, and so refunded the goods.[80] Aspinwall's thinking was clear; if Ottoman merchants did not find justice in British courts, why should Ottoman courts give justice to British merchants?

With so much damage being done, a British *taḳrīr* delivered on behalf of James Porter in Receb 1160/July 1747 was sent to the Porte, aimed at 'clarifying the affairs between the two states' (*taṣfiyet-i maṣlaḥat beynü'l-devleteyn*), which shows the diplomatic manoeuvres the ambassador employed to deflect liability and to salvage the situation.[81] Porter first admitted that, 'according to complaints of the merchants of the Muslim people, recently a British privateer committed usurpation and enslavement [*ġaṣb ve istirḳaḳ*]'; doubtless this was referring to Wright's attack on the pilgrim ship at Larnaca, and is notable for including the term in Islamic jurisprudence for tort theft, or usurpation, *ġaṣb*.[82] To prove that the British government was being proactive, he referred

76 Muhammad Khalid Masud, Rudolph Peters, & David S. Powers, 'Qāḍīs and their courts: An historical survey' in Muhammad Khalid Masud, Rudolph Peters, & David S. Powers (eds), *Dispensing Justice in Islam: Qadis and their Judgements* (Leiden, 2006), 1–47 at 27.

77 For a contemporary view of this trade, see: *Istoria degli stati di Algeri, Tunisi, Tripoli e Marocco* (London, 1754), 310–15.

78 TNA/SP97/32 Stanhope Aspinwall to the Duke of Newcastle, 13 October 1744; 6 December 1744; 29 March 1746.

79 TNA/SP97/32 Stanhope Aspinwall to the Duke of Newcastle, 9 February 1745/6.

80 TNA/SP97/33 Osman and Ahmed of Heraklion to Hacı Süleyman of Istanbul, end of Zilhicce 1160 [beginning of January 1747/8]; TNA/SP97/33 Duke of Bedford to James Porter, 3 June 1748; TNA/SP97/55 Memorial of the Governor and Company of Merchants of England trading into the Levant Seas, 17 November 1779.

81 BOA/C.HR/15/723, 26 Receb 1160 [3 August 1747]; TNA/SP97/33 James Porter to Hacı Mehmed Paşa, undated Italian letter (c. August 1747).

82 BOA/C.HR/15/723. See: Colin Imber, *Ebu's-su'ud: The Islamic Legal Tradition* (Stanford, 1997), 213–33 especially 222–5. For *ġaṣb* rulings of a seventeenth-century *Şeyhülislam*, see: ʿAli Efendi, *Fetāvā-yı ʿAlī Efendi maʿa'n-nuḳūl* (Istanbul, 1272 [1856]), 589–91.

to 'very strong and repeated warnings' (*tenbīhāt-ı ekīde-i mükerrere*) sent by the king to British ships in the Levant. The proviso was then added that there would be difficulty in paying dividends (*eyrād*) on losses without complete proofs (*ḫasāret bilā subūt kāmile*). Moreover, he emphasised that 'this your supplicant [i.e. the ambassador] will not undertake compensation; compensation must come from a collection being made [i.e. from the Company]' (*bu dāʿīleri tażmīnāt-ı müteʿahhīd olamayub tażmīni lāzım gelenden taḥṣīl etdirilmesine*).[83] This *taḳrīr* shows that the ambassador officially took a rather hard line with these claims in an attempt to discount liability, probably worried that he would have to pay from his own allowance. Whilst Porter wanted to only pay on strict criteria of proof, the Istanbul factory in Istanbul 'was rather of the opinion to finish the whole, than suffer any remains of demands to expose the people or the commerce'.[84] Here, we clearly see the concern of the British merchants that their trade would suffer if justice were not done for the Ottoman merchants.

British privateering in the Levant in the late 1740s did great damage to French trade, but was also disastrous for the Levant Company. The British ambassador was bound by the maritime regulations as they were decreed under Ottoman sultanic law, and was pressured by the Ottoman sufferers and the imperial government. Moreover, privateering did great damage to diplomatic practice. In the summer of 1746, the new grand vizier Haccı Mehmed Paşa laid out the Ottoman government's grievances against Britain in an oral address, berating them for failing to dispatch an ambassador in four years and for allowing their ships to abuse Ottoman subjects. Aspinwall reported back to the secretary of state that:

> All this was delivered to me in a very serious and emphatic tone, and there plainly appeared in the vizier's ancient countenance ... a kind of concern mixed with indignation at seeing themselves so neglected, and if I may dare to say it, ill-treated by friends.[85]

That sense of poor treatment by an ally translated into the regular requests of the ambassador, such as those relating to customs duties, being deferred; as Porter noted at the height of the compensation crisis in August 1747, 'all national affairs [are] suspended and at a stand'.[86] The privateering crisis threatened to break long-standing and peaceful relations between the two states.

When conflict again broke out in 1755, and a British privateer took a French ship inside the port of Milos, Porter made it very clear to the British government and the commanders of British ships that he did not want a repeat of the 1740s.[87] Moreover, a recent British treaty with Russia had made the

83 BOA/C.HR/15/723.

84 TNA/SP97/33 James Porter to the Duke of Newcastle, 29 August 1747.

85 TNA/SP97/32 Stanhope Aspinwall to the Duke of Newcastle, 20 August 1746.

86 TNA/SP97/33 James Porter to the Duke of Newcastle, 29 August 1747.

87 TNA/SP97/37 Commandamento diretto al Naib & alli Commandanti dell'Isola di Milo, middle of Ṣafer 1169 [1755].

Ottomans suspicious of British allegiances, and Porter warned that 'my credit will be wholly lost, and every representation I may make in vain'.[88] In a letter sent to the commanders of British ships, he explained Ottoman notions of maritime territoriality:

> The Turks understand their ports, open roads, havens, bays, or anchoring places on their coasts, whether there are forts, or castles, or governors or not ... to be sacred, and an asylum; all ships taken at anchor from thence, they will consider as a breach of friendship.[89]

This important final phrase, 'a breach of friendship', demonstrates that the British were fully aware of the implications of maritime violence, that the importance the Ottomans placed on the maintenance and display of *dostluk̨* was more than just capitulatory rhetoric. The British government took note following Porter's warnings and a petition by the Company, and two orders in council were issued forbidding British ships from taking enemy vessels in Ottoman ports, molesting Ottoman subjects, and from taking any ships going between Ottoman ports carrying Ottoman goods.[90] Nonetheless, captures were still being made within Ottoman waters, and Porter was sent a confidential note from the Ottoman government complaining of lost customs revenue, and proposing to reinstitute the maritime limits.[91] Moreover, Istanbul and other cities were suffering from shortages of bread and rice, and it is probable that the Ottoman government was wary of privateers taking desperately needed provisions.[92] Therefore, a formal declaration in 1171/1758 re-established the maritime limits between the Morea and the Gulf of Sirte.[93] This time, however, the combination of the maritime limits, and pressure from both the Ottoman and British authorities, managed to limit the violence compared to the previous conflict.

Following the outbreak of war again in 1778, Sir Robert Ainslie was afraid that renewed privateering would lead to 'continual avanias'.[94] When a Captain Baxter took a ship from Jaffa carrying pilgrims from Jerusalem, who were dumped on Kos minus their goods, Ainslie feared the worst, but a reissuing of the Orders in Council of 1756 temporarily placated the Ottoman government.[95] This, however, did not stop the privateers, and with food shortages in Istanbul and Anatolia, British disruption of French shipping was affecting the supply

88 TNA/SP97/37 James Porter to Sir Thomas Robinson, 5 December 1755.

89 TNA/SP97/37 Copy of Mr Porter's Letter to the Commanders of His Britannick Majesty's Ships of War and Cruizers &ca, 26 November 1755.

90 TNA/SP97/39 The King's Most Excellent Majesty in Council, 3 February 1756; Copy of an Order of Council, 1 June 1756

91 TNA/SP97/40 James Porter to William Pitt, 4 April 1758.

92 TNA/SP97/40 James Porter to William Pitt, 17 May 1758.

93 TNA/SP97/40 Translation of a Memorial or Request of the Ottoman Porte, undated (c. July 1758).

94 BOA/C.HR/184/9160, 14 Safer 1192 [14 March 1778]; TNA/SP97/54 Sir Robert Ainslie to Viscount Weymouth, 4 May 1778; 18 May 1778.

95 TNA/SP97/55 Sir Robert Ainslie to Viscount Weymouth, 18 June 1779; TNA/SP97/55 Viscount Weymouth to Sir Robert Ainslie, 16 July 1779.

of rice from Egypt, creating disorder in the Ottoman capital. When Charles Mackenzie took a ship carrying 20,000 *guruş*-worth of provisions from Egypt, Ainslie was given three months to secure compensation, and the Company petitioned that it could not bear the cost.[96] As a result of these actions, the Ottoman government formally notified the French and British ambassadors of the reinstitution of the maritime regulations, terming them '*ḳavāʿid-i deryā*' (the rules of the sea), which they had been preparing since earlier that year, and with the limits again set from the Morea to the Gulf of Sirte.[97] This was noted in a command to the Ottoman governors in the Mediterranean and naval officials in February 1780, declaring the 'Islamic borders' (*ḥudūd-u İslāmiye*) to be 'a supposed line' (*ḫaṭṭ- ı farż*) from Morea to Crete and down to Egypt in order to allow ships to pass in security and safety (*emnan ve sāliman*).[98] However, after discussions with the ambassadors, the Ottomans agreed to suspend the full implementation of the regulations to see how the European ships would behave, but warned that they would be fully enacted if 'the commands of the ambassadors are subsequently not observed, [and if the British and French] fight one another underneath the cannon of the castles, and near to the ports and islands, and within three [nautical] miles distance from land'.[99]

These revised Ottoman and renewed British orders led to a stricter approach to privateers from the embassy. A complaint had been received by the Ottoman government and British embassy from an Ottoman subject from Tinos, Mihal Droso, a non-Muslim subject, who had freighted a French ship from Acre to Izmir via Cyprus with a cargo of wheat (*ḥinṭa ḥamūlesile*) that was taken and seized (*aḫẕ ve girift*) by a British privateer off Chios.[100] After a number of similar violations, including a blockade by British ships of the port of Milos, Ainslie issued a stern warning that the Ottoman command should be respected:

> I do hereby in virtue of my full powers, enjoin all and every one of His Majesty's subjects whom it may concern to refrain from committing any the least infraction to this imperial command, which is conform to the instructions framed by the Lords of the Admiralty under which they act, as they shall answer it, at their utmost peril, and under pain of such punishment as by the law may be inflicted.[101]

96 TNA/SP97/55 Sir Robert Ainslie to Viscount Weymouth, 3 September 1779; TNA/SP97/55 Memorial of the Governor and Company of Merchants of England trading into the Levant Seas, 17 November 1779.

97 BOA/C.BH/273/12571, end of Rebiülevel 1193 [1779]; TNA/SP97/55 Comandamento Imperiale diretto a Dervish Mehemmed Bei Commandante attuale della Flotta Imperiale nell'Arcipelago, beginning of Rebiülevvel 1193 [middle of April 1779]; TNA/SP97/55 A motivo della Guerra, sussistente frà la Francia e l'Inghilterra quest'Esposizione ora è State messa in iscritta acciò Sia proposta ai Ministri, 11 Zilkade 1193 [20 November 1779].

98 BOA/C.HR/118/5877, middle of Safer 1193 [beginning of March 1779]; TNA/FO78/1 Italian Memorial of the Porte, 9 Safer 1194 [12 February 1780].

99 BOA/C.HR/118/5877.

100 BOA/C.HR/82/4099, 27 Rebiülevvel 1194 [3 April 1780].

101 TNA/FO78/1 Copy of a Letter of His Excellency Sir Robert Ainslie Addressed to all Commanders of British Privateers, and Armed Ships cruising in the Levant Seas, written at the desire of the Porte, 15 May 1780.

Crucially, this order was followed through. In June 1780, *The Salisbury Cutter* took French ships with many thousands of *guruş* belonging to Ottoman subjects off Sarafand (near Sidon) and in the harbour of Beirut, coming under fire from the guns of the Ottoman castle of that city.[102] Ainslie complained to London of having to be 'an intermediary between the Ottoman ministers, who with great reason complain, and of such of our cruisers who act like downright pirates, without any attention to their instructions, to the laws of nations, and to the rights of sovereigns'.[103] Estimating that the Company would be liable to pay £20,000 compensation (around £2 million today), he sent notice to the consuls in Cyprus, Aleppo, Syrian Tripoli, and Livorno to sequester the goods if the privateer arrived in their districts.[104] This tactic worked; when the captain, John Chandler, arrived at Larnaca, he was accosted by consul Michael de Vezin and forced to restore the Ottoman goods and compensate the merchants.[105] After almost a century, action was finally being taken against the violence of British privateers in the Mediterranean.

However, the general disregard that the British privateers and even Royal Navy ships had for Ottoman goods on French ships shows a serious breach of relations, and produced a dispute that was difficult to resolve due to its financial and political implications. It is evident that the Ottomans had a clear notion of their maritime territoriality, something clearly understood by the British. However, violations of those waters in the area around Izmir in the 1690s and 1700s had resulted in the extension of maritime jurisdiction out to sea. The increasing employment of French ships in freighting Ottoman goods meant that in the conflicts of the 1740s and 1770s, British attacks on shipping in the Levant threatened Ottoman food supplies. This led to the extension of the maritime limits, and Ottoman legal jurisdiction, to the furthest possible boundaries of Ottoman waters, and resulted in the successful prosecution for compensation. Although the British ambassadors formally objected to the new maritime boundaries, the Company was obliged to issue compensation under these new Ottoman laws. Ottoman decrees to their naval officials and to the European diplomats, along with the petitions and other documentation submitted by the sufferers, indicate that the maritime regulations were successfully implemented, especially considering that the Company was obliged to pay compensation when proof could be made under Ottoman law. Despite the expense, which greatly damaged the Company's finances, this was ultimately necessary to protect British merchants and their interests and maintain relations. Moreover, the ambassadors were unable to persuade the Ottomans to revoke the new maritime limits until strict guarantees for the

[102] TNA/FO78/1 Sir Robert Ainslie to the Earl of Hillsborough, 26 June 1780.

[103] TNA/FO78/1 Sir Robert Ainslie to the Earl of Hillsborough, 1 July 1780.

[104] Ibid.; TNA/FO78/1 Estratti degl'Ilami (o sia rappresentazioni) in idioma Arabo, venuti dalle parti di Saida, e Beirùt, undated (c. June 1780); TNA/FO78/1 Memorial Translate from the Turkish Original by Me Bartholemew Pisani British Drugoman, 30 June 1780; TNA/FO78/1 Sir Robert Ainslie to the Earl of Hillsborough, 17 July 1780; TNA/FO78/1 Copy of the Ambassador's Anser, to the Porte's Memorial, 3 July 1780.

[105] TNA/FO78/1 Sir Robert Ainslie to the Earl of Hillsborough, 17 August 1780.

privateers' behaviour had been formally issued and implemented by the British government.

The actions of British privateers provoked a diplomatic crisis, and provided a dispute quite unlike the more routine commercial cases. As Porter noted, so long as the British were unwilling to assist Ottoman merchants, the Ottoman government would be unwilling to see to the ambassador's business, whether it related to matters of foreign policy or of consular functions. In seeking to damage French commerce in the Levant, the British government's support for privateering concurrently damaged the Company's trade and the merchants' interests, as well as its reputation with the Ottoman government. Ill-conceived foreign policy decided in London had a direct and negative impact on the well-being of British merchants across the Ottoman realms. Perhaps most importantly from the perspective of diplomatic practice, as Aspinwall had observed, it was a very poor way to treat the subjects of an ally. If the main purpose of diplomatic relations – the primary aim of all the finance, all the gift-giving, and all the ceremonial – was to protect the interests of British merchants and increase their trade through maintaining a firm friendship with the Ottoman state, then the British policy of unrestrained privateering in the Eastern Mediterranean was just about the closest thing to breaking that friendship, and ruining British commerce. The privateering issue, however, shows the increasing separation of politics and commerce in the eighteenth century in pursuit of an ever-more aggressive foreign policy, a pursuit that would end centuries of peaceful friendship between the British and the Ottoman Empire.

## Political diplomacy: Manifestations of foreign policy

The primary focus of this study has been on diplomatic practice and its relationship with finance and commerce. Yet, the ambassador was also a minister of the Crown, and was expected to further the interests of British foreign policy as and when required. As we have seen from the policy of aggressive privateering, British foreign policy aims were not always compatible with the maintenance of friendly relations. However, violence was only part of the story of British–Ottoman political relations. For much of the later seventeenth and eighteenth centuries, a major foreign policy aim of the British was to secure the role of mediator in Ottoman treaty negotiations with a view to furthering Britain's political and economy clout at the Sublime Porte, notably via the peace treaties of Carlowitz (1699), Passarowitz (1718), and Sistova (1792). These negotiations, being separate from the direct aims of the Company and outside its diplomatic framework, were dealt with differently in rhetorical and financial terms. However, the final part of this story ends not with peace and friendship, but with war and betrayal, and it is important to ask why the long eighteenth century of British–Ottoman relations ended in conflict between the two states, and what that meant for the merchants who relied on ambassadorial protection.

Mediation became a key function of British foreign policy in the Ottoman Empire from the later seventeenth century. Negotiated settlements had existed for a long time in Ottoman history, yet peace treaties were ultimately, as with the Capitulations, often unilateral grants by the Ottoman state. This practice, however, began to change with the Treaty of Carlowitz in 1699, at which negotiation the Ottomans were represented by negotiators with a background in state administration rather than in the military. The settlement at Carlowitz, with the British and Dutch ambassadors acting as mediators (*mutavaṣṣıṭ*), was based on the principle of *uti possidetis*, meaning that at the end of the conflict, each party retained the land it had gained, unless otherwise specified.[106] In such a manner, the Ottomans accepted territorial losses, and, at the same time, concrete borders. For over a year after the signing of the treaty, Ottoman and Habsburg commissioners toured the borders to agree on set limits.[107] Maps would therefore prove increasingly important in such agreements, with a number of examples in the Ottoman archives showing the detailed level at which border commissions operated.[108] Shifting conceptions of borders and territorial integrity were accompanied by some soul-searching among the Ottoman elite, with the diplomat and historian Ahmed Vasıf Efendi examining the changes in diplomatic attitudes in his history of the late eighteenth century, published in 1804.[109] In the aftermath of the 1768–74 war with Russia, Ahmed Vasıf reflected on the territorial losses and reparations that peace had brought, assessing that 'the Sublime State was tired after six years of war with its enemies', and further blaming other states for instigating and exciting (*taḥrīk ve teşvīḳ*) the conflict.[110] Thus, the move towards diplomatic endeavours rather than conflict would be ultimately beneficial to the Ottoman state, yet there was clearly an element of distrust towards some of their enemies. He used what was a stock Ottoman phrase in the latter part of the eighteenth century in accusing Austria (*Nemçe*) and Russia (*Mosḳov*) of violating the treaty (*naḳż-ı ʿahd*) between them.[111] This phrase is of Qur'anic origin, from a number of suras (e.g. 2:27, 13:20–5, 16:91–2), but the most relevant in this case is sura 8:56, which describes the unbelievers as 'the ones with whom you made a treaty, but they break their covenant each time' (*yanquḍūna ʿahdahum fī kulli marratin*).

The notion of a treaty being violated is one that seems to have become of particular importance in Ottoman diplomatic discourse in the aftermath of

[106] For an Ottoman narrative, see: Mehmed Said Efendi, *Tārīḫ-i gülşen-i maʿārif*, 2 vols (Istanbul, 1252 [1836]), vol. II, 1033–6.

[107] SOAS/SC.PP/3/20 Baron Paget to Robert Sutton, 15 October 1700; SOAS/SC.PP/17/73 Robert Sutton to Baron Paget, 15 November 1700.

[108] See, for example: BOA.HRT.h/190, Ramazan 1152 [1739]; BOA.HAT/241/13504, undated (c. 1205/1791). This last map was part of a formal appendix to the Treaty of Sistova. See: *Separate Convention between the Emperor of Germany and the Ottoman Porte, signed at Sistovo, August 4, 1791* (London, 1792).

[109] Ahmed Vasıf Efendi, *Meḥāsinü'l-āsār ve ḥaḳāʾiḳü'l-āḫbār* (Istanbul, 1219 [1804]). A very interesting comparison has been made between this source and the works of Ahmed Resmi Efendi in the context of changing Ottoman political ideology in Aksan, *An Ottoman Statesman*, 102–15. See also: Aksan, 'Ottoman political writing'.

[110] Ahmed Vasıf Efendi, *Meḥāsinü'l-āsār*, vol. II, 308.

[111] Ibid.

Carlowitz. In the eighteenth century, the Ottoman government began to send justifications for their going to war with Russia or the Habsburgs to friendly European powers, particularly Britain as a mediator. The first of these was sent in late 1710, of which the Italian translation survives:

> The Muslim emperor, having established and confirmed the peace … with the king of the Muscovites, and the said king having made slaves of a number of Muslims living on the victorious borders of this Empire, and also done other actions by which means he violates the peace; and being so evident and established, in order to remedy the damage to the Muslim lands, it is permissible by law to send the army against the said king and declare war.[112]

There are two interesting points to take from this text. First, that war had to receive the sanction under Islamic law via the approval of the *ʿulemāʾ*, the Islamic scholars and jurists via a *fetvā*, something noted on the translation.[113] Second, the Ottomans did not justify going to war in the name of perpetual religious conflict, but in response to specific violations of treaties. In 1736, the grand vizier Seyyid Mehmed Paşa wrote to George II concerning Habsburg and Russian violations of their treaties, the English translation of which states:

> [A]ll imaginable care has ever been had, not to use any the least violence on their confines, before the term prescribed in the articles given them were expired, according to the precept of God, *You must wait 'till the time of the treaty you have with them be expired.*[114]

Quoting here directly from the Qur'an (9:4) to demonstrate the Ottomans' strict adherence to treaties as a religious duty, he then argued, again using the Qur'an (2:194), that war was the only correct option, as that verse commands an attack to be met with an attack. The grand vizier specifically emphasised that the Russians had violated the treaty, even under Christian law, saying that the Russian government was made up of 'religious men, though disregarding their faith, they should make no account of the precepts of Jesus Christ, but even slight and neglect them'.[115] This was overwhelming evidence, from the Ottoman perspective, of their right to go to war with Russia, and the letter announcing that the Russians had again violated their treaty, sent to London in 1768, aimed to show Ottoman patience in the face of Russian provocation:

> And to this time there is not found any behaviour or occurrence on the part of the Sublime State contrary to friendship or the imperial capitulations [*dostluġuñ ḫilāfa ve ʿahdnāme-i hümayūnuñ muġayir*]; while this matter was for three years, out of friendship, looked upon with a blind eye and deferred,

112 TNA/SP97/22 Sir Robert Sutton to the Earl of Sunderland, attachment: Resolution of the Porte.
113 Ibid. 'In riposta si dimanda se sia necessario? le Legge risponde è necessario.'
114 TNA/SP97/28 Seyyid Mehmed Paşa to George II, undated [1148/1736].
115 Ibid.

> the state of Russia, contrary to the peace and harmony [*muġāyir-i ṣulḥ ve ṣalāḥ*], has committed this ignorant violation of the treaty [*bu cehalet naḳż -ı ʿahd irtikāb*].[116]

This is the language of *dostluḳ*, friendship, betrayed, and of a justified distrust of the other contracting parties in peace treaties. The Ottoman declarations of war in the eighteenth century all received the approval of the *ʿulemāʾ*, not because there was an idea that some sort of perpetual war should exist between the *dār al-Islām* and *dār al-ḥarb*, but because those in treaty with the Ottomans were perceived to have broken their side of the agreement. Although the response was justified by Qur'anic verses, this was by no means a uniquely Islamic problem or response. Indeed, this sort of synthesis demonstrates the fact that the Ottomans developed their own pragmatic form of diplomacy, in some respects rooted in Islamic law and tradition, and in others reactive to current events. The violation was not contrary to Islam, but contrary to friendship and the Capitulations.

After Carlowitz, the Ottomans had reacted to changes in their political and military fortunes, and had embraced new concepts of peace-making, from defining and mapping solid borders, to adopting the conventions of mediation. Indeed, on more than one occasion the Ottoman government offered their own mediation to end conflicts between European powers, notably during the War of the Austrian Succession, when Ottoman subjects suffered, as has been seen, from privateering by British and French ships. The grand vizier Seyyid Hasan Paşa set forth his concerns to George II in 1745:

> [F]irst, the effusion of so much human blood, the misfortunes of so many ladies being exposed to dishonour, all the effects of war; secondly, the calamity and affliction, under which an infinite number of persons will sink next summer; and thirdly, the interruption of trade, as is said, for want of security, which is the support of the subjects.[117]

Here we see an almost textbook argument against war in terms of the human cost, but, with a nod to the dangers of European privateers in Ottoman waters, warning of the disruption to commerce. The Ottomans clearly understood that the Europeans hurt most when their trade was damaged. In a letter sent at the same time to the Duke of Newcastle as secretary of state, Seyyid Hasan argued that 'it is God almighty's express command not to hurt one another; but by such open variance trade is lost and ruined, the subjects in uncertainty even of keeping what is their own, for by both parties the people are sure to suffer'.[118]

116 TNA/SP97/44 Devlet-i ʿAliye dāʾim'ül-ḳarār ile olan muṣalaḥayı Rusiya devleti fesḫ ve naḳż-ı ʿahd eylediğini muşʿir-i beyānnāmedir, 1182 [1768]. There is also an attached Italian translation: TNA/SP97/44 Manifesto contente a rottura e violazione, che la Corte di Russia ha fatto, della pace avuta colla Fulgida Porta.

117 TNA/SP97/32 Seyyid Hasan Paşa to George II, undated (translated from Italian by Antonio Pisani 31 January 1744/5).

118 TNA/SP97/32 Seyyid Hasan Paşa to the Duke of Newcastle, undated (translated from Italian by Antonio Pisani 31 January 1744/5).

This was not the argument of universalist peace, but aimed specifically at a European mercantile audience.

The British never took up the Ottomans on their offers of peace mediation with the French. However, the Ottomans did employ the British on a number of occasions in that capacity; the question is, why? European geopolitics does not provide much of an answer. Britain and its allies were at war with France and its allies for much of the long eighteenth century; Britain tended to fight France, France tended to fight the Habsburgs, and the Habsburgs tended to fight the Ottoman Empire. It was therefore in Britain's interest that the Habsburgs did not have to fight on two fronts, against the French in the west and against the Ottomans in the east. The strategic benefits for Britain in persuading the Ottomans to make peace with the Habsburgs in such conflicts were therefore clear. It is not so clear how the Ottomans viewed this diplomatic mess, as, in theory, by being allied with the Habsburgs, the British were on the wrong side. Nonetheless, it was primarily this rationale that led the British to seek an end to the drawn-out conflict between the Ottoman Empire and the Habsburgs from the Siege of Vienna in 1683 until 1699. The idea of mediation as a political tool came to the fore earlier in the seventeenth century, notably with the efforts of Sir Thomas Roe to mediate peace between the Ottomans and the Poles.[119] After the restoration of the British monarchy in 1660, mediation seems to have been seen as a way to advance the glory of that battered institution on the global stage. Almost immediately on his arrival in 1661, Winchilsea wrote that he considered there to be 'opportunities in this place of advancing His Majesty's power and honour, as in any parts without his own dominions', to be achieved through Charles II's 'umpirage of peace' to end the Ottoman–Venetian war over Crete. Given the French involvement in that conflict against the Ottomans, this would also be a way to steal a march on the old enemy. For Winchilsea, there were personal benefits too, with mediation being for 'my master's glory, and my own honour'.[120] Despite early encouragement from the Venetian Senate, the plan did not come together, ultimately because there was little benefit for British interests.[121] Similarly, in the conflict that erupted following the siege of Vienna in 1683, Chandos suggested that James II 'concern himself as a mediator of peace', arguing that he 'would be heard better than any Christian prince in the world, and esteemed for so good a friend at the Porte, that he might command what privileges he had a desire of for encouragement of his merchants' trade in all parts of the Grand Signor's dominions'.[122] By Carlowitz, therefore, mediation was already well established in the British diplomatic arsenal in Istanbul.

[119] *The Negotiations of Sir Thomas Roe, in his Embassy to the Ottoman Porte, from the Year 1621 to 1628 Inclusive* (London, 1740); J.K. Fedorowicz, *England's Baltic Trade in the Early Seventeenth Century: A Study in Anglo-Polish Commercial Diplomacy* (Cambridge, 1980), 10–12.

[120] TNA/SP97/17 Earl of Winchilsea to Sir Edward Nicholas, 12 June 1661.

[121] TNA/SP97/17 Earl of Winchilsea to the Lord Treasurer, 30 September 1661; TNA/SP97/17 Giulio Cesare Alberti to the Earl of Winchilsea, 15 November 1661; TNA/SP97/18 Earl of Winchilsea to the Earl of Arlington, 8 October 1664.

[122] TNA/SP97/20 Baron Chandos to the Earl of Sunderland, 25 September 1685.

Table 9: *Baron Paget's travel and provision expenses at Carlowitz claimed on the British treasury, 1697–8*

| **Items claimed** | **Amount (£)** |
|---|---|
| Coaches, carts, wagons, horses, presents to the sultan's officers, on journey from Istanbul to Edirne | 240 |
| 'Turkish' clothes and furs for 100 servants | 1,700 |
| 90 horses | 500 |
| Saddles, bridgs, and housses for 140 horses, as well as mules and camels | 420 |
| 14 new tents | 280 |
| Cloth paling for camp enclosure | 60 |
| Trunks, bags, etc. | 30 |
| Allowances for 2 translators and 2 *giovanni di lingua* | 80 |
| 2 coaches | 90 |
| Salary for 50 servants at £1 5s per month for 6 months | 375 |
| Salary for 7 'Arabian' labourers at £1 10s per month | 63 |
| Allowance for secretary's journeys to London and Vienna | 321 |
| 2 silver watches given to Ottoman officers | 16 |
| English cloth and other furniture for the ambassador's lodgings, and the congress hall at Carlowitz | 90 |
| Ambassadors entertainment from 6 December 1697 to 6 December 1698 | 3,650 |
| Expenses for return to Edirne, including gifts | 5,640 |
| Ambassador's entertainment from 6 December 1698 to 6 October 1699 | 1,520 |
| Salary for 50 Greek and Armenian servants at £1 5s per month for 5 months | 252, 10s |
| Salary for 7 'Arab' labourers at £1 10s per month for 5 months | 52, 10s |
| Various waterproof items | 15 |
| 2 coaches and 2 sets of horses bought at Vienna | 780 |
| Allowance for secretary's journey to London | 200 |
| Salary for 6 janissaries at 5s per day between them for 1 year and 10 months | 167 |
| Gifts to ambassadors' officers at Carlowitz | 150 |
| Journey from Carlowitz to Belgrade | 40 |
| Gifts given on the ratification of the treaty | 50 |
| Gifts given to Ottoman officers at Belgrade | 100 |

Table 9 Cont.

| Items claimed | Amount (£) |
|---|---|
| River journey from Belgrade to Rusçuk (Ruse) with 37 boats | 656 |
| Gift of a gun and pair of pistols to a paşa | 10 |
| Gift of a gold watch to the qadi of Rusçuk | 17 |
| Journey from Rusçuk to Edirne | 10 |
| New boots and clothes for 150 servants at audience with grand vizier | 140 |
| Gifts to an ağa attending the ambassador | 100 |
| Gifts to Ottoman guards and officers | 50 |
| **Total** | **19,239** |

*Source*: SOAS/SC.PP/3/18 An Acc:t of Expenses &ca of which an allowance is pray'd. 1698.

In ascertaining how far the mediations improved the lot of the British merchants, however, it is necessary first to evaluate the cost of the mediation balanced against any privileges and freedoms received. The Company absolutely refused to contribute to the financial costs of mediation, indicating how little the merchants in London valued such endeavours. The government of William III, however, invested hugely in this geostrategic move. Unlike other sorts of diplomatic activities, mediations were not a burden on the merchants, but rather on British government. Table 9 shows the items of expenditure for mediating duties claimed by Baron Paget between 1697 and 1699, amounting to over £19,000, around £2 million in modern currency. On that particular occasion, the British government paid for the salaries of servants, translators, and labourers, allowances for messengers to London and Vienna, transportation, lodgings, and other necessities. A large amount was expended on gifts to Ottoman officials, including silver watches. Unlike the normal course of diplomatic business in Istanbul, at Carlowitz the British ambassador was given everything that he needed in order to conform to Ottoman conventions, including impressive lodgings and a substantial retinue.

Later expenditure on such occasions was nowhere near as extravagant, perhaps indicating the decreasing importance for the British of the use of mediation to attempt to influence the geopolitics of European conflicts, or perhaps simply an unwillingness to spend such vast amounts of money. In 1716, Sir Robert Sutton found himself given comparatively meagre expenses, complaining that '[t]hese orders do not allow so much as the expenses of a druggerman [*tercüman*] to attend the camp, or the dispatch of an express for the king's affairs, much less of the ambassador's removal to Adrianople [Edirne] or elsewhere, when necessary to carry on any negotiation'.[123] When

[123] TNA/SP97/23 Sir Robert Sutton to James Stanhope, 4 April 1716.

Sir Everard Fawkener attempted to mediate peace between the Ottomans and the Russians in 1739 (ultimately to be trumped by the French ambassador), he expended a total of £1,153 on travel, couriers, postage, and gifts (around £150,000 today).[124] Sir Robert Ainslie's successful involvement in the mediation of a peace between the Ottomans and Habsburgs at Sistova almost a century after Paget cost the British government 10,509 *guruş* (£904 in 1791, around £85,000 today) in equipage, correspondence, and gifts.[125] Despite being nowhere near the level of Carlowitz, these mediations and attempted mediations represented a substantial outlay for the British Crown, representing a significant investment in this policy.

As well as claiming expenses from the British government, the ambassador also had recourse to Ottoman benevolence when engaged as a mediator, paid through the *taʿyīn*, literally a ration or allowance. The *taʿyīn* was generally granted to nearby and neighbouring powers. For instance, John Murray in the 1770s recorded the Venetian ambassador as receiving 116 *guruş* per day, the Swedish envoy 60 *guruş* per day, and the Habsburg internuncio 100 *guruş* per day for up to nine months, after which time 12 *guruş* per day.[126] The *taʿyīn*s granted to the British ambassadors as mediators, however, were somewhat different, usually supplied through rations in kind rather than cash payments, and there are a number of documents in the Ottoman archives detailing just what the British ambassadors received. For instance, it was common for the Ottoman government to provide transportation, specifically carts (*ʿaraba*) and guards (*bekci*) for the ambassadors as they travelled in the Ottoman realms for specific official purposes, especially when the Ottoman capital was largely based in Edirne rather than Istanbul or when the high officials were with the army, such as the expenses provided for Trumbull from Edirne to Istanbul in 1102/1691, and to Sutton from Sofia to Istanbul in 1129/1717.[127] One detailed example of such costs comes from 1104/1693, when Sir William Harbord travelled to the imperial military camp (*ordu-u hümāyūn*), provided with twenty-five pack horses (*bargīr*) and twenty-six carts, the total cost amounting to the substantial sum of 734 *guruş*.[128]

In addition to transportation costs, the Ottoman government provided large quantities of provisions for mediating ambassadors, and the accounts for the conference at Carlowitz show the massive amounts of money and goods that negotiation cost the Ottoman state.[129] During Fawkener's unsuccessful

124 TNA/SP97/30 Sir Everard Fawkener his Majestys Ambassador & Plenipotentiary for mediating a peace between the Grand Signior & Her Czarish Majesty &c humbly craves allowance for his extraordinary expense in that service, 26 January 1738/9 to 26 April 1739; 26 April 1739 to 26 July 1739; 26 July 1739 to 26 October 1739.

125 TNA/FO78/12A Details of Extraordinary Expenditure respecting the Congress of Sistova, undated (January 1791).

126 TNA/SP97/50 John Murray to the Earl of Rochford, 3 October 1774; TNA/SP97/49 John Murray to the Earl of Rochford, 18 January 1773.

127 BOA/C.HR/96/4777, 15 Ramazan 1102 [9 June 1691]; BOA/İE.HR/14/1388, 26 Zilkade 1129 [31 October 1717].

128 BOA/İE.HR/3/316, 28 Rebiülahir 1104 [5 January1693].

129 BOA/MAD.d/7744, 20 Şevval to 20 Zilhicce 1110 [21 April to 18 June 1699].

attempt to secure British mediation in the late 1730s, he received rations from the Ottoman state whilst staying at the winter quarters of the Ottoman army at Hacıoğlu Pazarı (modern Dobrič in Bulgaria) in 1736. Fawkener and his retinue consumed 8,167 *akçe*s (68 *guruş*, around £1,000 today) of provisions, including 200 *akçe*s of chickens (*ṭavuḳ*), 180 *akçe*s of sugar (*şeker*), 540 *akçe*s of coffee (*ḳahve*), and 150 *okka*s (192kg) of unrefined vinegar (*ḫām sirke*) worth 1,800 *akçe*s.[130] When Fawkener sent a *taḳrīr* requesting his subsistence at the Ottoman military camp at Babadağ during the preliminary negotiations in 1738, he received an allowance of 3,000 *guruş* per month.[131] At actual negotiations, allowances were similarly generous. Sutton's secretary (noted in the documents as İngiltere elçisiniñ kātibi) received allowances (*maṣārifāt*) for his journey from the Ottoman fortress at Niš to the conference location (*maḥall-ı mukāleme*) at Passarowitz. He received provisions worth 7,108 *akçe*s (around £1,000 today), from foodstuffs such as unrefined vinegar (1,800 *akçe*s-worth), meat (*laḥm*), rice (*pirinç*), and clarified butter (*revġan-ı sāde*), to other necessaries such as firewood (*ḥaṭab*), candles (*mūm*), hay (*giyāh*), mules (*ḳatār*), and post horses (*manzil-bārgirī*).[132]

With the credit line extended by the British government, and the allowances and rations provided by the Ottoman state, the ambassadors were on the whole amply supplied, and the Company was spared an otherwise crippling burden. Geopolitics aside, in terms of actual benefits acquired by the Company as a result of British influence exerted on the political stage of the mediations, the results were, at best, mixed. Following Carlowitz, Paget himself noted that he could only hope that the peace 'may prove beneficial to the trade of the Honourable Levant Company', without aiming to secure any specific improvements to the Capitulations.[133] The British government had hoped that the mediation at Passarowitz would permit new commercial treaties with both Venice and the Ottoman Empire, with Wortley Montagu claiming that 'how far a mediation would be advantageous to the trade of the nation is known to everyone that is acquainted with this country'.[134] However, Sutton wrote to London following the signing of the treaty that, as the Ottoman and Venetian plenipotentiaries had received no instructions concerning British trade, 'all I was able to do in execution of His Majesty's commands in that respect was to recommend them to employ their credit with their respective masters in favour of such proposals'.[135] In contrast, following their successful mediation at Belgrade in 1739, the French were granted new and greatly improved Capitulations.[136]

[130] BOA/C.HR/175/8729, 19 Cemaziülevvel 1149 [25 September 1736].

[131] BOA/C.HR/165/8244, 2 Cemaziülahir 1151 [16 September 1738].

[132] BOA/C.HR/147/7340, 5 Cemaziülahir 1130 [6 May 1718].

[133] SOAS/SC.PP/3/19 Baron Paget to James Vernon, July 1699.

[134] TNA/SP97/24(2) Abraham Stanyan to James Craggs, 20 July 1718; TNA/SP97/24(1) Edward Wortley Montagu to Joseph Addison, 30 November 1717.

[135] TNA/SP97/24(3) Sir Robert Sutton to James Craggs, 22 August 1718.

[136] TNA/SP97/30 Sir Everard Fawkener to the Duke of Newcastle, 8 February 1738/9; TNA/SP97/31 Sir Everard Fawkener to the Duke of Newcastle, 29 May 1740; 13 August 1740;

The later years of the eighteenth century marked a change in the use of mediation, primarily due to shifts in British foreign policy. The British government gave substantial assistance to the Russians in the war of 1768–74, including provisioning the Russian fleet on its long journey from its Baltic base to the Mediterranean, where it inflicted a humiliating defeat on the Ottoman navy at Çeşme in 1770. This, as noted above, sparked riots against the British in Izmir, and political ill-will continued as the British half-heartedly offered mediation to end the conflict, the British monarch assuming the title of 'Mediator of the Treaty Carlowitz'.[137] The Ottomans, however, were not impressed. An 'explanatory letter of the truth' (*beyānnāme-i ṣıdıḳ*) sent to John Murray in 1187/1773 claimed that unreasonable Russian demands for the independence of the Crimean Khanate had restarted the conflict after initial talks broke down.[138] Despite appeals to 'our ancient and beloved friend' (*ḳadīmī muḥibb dostumuz*), nothing happened from the British side until one letter sent at the very end of the war authorising Murray to accept a mediation if requested by both Russia and the Ottomans, which rather unbelievably claimed that '[t]he strong proof of His Majesty's friendship manifested to the Porte at the breaking out of the war, and the early tender of his good offices to put an end to it, which was not listened to, have fully justified the king's dissatisfaction, and indisposition to receive any overtures that have been made to him since that time'.[139] Of course, the fact that the British had been anything but impartial during the war was not considered as a factor in the Ottoman reluctance to trust the British at that time. Through such actions, the ancient friendship began to fray.

As British self-confidence and aggression grew at the end of the eighteenth century, this sort of confrontational and arrogant tone would be more frequently employed. The British government, and indeed a number of the ambassadors in Istanbul, had long held a rather high opinion of their own nation compared to the Ottoman Empire. For instance, during a commercial dispute in the 1680s, Chandos considered whether it was worth threatening war to make the Ottomans more compliant, but concluded 'how ungrateful to the king will be the necessity of an expensive, tedious, hazardous war with this proud and almost as powerful Empire'.[140] Such a threat did have precedent. When Winchilsea was sailing to Istanbul from London, one of his stops was at Algiers, where he considered himself to have been poorly received. Engaging in some military espionage, he claimed that the right strategy – massive bombardment – would cause 'so great a damage to that city that forty years will scarce repair'.[141] On arriving in Istanbul, he further wrote that '[i]f His Majesty shall think that the ill-treatment I received at Algiers and their violation of the

Traduzione delle Capitolationi rinovati à favore della Nazione Francese coll'aggiunta di certa altri privilegi concessi dalla Porta Ottomana.

137 TNA/SP97/46 Viscount Weymouth to John Murray, 16 February 1770.

138 TNA/SP97/49 Ottoman memorial, 23 Muharrem 1187 [16 April 1773].

139 TNA/SP97/50 Earl of Rochford to John Murray, 25 February 1774 (Most Secret).

140 BL, Stowe 219 Baron Chandos to Sir John Buckworth, 22 January 1681/2.

141 TNA/SP97/17 Earl of Winchilsea to Charles II, 3/13 December 1660.

former peace shall deserve a revenge, I desire that His Majesty's design herein may first be communicated to me, that so I may use those endeavours as may notwithstanding preserve a right understanding here'.[142] These were not just empty threats, as the British bombardment of Tripoli in 1675 showed, and Sir John Finch opined that 'the peace with Tripoli, so honourably concluded by Sir John Narborough ... has given great reputation, and terror to His Majesty's arms in this court'.[143] Doubtless, Chandos had such actions in mind when he made his threats, but military action, the 'other means' of pursuing policy as von Clausewitz described it, although put into practice against the North African Regencies, was never really a serious option with regard to the Ottomans during the eighteenth century.

This, however, changed with the French Revolutionary and Napoleonic Wars (1789–1815), and particularly following the French invasion of Egypt in 1798, when France became, as one Ottoman *taḳrīr* termed it, 'a strong adversary and enemy' (*ḫaṣīm-i ḳavī ve düşmanı*).[144] *The London Gazette* reprinted the Ottoman declarations of war against France, including the decree that the French diplomats, merchants, and all of their goods were to be seized as a punishment for their government's hostility.[145] This, evidently, was devastating for French trade in the Ottoman Empire.[146] With the help of a British naval and military force, the French surrendered in Egypt in 1801, and this involvement of British forces marked something of a turning point.[147] A number of rewards were granted to the British for intervening on behalf of the Ottoman Empire, such as the sultan's giving the embassy freehold land for a new building. Crucially for the merchants, the chargé d'affaires John Spencer Smith had secured a new commercial agreement in 1799 granting British subjects the right to trade in the Black Sea.[148] A link was being forged in the Ottoman context between military involvement and material and commercial rewards.

This whole episode seems to have created a certain degree of overconfidence in British power and influence, and taught them the lesson that force could bring advantages. They did not, however, seem to take any heed to the fate of the French mercantile community in Istanbul. Instead, with the embassy severed from its commercial roots with the arrival of Charles Arbuthnot in 1805, and the cycle of friendship intimately connecting diplomatic finance and practice thus interrupted, foreign policy interests surged ahead of mercantile concerns. When

142 TNA/SP97/17 Earl of Winchilsea to Sir Edward Nicholas, 4 March 1660/1.

143 TNA/SP97/19 Sir John Finch to Joseph Williamson, 31 May 1676.

144 BOA/C.HR/46/2295, 27 Safer 1213 [10 August 1798].

145 TLG no.15074, 23–7 October 1798, 4–7.

146 Eldem, *French Trade*, 33. For an interesting examination of this period, see: Kahraman Şakul, 'What happened to Pouqueville's Frenchmen? Ottoman treatment of the French prisoners during the War of the Second Coalition (1798–1802)', *Turkish Historical Review* 3 (2012), 168–95.

147 See: Robert Thomas Wilson, *A History of the British Expedition to Egypt* (London, 1803); E. Driault, 'Les Anglais devant Constantinople et Alexandrie, 1807', *Revue Historique* 73:1 (1900), 24–60.

148 'No.2 Act (Black Sea). Constantniople, October 30, 1799' in *Treaties between Turkey and Foreign Powers*, 269.

the British attempted in 1806 to dissuade the Ottomans from going to war with Russia, Arbuthnot, the first ambassador to be appointed without any reference to the Company, told *reisülküttab* that '[i]f you follow the advice I am going to give, His Majesty will continue to be your friend; if you neglect it, you will lose your best ally'.[149] For a British ambassador to address the Ottoman government in this manner was unheard of, and was certainly not in the spirit of ancient friendship. At the same time, the British government had written to Arbuthnot, telling him that a strong naval force was on its way to Istanbul 'to give weight to, and if necessary to enforce an acquiescence in your representations'.[150] With the memory of the fate of the French ambassador and nation in 1798 still fresh, the British government dispatched a naval force to free Arbuthnot and the British merchants in the event of their detention.[151] All of this put great pressure on Arbuthnot, who was also given powers to order an attack on the Ottomans if he thought necessary, a power granted, according to the Foreign Office, because of the lack of means of a speedy communication between London and Istanbul.[152] The delay in communications had always been an issue, but never before had such a matter as a potential conflict been left in the hands of the ambassador, and one who was now detached from the old ideal of maintaining friendship for commercial interest.[153] The separation of the commercial and political aspects of the embassy, coupled with a new sense of military power and of political superiority, drew the British ever-closer to breaking with the Ottomans.

Arbuthnot's rationalisation for movements towards conflict were, however, partly based on commercial interests and basic freedoms, notably the new customs agreement that he had signed with the Ottoman government in 1806.[154] He claimed that the new tariff 'is everywhere shamefully eluded', and that 'in the instance also of protection, we perhaps of all nations have the greatest reason to complain'.[155] Before, this would have been an issue for *taḳrīr*s and other established forms of diplomatic practice; now, commercial disputes were a *causus belli*. When war broke out between the Ottomans and the Russians in January 1807, the pressure mounted, especially after the Ottoman government requested that the British fleet anchored off the Dardanelles move further away to Tenedos.[156] With rumours circulating that the Ottomans were about to seize HMS *Endymion* and take him and the merchants hostage, Arbuthnot hatched a secret plan to evacuate the British factory in Istanbul. [157] The merchants were told that they had been invited to

149 TNA/FO78/52 Copy of a Note from Mr Arbuthnot to the Reis Efendi, 21 December 1806.

150 TNA/FO78/52 Viscount Howick to Charles Arbuthnot, 12 November 1806.

151 TNA/FO78/52 Viscount Howick to the Lords Commissioners of the Admiralty, 21 November 1806.

152 Ibid.

153 TNA/FO78/55 Viscount Howick to Charles Arbuthnot, 13 January 1807.

154 BOA/C.HR/19/930, 21 Şevval 1220 [11 January 1806].

155 TNA/FO78/55 Charles Arbuthnot to Viscount Howick, 15 January 1807.

156 TNA/FO78/55 Charles Arbuthnot to Sir Thomas Louis, 13 January 1807; TNA/FO78/55 Sir Thomas Louis to Charles Arbuthnot, 11 January 1807.

157 TNA/FO78/55 Charles Arbuthnot to Viscount Howick, 27 January 1807; TNA/FO78/55 Charles Arbuthnot to Viscount Howick, 3 February 1807.

dine on board *Endymion* to celebrate George III's birthday. However, once Arbuthnot joined them on board, the ship weighed anchor, sailing for safety in Malta. Arbuthnot claimed that the merchants supported him; how far they did is unclear from the surviving records.

On 25 Zilkade 1221 (3 February 1807), an official declaration (*taḳrīr-i resmī*) was given to the ambassadors of all friendly states (*bilcümle dost devletleriñ elçilerine iʿṭā olundu*) by the Ottoman government.[158] After a number of messages between embassy and palace, the British ambassador's final course of action came as something as a shock; 'Suddenly,' the Ottoman government reported, 'and without any notice, he departed from the Abode of Felicity' (*nāgehān bilā ḫaber Der-Saʿādet'den mufāraḳat*).[159] Like the French a decade earlier, Britain had made a 'manifestation of hostility' (*iẓhār-ı ḫuṣūmet*), as one imperial note described it, without an official declaration of war (*iʿlām-ı ḥarb*), as Arbuthnot's departure was followed by British military assaults in the Dardanelles and later in Egypt.[160] The particular phrase 'manifestation of hostility' is the direct opposite of the capitulatory phrase that had been the bedrock of relations, the 'manifestation of amity' (*iẓhār-ı muṣāfāt*).

Arbuthnot asked the envoy of Denmark in Istanbul, Baron Hübsch, to act as chargé d'affaires in order to protect any remaining British subjects, especially the women and children left behind.[161] As well as that distress, there was the matter of material losses. Arbuthnot asked Hübsch 'to take care of the effects belonging to the [British] palace; those which our merchants have left behind them; and everything belonging to me personally'.[162] The newly completed embassy building was now left deserted. However, the merchants suffered the greatest losses. How big those losses were is difficult to calculate. On reconvening on 2 May 1809, the assembly of the British factory in Istanbul resolved 'that a statement of the losses which each individual commuted with the Right Worshipful Company had suffered on the occasion of the late rupture between England and the Porte, should be drawn up and a memoire be addressed to their worships praying that an indemnification be obtained, through their medium, for the same'.[163] On reflection, however, the merchants addressed this application to Arbuthnot instead.[164] To take just one example, an *ʿarżüḥāl* (petition) presented by one Anton Davudoğlu in 1222/1807 mentions the fate of the goods of a British merchant named as 'İzmit', presumably William Smith.[165] Smith was a resident of the Bereketzade neighbourhood of Galata, and in the spring of 1807, 'the greater part of his goods were collected [and]

[158] BOA/C.HR/149/7435, 25 Zilkade 1221 [3 February 1807].
[159] Ibid.
[160] BOA/HAT/142/5914, 21 Safer 1222 [29 April 1807].
[161] TNA/FO78/58 Charles Arbuthnot to Baron Hübsch, 29 January 1807; Baron Hübsch to Viscount Howick, 9 February 1807.
[162] TNA/FO78/58 Charles Arbuthnot to Baron Hübsch, 29 January 1807.
[163] TNA/SP105/212, Proceedings of an Assembly of the British Factory held at Pera, 2 May 1809.
[164] TNA/SP105/132 Isaac Morier to the Levant Company, 30 September 1809.
[165] BOA/C.ADL/36/2184, 15 Zilkade 1222 [13 January 1808].

taken away, with only a few meagre possessions remaining intact'.[166] The inventory of goods taken from his house in Bereketzade included glass bottles (*şīşe*), a new writing desk (*cedīd yāzıḫāne*), a number of chests (*ṣandūḳ*), and even his bedding (*yorġān*).

As with privateering, British foreign policy had proved disastrous to British subjects in the Ottoman Empire. Although much effort had been put into advancing British foreign policy in the Ottoman Empire through the mediation of peace treaties, these were of little use politically or commercially to the British state and subjects, and much of the Ottoman success in peace negotiations was due to the skill of their own plenipotentiaries, rather than the interposition of their European allies.[167] Thankfully for the British merchants, unlike regular diplomatic practices, mediations were financed by the Ottoman and British governments, although the Company's refusal to finance mediations demonstrates that they saw little utility for British commerce in such endeavours. The violence, of privateers, of rhetoric, and finally of arms, shows that by the end of the eighteenth century, the nature of relations had changed significantly. Neither the British involvement in mediating Ottoman peace treaties nor the first British–Ottoman War at the beginning of the nineteenth century is indicative of the 'rise' of Britain and the concurrent 'fall' of the Ottoman Empire. Rather, this marks the beginnings of aggressive imperial domineering, a far cry from a relationship based around the maintenance of friendship. From their intervention in Egypt in 1801, the British took the lesson of Ottoman military weakness and the rewards of their own naval strength. However, the disastrous military campaigns of 1807 and 1808 resulted in an Ottoman military victory and nothing gained except the restoration of the 1675 Capitulations. Ultimately, the implementation of British foreign policy in its diplomacy in the Ottoman Empire brought almost no benefit for British subjects there. On the contrary, British privateers in the mid-century threatened to ruin mutual commerce, British assistance to the Ottoman arch-enemy Russia in 1770 saw British merchants assaulted in the streets, and in 1807, at the outbreak of war after centuries of peaceful relations, the merchants lost everything.

## Conclusion

The negotiation of disputes in British–Ottoman relations in the long eighteenth century can be seen either from the perspective of the state or from the perspective of British and Ottoman subjects. In examining the daily concerns of freedom of movement and trade, it is clear that there was a well-established mechanism for ensuring that disputes that could not be resolved at a local level were negotiated through the use of *taḳrīr*s. Accompanied by the usual customs of gift-giving and ceremonial, the surviving *taḳrīr*s in the Ottoman

[166] Ibid.

[167] Rifa'at Ali Abou-El-Haj, 'Ottoman diplomacy at Karlowitz' in Yurdusev, *Ottoman Diplomacy*, 89–113.

archives show that the British ambassadors and translators operated within the Ottoman legal framework of petitions. In the case of preserving freedom of movement, there were standard documents submitted regularly, and in the case of more complex commercial disputes, ambassadors appealed to both the Capitulations and to Ottoman shari'a, sultanic and customary legal practices. Just as the British ambassadors were able to appeal to Ottoman law in order to secure satisfaction for their subjects, so too was the Ottoman state able to apply its own law when dealing with British infractions. Attacks by British privateers impacting on Ottoman trade and food supplies saw the extension of territorial sovereignty into the open seas of the Mediterranean in order to successfully gain compensation for Ottoman sufferers. Although the British ambassadors and government objected to the new Ottoman maritime regulations, the pressure from the sufferers and from the Ottoman state compelled the Levant Company, and on occasion the British government, to pay damages. By the end of the eighteenth century, the ambassadors were given powers by the British government to punish privateers who attacked Ottoman subjects, and this is what finally persuaded the Ottoman government to rescind their extended maritime limits. It took a century for the British government to assume responsibility for the actions of their privateering subjects, and that lack of care had ultimately damaged British–Ottoman relations, and the fortunes of British trading subjects. As with the proofs of patience the Ottomans provided in their rationales for war against Russia, the use of the maritime limits and legal compensation shows that the Ottomans valued the practice of diplomacy over the threat of violence.

In a secret letter to James Porter in May 1759, William Pitt instructed the ambassador to inform the grand vizier Koca Ragıb Paşa, that:

> The best and strongest bond of union between great powers, is unity of interest; that to have at heart the safety of the same friends, and to wish to pursue the destruction of the same enemies, cannot, in wisdom and policy, be less powerful motives of action, than the formality and letter of treaties.[168]

By the turn of the nineteenth century, that unity of interest had shifted, from ensuring commercial freedom and prosperity, to advancing political alliances. Although British policy in the seventeenth century had been enforced through violence elsewhere, specifically against the Ottoman North African Regencies, it had not been a viable or even desirable option for much of the eighteenth century. However, the British military intervention in Egypt against the French invasion had gained British merchants the rights to trade in the Black Sea, and part of the dispute with the Ottoman government in 1806 was framed in commercial terms. The separation of the embassy from the Company's interests with Arbuthnot's arrival in 1805 proved to be a disaster. He had been entrusted with a great amount of power at a time of political and military tension, but the subsequent crisis forcing the ambassador and the factory

[168] TNA/SP97/40 William Pitt to James Porter, 25 May 1759 (Most Secret).

from Istanbul resulted in the merchants losing all their goods and possessions. As with the mediations of the previous century, little was gained, and in this case, the two centuries-old British mercantile settlement in Istanbul was greatly damaged. In contrast to the diplomatic framework that saw the ambassador working within the context of Ottoman law and diplomatic culture, financed by the British merchants, and with the aim of preserving friendship and peaceful commerce, Arbuthnot wielded a new and brutal form of power. However, with commercial and political interests severed, it was the British merchants who literally ended up paying the price.

# Conclusions: De/re-constructing British–Ottoman diplomacy

The story of British–Ottoman relations in the long eighteenth century was marked by the arrival and departure of ships. In 1807, HMS *Endymion* left Istanbul with the British ambassador and factory on board, to be replaced by British warships tasked with cowing that city into submission. This final act could not have been more different from the narrative of the first relations between the two states, enshrined in the Capitulations, of the English queen sending her ships with her ambassador, gentlemen, and gifts. Within a few years of political and commercial interests being firmly separated, British foreign policy had brought disaster to the merchants trading in Istanbul. The framework of relations that had functioned for over two hundred years had seen the British merchants and ambassadors dependent on each other, the ambassadors for the finance brought in by successful commerce, and the merchants for the protection they gained from the ambassador's protection of their interests through gifts, ceremonial, and petitions that provided the displays of friendship required by the Ottoman state. The ambassadors' negotiations had a purpose, and set practices, for a tangible aim; the maintenance of peaceful commerce through displays of friendship. This aim was shared by the Ottomans, too. In a letter to the British government concerning the conflict of the 1740s, translated by Antonio Pisani, the head *tercüman* of the British embassy, the grand vizier Hassan Paşa provided a glimpse of an Ottoman vision of relations:

> The principal requisite [of existence] – which is that of providing in this life in order to attain afterwards the other – consists in being able to enjoy immunity and repose, as well as the necessary conveniences in their places of dwelling. Hence, it comes that mankind, to obtain that point [must] apply themselves in various sorts of traffic, and to the exercise of so many different arts. Yet the mass of the human body being composed of elements opposite to each other, there is moderation required in the manner of ruling the whole machine, to fit and to dispose the places of recourse according to the different factions.[1]

1 TNA/SP97/32 Hassan Paşa to the Duke of Newcastle, undated (translated by Antonio Pisani, 31 January 1744/5).

In this view, interactions between states and their subjects were part of a single system, yet a system nonetheless dominated by constant tensions requiring compromises. This idea of moderation and compromise returns to the exhortation of François de Callières at the beginning of this study calling on the prudent ambassador 'to accommodate himself to the manners and customs of the country where he is'.[2] That was the very essence of the diplomatic framework that the British merchants supported through their finance: the maintenance of peaceful relations through participation in Ottoman conventions of gift-giving, ceremonial, and petitioning.

British diplomacy in the Ottoman Empire in the long eighteenth century must be seen primarily in the context of commercial relations, rather than abstract political ties. Until the very end of the eighteenth century, the only treaty governing British-Ottoman relations was the 1086/1675 version of the Capitulations, a document concerned above all with trade. Given the unique position of the Levant Company in overseeing relations, and the content of other Ottoman–European treaties, this is hardly surprising. The purpose of the Company's initial incorporation was to provide security for a group of merchants travelling potentially dangerous routes to the Ottoman ports. However, the Company's primary objective soon developed into financing the institution that protected its interests, the embassy in Istanbul. The centrality of commerce was further reflected in the embassy's occupants, with a significant number of the ambassadors until the 1770s having strong links to the commercial or financial world, many being members of the Levant Company itself. Only with the decline in the Company's fortunes, and a concurrent and growing financial input from the British government, along with the professionalisation of the conduct of British and Ottoman foreign affairs in the later eighteenth century, did career diplomats begin to be routinely appointed to Istanbul. This change was equally reflected in the dispatch of the first resident Ottoman diplomats to London. Above all, the ambassador acted primarily in the interests of British trading subjects, with Arbuthnot's appointment and actions marking a violent break in that pattern.

The intimate link for most of the century between commerce and diplomatic practice is clear through an examination of British–Ottoman trade and the finances of the Levant Company. British trade over the course of the eighteenth century went through a series of peaks and troughs – a number of those troughs caused by the privateering conflict with France – but overall saw a decrease in the middle of the century and a recovery at its end. Difficult periods were caused by wars, changes in fashion, and above all by a reliance on one particular kind of trade, that of the exchange of woollen manufactures for raw silk. By the end of the century, the British and Ottoman merchants adapted to the new reality, and diversified the nature of their commerce. However, the declivity in the middle of the century had serious consequences for the Company's finances, affecting the finances of the ambassador. When the merchants were buying and selling fewer goods, the Company received

[2] De Callières, *The Art of Negotiating*, 164.

less in duties, and its diplomatic establishments, the maintenance of which required constant sources of finance to support gift-giving, ceremonial, and daily administration, would be unable to participate in the conventions of diplomacy in Istanbul. It was this pressure that saw the British government begin to contribute towards the ambassador's salary from 1746, and to several bailouts of the Company from 1768. The complaints of the ambassadors concerning their finances were so common, and so validated by the accounts ledgers, that there is little reason to doubt that financial pressures were a serious problem to the conduct of British diplomacy in the Ottoman Empire in this period. These financial issues helped to change the embassy from a merchant-financed institution to a government-funded one, which had consequent implications for its priorities and approaches.

These changes can be seen by observing those crucial practices of gift-exchange, ceremonial, and negotiating disputes. The three main categories of gift-giving represented different and changing aspects of British–Ottoman relations. *Ḫilʿat* gifts were formal exchanges of garments, and the clothing (*ilbās*) of the ambassador and the acceptance of his gifts represented the bond between the Ottoman state as a benefactor and the ambassador (and his state) as beneficiary, but towards the end of the eighteenth century began to include new forms of honours such as chivalric orders. The second sort of gift, the more tributary *pīşkeş* presented on the appointment of certain officials and on certain occasions, notably the *Ramazan Bayramı*, all but ceased by the end of the century due to changing attitudes and structures on the part of the Ottoman state, and growing resentment on the part of the European ambassadors. The final and perhaps most important sort of gift were *hibe* gifts, given by the British to a variety of Ottoman officials to establish and solidify working relationships and secure their commercial and political aims. Gift-giving was a crucial part of diplomatic interaction, formally and informally, and this, of course, cost money. Therefore, pressure on finances limited expenditure on gifts, something noted by the ambassadors themselves when compared to their diplomatic allies and rivals.

Such financial constraints were equally apparent in performative diplomacy, the audiences, ceremonies, and rituals that accompanied and drove diplomatic interactions. The regular meetings accompanied by coffee, sherbet, tobacco, and other treats, as well as the maintenance of liverymen, costs of banquets, feasts, and other sorts of celebration and entertainment, all required finance that was not always readily available, thus potentially denting the prestige of the British mission. This was evident in the maintenance of the British embassy building, which was in a far poorer state than those of the other European powers resident in Istanbul. Performative diplomacy also raised questions of representations. As with gift-giving, it was the implications of inferiority, rather than the cost of complying, that angered a number of commentators, including former ambassadors. However, on the whole, both gift-giving and performative diplomacy were viewed not only as necessary parts of engaging with the Ottoman state to maintain commerce and friendship but also, particularly in terms of ceremonial, as honourable. Indeed, when comparing the sorts of ceremonies that greeted the Ottoman ambassador to London in 1795, the core elements of military display, hospitality, and displays of wealth were common to both polities. They were also, above all, key components of Ottoman ceremonial to which the ambassador was obliged to conform, to give manifestations of friendship in order to deal with the most crucial part of relations, the welfare of British merchants and their trade through the maintenance of friendship with the Ottomans.

Perhaps unsurprisingly considering the nature of the appointment, commercial disputes between British and Ottoman merchants, and protecting the rights, freedoms, and securities of British subjects, topped the list of the ambassador's priorities, even if this was not prominent in the diplomatic correspondence. Acting within the framework of the provisions of the Capitulations and the tenets of the different Ottoman legal systems, the oral and written declarations that passed between palace and embassy should be seen within a wider Ottoman legal and petitionary context, with daily diplomacy as much a performative practice as gift-giving and ceremonial. It is in this realm of relations, however, that the small changes in attitude on the part of the British observed in those other main forms of practices become quite apparent. The major recurring dispute between the British and the Ottomans in the long eighteenth century, which revolved around the perceived violations of Ottoman waters and attacks on Ottoman merchants and goods by British privateers, was resolved by the Ottomans through similar means: meetings, declarations, memoranda, and royal letters. Although the British ambassadors often classified the attempts of the Ottoman state to gain restitution or compensation for its subjects as unjust impositions, in fact the Ottoman government made its case based on the Capitulations and on Ottoman legal practices, as well as on the idea of ancient friendship. That so much compensation was paid, and that the British eventually gave sufficient powers to their ambassador to rein in their privateers, demonstrates that this was a legitimate prosecution, achieved through a clever extension of Ottoman maritime boundaries when necessary. The fact that the Company paid most of the compensation also demonstrates that much of the policy emanating from London was damaging to the interests of British subjects residing in the Ottoman realms. Indeed, as we have just seen, British foreign policy in the Ottoman Empire, particularly through peace mediation, achieved little benefit for British merchants, and although there was some progress in gaining extra privileges following the British military involvement in Egypt at the end of the century, the British attempt to enforce its foreign policy vision on the Ottomans in the early nineteenth century saw military defeat and great losses for British merchants trading in the Ottoman realms.

From all of this, it is possible to draw a number of conclusions. The overall picture shows a gradual move towards a new set of practices based on interference, threats, and geopolitical balancing that would be a hallmark of the nineteenth century with regard to British dealings with the Ottoman realms. However, for most of the period examined here, the Ottoman and British sources show that British diplomacy in the Ottoman Empire in the long eighteenth century centred mainly on the peaceful resolution of commercial concerns and legal disputes, with British foreign policy a largely peripheral part of diplomatic interactions despite its heavy presence in the diplomatic correspondence to and from London. Moreover, the British ambassadors were only able to pursue negotiations in resolving disputes because they conformed to the conventions of Ottoman diplomatic culture, from the phrasing of their diplomatic notes, to participating in specific rituals and ceremonies, and, crucially, by engaging in set practices of gift-giving. Such practices were not static, evolving and changing as the century went on. Yet, without conforming to those conventions, it would have been simply impossible to engage in any serious business whatsoever, commercial or political. Moreover, such conventions were often an opportunity to display British power, and to market British goods, from timepieces to all-important textiles, and, within the Ottoman diplomatic framework, to make *iẓhār-ı muṣāfāt*, displays of friendship. All this required finance, and the way in which the embassy was funded caused a number of problems. Whereas mediating ambassadors could rely on generous allowances from the British government and rations from the Ottoman state, regular duties were primarily funded by the Company. Working on a tight budget, British ambassadors, even with increasing government contributions from the second half of the eighteenth century, were required to spend significant amounts on gifts, entertainments, and other essentials. In the face of decreasing and changing trade patterns, and damage to trade caused by wars and other external factors, the burden of this expenditure was too much for the Company to bear, and ultimately led to the British government assuming full control of the embassy by financing it entirely.

All of this together shows the interplay between finance, cultural convention, and legal considerations in the practice of diplomacy in the long eighteenth century. By looking at these different categories, it has been possible to construct a history of British–Ottoman relations in this period based not on abstractions of states and foreign policies, but rather on the daily concerns and practices of diplomats and mercantile subjects. This has been possible only by re-examining the diplomatic correspondence, as well as bringing in financial and commercial data, and, crucially, Italian and Ottoman Turkish sources from London and Istanbul, including correspondence, petitions, and treaty texts. Without a doubt, there are other sources waiting to be examined to add further dimensions to our understanding of diplomatic practices in the Ottoman Empire in this period. Above all, the research for this study emphasises the importance of considering the financial and material side of diplomatic practice in conjunction with other facets of diplomacy. In her study on Ahmed Resmi Efendi, Virginia Aksan raised the issue of finance in particular as one that was largely not understood in the Ottoman context:

> The entire question of support of foreign representatives by the host governments is in need of a thorough analysis, along with diplomatic practices in general. One of the recurrent themes of the dispatches of European diplomats is the lack of cash, and the indebtedness which occurred as a result of 'gifts'

> to Ottoman officials, a problem equally common to the Ottoman permanent missions in Europe when they began in 1793.[3]

I hope that this study has, in some measure, made a contribution to visualising the mechanics and implications of diplomatic funding in the particular case of the British embassy in Istanbul, through gifts and other practices. However, much work remains to fully understand the financial aspects of diplomacy in the Ottoman realms, and comparative cases will be particularly valuable.[4]

Friendship is a word that has occurred throughout this study, and it seems appropriate to finish by considering the significance of this idea. Friendship was a founding principle of British–Ottoman relations, and was only broken with the arrival of war in 1807. It is a word that has a number of synonyms in Ottoman Turkish, and its significance to diplomatic history has perhaps been understated. When Yusuf Agah was recalled from London, the Ottoman translators of a letter from George III phrased his achievement as having 'strengthened and reinforced beyond all expression the full and complete concord of love and affection that has happily and blessedly endured and persisted of old between your Sublime State and the state of Britain'. This translation gives an ostensibly British text an Ottoman voice. The key Ottoman phrasing here – *ez-ḳadīm*, 'of old', *vidd ve muḥabbet ve tām ve ḥüsn-ü mālākelāmıñ*, 'the full and complete concord of love and affection' – presents us with an ideal. It is the same ideal that spoke of the Ottoman court in the British Capitulations as 'the refuge of asylum of the sultans of the earth, the place of retreat of the sovereigns of the globe', in beautiful rhyming phrases as *melāẕ-ı melcāʾ-ı selāṭīn-i cihān ve penāh-ı mencā-ı ḫevāḳīn-i devrān*. It is a vision of diplomatic practice that saw peace and friendship as interchangeable goals of international relations. This is not to say that the Ottomans eschewed violence, or were beyond reproach in their diplomatic practices and aims. But if we are to reconstruct Ottoman diplomacy and its practices in the eighteenth century, then the idea of friendship – *dostluḳ* – and its various associated articulations seem to provide a pretty good starting point. If the physical manifestation of that friendship was an ambassador coming to the Ottoman court to renew and maintain the Capitulations, and those articles a beneficent gift – *iḥsān* – whose maintenance was achieved through displays of friendship – *iẓhār-ı muṣāfāt* – then in Ottoman diplomatic rhetoric the framework of relations already appears; friendship required ambassadors giving gifts, and performing in different forms of ceremonial within the Ottoman framework. For the British – and to some extent the Ottomans – peaceful commerce was the essence of friendship, which, through the added layer of mercantile finance, wove all of these interests and practices together at the British embassy in Istanbul.

[3] Aksan, *An Ottoman Statesman*, 44, fn.31.

[4] For an excellent study on this subject, see: Irena Fliter, 'The diplomats' debts: International financial disputes between the Ottoman Empire and Prussia at the end of the eighteenth century', *Osmanlı Araştırmaları / Journal of Ottoman Studies* 48 (2016), 399-416.

# Bibliography

## Archival sources

**Başbakanlık Osmanlı Arşivleri (Prime Ministry's Ottoman Archives, BOA), Istanbul**

Sadaret, Sadaret Defterleri (Grand Vizierate, Grand Vizierate Registers, A.)d)

Bab-ı Asafi, Düvel-i Ecnebiye Defterleri (Sublime Porte, Registers of Foreign States, A.DVN.DVE.d)

Bab-ı Asafi, Düvel-i Ecnebiye Defterleri, İngiltere (Sublime Porte, Registers of Foreign States, Britain, A.DVN.DVE.(3))

Ali Emre Tasnifi, II Ahmed (Ali Emre Series, Ahmed II, AE.SAMD.II)

Ali Emre Tasnifi, III. Ahmed (Ali Emre Series, Ahmed III, AE.SAMD.III)

Cevdet Tasnifi, Adliye (Cevdet Series, Judicial, C.ADL)

Cevdet Tasnifi, Askeriye (Cevdet Series, Military, C.AS)

Cevdet Tasnifi, Bahriye (Cevdet Series, Naval, C.BH)

Cevdet Tasnifi, Dahiliye (Cevdet Series, Internal, C.DH)

Cevdet Tasnifi, Hariciye (Cevdet Series, Foreign, C.HR)

Cevdet Tasnifi, İktisat (Cevdet Series, Economic, C.İKTS)

Cevdet Tasnifi, Maliye (Cevdet Series, Financial, C.ML)

Cevdet Tasnifi, Saray (Cevdet Series, Palace, C.SM)

Matbah-ı Amire Eminliği Defterleri (Registers of the Stewardship of the Imperial Kitchens, D.BŞM.MTE.d)

Hatt-ı Hümayun (Imperial Rescripts, HAT)

Haritalar (Maps, HRT.h)

İbnülemin Tasnifi, Bahriye (İbnülemin Series, Naval, İE.BH)

İbnülemin Tasnifi, Hariciye (İbnülemin Series, Foreign, İE.HR)

İbnülemin Tasnifi, Saray (İbnülemin Series, Palace, İE.SM)

Kamil Kepeci Tasnifi Defterleri (Kamil Kepeci Series Registers, KK.d)

Maliyeden Müdevver Defterler (Registers of Circulars from the Finance Office, MAD.d)

Topkapı Sarayı, Müze Arşivi Defterleri (Topkapı Palace, Museum Archive Registers, TS.MA.d)

**British Library (BL), London**
Additional Manuscripts (Add.)
Stowe Papers (Stowe)

**British Museum (BM), London**
Greek and Roman Antiquities (GRA)
Middle East (ME)
Britain, Europe, and Prehistory (PEC)

**Government Art Collection (GAC), United Kingdom**
online collection (http://www.gac.culture.gov.uk)

***The London Gazette* (*TLG*)**
online (http://www.thegazette.co.uk)

**London Metropolitan Archives (LMA)**
City of London Collections (CLC)
Manuscrupts (MS.)
Special Collections, Prints, Westminster (SC/PZ/WE)

**Museum of London (MOL)**
Permanent collection (PC)

**The National Archives (TNA), London**
Court of Chancery (C1)
Ledgers of Imports and Exports (CUST3)
States of Navigation, Commerce, and Revenue (CUST17)
Exchequer, Miscellaneous Ecclesiastica Documents (E135)
Foreign Office, Ottoman Empire (FO78)
Foreign Office, Confidential Print (FO881)
Extracted from the Foreign Office Records (MPK1)
Special Collections, Papal Bulls (SC7)
Special Collections, Ancient Petitions (SC8)
State Papers, Foreign, Turkey (SP97)
State Papers, Archives of British Legations (SP105)
State Papers, Foreign, Treaties (SP108)
Court of Star Chamber (STAC)
Treasury, Departmental Accounts (T38)

**National Maritime Museum (NMM), London**
Polar Equipment and Relics (REL)

**National Portrait Gallery (NPG), London**
Primary Collection (PC)

**Proceedings of the Old Bailey (POB)**
online archives (http://www.oldbaileyonline.org/)

**School of Oriental and African Studies (SOAS), London**
Special Collections, Paget Papers (SC.PP)

**Victoria and Albert Museum (VAM), London**
Ceramics Collection (CC)
Furniture and Woodwork Collection (FWC)
Metalwork Collection (MC)
Prints, Drawings, and Paintings Collection (PDPC)

**Walters Art Museum, Baltimore**
(online collections: http://www.thewalters.og/)
Manuscripts (Ms.)

**Printed primary sources**

Abu ʿAbd Allah Muhammad al-Idrisi, *Ẕikr al-Andalus Tālīf Sharīf al-Idrīs: Descripcion de España de Xerif Aledris*, trans. Josef Antonio de Conde. Madrid: Impr. Real, 1799.

Ahmed Cevdet, *Tārīḫ-i Cevdet,* 10 vols. Dersaadet: Matbaa-yı Osmaniye, 1309 [1891/2].

Ahmed Refik [Altınay], *Lāle Devri.* İstanbul: Muhtar Halid Kitabhanesi, 1331 [1915].

Ahmed Vasıf Efendi, *Meḥāsinü'l-āsār ve ḥaḳāʾiḳü'l-āḫbār.* İstanbul: Matbaa-yı Amire, 1219 [1804].

ʿAli Efendi, *Fetāvā-yı ʿAlī Efendi maʿa 'n-nuḳūl.* İstanbul: Tabhane-i Amire, 1272 [1856]).

*The Art of Tanning and of Currying Leather, With the Processes for Dying Leather Red and Yellow, As Practiced in Turkey*. Dublin: S. Powell, 1773.

Azuni, Domenico Alberto, *Origine et progrès du droit et de la législation maritime, avec des observations sur le consulat de la mer.* Paris: Cérioux, 1810.

Bickerstaff, Isaac, *The Sultan or, a Peep into the Seraglio.* Cork: For J. Sullivan, 1781.

Blount, Thomas Pope, *A Natural History*. London: For R. Bentley, 1693.

*Book of Gifts and Rarities: Kitāb al-Hadāyā wa al-Tuḥaf,* trans. Ghada al-Hijawi al-Qaddumi. Cambridge MA: Harvard University Press, 1996.

Burke, Edmund, *A Third Letter to a Member of the Present Parliament on the Proposals for Peace with the Regicide Directory of France*. Dublin: For P. Wogan et al., 1796.

Burke, Edmund, *Two Letters addressed to a Member of the Present Parliament on the Proposals for Peace with the Regicide Directory of France.* Dublin: For P. Wogan et al., 1796.

Busbecq, Ogier Ghiselin de, *The Turkish Letters of Ogier Ghiselin de*

*Busbecq, Imperial Ambassador at Constantinople, 1554–1562*, trans. Edward Seymour Forster. Oxford: Clarendon Press, 1927.

Bynkershoek, Cornelius van, *De lege Rhodia de Jactu Liber Singularis et de Dominio Maris Dissertatio.* The Hague, 1703.

Callières, François de, *The Art of Negotiating with Sovereign Princes*, trans. anonymous. London: For George Strahan, 1738.

Callières, François de, *The Art of Negotiating with Sovereign Princes*, trans. anonymous. London: For Geo. Strahan, 1716.

Callières, François de, *De la Manière de Negocier avec les Souverains*. Amsterdam: Pour la Compagnie, 1716.

*The Capitulations and Articles of Peace between the Majesty of the King of Great Britain, France, and Ireland &c. and the Sultan of the Ottoman Empire.* London: For J.S., 1679.

Carter, Charles, *The Compleat City and Country Cook: or, Accomplish'd Housewife*. London: For A. Bettesworth et al., 1732.

*The Case Fairly Stated between the Turky Company and the Italian Merchants.* London, 1720.

Charas, Moyse, *Theriaque d'Andromacus*. Paris: Laurent d'Houry, 1685.

Cobbett, W. (ed.), *The Parliamentary History of England from the Earliest Period to the Year 1803*, 12 vols. London: T.C. Hansard, 1806–20.

Collins, Arthur, *The Baronetage of England.* London: For John Stockdale, 1806.

Collins, John, *An Introduction to Merchants-Accompts: containing Seven distinct Questions or Accompts.* London: William Godbid, 1675.

*Considerations on the Dispute Between the Levant Company and the Italian Merchants, Relating to the Importation of Raw Silk from Leghorn.* London, 1720.

Cooper, Ambrose, *The Complete Distiller*. London: For P. Valliant & R. Griffiths, 1757.

*The Critical Review: Or, Annals of Literature*, 3rd series, 24 vols. London, 1808.

Dallaway, James, *Constantinople Ancient and Modern, with Excursions to the Shores and Islands of the Archipelago and to the Troad.* London: For T. Bensley, 1797.

Delisle, Guillaume, *Carte de Perse dressée puor l'usage du Roy*. Amsterdam, c. 1730.

*The Dictionary of Merchandize and Nomenclature in All Languages*. London, 1803.

*Encyclopædia Perthensis: or, Universal Dictionary of the Arts, Sciences, Literature etc,* 2 vols. Edinburgh: J. Brown, 1816.

Esad Efendi, *Teşrīfāt-ı ḳadīme*. İstanbul: Matbaa-yı Amire, 1287 [1870].

Esad Efendi, *Osmanlılarda Töre ve Törenler (Teşrifât-ı Kadîme)*, trans. Yavuz Ercan. İstanbul: Tercüme, 1979.

Eton, William, *A Survey of the Turkish Empire.* London: For T. Cadell et al., 1798.

Feridun Bey, *Mecmūʿa-ı Münşeʾātü's-selāṭīn*, 2 vols. [Istanbul]: Darüttıbattil'amire, 1265 [1849].

Gardner, John Dunn, *The Ionian Islands in Relation to Greece, with suggestions for advancing our trade with the Turkish countries of the Adriatic, and the Danube.* London: J. Ridgway, 1859.

Grotius, Hugo, *Le Droit de la Guerre et de la Paix*, trans. Jean Barbeyrac, 2 vols. Amsterdam: Chez Pierre de Coup, 1729.

Grotius, Hugo, *Of the Rights of War and Peace, In Three Volumes*, trans. anonymous, 3 vols. London: For D. Brown, 1715.

Grotius, Hugo, *The Most Excellent Hugo Grotius His Three Books Treating the Rights of War & Peace*, trans. William Evats, 3 vols. London: Thomas Basset, 1682.

Grotius, Hugo, *Opera Omnia Theologica in Tres Tomos Divisa*, 4 vols. Londini: Prostant venalia apud Mosem Pitt, 1679.

Grotius, Hugo, *De Jure Belli ac Pacis Libri Tres*. Amsterdami: Apud Guilielmum Blaew, 1631.

Grotius, Hugo, *Mare Liberum sive de jure quod Batavis competit ad Indicana commercia dissertatio.* Leiden: Ludovici Elzevirii, 1609.

Hakluyt, Richard (ed.), *The Principall Navigations, Voiages and Discoveries of the English nation, made by Sea or over Land, to the most remote and farthest distant Quarters of the earth at any time within the compasse of these 1500 yeeres.* London: Bishop & R. Newberie, 1589.

Hanway, Jonas, *An Answer, to the Appendix of a Pamphlet, entitled Reflextions upon Naturalization, Corporations and Companies, &c Relating to the Levant Trade and Turkey Company, As this Subject is occasionally mentioned in Hanway's Travels.* London: For R. Dodsley, 1753.

*The Historical Register, containing an Impartial Relation of all Transactions, Foreign and Domestick*, vol. XV. London: For R. Nutt, 1730.

Huxham, John, *An Essay on Fevers, and their Various Kinds, As Depending on Different Constitutions of the Blood.* London: For S. Austen, 1750.

*Indulgences issued to raise money to fight the Turks or to ransom captives.* Westminster: Caxton, c. 1480.

*Istoria degli stati di Algeri, Tunisi, Tripoli e Marocco.* London, 1754.

Jamal al-Din abu Bakr al-Qazwini [attributed as al-Khawarizmi], *Kitāb mufīd al-ʿulūm wa-mubīd al-humūm.* Damascus, 1333 [1906].

Johnson, Samuel, *A Dictionary of the English Language*, 3rd edn. Dublin: W.G. Jones, 1768.

*Journals of the House of Commons*, online edn., [http://parlipapers.chadwyck.co.uk/].

*Ḳānūnnāme-i hümāyūn-u ticāret-i baḥriye. İ*stanbul, 1280 [1864].

*Ḳānūnnāme-i ticāret.* İstanbul, 1281 [1865].

Kauffer, F., & Lechevalier, I.B., *Plan de Constantinople/Plan von Constantinopel*. Weimar: Verlang von Lorentz & Keil, 1807.

*Kitāb-ı ʿilm-i ādeb ve merāsīm-i ülfet ve ünsiyet*. Beirut: c. 1850.

*A Letter to Mr. Eton, from A Merchant in Turkey, in Answer to a Chapter in His Survey of the Turkish Empire, to prove the necessity of Abolishing the Levant Company*. London: For J. Mathews, 1799.

*Letters Writ by a Turkish Spy, Who liv'd five and forty Years undiscover'd at Paris*, 8 vols. London. For G. Strahan et al., 1734.

*The Levant Company's Orders and By-Laws.* London, 1800.

McCulloch, J.R., *A Dictionary, Practical, Theoretical, and Historical, of Commerce and Commercial Navigation*. London: Longmans, 1850.

MacFarlane, Charles, *Constantinople in 1828: A Residence of Sixteen Months in the Turkish Capital and Provinces.* London: Saunders & Otley, 1829.

MacGill, Thomas, *Travels in Turkey, Italy, and Russia, During the Years 1803, 1804, 1805, and 1806*, 2 vols. London & Edinburgh: J. Murray, 1808.

McPherson, David, *Annals of Commerce, Manufactures, Fisheries, and Navigation*, 4 vols. London: For Nichols & Son et al., 1803.

Madden, R.R., *Travels in Turkey, Egypt, Nubia, and Palestine, in 1824, 1825, 1826, and 1827*, 2 vols. London: Carey & Lea, 1829.

Mair, John, *Book-keeping Methodised: or, a Methodical Treatise of Merchant-Accompts, According to the Italian Form.* Dublin: H. Saunders, 1772.

Markham, Gervase, & Lawson, William, *A Way to get Wealth: containing Six Principall Vocations, or Callings, in which every good Husband or House-wife may lawfully imploy themselves*. London: E.H., 1668.

Massialot, François, *Le nouveau cuisinier royal et bourgeois*, 3 vols. Amsterdam: Aux depens de la Compagnie, 1734.

Mehmed Raşid Efendi, *Tārīḫ-i Rāşid*, 6 vols. [Istanbul]: Matbaa-i Amire, 1282 [1865]).

Mehmed Said Efendi, *Tārīḫ-i gülşen-i maʿārif*, 2 vols. İstanbul: Darü't-tıba'ati'l-amire, 1252 [1836].

Munis, Shir Muhamad Mirab, & Agahi, Muhammad Riza Mirab, *Firdaws al-Iqbāl: History of Khorezm*, trans. Yuri Bregel. Leiden: Brill, 1999.

*The Negotiations of Sir Thomas Roe, in his Embassy to the Ottoman Porte, from the Year 1621 to 1628 Inclusive*. London: S. Richardson, 1740.

Nisbet, Mary, *The Letters of Mary Nisbet of Dirleton, Countess of Elgin*, ed. Hamilton Grant Nisbet. New York: Appleton, 1928.

North, Roger, *The Life of the Honourable Sir Dudley North, Knt., Commissioner of the Customs, and Afterwards of the Treasury to His Majesty King Charles the Second.* London: For the Editor, 1744.

*Observations on the late Management of the Levant-Company, with Extracts of Letters from Constantinople and Smirna.* London, 1719.

Olearius, Adam, *The Voyages and Travels of the Ambassadors from the Duke of Holstein, to the Great Duke of Muscovy, and the King of Persia*, trans. John Davies. London: For Thomas Dring, 1662.

*Paragraphs of some Letters, among many others, from Aleppo, Smyrna, Constantinople, to prove the Reasonableness of the Levant Company's late Orders to carry on their Trade by General Ships.* London, 1719.

Pecquet, Antoine, *Discours sur l'Art de Negocier.* Paris: Chez Nyon fils, 1737.

Phillips, Richard, *Modern London, Being the History and Present State of the British Metropolis*. London: R. Phillips, 1804.

Pickering, Danby (ed.), *The Statutes at Large*, 46 vols. Cambridge: J. Bentham, 1762–1807.

Porter, James, *Observations on the Religion, Law, Government, and Manners, of the Turks*, 2 vols. London: For J. Nourse, 1768.

Pouqueville, F.C.H.L., *Travels through the Morea, Albania, and several other parts of the Ottoman Empire, to Constantinople, during the years 1798, 1799, 1800, and 1801*, trans. anonymous. London: Barnard & Sultzer, 1806.

*Reasons Against The Bill now depending in Parliament, Intitutled, A Bill for Inlarging and Regulating the Trade to the Levant Seas.* London, 1744.

*Reasons Humbly Offered to the Consideration of Both Houses of Parliament against the Exportation of Wooll out of England and Ireland.* London, 1700.

*Reasons Offer'd by the Merchants Trading to Italy, against the Bill desired by the Levant-Company, for Repealing a Clause in the Act of Navigation.* London, 1720.

*Reflections on the Expediency of Opening the Trade to Turkey.* London, 1753.

'Report from the Select Committee on Consular Establishments' in *Reports from Committees: Sixteen Volumes. (2) Army (Colonies); Consuls; Militia; General Darling* (London, 1835), vol. VI, 9.

Rósee, Pasqua, *The Vertue of the Coffee Drink, First publiquely made and sold in England by Pasqua Rosee*. London, 1666.

Rycaut, Paul, *The History of the Present State of the Ottoman Empire.* London: For John Starkey & Henry Brome, 1675.

Sandford, Francis, *The History of the Coronation of the Most High, Most Mighty, and Most Excellent Monarch, James I.* London: In the Savoy, 1687.

Scrofani, Xavier, *Voyage en Grèce, de Xavier Scrofani, Sicilien, Fait en 1794 et 1795*, trans. J.F.C. Blanvillain, 3 vols. Paris & Strasbourg: Chez Treuttel et Würtz, An IX [1801].

Selden, John, *Mare clausum sev de dominio maris libri duo*. London: Richardo Meighan, 1636.

*Separate Convention between the Emperor of Germany and the Ottoman Porte, signed at Sistovo, August 4, 1791*. London, 1792.

*A Short Reply to Mr. Eaton's Observations Respecting the Establishment of The Levant Company*. London, 1799.

Short, Thomas, *Medicina Britannica: or, a Treatise on such Physical Plants, as are Generally to be found in the Fields or Gardens in Great-Britain, Containing a particular Account of their Nature, Virtues, and Uses*. London: For Manby & Cox, 1746.

*Some Remarks on a Late Pamphlet, Intituled, Reflections on the Expediency of Opening the Trade to Turky.* London, 1753.

*The Statutes of the United Kingdom of Great Britain and Ireland, 6 George IV 1825*. London: His Majesty's Statute and Law Printers, 1825.

Struve, Johann Christian von, *Travels in the Crimea: A History of the Embassy from Petersburg to Constantinople, in 1793.* London: For G. & J. Robinson, 1802.

Tooke, William, *A New and General Biographical Dictionary*, 15 vols. London: For G.G. et al., 1798.

*Treaties &c. between Turkey and Foreign Powers, 1535–1855*. London: Foreign Office, 1855.

*The Treaties of Peace, 1919–1923*, 2 vols. New York: Carnegie Endowment for International Peace, 1924.

*A Treatise on the Cotton Trade in Twelve Letters Addressed to the Levant Company, West-India Planters, and Merchants*. London: John Abraham, 1789.

*The Turkey Merchants and their Trade Vindicated From the Aspersions and unjust Reproaches cast on them, In several Cases and Pamphlets Published in the Names of the Italian Merchants.* London, 1720.

Vattel, Emerich de, *The Law of Nations, or, Principles of the Law of Nature, Applied to the Conduct and Affairs of Nations and Sovereigns*, trans. anonymous. Dublin: Luke White, 1792.

Vattel, Emerich de, *Le Droit des Gens ou Principes de la Loi Naturelle Appliqués à la Conduite aux Affaires des Nations & des Souverains,* 2 vols. Leiden: Au depens de la Compagnie, 1758.

Vera y Figueroa Ávila y Zúñiga, Juan Antonio de, *Le Parfait Ambassadeur*, trans. anonymous. Leiden: Chez Theodora Haak, 1709.

Vera y Figueroa Ávila y Zúñiga, Juan Antonio de, *Le Parfait Ambassadeur*, trans. Sieur Lancelot. Paris: A. de Sommaville, 1635.

Vera y Figueroa Ávila y Zúñiga, Juan Antonio de, *El Enbaxador*. Seville: Por Fransisco de Lyra, 1620.

Walsh, Robert, *Account of the Levant Company: with Some Notices of the Benefits Conferred upon Society by its Officers, in Promoting the Cause of Humanity, Literature, and the Fine Arts.* London: For J & A Arch, 1825.

Walsh, Robert, *A Residence at Constantinople ... and Termination of the Greek and Turkish Revolutions*, 2 vols. London: Frederick Westley & A.H. Davis, 1836.

*The Weekly Amusement: or, the Universal Magazine,* 3 vols. London: For James Hoey, 1735.

Wicquefort, Abraham de, *The Ambassador and His Functions*, trans. Mr. Digby. London: For B. Lintott, 1716.

Wilson, Robert Thomas, *A History of the British Expedition to Egypt*. London: W. Corbet, 1803.

Yirmisekiz Mehmed Çelebi, *Relation de l'ambassade de Mohammed Effendi, texte turc.* Paris: Firmin Didot Frères, 1841.

## Secondary sources

Abou-El-Haj, Rifa'at Ali, 'Ottoman diplomacy at Karlowitz' in A. Nuri Yurdusev (ed.), *Ottoman Diplomacy: Conventional or Unconventional?* Basingstoke & New York: Palgrave, 2004, 89–113.

Abou-El-Haj, Rifa'at Ali, 'Ottoman attitudes toward peace making: The Karlowitz case', *Der Islam* 51:1 (1974), 131–7.

Abou-El-Haj, Rifa'at Ali, 'The formal closure of the Ottoman frontier in Europe, 1699–1703', *Journal of the American Oriental Society* 89:3 (1969), 467–75.

# Bibliography

Abou-El-Haj, Rifa'at Ali, 'Ottoman diplomacy at Karlowitz', *Journal of the American Oriental Society* 87:4 (1967), 498–512.

Adjaye, Joseph K., 'Indigenous African diplomacy: An Asante case study', *The International Journal of African Historical Studies* 18:3 (1985), 487–503.

Ágoston, Gábor, *Guns for the Sultan: Military Power and the Weapons Industry in the Ottoman Empire*. Cambridge: Cambridge University Press, 2005.

Aksan, Virginia, 'What's up in Ottoman studies', *Journal of the Ottoman Turkish Studies Association* 1:1–2 (2014), 3–21.

Aksan, Virginia, *An Ottoman Statesman in War and Peace: Ahmed Resmi Efendi, 1700–1783*. Leiden: Brill, 1995.

Aksan, Virginia, 'Ottoman political writing, 1768–1808', *International Journal of Middle East Studies* 25:1 (1993), 53–69.

Alam, Muzaffar & Subrahmanyam, Sanjay, *Indo-Persian Travels in the Age of Discoveries.* Cambridge: Cambridge University Press, 2007.

Allsen, Thomas T., *Commodity and Exchange in the Mongol Empire: A Cultural History of Islamic Textiles.* Cambridge: Cambridge University Press, 1997.

Allworth, Edward A., *The Modern Uzbeks: From the Fourteenth Century to the Present: A Cultural History.* Stanford: Hoover Institution Press, 1999.

[Altınay], Ahmet Refik, 'Türkler ve Kraliçe Elizabeth', *Darülfünun Edebiyat Fakültesi Mecmuası* 8:5 (1932), 3–28.

Anderson, M.S., *The Rise of Modern Diplomacy, 1450–1919.* Harlow: Longman, 1993.

Anzulovic, Branimir, *Heavenly Serbia: From Myth to Genocide.* New York: New York University Press, 1999.

Arı, Bülent, 'Early Ottoman diplomacy: Ad hoc period' in A. Nuri Yurdusev (ed.), *Ottoman Diplomacy: Conventional or Unconventional?* Basingstoke & New York: Palgrave, 2004, 36–65.

Arık, Sabire, 'Polonya kralı Jan Sobıeski'nin eşine yazdığı mektuplarında Türk olgusu' in Ekrem Causevic, Nenad Moacanin, & Vjeran Kursar (eds), *Perspectives on Ottoman Studies: Papers from the 18th Symposium of the International Committee of Pre-Ottoman and Ottoman Studies (CIEPO).* Münster: Lit Verlag, 2010, 81–97.

Armağan, Mustafa (ed.), *İstanbul armağanı: Lâle Devri.* İstanbul: İstanbul Büyükşehir Belediyesi Kültür İşleri Daire Başkanlığı, 2000.

Arslanova, Alsu A., 'Notes on the history of political relations between the Ulus of Djochi and the Uluses of the Khulaguyids' in Elena V. Boikova & Rostislav B. Rybakov (eds), *Kinship in the Altaic World: Proceedings of the 48th PIAC.* Wiesbaden: Harrasowitz, 2006, 25–42.

Atasoy, Nurhan, 'Processions and protocol in Ottoman Istanbul' in Karin Ådahl (ed.), *The Sultan's Procession: The Swedish Embassy to Sultan Mehmed IV in 1657–1658 and the Rålamb Paintings*. Istanbul: Swedish Research Institute, 2006, 74–113.

Ayalon, Yaron, *Natural Disasters in the Ottoman Empire: Plague, Famine, and Other Misfortunes*. Cambridge: Cambridge Univesrsity Press, 2014.

Aylmer, G.E., 'Slavery under Charles II: The Mediterranean and Tangier', *The English Historical Review* 114:456 (1999), 378–88.

Badem, Candan, *The Ottoman Crimean War (1853–1856)*. Leiden: Brill, 2010.

Bağış, Ali İhsan, *Britain and the Struggle for the Integrity of the Ottoman Empire: Sir Robert Ainslie's Embassy to Istanbul, 1776–1794*. Istanbul: Isis, 1984.

Bağış, Ali İhsan, *Osmanlı Ticaretinde Gayri-Müslimler: Kapitülasyonlar-Beratlı Tüccarlar Avrupa ve Hayrirye Tüccarları, 1750–1839*. Ankara: Turkhan Kitabevi, 1983.

Balfour-Paul, Jenny, *Indigo in the Arab World*. London: Curzon, 1997.

Barkey, Karen, *Empire of Difference: The Ottomans in a Comparative Perspective*. Cambridge: Cambridge University Press, 2008.

Bayly, C.A., *The Birth of the Modern World 1780–1914: Global Connections and Comparisons*. Oxford: Oxford University Press, 2004.

Bayly, C.A., *Rulers, Townsmen and Bazaars: North Indian Society in the Age of British Expansion, 1770–1870*. Cambridge: Cambridge University Press, 1983.

Bearman, P., Bianquis, T., Bosworth, C.E., Donzel, E. van, & Heinrichs, W.P., *Enyclopaedia of Islam, Second Edition*. Leiden: Brill, 1960–2005.

Beckett, John, *The Rise and Fall of the Grenvilles: The Dukes of Buckingham and Chandos, 1710 to 1921*. Manchester: Manchester University Press, 1994.

Beckwith, Sarah, 'Ritual, theater, and social space in the York Corpus Christi Cycle' in Barbara A. Hanawalt & David Wallace (eds), *Bodies and Disciplines: Intersections of Literature and History in Fifteenth-Century England*. Minneapolis: University of Minnesota Press, 1996, 63–86.

Bell, Gary M., *A Handlist of British Diplomatic Representatives, 1509–1688*. London: Royal Historical Society, 1990.

Ben-Amos, Ilana Krausman, *The Culture of Giving: Informal Support and Gift-Exchange in Early Modern England*. Cambridge: Cambridge University Press, 2008.

Bensoussan, Maurice, *Les particules alimentaires: naissance de la gastronomie au XVIe siècle*. Paris: Maisonneuve et Larose, 2003.

Bent, J. Theodore (ed.), *Early Voyages and Travels in the Levant*. London: For the Hakluyt Society, 1893.

Bent, J. Theodore, 'The English in the Levant', *The English Historical Review* 5:20 (1890), 654–64.

Berridge, G.R., *British Diplomacy in Turkey, 1583 to the Present: A Study in the Evolution of the Resident Embassy*. Leiden: Martinus Nijhoff, 2009.

Berridge, G.R., 'Dragomans and oriental secretaries in the British embassy in Istanbul' in A. Nuri Yurdusev (ed.), *Ottoman Diplomacy: Conventional or Unconventional?* Basingstoke & New York: Palgrave, 2004, 151–66.

Bierce, Ambrose, *The Cynic's Word Book*. London & New York: Doubleday, Page & Co., 1906.

Bindoff, S.T., Malcolm Smith, E.F., & Webster, C.K., *British Diplomatic Representatives, 1789–1852*. London: Royal Historical Society, 1934.

*The Biographical Dictionary of the Society for the Diffusion of Useful Knowledge*, 4 vols. London: Longman, 1842.

Birdal, Mehmet Sinan, *The Holy Roman Empire and the Ottomans: From Global Imperial Power to Absolutist States.* London & New York: IB Tauris, 2011.

Bolewski, Wilfried, *Diplomacy and International Law in Globalized Relations*. New York: Springer, 2007.

Borschberg, Peter, *Hugo Grotius, the Portuguese, and Free Trade in the East Indies*. Singapore: NUS Press, 2011.

Borschberg, Peter, 'The Euro-Asian trade in bezoar stones (approx. 1500 to 1700)' in Michael North (ed.), *Artistic and Cultural Exchanges between Europe and Asia, 1400–1900*. Farnham: Ashgate, 2010, 29–44.

Borschberg, Peter, 'Grotius' theory of trans-oceanic trade regulation: Revisiting Mare Liberum (1609)', *Institute for International Law and Justice Working Paper* 14 (2005).

Bostan, İdris, 'Mezamorta Hüseyin Paşa ve 1701 Tarihli Bahriye Kanunnamesi' in İdris Bostan & Salih Özbaran (eds), *Başlangıçtan XVII. Yüzyılın Sonuna Kadar Türk Denizcilik Tarihi 1.* İstanbul: Deniz Basımevi Müdürlüğü, 2009, 281–91.

Bostan, İdris, 'İzn-i Sefine Defterleri ve Karadeniz'de Rusya İle Ticaret Yapan Devlet-i Aliye Tüccarları, 1780–1846', *Türklük Araştırmaları Dergisi* 6 (1990), 28–35.

Bourdieu, Pierre, *Outline of a Theory of Practice*, trans. Richard Nice. Cambridge: Cambridge University Press, 1977.

Bowles, Edmund A., 'The impact of Turkish military bands on European court festivals in the 17th and 18th centuries', *Early Music* 34:4 (2006), 533–60.

Boyar, Ebru, & Fleet, Kate, *A Social History of Ottoman Istanbul.* Cambridge: Cambridge University Press, 2010.

Braudel, Fernand, *La Méditerranée et le Monde Méditerranéen a l'époque de Philippe II.* Paris: A. Colin, 1949.

Brenner, Robert, *Merchants and Revolution: Commercial Change, Political Conflict, and London's Overseas Traders, 1550–1653*. Princeton NJ: Verson, 1993.

Brown, Henry Phelps, & Hopkins, Sheila V., *A Perspective of Wages and Prices.* Cambridge: Cambridge University Press, 1981.

Brown, Peter, 'Dining by design' in Harlan Walker (ed.), *The Meal: Proceedings of the Oxford Symposium on Food and Cookery, 2001*. Totnes: Prospect, 2002, 58–66.

Brubaker, Leslie, 'The visualisation of gift giving in Byzantium and the mosaics at Hagia Sophia' in Davis & Fouracre (eds), *Languages of the Gift in the Early Middle Ages*. Cambridge: Cambridge University Press, 2010, 33–61.

Brummett, Palmira, *Mapping the Ottomans: Sovereignty, Territory, and Identity in the Early Modern Mediterranean.* New York: Cambridge University Press, 2015.

Bulut, Mehmet, 'XVII yüzyılda Osmanlılar ve merkantilistler', *Ekonom'k Yaklaşım Dergisi* 39 (2007), 23–36

Burian, Orhan, 'Türk-İngiliz münasebetinin ilk yıllar', *Anakara Üniversitesi Dil ve Tarih-Coğrafya Fakültesi Dergisi* 9:1–2 (1951), 1–41.

Burke, Bernard, *A Genealogical History of the Dormant, Abeyant, Forfeited, and Extinct Peerages of the British Empire*. London: Harrison, 1866.

Burke, John, *A Genealogical and Heraldic History of the Commoners of Great Britain and Ireland*, 4 vols. London: H. Colburn, 1836.

Burke, John, & Burke, John Bernard, *A Genealogical and Heraldic Dictionary of the Landed Gentry of Great Britain and Ireland*, 2 vols. London: H. Colburn, 1847.

Burke, John, & Burke, John Bernard, *A Genealogical and Heraldic History of the Extinct and Dormant Baronetcies of England, Ireland, and Scotland*, 2nd edn. London: J.R. Smith, 1844.

Butterfield, Herbert, *Man on his Past: The Study of the History of Historical Scholarship*. Cambridge: Cambridge University Press, 1955.

Cameron, Averil, 'The construction of court ritual: The Byzantine Book of Ceremonies' in David Cannadine & Simon Price (eds), *Rituals of Royalty: Power and Ceremonial in Traditional Societies.* Cambridge: Cambridge University Press, 1987, 106–37.

Canepa, Matthew P., *The Two Eyes of the Earth: Art and Ritual of Kingship between Rome and Sassanian Iran.* Berkeley & Los Angeles: University of California Press, 2009.

Carrió-Invernizzi, Diana, 'Gift and diplomacy in seventeenth-century Spanish Italy', *The Historical Journal* 51:4 (2008), 881–99.

Casale, Giancarlo, *The Ottoman Age of Exploration.* Oxford: Oxford University Press, 2010.

Cassidy-Geiger, Maureen (ed.), *Fragile Diplomacy: Meissen Porcelain for European Courts ca. 1710–63.* New Haven CT: Yale University Press, 2007.

Cawston, George, & Keane, Augustus Henry, *The Early Chartered Companies, A.D. 1296–1858*. London: E. Arnold, 1896.

Chaplais, Pierre, *English Diplomatic Practice in the Middle Ages.* Cambridge: Cambridge University Press, 2003.

Chencier, Robert, *Madder Red: A History of Luxury and Trade.* London: Curzon, 2005.

Chitnis, K.N., *Glimpses of Maratha Socio-Economic History*. New Delhi: Atlantic Publishers, 1994.

Christys, Ann, 'The queen of the Franks offers gifts to the caliph al-Muktafi'' in Wendy Davies & Paul Fouracre (eds), *The Languages of Gift in the Early Middle Ages.* Cambridge: Cambridge University Press, 2010, 149–70.

Clogg, Richard, *A Concise History of Greece.* Cambridge: Cambridge University Press, 1992.

Cole, W.A., 'Trends in eighteenth-century smuggling', *The Economic History Review* 10:3 (1985), 395–410.

Cole, W.A., 'The arithmetic of eighteenth-century smuggling: Rejoinder', *The Economic History Review* 28:1 (1975), 44–9.

Constable, Olivia Remie, *Housing the Stranger in the Mediterranean World: Lodging, Trade, and Travel in Late Antiquity and the Middle Ages*. Cambridge: Cambridge University Press, 2003.

Cosmo, Nicola Di, 'Kirghiz nomads on the Qing frontier: Tribute, trade, or gift-exchange?' in Nicola Di Cosma & Don J. Wyatt (eds), *Political Frontiers, Ethnic Boundaries, and Human Geographies in Chinese History*. London & New York: Routledge-Curzon, 2003, 351–72.

Cowan, Brian, *The Social Life of Coffee: The Emergence of the British Coffeehouse*. New Haven & London: Yale University Press, 2005.

Crapol, Edward P., 'Coming to terms with Empire: The historiography of late nineteenth-century American foreign relations' in Michael J. Hogan (ed.), *Paths to Power: The Historiography of American Foreign Relations to 1941*. Cambridge: Cambridge University Press, 2000, 79–116.

Croskey, Robert M., 'The diplomatic forms of Ivan III's relationship with the Crimean khan', *Slavic Review* 43:2 (1984), 257–69.

Çalış, B. Deniz, 'Gardens at the Kağıthane commons during the Tulip Period (1718–1730)' in Michael Conan (ed.), *Middle East Garden Traditions: Unity and Diversity*. Washington DC: Dumbarton Oaks, 2007, 239–68.

Çalışır, Deniz 'Osmanlı görsel kültüründe meyve teması: Geleneksel natürmort resimleri bağlamında bir değerlendirme', *Turkish Studies* 3:5 (2008), 65–86.

*Çırakman, Aslı, From the 'Terror of the World' to the 'Sick Man of Europe': European Images of the Ottoman Empire and Society from the Sixteenth Century to the Nineteenth*. Oxford: Peter Lang, 2002.

Çiçek, Kemal, 'Interpreters of the court in the Ottoman Empire as seen from the Sharia court records of Cyprus', *Islamic Law and Society* 9:1 (2002), 1–15.

Ćirković, Sima M., *The Serbs*. Oxford: Blackwell, 2004.

Dajani-Shakeel, Hadia, 'Diplomatic relations between Muslim and Frankish rulers, 1097–1153 A.D.' in Maya Shatzmiller (ed.), *Crusaders and Muslims in Twelfth-Century Syria*. Leiden: Brill, 1993, 190–215.

Dankoff, Robert, *An Ottoman Mentality: The World of Evliya Çelebi*. Leiden: Brill, 2004.

Darling, Linda, *Revenue-Raising and Legitimacy: Tax Collection and Finance Administration in the Ottoman Empire, 1560–1660*. Leiden: Brill, 1996.

Davis, Natalie Zemon, *The Gift in Sixteenth Century France*. Oxford: Oxford University Press, 2000.

Davis, Ralph 'English imports from the Middle East, 1580–1780' in M.A. Cook (ed.), *Studies in the Economic History of the Middle East from the Rise of Islam to the Present Day*. Oxford: Oxford University Press, 1970, 193–206.

Davis, Ralph, *Aleppo and Devonshire Square: English Traders in the Levant in the Eighteenth Century*. London: Macmillan, 1967.

Demirci, Süleyman, 'Complaints about avâriz assessment and payment in the avâriz-tax system: An aspect of the relationship between centre and periphery. A case study of Kayseri, 1618–1700', *Journal of the Economic and Social History of the Orient* 46:4 (2003), 437–74.

Dereli, Hâmit, *Kraliçe Elizabeth Devrinde Türkler ve İngilizler: Bir Araştırma.* İstanbul: Anil Matbaası, 1951.

Dickson, P.G.M., & Beckett, J.V., 'The finances of the Dukes of Chandos: Aristocratic inheritance, marriage and debt in eighteenth-century England', *The Huntington Library Quarterly* 64:3/4 (2001), 309–35.

Dijk, Wil O., *Seventeenth-Century Burma and the Dutch East India Company, 1634–1680.* Singapore: Singapore University Press, 2006.

Dillon, Janette, *The Language of Space in Court Performance 1400–1625.* Cambridge: Cambridge University Press, 2010.

Divitiis, Pagano de, *English Merchants in Seventeenth-Century Italy.* Cambridge: Cambridge University Press, 1997.

Driault, E., 'Les Anglais devant Constantinople et Alexandrie, 1807', *Revue Historique* 73:1 (1900), 24–60.

Duindam, Jeroen, *Vienna and Versailles: The Courts of Europe's Dynastic Rivals, 1550–1780.* Cambridge: Cambridge University Press, 2003.

Dursteler, Eric R., *Venetians in Constantinople: Nation, Identity, and Coexistence in the Early Modern Mediterranean.* Baltimore: Johns Hopkins University Press, 2006.

Eaton, Natasha, 'Between mimesis and alterity: Art, gift and diplomacy in colonial India, 1770–1800', *Comparative Studies in Society and History* 46:4 (2004), 816–44.

Eaton, Richard, *The Rise of Islam and the Bengal Frontier, 1204–1760.* Berkeley & Los Angeles: University of California Press, 1993.

Edgerton, Robert B., *The Fall of the Asante Empire.* London & New York: The Free Press, 1995.

Edmonds, John, *The History and Practice of Eighteenth Century Dyeing.* Little Chalfont: John Edmonds, 1999.

Elbl, Ivana, 'Cross-cultural trade and diplomacy: Portuguese relations with West Africa, 1441–1521', *Journal of World History* 3:2 (1992), 165–204.

Eldem, Edhem, 'Capitulations and Western trade' in Suraiya Faroqhi (ed.), *The Cambridge History of Turkey, Volume 3: The Later Ottoman Empire, 1603–1839*. Cambridge: Cambridge University Press, 2006, 283–335.

Eldem, Edhem, *French Trade in Istanbul in the Eighteenth Century*. Leiden: Brill, 1999.

Elliott, Mark C., *Emperor Qianlong: Son of Heaven, Man of the World.* Harlow & New York: Pearson Longman, 2009.

Emmer, P.C., *The Dutch Slave Trade, 1500–1850.* New York: Berghahn Books, 2006.

Epstein, M., *The Early History of the Levant Company*. London: Routledge, 1908.

Ergene, Boğaç A., *Local Court, Provincial Society and Justice in the Ottoman Empire: Legal Practice and Dispute Resolution in Çankırı and Kastamonu (1652–1744)*. Leiden: Brill, 2003.

Erimtan, Can, *Ottomans Looking West? The Origins of the Tulip Age and its Development in Modern Turkey*. London & New York: Tauris, 2008.

Esherick, Joseph, 'Cherishing sources from afar', *Modern China* 24:2 (1998), 135–61.

Espen, Moe, *Governance, Growth and Global Leadership: The Role of the State in Technological Progress, 1750–2000.* Aldershot & Burlington VT: Ashgate, 2007.

Ewers, John C., *Indian Life on the Upper Missouri.* Norman: University of Oklahoma Press, 1968.

Fagan, Margaret M., 'The uses of insect galls', *The American Naturalist* 52:614 (1918), 155–76.

Fairlie, Susan, 'Dyestuffs in the eighteenth ccntury', *The Economic History Review* 17:3 (1965), 488–510.

Faroqhi, Suraiya, *The Ottoman Empire and the World Around It*. London: IB Tauris, 2006.

Faroqhi, Suraiya, 'Declines and revivals in textile production' in Suraiya Faroqhi (ed.), *The Cambridge History of Turkey, Volume 3: The Later Ottoman Empire, 1603–1839*. Cambridge: Cambridge University Press, 2006, 356–75.

Faroqhi, Suraiya, 'Introduction' in Suraiya Faroqhi & Cristoph K. Neumann (eds), *The Illuminated Table, the Prosperous House: Food and Shelter in Ottoman Material Culture*. Würzburg: Ergon, 2003, 9–34.

Faroqhi, Suraiya, *Subjects of the Sultan: Culture and Daily Life in the Ottoman Empire*. London & New York: IB Tauris, 1995.

Faroqhi, Suraiya, 'Mohair manufacture and mohair workshops in seventeenth century Ankara', *İstanbul Üniversitesi İktisat Fakültesi Mecmuası* 41:1–4 (1982–3), 211–36.

Feavearyear, Albert, *The Pound Sterling: A History of English Money*, 2nd edn. Oxford: Oxford University Press, 1963.

Fedorowicz, J.K., *England's Baltic Trade in the Early Seventeenth Century: A Study in Anglo-Polish Commercial Diplomacy.* Cambridge: Cambridge University Press, 1980.

Feinberg, Harvey M., 'Africans and Europeans in West Africa: Elminans and Dutchmen on the Gold Coast during the eighteenth century', *Transactions of the American Philosophical Society* 79:7 (1989), 1–186.

Fenton, William N., 'Structure, continuity, and change in the process of Iroquois treaty making' in Francis Jennings (ed.), *The History and Culture of Iroquois Diplomacy: An Interdisciplinary Guide to the Treaties of the Six Nations and Their League.* Syracuse NY: Syracuse University Press, 1985, 3–37.

Ferrier, Ronal, 'Trade from the mid-14th century to the end of the Safavid period' in Peter Jackson & Laurence Lockhart (eds), *The Cambridge History of Iran 6*. Cambridge: Cambridge University Press, 1986, 412–90.

Field, Ophelia, *The Kit-Cat Club: Friends Who Imagined a Nation.* London: Harper, 2008.

Fielding, Andrew, & Fielding, Annelise, *The Salt Industry*. Princes Risborough: Shire Publications, 2006.

Findley, Carter Vaughn, *The Turks in World History*. Oxford: Oxford University Press, 2005.

Findley, Carter Vaughn, *Bureaucratic Reform in the Ottoman Empire: The Sublime Porte, 1789–1922*. Princeton: Princeton University Press, 1980.

Findley, Carter Vaughn, 'The legacy of tradition to reform: Origins of the Ottoman foreign ministry', *International Journal of Middle East Studies* 1:4 (1970), 334–57.

Firges, Pascal W., Graf, Tobias P., Roth, Christian, & Tulasoğlu, Gülay (eds), *Well-Connected Domains: Towards an Entangled Ottoman History*. Leiden: Brill, 2014.

Fissell, Mark, & Goffman, Daniel, 'Viewing the scaffold from Istanbul: The Bendysh-Hyde affair, 1647–1651', *Albion* 22:3 (1990), 421–48.

Fleet, Kate, *European and Islamic Trade in the Early Ottoman State: The Merchants of Genoa and Turkey*. Cambridge: Cambridge University Press, 2006.

Fliter, Irena, 'The diplomats' debts: International financial disputes between the Ottoman Empire and Prussia at the end of the eighteenth century', *Osmanlı Araştırmaları / Journal of Ottoman Studies* 48 (2016), 399–416.

Flood, Finbarr B., *Objects of Translation: Material Culture and Medieval 'Hindu-Muslim' Encounter*. Princeton NJ: Princeton University Press, 2009.

Foster, Joseph, *Alumni Oxoniensis: The Members of the University of Oxford, 1500–1714*. Oxford: Parker & Co., 1892.

Foster, William (ed.), *The Travels of John Sanderson in the Levant, 1584–1602*. London: Hakluyt Society, 1931.

Frangakis-Syrett, Elizabeth, 'Monetary shortage and the Ottoman economy: Late seventeenth to late eighteenth centuries' in Walid Arbid, Salgur Kancal, Jean-David Mizrahi, & Samir Saul (eds), *Méditerranée, Moyen-Orient: Deux siècles de relations internationales*. Paris: Editions L'Hartmann, 2003, 109–31.

Freeman, Charles W., *Arts of Power: Statecraft and Diplomacy*. Washington DC: United States Institute of Peace Press, 1997.

Freeman, Charles W., *The Diplomat's Dictionary*. Washington DC: United States Institute of Peace Press, 1994.

French, David, 'A sixteenth century English merchant in Ankara?', *Anatolian Studies* 22 (1972), 241–7.

Fridell, Gavin, *Fair Trade Coffee: The Prospects and Pitfalls of Market-Driven Social Justice*. Toronto: University of Toronto Press, 2007.

Frigo, Daniela, 'Prudence and experience: Ambassadors and political cultures in early modern Italy', *The Journal of Medieval and Early Modern Studies* 38:1 (2008), 35–55.

Fusaro, Maria, 'After Braudel: A reassessment of Mediterranean history between the Northern Invasion and the *Caravane Maritime*' in Maria Fusaro, Colin Heywood, & Mohamed-Salah Omri (eds), *Trade and Cultural*

*Exchange in the Early Modern Mediterranean: Braudel's Maritime Legacy.* London: Tauris, 2010, 1–22.

Fusaro, Maria, 'Les Anglais et les Grecs: Un réseau de coopération commerciale en Méditerranée vénitienne', *Annales HSS* 58:3 (2003), 605–25.

Fusaro, Maria, *Uva Passa: Una guerra comerciale tra Venezia e l'Inghilterra, 1540–1640.* Venice: Il Cardo, 1997.

Genç, Mehmet, *Osmanlı İmparatorluğunda Devlet ve Ekonomi.* İstanbul: Otüken, 2000.

Ghobrial, John-Paul, *Whispers of Cities: Information Flows in Istanbul, London, and Paris in the Age of William Trumbull.* Oxford: Oxford University Press, 2013.

Gienow-Hecht, Jessica C.E., 'What bandwagon? Diplomatic history today', *The Journal of American History* 94:5 (2009), 1083–6.

Ginio, Eyal, 'Aspects of Muslim culture in the Ottoman Balkans: A view from eighteenth-century Salonica' in Dimitris Tziovas (ed.), *Greece and the Baltans: Identities, Perceptions, and Cultural Encounters since the Enlightenment.* Aldershot & Burlington VT: Ashgate, 2003, 114–26.

Ginio, Eyal, 'Piracy and redemption in the Aegean Sea during the first half of the eighteenth century', *Turcica* 33 (2001), 135–47.

Goffman, Daniel, 'Negotiating with the Renaissance state: The Ottoman Empire and the new diplomacy' in Virginia Aksan & Daniel Goffman, *The Early Modern Ottomans: Remapping the Empire.* Cambridge: Cambridge University Press, 2007, 61–74.

Goffman, Daniel, *The Ottoman Empire and Early Modern Europe.* Cambridge: Cambridge University Press, 2002.

Gordon, Stewart, 'Introduction: Ibn Battuta and a region of robing' in Stewart Gordon (ed.), *Robes of Honour: Khil'at in Pre-Colonial and Colonial India.* Oxford: Oxford University Press, 2003, 1–30.

Gough, Kathleen, *Rural Society in Southeast India.* Cambridge: Cambridge University Press, 1981.

Göçek, Fatma Müge, *East Encounters West: France and the Ottoman Empire in the Eighteenth Century.* New York & Oxford: Oxford University Press, 1987.

Grehan, James, *Everyday Life and Consumer Culture in Eighteenth-Century Damascus.* Seattle: University of Washington Press, 2007.

Groot, Alexander H. de, 'The historical development of the capitulatory regime in the Ottoman Middle East from the fifteenth to the nineteenth centuries', *Oriente Moderno* 22(83):3 (2003), 575–694.

Groot, Alexander H. de, 'Dragomans' careers: The change of status in some families connected with the British and Dutch embassies at Istanbul, 1785–1829' in Alastair Hamilton, Alexander H. de Groot, & Maurits H. van den Boogert, *Friends and Rivals in the East: Studies in Anglo-Dutch Relations in the Levant from the Seventeenth to the Early Nineteenth Century.* Leiden: Brill, 2000, 223–46.

Gülsoy, Ersin, *Girit'in Fethi ve Osmanlı İdaresinin Kurulması, 1645–1670.* İstanbul: Tatav-Tarih ve Tabiat Vakfı Yayınları, 2004.

Gürkan, Emrah Safa, 'Mediating boundaries: Mediterranean go-betweens and cross-confessional diplomacy in Constantinople, 1560–1600', *Journal of Early Modern History* 19 (2015), 107–28.

Gürkan, Emrah Safah, 'Espionage in the 16th century Mediterranean: Secret diplomacy, Mediterranean go-betweens, and the Ottoman–Habsburg rivalry', PhD thesis. Georgetown University, 2012.

Hale, William, & Bağış, Ali İhsan (eds), *Four Centuries of Turco-British Relations: Studies in Diplomatic, Economic and Cultural Affairs*. Beverley: Eothern, 1984.

Halenko, Oleksander, 'Wine production, marketing, and consumption in the Ottoman Crimea, 1520–1542', *Journal of the Economic and Social History of the Orient* 47:4 (2004), 507–47.

Hall, Joseph M., *Zamumo's Gifts: Indian–European Exchange in the Colonial Southeast*. University Park: Pennsylvania State University Press, 2009.

Hamadeh, Shirine, 'Public spaces and the garden culture of Istanbul in the eighteenth century' in Virginia Aksan & Daniel Goffman (eds), *The Early Modern Ottomans: Remapping the Empire*. Cambridge: Cambridge University Press, 2007, 277–312.

Hambly, Gavin R.G., 'The emperor's clothes: Robing and "robes of honour" in Mughal India' in Stewart Gordon (ed.), *Robes of Honour: Khil'at in Pre-Colonial and Colonial India.* Oxford: Oxford University Press, 2003, 31–49.

Hamilton, Keith, & Langhorne, Richard, *The Practice of Diplomacy: Its Evolution, Theory and Administration*, 2nd edn. Abingdon & New York: Routledge, 2011.

Hannay, David, *The Great Chartered Companies.* London: Williams & Norgate, 1926.

Harlaftis, Gelina, 'The "Eastern invasion": Greeks in the Mediterranean trade and shipping in the eighteenth and nineteenth centuries' in Maria Fusaro, Colin Heywood, & Mohamed-Salah Omri (eds), *Trade and Cultural Exchange in the Early Modern Mediterranean: Braudel's Maritime Legacy.* London: Tauris, 2010, 223–52.

Harvey, John H., 'Turkey as a source of garden plants', *Garden History* 4:3 (1976), 21–42.

Hathaway, Jane, *The Arab Lands Under Ottoman Rule, 1516–1800.* Harlow: Pearson Longman, 2008.

Hathaway, Jane, 'Rewriting eighteenth-century Ottoman history', *Mediterranean Historical Review* 19:1 (2004), 29–53.

Hattox, Ralph S., *Coffee and Coffeehouses: The Origins of a Social Beverage in the Medieval Near East*. Seattle: University of Washington Press, 1985.

Haynes, Douglas E., *Rhetoric and Ritual in Colonial India: The Shaping of a Public Culture in Surat City, 1852–1928*. Berkeley & Los Angeles: University of California Press, 1991.

Hevia, James L., *Cherishing Men from Afar: Qing Guest Ritual and the Macartney Embassy of 1793*. Durham NC: Duke University Press, 2002.

Heywood, Colin, 'Ottoman territoriality versus maritime usage: The Ottoman islands and English privateering in the wars with France, 1689–1714' in Nicolas Vatin & Gilles Veinstein (eds), *Insularités ottomanes*. Paris: Maisonneuve & Larose, 2004, 145–73.

Heywood, Colin, 'The Kapudan Pasha, the English ambassador and the Blackham frigate: An episode in Anglo-Ottoman maritime relations (1697)' in E. Zachariadou (ed.), *The Kapudan Pasha, his Office and his Domain: Halcyon Days in Crete IV: A Symposium held in Rethymnon 7–9 January 2000.* Rethymnon: Crete University Press, 2002, 409–38.

Heywood, Colin, 'The frontier in Ottoman history: Old ideas and new myths' in Daniel Power & Naomi Standen (eds), *Frontiers in Question: Eurasian Borderlands, 700–1700*. London: St Martin's Press, 1999, 228–50.

*History of Parliament Online*, [http://www.historyofparliamentonline.org/].

Hoh-Cheung & Mui, Lorna H., '"Trends in eighteenth-century smuggling" reconsidered', *The Economic History Review* 28:1 (1975), 28–43.

Holmes, Catherine, 'Treaties between Byzantium and the Islamic world' in Philip da Souza & John France (eds), *War and Peace in Ancient and Medieval History*. Cambridge: Cambridge University Press, 2008, 141–57.

Holt, P.M., *Early Mamluk Diplomacy, 1260–1290: Treaties of Baybars and Qalāwūn with Christian Rulers*. Leiden: Brill, 1995.

Horn, D.B., *British Diplomatic Representatives, 1689–1789*. London: Royal Historical Society, 1932.

Horniker, Arthur Leon, 'Review: The despatches of Sir Robert Sutton, ambassador in Constantinople, 1710–1714', *The Journal of Modern History* 27:4 (1955), 421–2.

Horniker, Arthur Leon, 'Anglo-French rivalry in the Levant from 1583 to 1612', *The Journal of Modern History* 18:4 (1946), 289–305.

Horniker, Arthur Leon, 'William Harborne and the beginning of Anglo-Turkish diplomatic and commercial relations', *The Journal of Modern History* 14:3 (1942), 289–316.

Howland, D.R., *Borders of Chinese Civilization: Geography and History at Empire's End.* Durham NC: Duke University Press, 1996.

Huff, Toby E., *Intellectual Curiosity and the Scientific Revolution: A Global Perspective.* Cambridge: Cambridge University Press, 2010.

Hurewitz, J.C., 'The Europeanization of Ottoman diplomacy: The conversion from unilateralism to reciprocity in the nineteenth century', *Belleten* 25:99 (1961), 455–66.

Hütteroth, Wolf-Dieter, 'Ecology of the Ottoman lands' in Suraiya Faroqhi (ed.), *The Cambridge History of Turkey, Volume 3: The Later Ottoman Empire, 1603–1839.* Cambridge: Cambridge University Press, 2006, 18–43.

Ibn Fāyiʿ, ʿAbd ar-Raḥmān ibn Aḥmad ibn Muḥammad, *Aḥkām al-Baḥr fī al-Fiqh al-Islāmī.* Jeddah: Dār al-Andalus al-Khaḍrā, 2000.

Ilardi, Vincent, *Renaissance Vision from Spectacles to Telescopes.* Philadelphia: American Philosophical Society, 2007.

Imber, Colin, *Ebu's-suʿud: The Islamic Legal Tradition.* Stanford: Stanford University Press, 1997.

Irvin, Benjamin H., *Clothed in the Robes of Sovereignty: The Continental*

*Congress and the People Out of Doors*. Oxford: Oxford University Press, 2011.

Irwin, Robert, *For Lust of Knowing: The Orientalists and their Enemies*. London: Penguin, 2006.

Isom-Verhaaren, Christine, *Allies with the Infidel: The Ottoman and French Alliance in the Sixteenth Century*. London: IB Tauris, 2013.

Israel, Jonathan I., *Dutch Primacy in World Trade, 1585–1740*. Oxford: Oxford University Press, 1989.

Işıksel, Güneş, 'Méandres d'une pratique peu institutionalisée: La diplomatie ottomane, Xve–XVIIIe siècle', *Revue Monde(s)* 5:1 (2014), 43–55.

İnalcık, Halil (ed.), *An Economic and Social History of the Ottoman Empire, 1300–1914*. Cambridge: Cambridge University Press, 1994.

İnalcık, Halil, 'When and how British cotton goods invaded the Levant markets' in Huri İslamoğlu-İnan (ed.), *The Ottoman Empire and the World-Economy*. Cambridge: Cambridge University Press, 1987, 374–83.

Jacobs, Els M., *Merchant in Asia: The Trade of the Dutch East Company during the Eighteenth Century*. Leiden: CNWS, 2006.

Jacobs, Wilbur R., *Diplomacy and Indian Gifts: Anglo-French Rivalry Along the Ohio and Northwest Frontiers, 1748–1763*. Stanford: Stanford University Press, 1950.

Jansson, Maija, & Rogozhin, Nikolai, *England and the North: The Russian Embassy of 1613–1614*, trans. Paul Bushkovitch. Philadelphia: Amer Philosophical Society, 1994.

Jenkins, Susan, *Portrait of a Patron: The Patronage and Collecting of James Brydges, 1st Duke of Chandos (1674–1744)*. Aldershot & Burlington VT: Ashgate, 2007.

Jennings, Ronald C., 'Kadi, court, and legal procedure in 17th C. Ottoman Kayseri', *Studia Islamica* 48 (1978), 133–72.

Jirousek, Charlotte, 'The transition to mass fashion system dress in the Ottoman Empire' in Donald Quataert (ed.), *Consumption Studies and the History of the Ottoman Empire, 1550–1922: An Introduction.* Albany NY: SUNY Press, 2000, 201–42.

Johnson, Carina L., *Cultural Hierarchy in Sixteenth-Century Europe: The Ottomans and Mexicans*. Cambridge: Cambridge University Press, 2011.

Jones, Lynn, '‘Abbasid suzerainty in the medieval Caucasus: Appropriation and adaptation of iconography and ideology', *Gesta* 43:2 (2004), 143–50.

Jones, Martin, *Feast: Why Humans Share Food.* Oxford: Oxford University Press, 2007.

Jones, Raymond, *The British Diplomatic Service, 1815–1914*. Gerrards Cross: Smythe, 1983.

Kadı, İsmail Hakkı, *Ottoman and Dutch Merchants in the Eighteenth Century: Competition and Cooperation in Ankara, Izmir, and Amsterdam.* Leiden: Brill, 2012.

Kappeler, Dietrich, 'Texts in diplomacy' in Jovan Kurbalija & Hannah Slavik (eds), *Language and Diplomacy*. Msida: University of Malta, 2001, 201–6.

Karateke, Hakan T. (ed.), *An Ottoman Protocol Register Containing*

*Ceremonies from 1736 to 1808: BEO Sadaret Defterleri 350 in the Prime Ministry Ottoman State Archives, Istanbul.* Istanbul & London: Royal Asiatic Society, 2007.

Karpat, Kemal H., *Studies on Ottoman Social and Political History: Selected Articles and Essays*. Leiden: Brill, 2002.

Khalileh, Hassan S., *Islamic Maritime Law: An Introduction*. Leiden: Brill, 1998.

Kia, Mehrdad, *Daily Life in the Ottoman Empire*. Santa Barbara CA: Greenwood, 2011.

King, Brenda M., *Silk and Empire*. Manchester: Manchester University Press, 2005.

Kołodziejczyk, Dariusz, *Ottoman–Polish Diplomatic Relations, 15th–18th Century: An Annotated Edition of 'Ahdnames and Other Documents*. Leiden: Brill, 2000.

Konadu, Kawsi, *The Akan Diaspora in the Americas*. Oxford: Oxford University Press, 2010.

Kotzageorgis, Phokion P., 'About the fiscal status of the Greek Orthodox Church in the 17th century', *Turcica* 40 (2008), 67–80.

Koziol, Geoffrey, *Begging Pardon and Favour: Ritual and Political Order in Early Medieval France*. Ithaca NY: Cornell University Press, 1992.

Köprülü, Tuna, *İstanbul'daki Yabancı Saraylar*. İstanbul: İstanbul Büyükşehir Belediyesi Kültür Yayınları, 2005.

Kurat, Akdes Nimet, *Türk-İngiliz Münâsebetlerinin Başlangıcı ve Gelişmesi (1553–1610)*. Ankara: Türk Tarih Kurumu Basımevi, 1953.

Kurat, Akdes Nimet (ed.), *The Despatches of Sir Robert Sutton, Ambassador in Constantinople, 1710–1714*. London: Royal Historical Society, 1953.

Kurat, Akdes Nimet, 'İngiliz devlet arşivinde ve kütüphanelerinde Türkiye tarihine ait bazı malzemeye dair', *Ankara Üniversitesi Dil ve Tarih-Coğrafya Fakültesi Dergisi* 7:1 (1949), 1–18.

Kurlansky, Mark, *Salt: A World History*. London: Jonathan Cape, 2003.

Kurz, O., *European Clocks and Watches in the Near East*. Leiden: Brill, 1975.

Kütükoğlu, Mübahat, *Osmanlı-İngiliz İktisâdi Münasebetleri, I: 1580–1838*. Ankara: Türk Kültürünü Araştırma Enstitütü, 1974.

Laidlaw, Christine, *The British in the Levant: Trade and Perceptions of the Ottoman Empire in the Eighteenth Century*. London & New York: IB Tauris, 2010.

Laiou, Angeliki E., 'Byzantine trade with Christians and Muslims and the Crusades' in Angeliki E. Laiou & Roy Parviz Mottahedeh, *The Crusades from the Perspective of Byzantium and the Muslim World*. Washington DC: Dumbarton Oaks, 2001, 157–96.

Laiou, Angeliki E., & Morrison, Cécile, *The Byzantine Economy*. Cambridge: Cambridge University Press, 2007.

Lair, Anne, 'The ceremony of dining at Napoleon III's court between 1852 and 1870' in Daniëlle de Vooght (ed.), *Royal Taste: Food, Power and Status at the European Courts after 1789*. Farnham: Ashgate, 2011, 143–70.

Lambton, Anne K.S., '"Pīshkash": Present or tribute?', *Bulletin of the School of Oriental and African Studies* 57:1 (1994), 145–58.

Lambton, Ann K.S., *Continuity and Change in Medieval Persia.* Albany NY: Tauris, 1988, 185–220.

Langholtz, Harvey J., 'The psychology of diplomacy' in Harvey J. Langholtz & Chris E. Stout (eds), *The Psychology of Diplomacy.* Westport CT: Praeger, 2004, 1–18.

Lashley, Conrad, 'Towards a theoretical understanding' in Conrad Lashley & Alison Morrison (eds), *In Search of Hospitality: Theoretical Perspectives and Debates.* Oxford: Butterworth-Heinemann, 2000, 1–17.

Laven, Mary, *Mission to China: Matteo Ricci and the Jesuit Encounter with the East.* London: Faber & Faber, 2011.

Lev, Y., 'Charity and gift giving in medieval Islam' in Miriam Fenkel & Yaacov Lev (eds), *Charity and Giving in Monotheistic Religions*. Berlin: Walter de Gruyter, 2009, 235–64.

Lewis, Ioan M., *Social and Cultural Anthropology in Perspective*, 3rd edn. New Brunswick NJ: Transaction, 2003.

Loomba, Ania, 'Of gifts, ambassadors, and copy-cats: Diplomacy, exchange, and difference in early modern India' in Brinda Charry & Gitanjali Shahni (eds), *Emissaries in Early Modern Literature and Culture: Mediation, Transmission, Traffic, 1550–1700.* Farnham: Ashgate, 2009, 41–76.

Luke, Harry, *Cyprus under the Turks, 1571–1878* (London, 1921).

McCaskie, T.C., *State and Society in Pre-Colonial Asante*. Cambridge: Cambridge University Press, 1995.

McClanan, Anne, *Representations of Early Byzantine Empresses: Image and Empire.* Basingstoke & New York: Palgrave Macmillan, 2002.

McCullough, A.B., *Money and Exchange in Canada to 1900.* Toronto: Dundum Press, 1984.

McCusker, John, *Money and Exchange in Europe and America, 1600–1775.* London: Macmillan, 1978.

McCusker, John J., 'The current value of English exports, 1697–1800', *The William and Mary Quarterly* 28:4 (1978), 607–28.

McGowan, Bruce, *Economic Life in Ottoman Europe: Taxation, Trade and the Struggle for Land, 1600–1800*. Cambridge: Cambridge University Press, 1981.

McLane, John R., *Land and Local Kingship in Eighteenth-Century Bengal.* Cambridge: Cambridge University Press, 1993.

MacLean, Gerald, 'Courting the Porte: Early Anglo-Ottoman diplomacy', *University of Bucharest Review* 10:2 (2008), 80–8.

MacLean, Gerald, *Looking East: English Writing and the Ottoman Empire before 1800.* Basingstoke: Palgrave Macmillan, 2007.

Magalhães, José Calvet de, *The Pure Concept of Diplomacy*, trans. Bernardo Futcher Pereira. London & New York: Greenwood, 1988.

Maier, Charles S., 'Marking time: The historiography of international relations' in Michael Kammen (ed.), *The Past Before Us: Contemporary Historical*

*Writing in the United States*. Ithaca NY: Cornell University Press, 1980, 355–87.

Makdisi, Ussama, *The Culture of Sectarianism: Community, History, and Violence in Nineteenth-Century Ottoman Lebanon.* Berkeley & Los Angeles: University of California Press, 2000.

Martin, Janet, *Treasure of the Land of Darkness: The Fur Trade and its Significance for Medieval Russia.* Cambridge: Cambridge University Press, 1986.

Mason, Paul, *Histoire du commerce français dans le Levant au XVIIIe siècle.* Paris: Hachette, 1911.

Mason, Paul, *Histoire du commerce français dans le Levant au XVIIe siècle.* Paris: Hachette, 1896.

Masud, Muhammad Khalid, Peters, Rudolph, & Powers, David S., 'Qāḍīs and their courts: An historical survey' in Muhammad Khalid Masud, Rudolph Peters, & David S. Powers (eds), *Dispensing Justice in Islam: Qadis and their Judgements*. Leiden: Brill, 2006, 1–47.

Matar, Nabil, *Turks, Moors and Englishmen in the Age of Discovery*. New York & Chichester: Columbia University Press, 1999.

Matar, Nabil, *Islam in Britain, 1558–1685*. Cambridge: Cambridge University Press, 1998.

Matar, Nabil, *Britain and Barbary, 1589–1689*. Gainesville: University of Florida Press, 1998.

Mather, James, *Pashas: Traders and Travellers in the Islamic World.* New Haven: Yale University Press, 2009.

Mauss, Marcel, 'Essai sur le don: forme et raison de l'échange dans les sociétés archaïques', *L'Année Sociologique* 1 (1925), 30–186.

Metcalf, Thomas R., *Ideologies of the Raj.* Cambridge: Cambridge University Press, 1995.

Michael, Bernardo A., 'When soldiers and statesmen meet: "Ethnographic moments" on the frontiers of empire, 1800–15' in Stewart Gordon (ed.), *Robes of Honour: Khil'at in Pre-Colonial and Colonial India.* Oxford: Oxford University Press, 2003, 80–94.

Minchinton, E., & French, C.J., *Customs 3 (1696–1780) in the Public Record Office, London.* East Ardsley: Microform Academic Publishers, 1964.

Minkov, Anton, *Conversion to Islam in the Balkans: Kisve Bahası Petitions and Ottoman Social Life, 1670–1730.* Leiden: Brill, 2004.

Mintz, Sidney W., & Du Bois, Christine M., 'The anthropology of food and eating', *Annual Review of Anthropology* 31 (2002), 99–119.

Mitler, Louis, 'The Genoese in Galata: 1453–1682', *International Journal of Middle East Studies* 10:1 (1979), 71–91.

Moore, Arthur William, *Manx Worthies.* Douglas: S.K. Broadbent, 1901.

Mori, Jennifer, *The Culture of Diplomacy: Britain in Europe, 1750–1830.* Manchester: University of Manchester Press, 2011.

Morineau, Michel, 'Les frappes monétaires français de 1726 à 1793: premières considérations' in John Day (ed.), *Études d'histoire monétaire, XIIe–XIXe siècles.* Lille: Presses Universitaires de Lille, 1984, 69–141.

Muhanna, Elias I., 'The sultan's new clothes: Ottoman–Mamluk gift exchange in the fifteenth century', *Muqarnas* 27 (2010), 189–206.

Muir, Edward, *Ritual in Early Modern Europe*. Cambridge: Cambridge University Press, 1997.

Muldoon, James, 'Is the sea open or closed? The Grotius–Selden debate renewed' in Kenneth Pennington & Melodie Harris Eichbauer (eds), *Law as Profession and Practice in Medieval Europe: Essays in Honor of James A. Brundage.* Farnham: Ashgate, 2011, 117–36.

Nazır, Bayram, *Ottoman Hospitality and Its Impact on Europe*. Istanbul: İTO, 2008.

Necipoğlu, Gülru, 'Framing the gaze in Ottoman, Safavid, and Mughal palaces', *Ars Orientalis* 23 (1993), 303–42.

Newby, L.J., *The Empire and the Khanate: A Political History of Qing Relations with Khoqand c.1760–1860*. Leiden: Brill, 2005.

Nicol, D.M., *Byzantium and Venice: A Study in Diplomatic and Cultural Relations.* Cambridge: Cambridge University Press, 1988.

Nicol, D.M., 'A Byzantine emperor in England: Manuel II's visit to London in 1400–1401', *University of Birmingham Historical Journal* 12:2 (1971), 204–25.

Nowkeji, G. Ugo, *The Slave Trade and Culture in the Bight of Biafra: An African Society in the Atlantic World*. Cambridge: Cambridge University Press, 2010.

O'Day, Rosemary (ed.), *Cassandra Brydges, Duchess of Chandos, 1670–1735: Life and Letters*. Woodbridge: Boydell & Brewer, 2007.

Officer, Laurence H., & Williamson, Samuel H., 'Purchasing power of British pounds from 1245 to present', *MeasuringWorth* [http://www.measuring-worth.com/ppoweruk/].

O'Gorman, Kevin, McLellan, L.R., & Baum, Tom, 'Tourism in Iran: Central control and indigeneity' in Richard Butler & Tom Hinch (eds), *Tourism and Indigenous Peoples: Issues and Implications*. Oxford: Butterworth-Heinemann, 2007, 251–64.

Olnon, Merlijn, 'Towards classifying avanias: A study of two cases involving the English and Dutch nations in seventeenth-century Izmir' in Alastair Hamilton, Alexander H. de Groot, & Maurits H. van den Boogert (eds), *Friends and Rivals in the East: Studies in Anglo-Dutch Relations in the Levant from the Seventeenth to the Early Nineteenth Century*. Leiden: Brill, 2000, 159–86.

Onnekink, David, & Rommelse, Gijs, 'Introduction' in David Onnekink & Gijs Rommelse (eds), *Ideology and Foreign Policy in Early Modern Europe, 1650–1750*. Farnham: Ashgate, 2011, 1–10.

Oresko, Robert, Gibbs, G.C., & Scott, I.M., 'Introduction' in Robert Oresko, G.C. Gibbs, & I.M. Scott (eds), *Royal and Republican Sovereignty in Early Modern Europe*. Cambridge: Cambridge University Press, 1997, 1–42.

*The Origin and Early History of the Russia or Muscvoy Company*. London, 1830.

*Oxford Dictionary of National Biography*, online edn, [http://www.oxforddnb.com/view/].

Özdemir, Kemal, *Ottoman Clocks and Watches*. İstanbul: Creative Yayıncılık, 1993.

Özmucur, Süleyman, & Pamuk, Şevket, 'Real wages and standards of living in the Ottoman Empire, 1489–1914', *The Journal of Economic History* 62:2 (2002), 293–321.

Pamuk, Şevket, 'Prices in the Ottoman Empire', *International Journal of Middle East Studies* 36:3 (2004), 451–68.

Pamuk, Şevket, İstanbul ve Diğer Kentlerde 500 Yıllık Fiyatlar ve Ücretler, 1469–*1998*. Ankara: T.C. Başbakanlık Devlet İstatistik Enstitüsü, 2000.

Pamuk, Şevket, *A Monetary History of the Ottoman Empire*. Cambridge: Cambridge University Press, 1999.

Pamuk, Şevket, 'In the absence of domestic currency: Debased European coinage in the seventeenth-century Ottoman Empire', *The Journal of Economic History* 57:2 (1997), 345–66.

Pamuk, Şevket, *The Ottoman Empire and European Capitalism, 1820–1913*. Cambridge: Cambridge University Press, 1987.

Panaite, Viorel, 'French Capitulations and consular jurisdiction in Egypt and Aleppo in the late sixteenth and early seventeenth centuries' in Pascal W. Firges, Tobias P. Graf, Christian Roth, & Gülay Tulasoğlu (eds), *Well-Connected Domains: Towards an Entangled Ottoman History*. Leiden: Brill, 2014, 71–87.

Panzac, Daniel, *La caravane maritime: marins européens et marchands ottomans en Méditerranée, 1680–1830*. Paris: CRNS Editions, 2004.

Panzac, Daniel, *Commerce et navigation dans l'Empire Ottoman au XVIIIe siècle*. Istanbul: Isis, 1996.

Panzac, Daniel, 'Les échanges maritimes dans l'Empire ottoman au XVIIIe siècle', *Revue de l'Occident Musulman et de la Méditerranée* 39:1 (1985), 177–88.

Papalas, Anthony J., *Rebels and Radicals: Icaria 1600–2000*. Wauconda IL: Bolchazy-Carducci, 2005.

Paris, Robert, *Histoire du commerce de Marseille*, vol. V, 'De 1660 à 1789, le Levant'. Paris: Libraire Plon, 1957.

Parry, V.J., 'Materials of war in the Ottoman Empire' in M.A. Cook (ed.), *Studies in the Economic History of the Middle East from the Rise of Islam to the Present Day*. Oxford: Oxford University Press, 1970, 219–29.

Peabody, Norbert, *Hindu Kingship and Polity in Precolonial India*. Cambridge: Cambridge University Press, 2003.

Pearson, J.B., *A Biographical Sketch of the Chaplains to the Levant Company, Maintained at Constantinople, Aleppo and Smyrna, 1611–1706*. Cambridge: Deighton, Bell & Co., 1883.

Pelz, Stephen, 'Toward a new diplomatic history: Two and a half cheers for international relations methods' in Colin Elman & Mirian Fendius Elman (eds), *Bridges and Boundaries: Historians, Political Scientists, and the Study of International Relations*. Cambridge MA: MIT Press, 2001, 85–110.

Pelz, Stephen, 'Essay and reflection: On systematic explanation in international history', *The International History Review* 12:4 (1990), 762–81.

Perry, Norma, *Sir Everard Fawkener, Friend and Correspondent of Voltaire.* Banbury: Voltaire Foundation, 1975.

Philippides, Marios, & Hanak, Walter K., *The Siege and the Fall of Constantinople in 1453: Historiography, Topography, and Military Studies.* Farnham: Ashgate, 2011.

Pinckney Stetkevych, Suzanne, *The Mantle Odes: Arabic Praise Poems to the Prophet Muḥammad.* Bloomington: Indiana University Press, 2010.

Piot, Charles, 'Of slaves and the gift: Jabre sale of kin during the era of the slave trade', *The Journal of African History* 37:1 (1996), 31–49.

Piterberg, Gabriel, *An Ottoman Tragedy: History and Historiography at Play.* Berkeley & Los Angeles: University of California Press, 2003.

Plöger, Karsten, *England and the Avignon Popes: The Practice of Diplomacy in Late Medieval Europe.* London: Legenda, 2005.

Popović, Tatyana, *Prince Marko: The Hero of South Slavic Epics.* Syracuse NY: Syracuse University Press, 1988.

Quataert, Donald, *Ottoman Manufacturing in the Age of Industrial Revolution.* Cambridge: Cambridge University Press, 1993.

Rambert, Gaston (ed.), *Histoire du commerce de Marseille*, 8 vols. Paris: Libraire Plon, 1949–66.

Rawlinson, H.G., 'The embassy of William Harborne to Constantinople, 1583–8', *Transactions of the Royal Historical Society* 4:5 (1922), 1–27.

Rawlinson, H.G., 'Early trade between England and the Levant', *Journal of Indian History* 2 (1922), 107–16.

Ray, Arthur J., *Indians in the Fur Trade.* Toronto: University of Toronto Press, 1998.

Reindl-Kiel, Hedda, 'East is East and West is West, and sometimes the twain did meet: Diplomatic gift-exchange in the Ottoman Empire' in Colin Imber, Keiko Kiyotaki, & Rhoads Murphey (eds), *Frontiers of Ottoman Studies: State, Province, and the West*, 2 vols. London & New York: IB Tauris, 2004, vol. II, 113–24.

Reindl-Kiel, Hedda, 'The chickens of paradise: Official meals in the mid-seventeenth century Ottoman palace' in Suraiya Faroqhi & Cristoph K. Neumann (eds), *The Illuminated Table, the Prosperous House: Food and Shelter in Ottoman Material Culture.* Würzburg: Ergon, 2003, 59–88.

Rice, Warner Grenelle, 'Early English travellers to Greece and the Levant' in *Essays and Studies in English and Comparative Literature.* Ann Arbor: University of Michigan Press, 1933, 205–60.

Roosen, William, *Daniel Defoe and Diplomacy.* London: Associated University Press, 1986.

Roosen, William, 'Early modern diplomatic ceremonial: A systems approach', *The Journal of Modern History* 52:3 (1980), 452–76.

Rosedale, H.G., *Queen Elizabeth and the Levant Company: A Diplomatic and Literary Episode of the Establishment of our Trade with Turkey.* London: Royal Society of Literature, 1904.

Rosenthal, Franz, 'Gifts and bribes: The Muslim view', *Proceedings of the American Philosophical Society* 108:2 (1964), 135–44.

Rowland, Albert, *Studies in English Commerce and Exploration in the Reign of Elizabeth*. Philadelphia: University of Philadelphia Press, 1924.

Rozen, Minna, *A History of the Jewish Community in Istanbul: The Formative Years, 1453–1566*. Leiden: Brill, 2002.

Rudolph, Harriet, 'The material culture of diplomacy: The impact of objects on the dynamics of Habsburg–Ottoman negotiations at the Sublime Porte (1530–1650)' in Gunda Barth-Scalmani, Harriet Rudolph, & Christian Steppan (eds), *Politische Kommunkation zwischen Imperien: Der diplomatische Aktionsraum Südost- und Osteuropa* (Innsbruck, 2013), 211–37.

Rule, John C., 'Review article: Gathering intelligence in the age of Louis XIV', *The International History Review* 14:4 (1992), 732–52.

Sack, Robert D., *Human Territoriality: Its Theory and History*. Cambridge: Cambridge University Press, 1986.

Sajdi, Dana, 'Decline, its discontents, and Ottoman cultural history: By way of introduction' in Dana Sajdi (ed.), *Ottoman Tulips, Ottoman Coffee: Leisure and Lifestyle in the Eighteenth Century*. London & New York: IB Tauris, 2007, 1–40.

Salzmann, Ariel, *Tocqueville in the Ottoman Empire: Rival Paths to the Modern State*. Leiden: Brill, 2004.

Salzmann, Ariel, 'The age of tulips: Confluence and consumer culture (1550–1730)' in Donald Quataert (ed.), *Consumption Studies and the History of the Ottoman Empire, 1550–1922: An Introduction*. Albany NY: SUNY Press, 2000, 83–106.

Samancı, Özge, 'Pilaf and bouchées: The modernization of official banquets at the Ottoman palace in the nineteenth century' in Daniëlle de Vooght (ed.), *Royal Taste: Food, Power and Status at the European Courts after 1789*. Farnham: Ashgate, 2011, 111–42.

Satow, Ernest, *Satow's Diplomatic Practice*, 6th edn, ed. Ivor Roberts. Oxford: Oxford University Press, 2009.

Schafer, Edward H., *The Golden Peaches of Samarkand: A Study of T'ang Exotics*. Berkeley & Los Angeles: University of California Press, 1963.

Scott, Hamish, 'Diplomatic culture in old regime Europe' in Hamish Scott & Brendan Simms (eds), *Cultures of Power in Europe during the Long Eighteenth Century*. Cambridge: Cambridge University Press, 2007, 58–88.

Sen, Sudipta, *Empire of Free Trade: The East India Company and the Making of the Colonial Market Place*. Philadelphia: University of Pennsylvania Press, 1998.

Sennett, Richard, *Together: The Rituals, Pleasures and Politics of Co-operation*. New Haven: Yale University Press, 2012.

Shefer-Mossensohn, Miri, *Ottoman Medicine: Healing and Medical Institutions, 1500–1700*. Albany NY: SUNY Press, 2009.

Shumway, Rebecca, *The Fante and the Transatlantic Slave Trade*. Rochester NY: University of Rochester Press, 2011.

Singer, Amy, 'The "Michelin Guide" to public kitchens in the Ottoman

Empire' in Amy Singer (ed.), *Starting with Food: Culinary Approaches to Ottoman History*. Princeton NJ: Princeton University Press, 2011, 69–92.

Skilliter, S.A., *William Harborne and the Trade with Turkey 1578–1582: A Documentary Study of the First Anglo-Ottoman Relations*. Oxford: Oxford University Press, 1977.

Skilliter, S.A., 'Turkish documents relating to Edward Barton's embassy to the Porte (1588–1598)', PhD thesis, University of Manchester, 1965.

Smith, Thomas W., *History and International Relations*. London: Routledge, 1999.

Smith, Woodruff D., *Consumption and the Making of Respectability, 1600–1800.* London & New York: Routledge, 2002.

Smolenski, John, 'The death of Sawantaeny and the problem of justice on the frontier' in William A. Pencak & Daniel K. Richter (eds), *Friends and Enemies in Penn's Woods: Indians, Colonists, and the Racial Reconstruction of Pennsylvania.* University Park: Pennsylvania State University Press, 2004, 104–28.

Soumonni, Elishée, 'The compatibility of the slave and palm oil trades in Dahomey, 1818–1858' in Robin Law (ed.), *From Slave Trade to 'Legitimate' Commerce: The Commercial Transition in Nineteenth-Century West Africa.* Cambridge: Cambridge University Press, 1995, 78–92.

Spence, Jonathan D., *The Memory Palace of Matteo Ricci*. London: Penguin, 1985.

Spohr Readman, Kristina, 'Memoranda' in Miriam Dobson & Benjamin Zieman (eds), *Reading Primary Sources: The Interpretation of Texts from 19th and 20th Century History.* Abingdon & New York: Routledge, 2009, 123–40.

Steele, Ian K., 'The Shawnees and the English: Captives and war, 1753–1763' in Daniel P. Barr (ed.), *The Boundaries between Us: Natives and Newcomers along the Frontiers of the Old Northwest Territory, 1750–1850*. Kent OH: Kent State University Press, 2006, 1–24.

Steele, M. William, *Alternative Narratives in Modern Japanese History.* London: Routledge-Curzon, 2003.

Stillman, Yedida Kalfon, *Arab Dress from the Dawn of Islam to Modern Times: A Short History*, ed. Norman A. Stillman. Leiden: Brill, 2000.

Stout, Chris E., 'A psychologist in the diplomat's court: A primer' in Harvey J. Langholtz & Chris E. Stout (eds), *The Psychology of Diplomacy.* Westport CT: Praeger, 2004, 19–28.

Subramanyam, Sanjay, 'Frank submissions: The Company and the Mughals between Sir Thomas Roe and Sir William Norris' in H.V. Bowen, Margarette Lincoln, & Nigel Rigby (eds), *The Worlds of the East India Company.* Woodbridge & Rochester NY: D.S. Brewer, 2002, 69–96.

Sürücüoğlu, Metin Saip, 'Osmanlı İmparatorluğu'nda mutfak teşkilatı protokol tören ve şenlik yemekleri' in Kamil Toygar (ed.), *Türk Mutfak Kültürü Üzerine Araştırmalar*. Ankara: Türk Halk Kültürünü Araştırma ve Tanıtma Vakfı. 1999, 49–81.

Şakul, Kahraman,'What happened to Pouqueville's Frenchmen? Ottoman treatment of the French prisoners during the War of the Second Coalition (1798–1802)', *Turkish Historical Review* 3 (2012), 168–95.

Tabakoğlu, Hüseyin Serdar, 'The re-establishment of Ottoman–Spanish relations in 1782', *Turkish Studies / Türkoloji Araştırmaları* 2/3 (2007), 496–524.

Takats, Sean, *The Expert Cook in Enlightenment France.* Baltimore: Johns Hopkins University Press, 2011.

Takeda, Junko Thérèse, *Between Crown and Commerce: Marseille and the Early Modern Mediterranean.* Baltimore: Johns Hopkins University Press, 2011.

Talbot, Michael, 'A treaty of narratives: Friendship, gifts, and diplomatic history in the British Capitulations of 1641', *Osmanlı Araştırmaları / The Journal of Ottoman Studies* 48 (2016), 357–398.

Talbot, Michael, 'Accessing the Shadow of God: Spatial and performative ceremonial at the Ottoman court' in Dries Raeymaekeres & Sebastiaan Derks (eds), *The Key to Power? The Culture of Access in Princely Courts, 1400–1750.* Leiden: Brill, 2016, 101–23.

Talbot, Michael, 'Gifts of time: Watches and clocks in Ottoman–British diplomacy, 1693–1803', *Jahrbuch für Europäische Geschichte* 17 (2016), 55–79.

Talbot, Michael, 'Petitions of the supplicant ambassador: British commercial representations to the Ottoman state in the eighteenth century', *Osmanlı Araştırmaları / Journal of Ottoman Studies* 46 (2015), 163–91.

Talbot, Michael, 'Feeding an elephant in eighteenth-century Istanbul', *Tozsuz Evrak* (September 2013), [docblog.ottomanhistorypodcast.com].

Talbot, Michael, 'A Jacobite lady in Constantinople: The story of Lady Mary Gerard of Gerard's Bromley', *Staffordshire History* 53 (2011), 3–14.

Telfer, Elizabeth, 'The philosophy of hospitableness' in Conrad Lashley & Alison Morrison (eds), *In Search of Hospitality: Theoretical Perspectives and Debates.* Oxford: Butterworth-Heinemann, 2000, 38–55.

Tezcan, Baki, *The Second Ottoman Empire: Political and Social Transformation in the Early Modern World.* Cambridge: Cambridge University Press, 2010.

Tezcan, Hülya, 'The imperial robe collection at Topkapı Palace Museum' in Patricia L. Baker, Hülya Tezcan, & Jennifer Wearden (eds), *Silks for the Sultans: Ottoman Imperial Garments from Topkapı Palace.* Istanbul: Ertuğ & Kocabiyik, 2007, 10–30.

Tezcan, Hülya, *19.yy Sonuna Ait Bir Terzi Defteri: A Late 19th Century Tailor's Order-Book.* İstanbul: Sadberk Hanım Müzesi, 1992.

Thoen, Irma, *Strategic Affection? Gift-Exchange in Seventeenth Century Holland.* Amsterdam: Amsterdam University Press, 2007.

Thomas, Clive Y., 'Coffee production in Jamaica', *Social and Economic Studies* 13:1 (1964), 188–217.

Tooker, Elisabeth, *An Ethnography of the Huron Indians, 1615–1649.* Syracuse NY: Columbia University Press, 1991.

Toomer, G.J., *Eastern Wisedome and Learning: The Study of Arabic in Seventeenth-Century England.* Oxford: Oxford University Press, 1996.

Tor, D.G., 'The Islamization of Central Asia in the Sāmānid era and the reshaping of the Muslim world', *Bulletin of the School of Oriental and African Studies* 72:2 (2009), 279–99.

Torab, Azam, *Performing Islam: Gender and Ritual in Iran.* Leiden: Brill, 2007.

Trexler, Richard C., *Public Life in Renaissance Florence.* Ithaca NY: Academic Press, 1991.

Unat, Faik Reşit, *Osmanlı Serfirleri ve Sefaretnâmeleri*. Ankara: Türk Tarih Kurumu, 1968.

Urbach, Karina, 'Diplomatic history since the cultural turn', *The Historical Journal* 46:4 (2003), 991–7.

Ursinus, Michael, *Grievance Administration (Şikayet) in an Ottoman Province: The Kaymakam of Rumelia's 'Record Book of Complaints' of 1781–1783.* Abingdon & New York: Routledge-Curzon, 2005.

Uzunçarşılı, İsmail Hakkı, *Osmanlı Devletinin Saray Teşkilâtı.* Ankara: Türk Tarih Kurumu, 1945.

Van den Boogert, Maurits, *The Capitulations and the Ottoman Legal System: Qadis, Consuls and Beratlıs in the 18th Century.* Leiden: Brill, 2005.

Van den Boogert, Maurits, 'Redress for Ottoman victims of European privateering: A case against the Dutch in the Divan-i Hümayun (1708–1715)', *Turcica* 33 (2001), 91–118.

Vashishta, H.B., *Land Revenue and Public Finance in Maratha Administration.* Delhi: Oriental Publishers, 1975.

Veinstein, Gilles, 'Commercial relations between India and the Ottoman Empire (late fifteenth to late eighteenth centuries): A few notes and hypotheses' in Sushil Chaudhury & Michel Morineau (eds), *Merchants, Companies and Trade: Europe and Asia in the Early Modern Era.* Cambridge: Cambridge Univesrity Press, 1999, 95–115.

Venn, John, & Venn, J.A., *Alumni Cantabrigienses*, 10 vols. Cambridge: Cambridge University Press, 1922–7.

Vroom, Joanita, '"Mr. Turkey goes to Turkey," or: How an eighteenth-century Dutch diplomat lunched at Topkapı Palace' in Amy Singer (ed.), *Starting with Food: Culinary Approaches to Ottoman History*. Princeton NJ: Princeton University Press, 2011, 139–76.

Walker, Jeffrey K., 'Fiction versus function: The persistence of "representative character" theory in the law of diplomatic immunity' in Harvey J. Langholtz & Chris E. Stout (eds), *The Psychology of Diplomacy.* Westport CT: Praeger, 2004, 243–68.

Wallwork, K.L., 'The mid-Cheshire salt industry', *Geography* 44:3 (1959), 171–86.

Wansbrough, John, 'Venice and Florence in the Mamluk commercial privileges', *Bulletin of the School of Oriental and African Studies* 28:3 (1965), 483–523.

Watkins, John, 'Toward a new diplomatic history of medieval and early modern Europe', *Journal of Medieval and Early Modern Studies* 38:1 (2008), 1–14.

Wearden, Jennifer, 'The technical skill of Ottoman craftsmen' in Patricia L. Baker, Hülya Tezcan, & Jennifer Wearden (eds), *Silks for the Sultans: Ottoman Imperial Garments from Topkapı Palace.* Istanbul: Ertuğ & Kocabiyik, 2007, 45–56.

Webb, Nigel, & Webb, Caroline, *The Earl and His Butler in Constantinople: Introducing the Diary of Mr Samuel Medley, Butler, 1733–36.* Oakham: Legini, 2006.

Webb Yıldırmak, Gülay, *XVIII. Yüzyılda Osmanlı-İngiliz Tiftik Ticareti.* Ankara: Türk Tarih Kurumu, 2011.

Weiker, Walter F., *Ottomans, Turks and the Jewish Polity: A History of the Jews of Turkey.* Jerusalem: Jerusalem Centre for Public Affairs, 1992.

White, Richard, *The Middle Ground: Indians, Empires, and Republics in the Great Lakes Region, 1650–1815.* Cambridge: Cambridge University Press, 2011.

Willan, T.S., 'Some aspects of English trade with the Levant in the sixteenth century', *The English Historical Review* 70:276 (1955), 399–410.

Windler, Christian, 'Diplomatie et interculturalité: les consuls français à Tunis, 1700–1840', *Revue d'Histoire Moderne et Contemporaine* 50:4 (2003), 63–91.

Windler, Christian, *La diplomatie comme expérience de l'autre: consuls français au Maghreb (1700–1840).* Geneva: Droz, 2002.

Windler, Christian, 'Diplomatic history as a field for cultural analysis: Muslim–Christian relations in Tunis, 1700–1840', *The Historical Journal* 44:1 (2001), 79–106.

Wishnitzer, Avner, *Reading Clocks Alla Turca: Time and Society in the Late Ottoman Empire.* Chicago: University of Chicago Press, 2015.

Wood, Alfred C., *A History of the Levant Company.* Oxford: Oxford University Press, 1935.

Wood, Alfred C., 'The English embassy at Constantinople, 1660–1762', *The English Historical Review* 40:160 (1925), 533–61.

Yalçınkaya, Mehmet Alaaddin, *The First Permanent Ottoman Embassy in Europe: The Embassy of Yusuf Agâh Efendi, 1793–1797.* Istanbul: Isis, 2010.

Yalçınkaya, Mehmet Alaaddin, 'III. Selim Döneminde Dış Temsilciliklerin Kurulması' in Seyfi Kenan (ed.), *Nizâm-ı Kadîm'den Nizâm-ı Cedîd'e: Üçüncü Selim ve Dönemi.* İstanbul: İSAM, 2010, 593–624

Yalçınkaya, Mehmet Alaaddin, 'Mahmud Raif Efendi as the chief secretary of Yusuf Agah Efendi, the first permanent Ottoman-Turkish ambassador to London (1793–1797)', *Ankara Üniversitesi Osmanlı Tarihi Araştırma ve Uygulama Dergisi* 5 (1994), 385–434.

Yarak, Larry W., 'A Dutch embassy to Asante in 1857: The journal of David Mill Graves', *History in Africa* 24 (1997), 363–80.

Yonan, Michael Elia, *Empress Maria Theresa and the Politics of Habsburg Imperial Art.* University Park: Pennsylvania State University Press, 2011.

Yosmaoğlu, İpek K., 'Constructing national identity in Ottoman Macedonia' in William Zartman (ed.), *Understanding Life in the Borderlands*. Athens: University of Georgia Press, 2010, 160–88.

Young, G.M., *Victorian England: Portrait of an Age.* Oxford: Oxford University Press, 1936.

Yurdusev, A. Nuri (ed.), *Ottoman Diplomacy: Conventional or Unconventional?* Basingstoke & New York: Palgrave, 2004.

Yurdusev, A. Nuri, 'The Ottoman attitude toward diplomacy' in A. Nuri Yurdusev (ed.), *Ottoman Diplomacy: Conventional or Unconventional?* Basingstoke & New York: Palgrave, 2004, 5–35.

Zeiler, Thomas W., 'The diplomatic history bandwagon: A state of the field', *The Journal of American History* 95:4 (2009), 1053–73.

Zilfi, Madeline C., 'Goods in the mahalle: Distributional encounters in eighteenth-century Istanbul' in Donald Quataert (ed.), *Consumption Studies and the History of the Ottoman Empire, 1550–1922: An Introduction.* Albany NY: SUNY Press, 2000, 289–312.

Zorlu, Tuncay, *Innovation and Empire in Turkey: Sultan Selim III and the Modernisation of the Ottoman Navy*. London & New York: IB Tauris, 2008.

# Index

Lightning Source UK Ltd.
Milton Keynes UK
UKHW021324220319
339682UK00003B/205/P

9 781783 272020